OCR GCSE HISTORY

EXPLAINING THE MODE

C000263097

WAR & SOCIETY

- ■ 'War & British Society' thematic study
- ■ 'Personal Rule to Restoration' depth study
- ■ 'Castles' study of the historic environment

BEN WALSH
ALAN FARMER
PAUL SHUTER
TOM WHEELEY

AN HACHETTE UK COMPANY

This resource is endorsed by OCR for use with specification OCR GCSE (9–1) in History A (Explaining the Modern World) (J410). In order to gain OCR endorsement, this resource has undergone an independent quality check. Any references to assessment and/or assessment preparation are the publisher's interpretation of the specification requirements and are not endorsed by OCR. OCR recommends that a range of teaching and learning resources are used in preparing learners for assessment. OCR has not paid for the production of this resource, nor does OCR receive any royalties from its sale. For more information about the endorsement process, please visit the OCR website, www.ocr.org.uk.

Note: The wording and sentence structure of some written sources have been adapted and simplified to make them accessible to all students, while faithfully preserving the sense of the original.

Although every effort has been made to ensure that website addresses are correct at time of going to press, Hodder Education cannot be held responsible for the content of any website mentioned in this book. It is sometimes possible to find a relocated web page by typing in the address of the home page for a website in the URL window of your browser.

Hachette UK's policy is to use papers that are natural, renewable and recyclable products and made from wood grown in sustainable forests. The logging and manufacturing processes are expected to conform to the environmental regulations of the country of origin.

Orders: please contact Bookpoint Ltd, 130 Milton Park, Abingdon, Oxon OX14 4SE. Telephone: (44) 01235 827720. Fax: (44) 01235 400454. Email education@bookpoint.co.uk Lines are open from 9 a.m. to 5 p.m., Monday to Saturday, with a 24-hour message answering service. You can also order through our website: www.hoddereducation.co.uk

ISBN: 978 1 4718 6247 2

© Ben Walsh, Alan Farmer, Paul Shuter, Tom Wheeley 2017

First published in 2017 by
Hodder Education,
An Hachette UK Company
Carmelite House
50 Victoria Embankment
London EC4Y 0DZ

www.hoddereducation.co.uk

Impression number   10 9 8 7 6 5 4 3 2 1

Year   2021 2020 2019 2018 2017

Cover photo © The Art Archive/Alamy Stock Photo

Artworks by Ron Dixon

Typeset by White-Thomson Publishing Ltd

Printed in Italy

A catalogue record for this title is available from the British Library.

The publishers and authors would like to thank Rob Bircher and David Bryant for their thoughtful and creative contributions to shaping the material in the thematic study.

Contents

Prologue: The historian's mind-set

How historians work

If you think that history means reading a lot of information from a textbook and then memorising it all, you are wrong. If you try to learn history in this way, you will probably end up feeling a bit like the picture above!

Even historians get overwhelmed by the amount of historical information to be found in books, archives and other sources. They use a range of techniques to help them make sense of it all.

Focus

No historian can study every aspect of a period of history. To make the subject manageable, historians focus on particular areas. This book does the same – each of the studies focuses on selected parts of the story. In doing so we miss out other historical information, such as science and technology or the economy.

Ask questions

Historians are investigators rather than just collectors of information. They search for new information about the past in order to tackle important questions.

Historians have different interests. They do not all investigate the same questions. So when studying the Norman Conquest, for example, Historian A may be most interested in why the Normans succeeded in conquering England, while Historian B may concentrate on the social impact of the Norman Conquest. A bit like two different builders, they use the same or similar materials but they ask different questions and tell different stories.

You will follow the same sort of process when preparing for your history exam. You need to learn the content of the specification, but you also need to practise *using this content* to answer important questions. The text in this book, as well as the Key Questions and Focus Tasks for each topic, are designed to help you think in this way.

Select

Another vital technique that historians use is selection. From all the material they study, historians must select just the parts that are relevant and useful to answer a question.

Selection is hard for a historian, but it may be even harder for you under the time pressure of an exam. You have learnt a lot of history facts and you want to show the examiner how much you know – but this is the wrong way of thinking. To begin with, you risk running out of time. Even more serious, you may end up not answering the question clearly because you have included things that are not relevant or helpful. Compare this process to a wardrobe full of clothes. You never wake up in the morning and put on every item of clothing you own! You choose what to wear depending on different factors:

- the weather
- what you will be doing that day (going to school, a wedding, a Saturday job, a sports match).

Selecting information carefully will make your writing more focused and relevant. Thinking carefully about each fact as you select what is relevant and reject what is not will also help you remember the information.

Organise

Once historians have selected the relevant information, they then have to choose what order to present it in to create a coherent argument. You must do the same. If you are responding to the question 'Why did the Vikings invade Britain in the medieval period?', you must build an argument that shows what you think is the most important reason. Listing all the events that led up to the Viking raids does not necessarily explain why the Vikings attacked, or why they attacked in particular places or at particular times. You must link the events to the outcomes.

Fine tune

But don't stop there. Even the most skilled historians make mistakes when they write, and you might too. When you have finished writing, re-read your text and fine tune it to make it as clear and accurate as possible. When you are about to go out, what is the last thing you do before you leave the house? Check your hair? Check your make-up? That is fine tuning. It is a history skill too, and could make a real difference to how much an examiner enjoys reading what you write.

So remember:

- focus
- ask questions
- select
- organise
- fine tune.

Keep these points in mind as you work through your course. Good luck!

Features of this book

Focus

In every topic there is a Focus box. This sets out the main events and developments that will be covered. It also highlights the issues and questions that we will help you think about and develop your views on.

Key Questions

These are the questions that take a really big view of a topic. These questions will help you prepare for the big questions at the end of your exam.

Factfile

Factfiles are more or less what they say – files full of facts! These give you important background information to a story, without interrupting the narrative too much.

Focus Task

Focus Tasks are the main tasks for really making sure you understand what you are studying. They will never ask you to just write something out, take notes or show basic comprehension. These tasks challenge you to show that you know relevant historical information and can use that information to develop an argument.

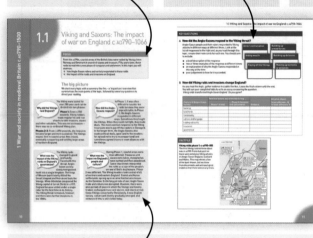

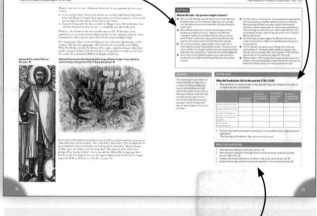

The Big Picture

At the start of each topic in Part 1, we summarise the big picture – in fact, since the whole thematic study is a big picture we probably should have called it 'the really big picture'! This feature sums up the big questions that historians ask about this period and their thinking about those questions. We hope that it will help you keep an overview of the period in your head and that it will be a useful revision tool.

Practice Questions

These questions come at the end of major sections. They are designed to help you think about the kinds of questions you may come across in your exam. We do not know the exact questions you will be asked, but we know the *style* of question. Usually we have shown you the marks that might be available to give you a sense of how much time to spend on it. The question types are explained in the Assessment Focus sections.

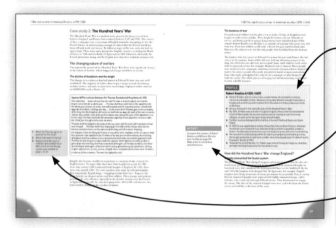

Profile

Profiles are essentially factfiles about people, summarising the key facts about a historical figure.

Activity

Activities help you think through a particular issue, usually as a building block towards a Focus Task.

Margin Questions

These are designed to keep you on track. They usually focus on a source or a section of text to make sure you have fully understood the important points in there.

Assessment Focus

This section takes you through the types of questions in the exam paper, how they are assessed and possible ways to answer them.

Glossary and Key terms

Glossary terms are highlighted LIKE THIS and defined in the Glossary on page 264. Key Terms are listed at the end of each chapter.

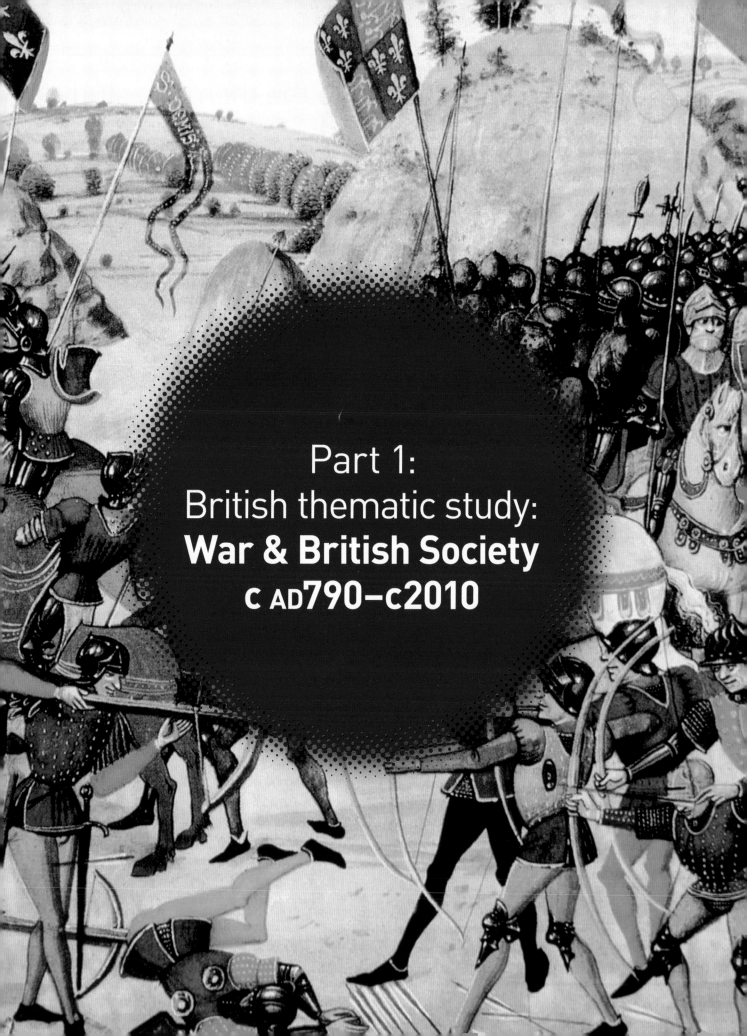

Part 1:
British thematic study:
War & British Society
c AD790–c2010

Introduction to the thematic study

The big picture: War and British society c790–c2010

This part of the course covers the story of how warfare affected British people and British society over a period of a thousand years. You will examine key issues about the causes of wars, types of wars, effects of wars, and how wars affected both the people who fought them and those who were not directly involved in the fighting. Each chapter covers a particular period in British history: medieval, early modern and modern. In each period we will focus on the following information:

Different types of war: Wars of conquest, invasion, defence, empire, ideology, religion, civil war, and many more.	**Attitudes and responses to war:** How the majority of the population felt about various wars, the extent to which they supported or opposed the wars, or how the wars were fought.	**Impacts of war on people:** The extent to which different groups in society were affected by different wars at different times.	**Impacts of war on government and politics:** How wars affected the way governments worked, and how wars affected the relationship between rulers and governments and the people they ruled.

The key players

One of the things you will see in the story of war and society is that the key players change. In the early part of the story, the significant figures were the monarchs and the barons (also referred to as the nobles or the aristocracy). However, ordinary people were also involved in this early period. Many of them took part in the fighting. Many of them were directly affected by wars, as victims or perhaps as refugees fleeing war. This pattern remained the same for much of our story, but from the later medieval period it started to change. As wars became more expensive, monarchs and governments increasingly found that they needed the support of the people, so they began to play a more influential part. At first this was through parliament, but later it was directly through public opinion in the press and other types of media.

The medieval period (c AD790–c1550): Nobles, knights and feudal service

In the medieval period, war was a part of life for almost everyone. Anglo-Saxon society was dominated by the concept of the war band. The king was supported by his most loyal followers – the earls. He gave them wealth and land, and in return they led his armies. This idea filtered down through society. Earls gave land and wealth to thegns, who fought for the earls. The thegns protected their local village and in return the villagers provided food, horses and other essentials in times of war. This pattern dominated English society throughout the medieval period.

When the Normans invaded in 1066 they had the same basic system of military service in return for land, often referred to as feudalism. There were some interruptions and violent clashes between barons and monarchs, but the basic feudal arrangement remained for many centuries. It even became an art form, with books, songs and poems about heroic knights who obeyed the code of chivalry. Ordinary people played a part in this. Without their contribution in terms of providing food and horses, or making weapons, armour and other equipment, the knights would have been powerless.

Over time, the scale of warfare increased. Instead of wars being between princes and dukes, they became wars between countries – most of the time England fought against France, but also against Wales and Scotland. Armies grew larger and more professional. The feudal system began to break down as it struggled to meet the demands of war. Instead, monarchs began collecting taxes to pay professional troops, rather than summoning their knights to fight. By the 1300s, even this was not enough and still more money and taxes were needed. The only way to collect these was to get the approval of parliament. As a result, parliament became increasingly powerful and important.

The early modern period c1500–c1750: New wars, new ways of fighting them

In the early modern period, the nature of war began to change. War was still fought between countries, but religion became a critical cause after Europe divided into Catholic and Protestant countries (England became Protestant in 1534). Convinced that God was on their side, armies fought across Europe with new tactics. New weapons emerged, particularly gunpowder. Knights and castles were no longer the key elements of armies. For England, sea power increased in importance. Faced by the great Catholic powers of France and Spain, England had to use its superior sea power to defend its shores and launch attacks on its more powerful enemies.

War continued to be expensive, which increased the importance of parliament still further. As the costs of war increased, so did the burden on ordinary people. Elizabeth I wisely decided to devote time and attention to winning over the support of her people with a powerful propaganda campaign. War, religion, money and parliament proved to be difficult forces for governments to control. Elizabeth I managed it well, as did her successor James I. However, James's son Charles I proved unequal to the task and the result was years of civil war throughout the 1640s. Parliament became more powerful than ever, and for the first time England had a permanent standing army.

This did not solve the divisions within Britain, though. Scotland and England had been bitter rivals since the 1300s and there would be more bloodshed and rebellion before England and Scotland agreed an Act of Union. By the 1750s, Britain was at peace – internally at least. Several hundred years of warfare had turned it into a formidable military and maritime power.

The modern period c1750–c2010: Global war to asymmetric conflict

In the modern period, Britain built on the foundations of the earlier centuries to become the dominant global power. Britain fought wars in distant countries as well as closer to home against its major rival France. By the early 1900s, Britain was the world's most powerful state, with a huge empire and the greatest navy to protect that empire and control the seas.

The rise to global power was generally popular, and it was supported by the British people. However, there were mistakes and problems along the way. It became increasingly clear that in a modern state the government needed the support of the people to fight wars. This proved to be particularly true in the World Wars, in which the entire population was mobilised either in the armed forces or in essential industries, or simply in conserving and recycling vital resources. Britain declined after the Second World War. While it was still a leading power, it was no longer a match for the new superpowers, the USA and the USSR. The British people on the whole accepted the way governments managed this change. Wars did not end, but the days of major global wars seemed to be over. New wars, involving asymmetric warfare – terrorist tactics – emerged, and both governments and people were required to play key roles in terms of support, information and ideas.

1.1 Viking and Saxons: The impact of war on England c AD790–1066

FOCUS

From the AD790s, coastal areas of the British Isles were raided by Vikings from Norway and Denmark in search of slaves and treasure. Fifty years later, these raids turned into a new phase of conquest and settlement. In this topic you will examine:
- how Anglo-Saxon rulers and society responded to these raids
- the impact of the raids and invasions on England.

The big picture

We start every topic with a summary like this – a 'big picture' overview that summarises the main points of the topic, followed by some key questions to direct your reading.

Why did the Vikings raid England?

The Viking wars lasted for over 200 years and can be divided into two phases:

Phase 1: From AD750 onwards, Viking raiders made regular hit-and-run attacks to take treasure, slaves and other valuables. This was not an invasion – there was no co-ordinated Viking plan.

Phases 2–3: From AD850 onwards, the invasions became larger and more sustained. The Vikings stayed, first in coastal areas then inland, eventually conquering and settling large areas of northern England.

How did the Anglo-Saxons respond?

In Phase 1, it was often difficult to counter the raids because they were unpredictable. In Phase 2, the Anglo-Saxons responded in different ways. Sometimes they fought the Vikings. When they could not fight, they made deals. The most common response to the Viking incursions was to pay off the raiders in Danegeld. In the longer term, the Anglo-Saxons also made political deals, gave land to the invaders (or agreed not to try to reconquer land) and sometimes agreed truces or even alliances with the Vikings.

What was the impact of the Viking raids on England's government?

The Viking raids changed England profoundly. Faced with this threat, Anglo-Saxon society slowly reorganised itself into a single kingdom. The kings of Wessex (particularly Alfred the Great) stopped and then drove back the Vikings. When Athelstan conquered the Viking capital of Jorvik (York) in AD927, England became united under a single ruler for the first time in its history. The Viking threat remained, however, and there were further invasions in the 1000s.

What was the impact on England's people and culture?

During Phase 1, coastal areas were most affected. Treasures and slaves were taken, monasteries were sacked and then abandoned. Some churchmen interpreted the raids as a sign of the people's sin and of God's displeasure. Phase 2 was different. The Viking invaders took control of all of northern and eastern England. Danish and Norse settlements sprang up in an area that became known as the Danelaw. In the long periods of war, Anglo-Saxon trade and culture was disrupted. However, there were also periods of peace in which the Vikings and Saxons traded, exchanged music and stories, and intermarried. Some Vikings converted to Christianity. A new English society, culture and identity gradually emerged, and evidence of this is still visible today.

KEY QUESTIONS

A How did the Anglo-Saxons respond to the Viking threat?

Anglo-Saxon people and their rulers responded to Viking attacks in different ways at different times. Look at the list of responses to the right and, as you read through this topic, create short note cards for each one. You should aim to include:

- a brief description of the response
- two or three examples of the response at different times
- an explanation of why the Anglo-Saxons responded in this way at the time
- your judgement on how far it succeeded.

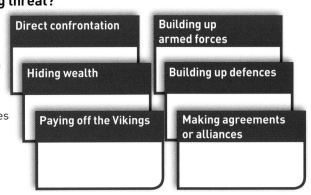

Direct confrontation

Building up armed forces

Hiding wealth

Building up defences

Paying off the Vikings

Making agreements or alliances

B How did Viking raids and invasions change England?

As you read this topic, gather evidence in a table like this. Leave the final column until the end.
You will use your completed table to write an essay answering the question:
'Viking raids transformed Anglo-Saxon England.' Do you agree?

Feature of Anglo-Saxon Society	How this feature was affected during ...		Evidence	Relative impact (most affected = 10 to least affected = 1)
	... Phase 1 (raids)	... Phase 2 (invasion and settlement)		
farming				
local lords				
Christianity				
culture and language				
trading networks				
treasures				
government				

FACTFILE

Viking raids phase 1: c AD790–855
The first Viking raid we know about was in AD789. From that point on there were extensive Viking attacks on Anglo-Saxon England, Scotland and Wales. This map shows a few of the best-known, but we know from documents and archaeological evidence that there were many more.

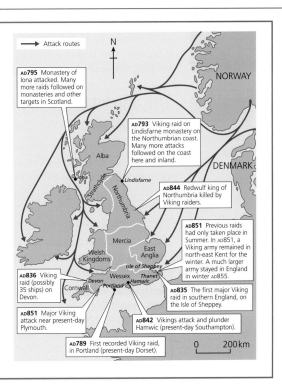

→ Attack routes

N

NORWAY

DENMARK

AD795 Monastery of Iona attacked. Many more raids followed on monasteries and other targets in Scotland.

AD793 Viking raid on Lindisfarne monastery on the Northumbrian coast. Many more attacks followed on the coast here and inland.

AD844 Redwulf king of Northumbria killed by Viking raiders.

AD851 Previous raids had only taken place in Summer. In AD851, a Viking army remained in north-east Kent for the winter. A much larger army stayed in England in winter AD855.

AD836 Viking raid (possibly 35 ships) on Devon.

AD835 The first major Viking raid in southern England, on the Isle of Sheppey.

AD851 Major Viking attack near present-day Plymouth.

AD842 Vikings attack and plunder Hamwic (present-day Southampton).

AD789 First recorded Viking raid, in Portland (present-day Dorset).

Alba, Iona, Strathclyde, Lindisfarne, Northumbria, Mercia, East Anglia, Welsh Kingdoms, Wessex, Isle of Sheppey, Thanet, Hamwic, Devon, Portland, Cornwall

0   200km

Phase 1 c AD790–855: How devastating were the Viking raids, and why?

Historians have long debated this question. To answer it, we obviously need to look at the VIKINGS, but we also need to consider the people they were attacking: the Anglo-Saxons.

The Vikings were prepared

'Viking' is a general term for the people of Scandinavia – particularly present-day Norway and Denmark. For centuries, Anglo-Saxon England and the Frankish Empire (modern France and Germany) had traded peacefully with the Scandinavians. However, a growing population and disruptions in trade with the Frankish Empire led them to turn from trading to raiding.

The Vikings were well suited to the role of raiders. Evidence such as the Stora Hammars stones (see Source 1) show us how important courage and warfare were to them. The Vikings were also excellent seafarers, shipbuilders and navigators. Their longships could cross the open sea or sail quite long distances up fairly shallow rivers. This was a huge advantage for raiders, because it meant they could appear unexpectedly off the coast or even inland without warning.

Anglo-Saxon England was not prepared

The Anglo-Saxons had come to Britain in waves from around AD430 to the 600s, and had settled in small communities under the AUTHORITY of a local lord or chief. War was very much part of Anglo-Saxon society, but not the kind of mobile raiding warfare the Vikings unleashed. There were simply not enough Anglo-Saxon warriors to guard all the places where a Viking raid might occur.

Another problem for the Anglo-Saxons was that their most valuable sites were undefended. By the AD790s, Christianity had taken a strong hold in England and monasteries such as Lindisfarne were important centres of worship, learning and culture. Anglo-Saxon kings and lords gave money and land to the Church, hoping for God's favour. No Anglo-Saxon leader would attack a church, so despite housing great wealth, these sites were thought to be safe from attack.

The impact of the raids on Anglo-Saxon England

Shock and awe

Most of the histories of this period were written by the monks who came under attack from the Vikings. These accounts probably give exaggerated accounts of the raids, but they also give a strong sense of the shock the raids caused. A common prayer in church services at the time was 'From the fury of the Northmen, O Lord deliver us'. 'Northmen' became another word for devil or demon.

Source 1 A modern photograph of one of the Stora Hammars stones, part of a series of Viking memorials in Sweden. ▼

ACTIVITY

Study Source 1 carefully. It is a valuable source of evidence about Vikings and the importance of ships, the sea, warfare and Viking beliefs. These help us understand why they were effective raiders.

EITHER use a copy of the photograph and label it to show the main features of the stone and how it provides evidence about the Vikings.

OR write and record an audio guide for a visitor looking at the stone who knows nothing about the Vikings.

> **Source 2** An account of the Viking attack on Holy Island in AD792, from the *Anglo-Saxon Chronicle*.
>
> *In this year dire forewarnings came over the land of the Northumbrians, and miserably terrified the people: these were extraordinary whirlwinds and lightnings, and fiery dragons were seen flying in the air. A great famine soon followed these omens; and soon after that, in the same year, on the sixth of the ides of Ianr [8 June], the havoc of heathen men miserably destroyed God's church on Lindisfarne, through rapine and slaughter.*

Source 3 A reliquary box made in the eighth century to hold a saint's relic. It was taken by a Viking raider and eventually became a Norwegian lady's jewellery casket in the tenth century. An inscription on the base reads 'Ranvaik owns this casket'. ▼

Economic damage

It was not just hysteria. The raids in Phase 1 of the Viking attacks had a significant effect on England. Archaeologists in Scandinavia have found large quantities of Anglo-Saxon coins, jewellery and other treasure in Viking settlements, suggesting large-scale looting and piracy. Evidence from skeletons also suggests that many Anglo-Saxons were taken back to Scandinavia as slaves.

In England, archaeologists have found examples of graves indicating large-scale fighting and death – probably the result of Viking raids. There is also evidence of disruption to trade and the economy. For example, some Anglo-Saxon coins found in Northumbria are made mostly from tin rather than silver, suggesting that silver was either hard to get hold of at the time or that the economy was damaged (or both).

A new identity?

Another important impact of the early Viking raids was that they contributed to the emergence of a new Anglo-Saxon culture and identity. Leading CHURCHMEN like Alcuin of York emphasised the idea that this was a religious threat as well as a military one. The Church propaganda machine created a powerful idea. Anglo-Saxon lords and princes who had fought and quarrelled with each other before the Viking raids now began to see themselves as one people, united as Christians against the Northmen.

Source 4 An illustration of the murder of Edmund, king of East Anglia, in AD869, from a church chronicle. After his death, he was created St Edmund the Martyr – a powerful propaganda device. ▼

FOCUS TASK

Why did the early Viking raids have such a powerful impact on Anglo-Saxon England?

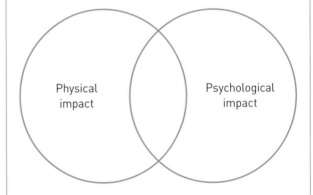

Physical impact

Psychological impact

1 Make your own copy of this diagram, but decide whether one factor was more important. If you think it was, make that circle bigger. Add notes in each circle explaining that factor. Think carefully about which points belong in the overlapping section.
2 Add any relevant points from these two pages to your note cards for Key Question A on page 11.
3 Add any relevant points from these two pages to your table for Key Question B on page 11.

1 Look back at pages 12–13 (how devastating the raids were). Explain why these measures would have been effective against Viking attacks.

Phase 2 AD865–990: **Invasion and its impact**

In the ninth century, the early Viking raids evolved into a full-scale invasion. In AD865, the first 'great army' of Vikings landed. This was a different type of war – the Vikings' aim was conquest and settlement. This time they moved deep inland (see Factfile). They overran Northumbria and established their own kingdom based on York. They took control of Mercia and East Anglia.

Wessex resists

Despite being surrounded, the kingdom of Wessex remained strong. In AD871, Alfred became king of WESSEX. Alfred is now known as 'Alfred the Great' because he took Wessex from the brink of defeat to victory over the Danes. At one point, however, the kingdom seemed lost. At Christmas AD878, the Danish leader Guthrum launched a surprise attack. Alfred was forced to flee for his life and his forces were scattered. Despite this setback, Alfred rallied his troops and fought a campaign using GUERRILLA tactics to harass the Danes and stop them gaining full control of Wessex. By April AD878 he had reorganised his forces and won a major victory at the Battle of Edington in Wiltshire. After this, the Vikings agreed to stay out of Wessex and Guthrum was baptised a Christian.

PROFILE

Alfred the Great

- Alfred was the fourth son of king Ethelwulf, so he never expected to become king.
- His elder brothers all died so he took the throne in AD871, at the height of Viking domination.
- Despite early setbacks, he first defeated the Vikings and then established defences against future attacks.
- He is mainly remembered as a military leader, but could claim other important achievements. He revised English law, basing it all on Christian principles. He supported the Church and recruited the best churchmen from around England to translate famous works and set up schools.

FACTFILE

Viking raids phase 2: c AD865–990.

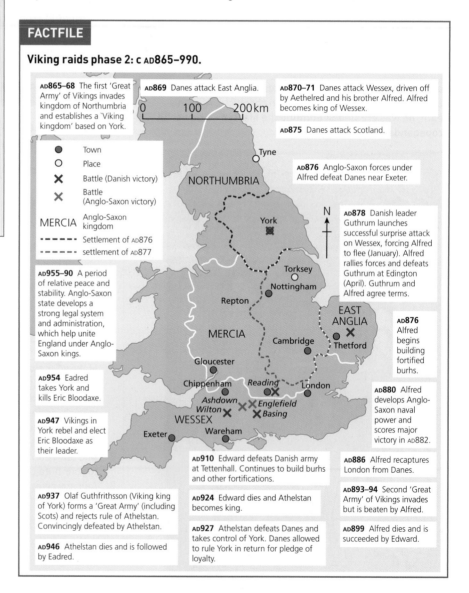

AD865–68 The first 'Great Army' of Vikings invades kingdom of Northumbria and establishes a 'Viking kingdom' based on York.

AD869 Danes attack East Anglia.

AD870–71 Danes attack Wessex, driven off by Aethelred and his brother Alfred. Alfred becomes king of Wessex.

AD875 Danes attack Scotland.

AD876 Anglo-Saxon forces under Alfred defeat Danes near Exeter.

AD878 Danish leader Guthrum launches successful surprise attack on Wessex, forcing Alfred to flee (January). Alfred rallies forces and defeats Guthrum at Edington (April). Guthrum and Alfred agree terms.

AD876 Alfred begins building fortified burhs.

AD880 Alfred develops Anglo-Saxon naval power and scores major victory in AD882.

AD955–90 A period of relative peace and stability. Anglo-Saxon state develops a strong legal system and administration, which help unite England under Anglo-Saxon kings.

AD954 Eadred takes York and kills Eric Bloodaxe.

AD947 Vikings in York rebel and elect Eric Bloodaxe as their leader.

AD910 Edward defeats Danish army at Tettenhall. Continues to build burhs and other fortifications.

AD886 Alfred recaptures London from Danes.

AD937 Olaf Guthfrithsson (Viking king of York) forms a 'Great Army' (including Scots) and rejects rule of Athelstan. Convincingly defeated by Athelstan.

AD924 Edward dies and Athelstan becomes king.

AD893–94 Second 'Great Army' of Vikings invades but is beaten by Alfred.

AD946 Athelstan dies and is followed by Eadred.

AD927 Athelstan defeats Danes and takes control of York. Danes allowed to rule York in return for pledge of loyalty.

AD899 Alfred dies and is succeeded by Edward.

Map legend:
- ● Town
- ○ Place
- ✗ Battle (Danish victory)
- ✗ Battle (Anglo-Saxon victory)
- MERCIA Anglo-Saxon kingdom
- – · – · – Settlement of AD876
- – – – – settlement of AD877

Map labels: Tyne, NORTHUMBRIA, York, Torksey, Nottingham, Repton, EAST ANGLIA, MERCIA, Cambridge, Thetford, Gloucester, Chippenham, Reading, London, Ashdown, Englefield, Wilton, Basing, WESSEX, Exeter, Wareham

0   100   200km

N

A map showing burhs established by Alfred and Aethelflaed in Wessex and Mercia.

In designing the burhs, Alfred had learned from how the Romans defended Britain:

- Burhs were linked by roads.
- They were never further than half a day's march from each other.
- They guarded strategic points such as rivers and bridges.

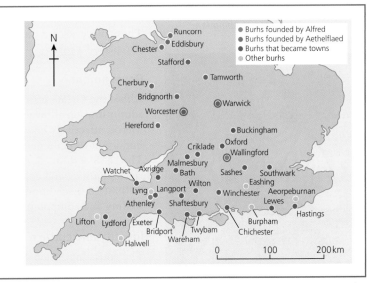

How great was Alfred?

1 When the Normans invaded Anglo-Saxon England in 1066, they tried to stop people telling stories about Alfred and instead encouraged legends about the mythical King Arthur. What does this tell you about the importance of Alfred to the Anglo-Saxon people?

2 Do you think Alfred's reputation as 'great' is deserved?

3 Look back over your work on pages 16–17 and add any relevant points to Key Questions A or B on page 11.

Alfred was wise and experienced enough to know that the Vikings would probably renege on this promise. He used the period of peace that followed the Battle of Edington to reorganise Wessex's defences.

- **Army:** Alfred realised that it took Wessex too long to raise an army. He reorganised his army so that, according to the ANGLO-SAXON CHRONICLE, 'always half its men were at home, and half out on service'.
- **Burhs:** He saw that Viking raids were only ever made on vulnerable targets. They would raid then retreat. Alfred set up a chain of BURHS (fortified towns) across southern England, which were permanently manned by soldiers from his newly reorganised army. These were expensive, but they worked well.
- **Navy:** Alfred wanted a navy that could disrupt the Vikings at sea. In AD896 he ordered a new type of boat that could do battle with the Viking longships around the English coast. These ships were twice the size of the longships.
- **Money:** Alfred used the efficient administration of Wessex to collect taxes to pay for all this.

When the Viking invaders returned in AD891–92 they faced much greater resistance than they had in the past. After four years, they stopped trying to conquer Wessex. Alfred allied Wessex with Mercia by marrying his daughter Aethelflaed to Ethelred of Mercia. By the time Alfred died in AD899 he controlled all England south of a line from London to Chester. North and north-east England (known as the DANELAW) remained under Viking control.

Building on Alfred's achievements

Alfred's successors continued to extend Wessex's control. His daughter Aethelflaed became a strong ruler in her own right. Known as 'The Lady of the Mercians', she built fortified towns along the border of her territory just as Alfred had done. She led her armies in capturing Derby and defeating Viking forces at Leicester. Under her rule, the Saxons pushed further into Danish-held territory until most of Mercia was free from Viking control.

Alfred's son Edward continued his work in Wessex, and his grandson Athelstan went further still, capturing York in AD927. Kings from Scotland and Wales also acknowledged Athelstan's authority. To celebrate, Athelstan had coins made with an inscription that read: 'Athelstan, king of all Britons' (see Source 6 on page 16).

Source 5 Aethelflaed, from *The Cartulary and Customs of Abingdon Abbey*, c1220. ▼

Source 6 A coin from Athelstan's reign, showing the Latin inscription meaning 'Athelstan, king of all Britons'. ▼

Reasons for success

These successes did not only come about due to military skills. Other factors also played a part.

Government

Alfred the Great's efficient system of law, tax collection, justice and administration allowed him and his successors to administer Wessex and Mercia effectively enough to win these wars. The royal princes and most important NOBLES met in a council called the WITAN, which advised the king. The LESSER NOBLES, or THEGNS, carried out key administrative roles such as law and justice and collecting taxes. SHIRES were divided into districts called HUNDREDS. Each hundred had its own law courts and was responsible for finding and equipping one hundred soldiers when the king required an army.

Identity and culture

The emerging Anglo-Saxon identity based on the adoption of Christianity was continually reinforced by the Church. A good example is the legend of Alfred. Although he was certainly an effective leader, the churchmen who wrote his story made his achievements even more spectacular. For example, there is a legend that Alfred disguised himself as a minstrel in order to get into the Danish camp and spy on the enemy. Anglo-Saxons were proud to be ruled by descendants of Alfred the Great, and this built loyalty and commitment to the campaigns against the Vikings.

Compromise

The CHRONICLES of the time tend to leave out one important factor: compromise. Although Athelstan captured York, he did not try to force the Vikings out of Northumbria and East Anglia. During the ninth century, Alfred and his successors got to know more about the Danes and other Vikings, and slowly stopped regarding them as the enemy. Records generally stop using the word 'Northmen' and start to use terms like 'Danes' or 'Norwegians'.

1 Source 5 is not meant to be a representation of what Aethelflaed really looked like. What is it trying to achieve?
2 How can you tell that Aethelflaed was important?
3 Study Source 6. Is it an example of coinage or propaganda? Explain your answer.

Source 7 Historian Ryan Lavelle, writing in 2015.

Although the expansion of Wessex in the early 900s saw English Christians forcing Danes and other Vikings into submission through strong-arm tactics, 'Danes' and 'English' continued to make agreements and negotiate over territory in a way that mirrored the diplomacy between the old rival Anglo-Saxon kingdoms. In fact, the descendants of ninth-century Scandinavian lords became the loyal allies of English rulers – particularly Edward the Elder (899–924) and Athelstan (924–39). These rulers allowed their new subjects to keep their lands in return for a submission to lordship. So this was not purely a story of nationhood or of the triumph of one group over another. Instead, the Vikings' role in the making of 'England' demonstrated that different peoples' dealings with one another involved flexibility and compromise as much as factionalism and conflict.

FOCUS TASK

Why did Wessex win?

1 Make your own copy of this diagram. Decide whether one factor was more important than the others. If you think it was, make that segment bigger. Add notes in each segment explaining the factor.
2 Fill in any relevant points from this section in your note cards for Key Question A on page 11.
3 Fill in any relevant points from this section in your table for Key Question B on page 11.

The impact of the Viking wars and invasions

There are no detailed records of the impact that these 90 years of invasion and war had on the local Anglo-Saxon population, but it was probably traumatic. As well as major battles such as Edington there were many small-scale clashes. This was a war of survival, and the fighting was savage.

One of the most important sources of evidence we have are hoards of treasure that have been unearthed around the country. These demonstrate the insecurity and unrest of this period. The Anglo-Saxons in southern England clearly hid wealth from the Vikings. In the north, the Vikings hid their treasures from the Anglo-Saxons.

The greatest asset of all was the land. Viking commanders shared out the farmlands of Northumbria among their warriors, who then brought over their wives and children to settle there. It is almost certain that many Anglo-Saxon lords were killed or forced to flee from their lands. There is archaeological evidence to suggest violence, including mass graves and layers of ash where settlements were burnt down.

It is also likely that many Anglo-Saxon villagers were dispossessed. They may even have been enslaved and forced to work on land that they had previously owned. Even when the Vikings did not take land for themselves, they usually forced Anglo-Saxon communities to pay tribute. In addition to this, Anglo-Saxon villagers would also have been required to supply their own forces with food, equipment and troops.

Despite this, over time the Anglo-Saxons and Vikings began to trade with each other, especially in the relatively peaceful period from AD955 to 990. Many Vikings converted to Christianity, and Christian objects such as crosses and prayer beads have been found in Viking settlements. There are also examples of Viking graves with Anglo-Saxon goods in them and vice versa. Modern DNA techniques have shown that Anglo-Saxons and Vikings intermarried.

ACTIVITY

Complete this paragraph about the impact of the Viking wars and invasions:

Whilst the achievements of Wessex were impressive we should remember they came at a heavy cost. Although we cannot be sure, the wars and invasions affected people in many ways. For example …

Source 8 A runestone in Sweden, put there by a Viking in commemoration of his receiving Danegeld in England. ▼

Viking raids phase 3: AD991–1066

AD991   Vikings defeat Anglo-Saxons at Battle of Maldon. The Vikings are paid 10,000 pounds in Danegeld.

AD994   Sweyn Forkbeard lays siege to London. He is paid off with 22,000 pounds in Danegeld.

1007   Aethelred buys two years of peace with 36,000 pounds of Danegeld.

1012   Vikings sack Canterbury and murder the archbishop. They are paid off with 48,000 pounds in Danegeld. Aethelred introduces an annual land tax to pay Viking mercenaries to defend England from other Vikings.

1013   Full-scale invasion by Sweyn Forkbeard meets little resistance and he becomes king. Aethelred flees the country.

1017   Sweyn dies in 1014. After a short struggle, his son Cnut becomes king of England as part of an empire which includes Denmark and Norway.

1035   Cnut dies, leading to a seven-year period of turmoil and rivalry.

1042   Edward the Confessor becomes king and rules until 1066.

1   Compare Sources 9 and 10. How do they differ in their attitude to paying Danegeld?

2   Why do you think they differ?

Phase 3 AD991–1066: Completing the Viking conquest

Thirty years later, a new generation of Viking leaders emerged. In AD991, a large Viking army defeated the Anglo-Saxons under the leadership of the young King Aethelred at the Battle of Maldon in Essex. In the wake of this defeat, Aethelred consulted the Witan and they did what previous rulers had done – they paid off the Vikings with DANEGELD, but the Viking attacks continued (see Factfile).

Aethelred was in a weak position. He was king of England, but beyond Wessex the local lords had no faith in his ability to protect them from the Vikings. In 1002, he sent out an order to kill all Danes living among the Anglo-Saxons, but many noblemen in charge of carrying out this slaughter simply refused to do so, fearing revenge raids.

Aethelred proved unable to unite his nobles behind him or enforce his authority on them. When the Danish king Sweyn Forkbeard launched a full-scale invasion in 1013 he faced little resistance. The Anglo-Saxons felt that they were not being properly protected and most of them gave in. Aethelred fled into exile in Normandy.

Source 9 An extract from the *Anglo-Saxon Chronicle* commenting on events of 1011.

All these misfortunes befell us through lack of decision, in that they were not offered tax in time; but when they had done great evil, then truce was made with them.

Source 10 An extract from an old poem about the Battle of Maldon. Byrhtnoth (the Anglo-Saxon commander at the Battle of Maldon in AD991) is addressing the Vikings in response to their demand for Danegeld. Byrhtnoth died in the battle.

Byrhtnoth lifted his shield, shook his slender ash-spear, and spoke with single-minded anger:

'Seafarer, hear what I have to say! Spears will we give you as tribute. Messenger, tell your people that here stands a good earl with his war-band, who will defend this homeland, Aethelred's land, land of my prince, my folk and my fold.

In battle, now, you heathen must fall. Too shameful it seems that you should sail away bearing our wealth, without a fight. Not so softly shall you carry off riches. The point of the dagger and the edge of the sword must first meet in grim battle, before we pay you tribute.'

Was Aethelred 'unready'?

Today Aethelred 'the Unready' has a poor reputation. However, 'unready' is a mistranslation of an Old English word, *unraed*, which means 'badly advised'. Historians point out that the Witan advised the king to pay Danegeld to the Vikings when they began their attacks, and that many of Aethelred's predecessors had done the same. The sheer scale and effectiveness of the Viking attacks would have made it very difficult for any ruler to resist. Also, when Sweyn died in 1014, the leading nobles in England refused to accept his son Cnut as their king. Instead they asked Aethelred to come back and lead them, suggesting they wanted him as king. Aethelred returned to battle Cnut for the throne, but he died in April 1016. By October that year Cnut had conquered the country.

The Viking victory

Cnut did not try to make England a Viking country. He kept the Anglo-Saxon system of law and government, and extended it into the Danelaw. He surrounded himself with men he could trust, including the Anglo-Saxon Godwin, who became EARL of Wessex and Cnut's right-hand man.

After Cnut's death power returned to the Anglo-Saxon king Edward, and the most powerful figure in the land was the Anglo-Saxon Earl Godwin. By 1066, Godwin's family was effectively ruling the country, including Viking Northumbria.

KEY QUESTION REVIEW

A How did the Anglo-Saxons respond to the Viking threat?

Through the two and a half centuries of conflict between Anglo-Saxons and Vikings in England, the Anglo-Saxons faced different kinds of war and they responded in different ways.

Offence: Anglo-Saxon England was a warrior society. They fought back when they could, and with the right leadership they won some significant victories.

Defence: Alfred reorganised Anglo-Saxon society effectively to defend his territory and repel the Vikings. In particular, the burhs were a major breakthrough in keeping the enemy out of Wessex.

Responses to invasion

Appeasement: Aethelred's payment of Danegeld has earned him a bad reputation, but it is clear that from the earliest raids it was common for the Anglo-Saxons to pay off the Vikings. In fact, extracting tribute had been a normal part of the practice of war for centuries.

Compromise: Eventually, warring parties have to learn to live together – and this usually involves compromise. This happened in England with the emergence of the Danelaw, and eventually Anglo-Saxon England accepted a Viking king, Cnut.

1 Use your completed cards from page 11 to supply examples of each type of response.
2 Use your examples to write an answer to the following question:
   'The Anglo-Saxons were powerless against the Viking threat.' How far do you agree?

B How did Viking raids and invasions change England?

Look back at your completed table from page 11.
1 Use the final column to rank these impacts.
2 Use your completed table to write an answer to this question:
   'Viking raids transformed Anglo-Saxon England.' Do you agree?

PRACTICE QUESTIONS

1 Describe the Viking attacks on Anglo-Saxon England in the period AD790–c900. (4)
2 Describe two ways in which Anglo-Saxon society responded to the threat of Viking raids. (4)
3 How significant were the Viking attacks on England in the period AD790–1066? (14)
4 How effective were the responses of Anglo-Saxon society to the threat of Viking raids? (14)

1.2

The Norman Conquest and its impact

FOCUS

After the Saxon-Viking wars, England developed into a stable, well-governed and wealthy state. However, when Edward the Confessor died in 1066 without a son to take over the kingdom, powerful rivals fought for the throne. The winner was William of Normandy, who became William I. In this topic you will examine:
- why the Norman invasion and Conquest was successful
- how the Norman Conquest affected the way England was run
- how the Norman Conquest affected English society.

The big picture

The Norman Conquest and its impact

What type of war was this?

For the Normans and their leader, Duke William, this was a war of ambition and conquest. William had a claim on the English throne, but he could only enforce it using violence. William had his eye on the wealth of England and the power this would give him. He could reward his loyal followers and they in turn would support him in his wars with rival rulers in France.

For the English leader, Harold Godwinson, it was also a war of ambition. Having been appointed king by the English nobles in the Witan, he had the strongest claim to the throne. However, when William attacked, this also became a war of defence and survival for Harold.

Harold was defeated and killed at Hastings in October 1066, and resistance to William soon collapsed. However, people soon began to rebel against their new leaders, and a long period of bloody and brutal warfare followed.

How did the Norman Conquest change government in England?

The Conquest changed English society. It became a war of suppression for the Normans, and a war of survival for the Anglo-Saxon noble class. In the short term William combined ruthless violence and a network of castles to crush resistance. He then turned the efficient Anglo-Saxon system of government to his own advantage. He and his followers built new cathedrals as a way to stamp their identity on the defeated English. Within 20 years of their invasion had effectively taken over all the main areas of power in England and they wiped out the Anglo-Saxon nobility.

How did the Norman Conquest affect ordinary people in England?

Thousands died in the invasion and the consolidation of Norman power that followed. William's infamous 'Harrying of the North' was particularly brutal, and it was decades before the northern part of the kingdom recovered. Historians are still debating the full impact of the Norman Conquest, particularly the question of whether it introduced a 'Norman yoke' – a harsh regime of restrictive laws that were unfairly enforced. Most historians believe the impact was mixed. Certainly the class of thegns was virtually wiped out; many tenants lost their land and others suffered high rents and heavy taxes. However, there was greater freedom for some and probably continuity and stability for many others.

KEY QUESTIONS

A Why was the Norman Conquest successful?

The table below lists several factors behind the Normans' success in the 20 years or so after the Conquest. Copy the table and use it to record examples of each factor at work. Record this in the second column. You will complete the third column at the end of the unit.

Factor affecting Norman success	Evidence and examples of this factor at work	Importance (rank from most to least)
luck		
use of the law and administration		
effective leadership		
loyal support		
the Church		
military power		
castles		
other		

B How did the Norman Conquest change England?

The table below lists some features of Norman England. As you work through this topic, look for evidence of change or continuity from Anglo-Saxon England. Add more rows if you need them.

Feature of Anglo-Saxon England	Evidence of change	Evidence of continuity
the church		
land ownership		
government, law and administration		
life for ordinary people		
other		

Source 1 The Great Seal of William the Conqueror. This was issued once William was fully in control of England. The seal would be attached to official documents to show that they carried the king's approval and authority. ▼

ACTIVITY

Source 1 can tell us a great deal about the qualities of William the Conqueror and the image he wanted to present to his people. Work in two stages:

1 Look closely at the two sides of the seal and list all the images and symbols you can see. Do not worry if you are not sure what some of them are.
2 Read through the rest of this topic, then write a full commentary explaining what the seal shows and what it reveals about William the Conqueror.

Why was the Norman invasion of 1066 successful?

When Edward the Confessor died in 1066, three powerful rivals claimed the throne:

- Harald Hardrada, the king of Norway
- William, the duke of Normandy
- Harold Godwinson, the earl of Wessex.

The English nobles in the Witan appointed Harold Godwinson, but the other two claimants were prepared to fight. Harold Godwinson gathered his forces and waited to see which of his two rivals would act first. The Factfile below shows what happened next.

So why did the Norman invasion succeed? Was it simply bad luck – Harold having to fight two enemies in a short space of time? Were the Normans the superior force on the day of the Battle of Hastings? Or was there something else about the Norman war machine that secured William's victory?

FACTFILE

The key events of 1066.

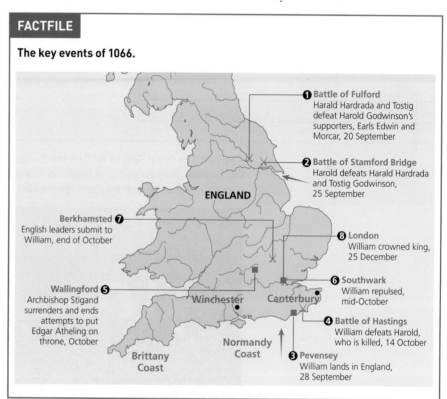

❶ **Battle of Fulford**
Harald Hardrada and Tostig defeat Harold Godwinson's supporters, Earls Edwin and Morcar, 20 September

❷ **Battle of Stamford Bridge**
Harold defeats Harald Hardrada and Tostig Godwinson, 25 September

❼ Berkhamsted
English leaders submit to William, end of October

❽ **London**
William crowned king, 25 December

❺ Wallingford
Archbishop Stigand surrenders and ends attempts to put Edgar Atheling on throne, October

❻ **Southwark**
William repulsed, mid-October

❹ **Battle of Hastings**
William defeats Harold, who is killed, 14 October

❸ **Pevensey**
William lands in England, 28 September

ENGLAND
Winchester
Canterbury
Normandy Coast
Brittany Coast

Superior forces

Some historians believe that while the English military system was impressive, the Norman one was even more formidable:

- Harold and his HOUSECARLS were a tight-knit, loyal band, but William's closest KNIGHTS were arguably even more loyal. William's closest lieutenants were his half-brothers, Odo and Robert.
- Harold had many well-equipped soldiers. The Normans had about the same number but they were even better equipped.
- The Norman war machine was more flexible. William had foot soldiers, horsemen and archers, so they could change tactics more easily than the English, who were mainly foot soldiers. English fighting tactics had not changed much for a century.

Source 2 A scene from the Bayeux Tapestry, showing fighting at the Battle of Hastings. ▼

1. Study Source 2. The Bayeux Tapestry is a biased source as it was commissioned by William of Normandy's brother. Does this mean it is of no use to historians?
2. How far does Source 2 support what David Carpenter says in Source 3?

Source 3 Historian David Carpenter, writing in 2004.

Hastings was a killing match and the Normans had more effective means of killing: horsemen, and also archers. The lack of English archers is one of the puzzles of the battle. Only one English bowman is shown on the tapestry, the consequence perhaps of the haste with which the army had been assembled. By contrast the shields and bodies of the English bristle with Norman arrows.

Experience of warfare

One of the most significant factors was the experience that the Norman knights and troops had in fighting. William of Normandy had been battling for his dukedom since he was a boy. The great lords of France were constantly at war, besieging castles as well as fighting openly. The duke of Normandy had to guard his territory against the king of France. England, meanwhile, had been relatively stable, without any serious civil war or invasion since 1016. So while Harold and the English thegns were no strangers to warfare, William and the Normans were even more experienced.

Leadership and decision making

The differences between the two sides can be seen clearly in the approaches taken by Harold and William. Harold was a strong leader, as his victory against Harald Hardrada demonstrated, but by turning his forces around and marching straight back south to do battle with the Normans he risked overstretching his resources. In contrast, William refused to strike inland immediately after he landed in England. Instead he stayed near the coast, secured his supply lines to Normandy and rested his troops while waiting for Harold to come to him. This turned out to be a wise decision.

FOCUS TASK

Why was the Norman invasion successful?

1. Add examples from these two pages to your table for Key Question A on page 21.
2. Which factor do you think was most important in the success of the Norman *invasion*?

23

How did the Normans take control of England 1066–75?

Winning the Battle of Hastings did not automatically make William king of England. The ARCHBISHOP of Canterbury, Stigand, tried to rally support among the thegns for Edgar ATHELING, the heir to the royal house of Wessex, to be the new king. William had to fight his way from Hastings to London to deal with the challenge. He destroyed the town of Dover, fought Anglo-Saxon forces at Canterbury, and by December 1066 had set up camp just outside London as he was unsure whether or not he would be able to enter the city. However, English forces had been greatly weakened and the thegns decided to support William's claim to the throne.

FACTFILE

A map showing the revolts against William, 1067–75.

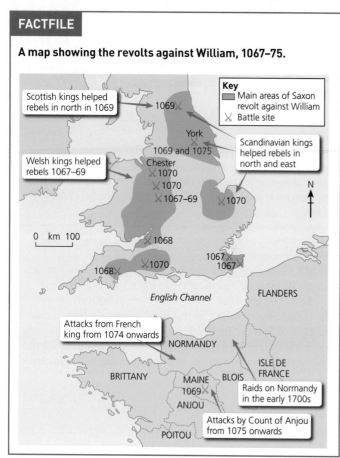

Key
- Main areas of Saxon revolt against William
- X Battle site

Scottish kings helped rebels in north in 1069 → 1069 X

York X

1069 and 1075

Chester X 1070

X 1070

X 1067–69

X 1070

Welsh kings helped rebels 1067–69

Scandinavian kings helped rebels in north and east

N ↑

0 km 100

X 1068

X 1070

1067 X 1067

1068 X

English Channel

FLANDERS

Attacks from French king from 1074 onwards

NORMANDY

ISLE DE FRANCE

BRITTANY

MAINE 1069 X

BLOIS

Raids on Normandy in the early 1700s

ANJOU

Attacks by Count of Anjou from 1075 onwards

POITOU

Ten weeks after his victory at Hastings – on Christmas Day 1066 – William was crowned king of England. But this still did not mean that he controlled the country. There were around 10,000 Normans trying to control 2 million Anglo-Saxons, most of whom were hostile to their conquerors. This hostility soon turned into rebellion. There were serious revolts against Norman rule every year between 1067 and 1075 (see Factfile), all over the country. So how did the Normans survive and thrive in England?

Factor 1: Military efficiency and ruthless violence

The Factfile shows the many revolts against Norman rule. Several were serious, but they never represented a truly united effort to overthrow the Normans. Firstly, there was no obvious leader to rally round, in the way that Alfred the Great had rallied the English against the Vikings (see pages 14–15). There was also no obvious place, such as a royal fortress, for the rebels to join forces and make a stand. Years of stability had left the English unprepared for a fight, and the Normans were able to deal with each rebellion as it occurred. They inflicted tens of thousands of casualties and carried out many atrocities against civilians.

At first William chose to show mercy to those who opposed him, in keeping with the Norman ideal of chivalry. After the Battle of Hastings, English nobles who surrendered were not executed. In fact, William was much more merciful than the Anglo-Saxons or Vikings had traditionally been to those they defeated in battle. When the people of Exeter rose up against him, William crushed the revolt but accepted their surrender without issuing any punishment.

However, as the revolts continued William began to deal more harshly with the rebels. The most serious threat came in 1069, when the northern English earls joined forces with the king of Scotland and a Viking fleet to oppose William. William's castles in York were destroyed and his garrison killed. William marched north, arriving in York in December 1169. He paid off the Danes and then proceeded to make sure the north never troubled him again. He drove off the rebel forces and destroyed large areas, burning homes, barns and other buildings, and killing animals. This event became known as the HARRYING OF THE NORTH (see Sources 4 and 5). It was rumoured that people ate horses, cats, dogs and even human flesh to survive. Many thousands probably still died of starvation. It was decades before the area recovered.

> **Source 4** Part of a speech given by William the Conqueror shortly before he died in 1087. It was recorded by the English chronicler Orderic Vitalis in the 1120s.
>
> *I attacked the English of the northern shires like a lion. I ordered their houses and corn, with all their implements and belongings, to be burnt without exception and large herds of cattle and beasts of burden to be destroyed wherever they were found. It was there that I took revenge on masses of people by subjecting them to a cruel famine; and by doing so – alas! – I became the murderer of many thousands, both young and old, from that fine race of people.*

How and why did William's attitude towards his enemies change in 1069?

> **Source 5** Orderic Vitalis, writing in 1070.
>
> *My narrative has frequently had occasion to praise William, but for this act which condemned the innocent and the guilty alike to die by slow starvation I cannot commend him. For when I think of helpless children, young men in the prime of life, and hoary greybeards perishing alike of hunger, I am so moved to pity that I would rather lament the grief and sufferings of the people than make a vain attempt to flatter the perpetrator of so much infamy.*

Factor 2: Castles

The strategic importance of castles

Castles originated in France, where rival rulers often attacked and invaded each other's lands and there were few natural barriers to stop them. The castle emerged as the best way to protect territory and repel invaders. A few dozen soldiers in a castle could control the surrounding area and slow down invaders even if they were outnumbered. The Normans knew that swiftly establishing a series of castles in England would be key to controlling the Anglo-Saxons. The BAYEUX TAPESTRY shows how the Normans built a castle at Pevensey almost as soon as they landed.

By contrast, the English had no castles to help defend their land – there had been no need for them in the relatively peaceful period before the Norman Conquest. There were some fortified houses, but these were too small to provide effective resistance. Two centuries earlier Alfred had built burhs, which proved effective against the Vikings (see page 15), but by the 1060s English towns were large and usually unwalled (another result of Anglo-Saxon prosperity). It would have required a huge number of soldiers to defend them effectively. If the Normans had been forced to besiege a series of English castles, one by one, it would have slowed the progress of the Conquest and might eventually have worn down the invaders. Without them, the English had few defences.

> **Source 6** Historian David Carpenter, writing in 2004.
>
> *Cavalry and castles were integral to the intensely competitive military and political environment in France, where small principalities – Anjou, Maine, Brittany, Normandy, the French kingdom – were engaged in constant fast-moving warfare across great plains and open frontiers. England was very different. Since Cnut's accession in 1016 it had suffered neither invasion nor civil war. Harold had triumphed in Wales, but this was not cavalry territory. There had been no need to develop either cavalry or castles. The English state had been too successful for its own good.*

FACTFILE

The early phase of castle building and the Marcher lordships.

The earls of Chester, Shrewsbury and Hereford were almost independent rulers known as 'marcher lords'. Their job was to make sure there was no threat to William from Wales.

Key
- Marcher lordship
- Castle

The Bishop of Durham was given the same role in the north. His job was to stop any threat from Scotland.

N

0   km   100

The symbolic importance of castles

Norman castles also had a symbolic role. The first Norman castles were simple buildings with ditches and wooden fences. They could be built fairly quickly, and local peasants were forced to construct the mottes (huge mounds of earth) and put up the defences. Today we visit castles for pleasure, but in 1066 they would have been a blot on the landscape, surrounded by felled trees and churned-up earth. For the English it must have felt like they were being forced to build their own prisons. Each castle and the surrounding area could be defended by a small number of Norman knights, and the buildings stood as a constant reminder of who was now in charge.

As the Normans secured their hold in each area, they forced local people to reinforce the temporary castles to make them stronger. During the next 30 years, they built around 500 new castles (the Factfile shows the location of just some of them). William paid for this programme of castle building with a massive TAX on the Church, forcing the great monasteries and cathedrals to pay for military service just like any other landholder.

> 1   Norman castles usually had three main aims: protection, control and intimidation. Study Source 7 and look for evidence of how castles achieved these aims.

Source 7 An artist's impression of how Pickering Castle in Yorkshire might have looked soon after 1066. ▼

Factors 3 and 4: A network of loyal supporters ... and land

William had a close band of supporters – people he trusted and who were personally loyal to him. The inner circle was made up of William's family and closest friends, but the key to loyalty beyond this group was land. William took land away from English thegns and gave it to his loyal Norman barons. They then sub-divided these lands to reward their followers, and so on. In return for land William got loyalty. This system is sometimes known as FEUDALISM after the Latin term *feodum*, which means 'a piece of land'. However, historians today do not use the word very much and certainly nobody at the time would have used it.

These loyal Normans were the key to consolidating control of England. Each area of land was controlled by a BARON and his knights with their network of castles. The Marcher lords, who were given the task of controlling the most rebellious areas (see Factfile), were particularly important.

It says a lot about this system that after 1075 William was away fighting in France for most of the time, yet Norman control in England was not seriously threatened again. As well as his barons, William had a loyal group of churchmen who helped him to administer England. Lanfranc, his Archbishop of Canterbury, effectively ran England in William's absence.

> **2** 'William used land ownership as a weapon of conquest.' Do you agree with this statement?

Factor 5: Making use of Anglo-Saxon administration

William emphasised that he was not 'seizing' England, he was simply inheriting it from Edward as, he claimed, Edward had promised. This air of legality helped him persuade officials in the royal government and SHERIFFS out in the shires to carry out his orders because he was their legal king (although some officials probably needed more persuading than others). These officials collected taxes, raised armies and maintained law and order, carrying out royal commands through WRITS. William now used the strength of this system to his own advantage (see Source 8). As time passed, English sheriffs and other officials were replaced by Normans, or by people who worked faithfully for Norman lords, and this gave William even greater control.

> **Source 8** Historian Geoffrey Hindley, writing in 2006.
>
> *The shire court lies behind the success of the Norman settlement. A Norman who had been granted land by the king needed only to present himself with a sealed writ. If it was agreed to be authentic by the sheriff and other officials of the court it was accepted. The local officials had to inform the newcomer of all the lands he now owned and even help him take possession of them.*

Factor 6: A new English Church

The Church in Anglo-Saxon England had been wealthy and influential. In fact, it played a key role in the Anglo-Saxon state, supporting the king and giving the English people a strong sense of identity. William also set about turning this strength to his own advantage. He removed the Anglo-Saxon BISHOPS and abbots presiding over the major monasteries, and replaced them with Normans. By 1070, only three of the country's 15 bishops were English.

FOCUS TASK

Why was the Norman Conquest successful?

1   Add further examples from these two pages to your table for Key Question A.
2   Which factor do you think was the most important in the success of the Norman *Conquest*? Why?

Source 9 An extract from the *Anglo-Saxon Chronicle*, referring to the Domesday Book.

[King William] sent his men over all England into every shire and had them find out how many 100 hides there were in the shire, or what land and cattle the king himself had in the country or what dues he ought to have in the 12 months from the shire. He also recorded how much land his archbishops had and his bishops and his abbots and his earls, how much each man who was a landholder in England had in land or livestock and how much money it was worth.

1   Look at Source 9. Before you read any further, ask yourself what questions might be answered about the Norman Conquest by studying a document that records land ownership.

The impact of the Norman Conquest

One problem for historians looking at the medieval period is that there are relatively few records dating from this period. However, on the topic of how England changed after the Norman Conquest we have one spectacular resource – the DOMESDAY BOOK – which records exactly who owned what in England in 1086.

The DOMESDAY SURVEY was carried out for practical reasons. In the 20 years after the Norman invasion almost all land in England had been seized, transferred, subdivided or sold off. Disputes over land ownership inevitably arose, because land meant wealth and power. William commissioned the survey to find out exactly who had owned what in 1066 and what had changed in the two decades that followed. He used the efficient Anglo-Saxon network of scribes, officials, local courts and sheriffs to carry out the survey, and every community had to answer 20 questions set by the Domesday Commissioners. The survey was a staggering achievement, taking testimony from thousands of landowners and even peasants across the country. It was completed in less than a year.

All this information was written up in the Domesday Book – a source that has survived to give us valuable insight into how Norman rule changed England.

Removal of the English nobility

It is not clear whether William set out with the intention of wiping out the English aristocracy. Certainly in the months after the Norman invasion many thegns pledged loyalty to William and were allowed to keep their lands. However, that situation changed rapidly, partly because William wanted to reward his Norman followers by giving them English land, but also because of rebellions against Norman rule. Rebels always lost their lands.

The Domesday Book gives us a very clear picture of the destruction of the English noble class. It shows that by 1086 only four major English lords survived. Many lords had been killed at Hastings or in the various rebellions. Many thegns had died too. But those who survived now found themselves working as tenants for Norman lords. More than 4,000 thegns had lost their lands and had been replaced by around 200 barons who were loyal to William.

Source 10 An aerial photograph of Winchester Cathedral. The outlines to the left of the cathedral show the layout of the old Anglo-Saxon cathedral that was knocked down and replaced with this one. ▼

Changes to the English Church

William purged the bishops and abbots of the major monasteries, replacing them with Norman bishops and abbots. Many churches were renamed and dedicated to different saints – wiping out the memory of many of the Anglo-Saxon saints traditionally honoured by the English people. William and his fellow Normans started a massive church-building programme and over the next 50 years every English cathedral and most of the main abbey churches were destroyed and rebuilt in the Norman style. The Normans were building these churches to give thanks to God for their victory, but at the same time they were trying to wipe out the old Anglo-Saxon culture and identity and replace it with their own.

2   Study Source 10. Why do you think the Normans bothered to leave the outline of the old cathedral when they built the new one?

The Norman 'yoke'?

It is harder to know how the Norman Conquest affected people further down the social scale. Life probably became more difficult for the peasants. The new Norman lords wanted to recover the money they had spent in the Conquest so rents probably rose. The new landlords also imposed new conditions on their tenants. The Domesday Book often mentions individual freemen with the phrase 'he is now a VILLEIN' (a tenant with restricted freedom and rights). After the Conquest, the number of SERFS (people who were owned by the lord) rose sharply and the number of freemen fell. In Cambridgeshire, for example, the number of freemen fell from 900 to 177. Latin replaced English as the language of government while at the local level Englishmen had to learn Norman French if they wished to be understood by their lords.

These changes, along with the dispossession of the thegns, the changes to the Church and the way William used the Anglo-Saxon legal and administrative system to control the country, gave rise to the idea of the 'Norman yoke' on the shoulders of the English people (a yoke is the harness worn by an ox pulling a plough and it is a heavy burden). However, most historians express doubt that Norman rule was significantly harsher on ordinary people than Anglo-Saxon rule had been. For example, the Normans abolished slavery, under pressure from the Church. This actually cost William financially, so historians assume it was done for moral reasons – the king had previous abolished slavery in Normandy.

> **Source 11 Historian Marc Morris, writing in 2012.**
>
> *There is still a widespread assumption that the Normans are 'them' and the English are 'us'. The Normans are the villains of the story, introducing bad things like feudalism and the class system. The notion persists that pre-Conquest England had been freer, more liberal with representative institutions and better rights for women. But almost all of this is a myth ... the Normans come across as arrogant, warlike, pleased with themselves and holier than thou. But the English are no better with their binge drinking, slavery and political murders. Whoever these people are they are not us. They are our forebears from 1000 years ago.*

KEY QUESTION REVIEW

A Why was the Norman Conquest successful?

1 You have been gathering evidence for the role of different factors in the Norman Conquest. Complete the table on page 21 by using the third column to rank the factors.

2 The real point of the research stage is to prepare you for some serious thinking. Complete one of these tasks.
   EITHER write an essay:
   'The Norman Conquest was successful because of castles.' Do you agree?
   The question is guiding you to one factor: castles. However, you also need to consider whether other factors were more or less important. Your completed table should give you some ideas.
   OR plan a TV documentary:
   A TV company want you to make a documentary to explain the Norman success from 1066 to 1087, but you only have half an hour. You will need to include all the elements in your table but it is up to you how long you give to each and what goes into each section. Make a plan for how to divide up the time. You could write up your plan as written explanation or as a storyboard.

B How did the Norman Conquest change England?

Review your change and continuity table from page 21. Use your completed table to answer this practice question:
How significant was the Norman Conquest for England?

PRACTICE QUESTIONS

1 Describe two examples of Norman military tactics. (4)
2 Explain why the Normans were able to hold on to England after 1066 despite English resistance. (8)

1.3 Medieval war and society: The rise and fall of the feudal system

FOCUS

The Norman Conquest changed England and set a pattern for subsequent centuries. Society was dominated by the demands of warfare. In this topic you will study the ways in which war and society evolved through the Middle Ages.

In Part A, you will examine the period 1100–1215, including:
- how the feudal system was supposed to work
- how and why it sometimes went wrong.

In Part B, you will examine the period 1290–1450, focusing on:
- how the approach to war changed in Edward I's reign
- how this evolution continued after Edward I's death.

The big picture

Why was war so central to medieval society?

For the upper end of medieval society (knights, barons and monarchs), war was a way of life and, in some respects, a business. The king was effectively 'chief warrior', his barons provided military service for him and the knights provided military service for their barons. If a king could fight successful wars, defend his lands, capture new lands and reward his followers (as Henry I and Henry II managed to do), then all was well. If not, then the consequences could be disastrous (such as the rebellion against King John). Over time, the nature of war changed as military service declined and a standing army emerged.

How did society view warfare?

For the ruling classes, war was romanticised. A whole culture grew up around the role of knighthood, known as chivalry. The ideal knight was noble, honourable and protective towards women and those who were not warriors. The Church promoted the ideals of chivalry. Many monks who wrote the chronicles of these times came from the same families as the noble knights. This shows in the way they wrote about war, idealising it in songs, stories and poems.

What was the relationship between war and government?

William the Conqueror and the kings who followed him gave land to their loyal followers. In return, great barons paid homage (promised loyalty) to the king and promised to provide knights when he called. Over time, as armies became larger and fought virtually full time, feudal service became less practical. Kings preferred to collect taxes and hire their own professional armies. To raise these taxes, kings needed a wider base of support from those they ruled. This led to the emergence of parliament, which agreed taxes in return for being more involved in running the country.

How did warfare affect ordinary people?

The majority of the population did not fight, but they paid for wars through their labour and their taxes. If you were directly caught up in warfare the experience was horrific. You might be forced to serve as a foot soldier. You might have your goods stolen or looted to feed the visiting army, or you might be forced to give them shelter and feed their horses. Over time, wars helped shape the identity of the population, creating an English, French, Scottish and Welsh identity as these states fought each other.

Source 1 An image of the Battle of Hastings (1066) from the Bayeux Tapestry. ▼

ACTIVITY

Study Sources 1 and 2 carefully. What similarities and differences can you see in the nature of warfare in 1066 and 1346?

Source 2 An image of the Battle of Crécy between English and French forces in 1346, during the Hundred Years' War. ▼

KEY QUESTIONS

A Why was warfare such a significant element of medieval society?

Look at these features of medieval society:
- land
- wealth
- equipment
- civil wars
- national wars
- chivalry
- leadership
- homage
- religion and the Church
- national identity.

Make a card for each feature. As you work through this topic, add notes to the cards explaining the role of each feature in medieval England.

B How and why did the business of war evolve during the medieval period?

Make a copy of the table below. As you work through this topic, complete the second and third columns to note down the reasons for the way warfare changed during this period and the impact the change had.

Change	Reason for change	Impact of change
shift from feudal military service to professional armies		
paying for wars and how this affected government		
importance of knights in warfare		
greater involvement of whole population		

1.3A Feudalism in theory and practice 1100–1215

FOCUS

How do you set up society to be ready to wage war at any time? The early medieval answer was feudalism. In this part of the topic you will investigate how this was supposed to work – and what happened when it failed.

Land, military service and dues

The key asset in medieval times was land. Land meant wealth and power. Monarchs owned huge amounts of land and they used the rents and other money generated by the land to run the country, raise armies and fight wars. War was the key activity for a ruler.

However, monarchs could not do all this alone. They relied on their close allies, the great barons and bishops. In return for land or positions of power, barons, bishops and knights offered loyalty and military service in the form of knights and foot soldiers. The barons also made sure the law was obeyed, taxes were collected and order was kept. In return for this, they received a share of the taxes collected and the fines imposed in their law courts. It was not all one way, though. Barons had to pay 'feudal dues' and accept control over important aspects of their lives. This included getting the king's permission to marry and usually paying a fee when lands were bought and sold, as well as when a baron died and his children inherited the land. This was partly a way of making money for the Crown and partly a way of preventing certain barons gaining too much land.

This give-and-take system filtered further down the social scale. Tenants-in-chief had sub-tenants. These were lesser nobles – local lords or knights. They provided military service in return for land. They also represented royal authority at the local village level – for example, acting as judges in the courts. At the lower end of society were the peasants who worked on land belonging to the lords and knights in return for a small plot of land and possibly a cottage.

Source 1 Extracts from Henry I's coronation charter, 1100, in which the new king promised to respect ancient rights and customs.

If any baron or earl of mine shall die, his heirs shall not be forced to purchase their inheritance, but shall receive it through force of law and custom.

Any baron or earl who wishes to betroth his daughter or other women kinsfolk in marriage should consult me first, but I will not stand in the way of any prudent marriage. Any widow who wishes to remarry should consult with me, but I shall abide by the wishes of her close relatives, the other barons and earls. I will not allow her to marry one of my enemies.

If any of my barons commit a crime, he shall not bind himself to the crown with a payment as was done in the time of my father and brother, but shall stand for the crime as was custom and law before the time of my father, and make amends as are appropriate. Anyone guilty of treachery or other heinous crime shall make proper amends.

Those knights who render military service and horses shall not be required to give grain or other farm goods to me.

Source 2 An image of a knight paying homage to his king, c1275. ▶

1   Read Source 1. What is Henry I offering the barons?
2   What is he expecting in return?
3   Do you think Source 1 or Source 2 is more useful as evidence about feudalism?

Castles

Castles were a vital part of the feudal system. By 1086, there were an estimated 500 castles in England and Wales (see Factfile on page 26). Some castles were ROYAL CASTLES, built and controlled by the king to guard strategic points, but most were BARONIAL CASTLES. A baron would build a castle to control his lands, to house his knights and to use as a residence. A castle was the most powerful military weapon of the period. Kings kept a close eye on baronial castles and barons needed royal permission to build castles, extend them or improve their fortifications.

Source 3 A photograph of Framlingham Castle and town today. Framlingham was a baronial castle belonging to the powerful Bigod family. ▼

4 Why might Framlingham Castle have caused concern to a monarch?

FOCUS TASK

Feudalism in theory

Historians have offered the following descriptions of feudal society:
● A rigid hierarchy where every person knew their place.
● A flexible system of give and take.
● A clever system designed to maintain the monarch's hold on power.

Decide how far you agree with each of the above statements. Rearrange them in order of how far they are supported by evidence.

Feudalism in practice

Of course, like many social systems, feudalism did not always work the way it was intended. Medieval England was characterised by personal rivalry, betrayal and disloyalty – probably at all social levels. There is evidence to suggest that whenever someone in a particular position showed signs of weakness, there was always someone one step below them – an upstart or an ambitious newcomer – ready to take advantage. The case studies that follow show what happened when the feudal system broke down.

Case study 1: The Anarchy under Stephen and Matilda

Why was there a civil war?

From the 1130s to the 1150s, there was a period of turmoil and war in England that historians later called the ANARCHY. When Henry I died in 1135, he had no legitimate son. He persuaded his barons to accept his daughter Matilda as queen. However, when Henry died, Matilda was away in France and her cousin Stephen of Blois – the richest baron in England – seized the throne for himself.

Source 4 An image of the Battle of Lincoln in 1141. ▼

Civil war followed. Stephen and Matilda fought for control of key castles and tried to recruit barons to their side. The war swung back and forth. Matilda beat Stephen at the Battle of Lincoln in 1141, captured him and headed for London. However, Stephen's supporters continued to fight and defeated Matilda's forces at Winchester. Stephen escaped from prison and became king again. From 1143 to 1146 there was a stalemate. Neither side was in control and royal authority broke down. Eventually the barons forced Stephen and Matilda to reach a deal. Matilda left England and Stephen ruled until his death, but he would be succeeded by Matilda's son, the future Henry II (see page 36).

What was the impact of the civil war?

With the two sides more concerned with fighting each other than running the country, law and order began to break down and some barons exploited this (see Source 5). Stephen tried to exert his control, besieging the castles of many rebel nobles, but he lacked the authority to make his lords follow his orders.

1   Read Source 5, then answer these questions:
    a   Who does the chronicler blame for the Anarchy?
    b   What are the consequences of the Anarchy?
    c   Which of these would have the most impact on ordinary people?
    d   What is the chronicler's attitude to the Anarchy?

> **Source 5** An extract from the *Peterborough Chronicle*, 1137.
>
> *When the traitors saw that Stephen was a good-humoured, kindly, and easy-going man who inflicted no punishment, then they committed all manner of horrible crimes ....*
>
> *For every great man built him castles and held them against the king; and they filled the whole land with these castles. They sorely burdened the unhappy people of the country with forced labour on the castles; and when the castles were built, they filled them up with devils and wicked men.*
>
> *By night and by day they seized those whom they believed to have any wealth, whether they were men or women; and in order to get their gold and silver, they put them into prison and tortured them with unspeakable tortures.*

Historians still debate the impact of this civil war. Although Victorian historians named this period the 'Anarchy', more recent studies suggest that the problems were localised and that the fighting was not constant throughout Stephen's reign. They think that the *Peterborough Chronicle* (Source 5) is unrepresentative because while the eastern part of England saw a lot of fighting, many other areas were untouched.

Why did the feudal system fail during the Anarchy?

Failure of monarchy?

The key problem was that Stephen was unable to enforce his authority. He tried to win the loyalty of the barons when he took power, but he probably went too far. He relaxed many of Henry I's restrictions on them and gave 30 of them the prestigious title of earl. His main problem, of course, was that he had to fight a civil war for much of his reign. So in that respect the Anarchy was the fault of Stephen – and possibly Matilda, although she could hardly be blamed for trying to claim her inheritance.

Was it the barons' fault?

In some areas, local lords and barons simply wanted stability so they ignored Stephen and Matilda and made their own peace agreements with rival lords. In other parts of the country, local lords took advantage of the lack of royal authority to build up their own power, seize lands from their neighbours, and extend and strengthen their castles without royal permission. Sometimes they effectively took control of the sheriffs. Sheriffs were royal officials, but with no effective government they lost their authority. Many simply followed the orders of local lords or were replaced by men loyal to those lords. In a society dominated by men of war, conflict was bound to break out when this happened. This was especially true because knights and barons faced relatively low risks – the rules of chivalry meant that if they were taken prisoner, they would be freed on payment of a ransom.

Source 6 An effigy of Geoffrey of Mandeville. He was denied a Christian burial because he had been excommunicated, so his body was wrapped in lead and taken to the Templar community in London. The Templars were an order of religious knights sworn to regain the Holy Land from the Muslims. ▼

The story of Geoffrey of Mandeville illustrates some of the issues that arose during this period of civil war. In 1140, Geoffrey inherited his father's lands in the east and south-east of England. However, a large proportion of the family lands in Essex were held by the king as a result of a fine imposed by Henry I on Geoffrey's father. Geoffrey was ambitious and ruthless. When Henry I died in 1135, he decided to exploit the situation to regain his father's lands. In 1140, he declared his support for Stephen and in exchange Stephen returned the most valuable lands in Essex to Geoffrey. When Stephen was captured in 1141, Geoffrey immediately declared his support for Matilda in return for the cancellation of his father's debts to the Crown and the return of other family lands. He was also made sheriff of Essex and Hertfordshire. When Stephen escaped, Geoffrey switched sides again, but in 1143 the two men fell out and Stephen ordered Geoffrey's arrest. Geoffrey rebelled and the king besieged him in Burwell, Cambridgeshire, in 1144. Geoffrey was killed in the fighting.

Geoffrey was probably one of the more extreme examples of ambitious barons during this period, but there were plenty of them, including the powerful Hugh Bigod. When civil war broke out, Hugh seized Norwich Castle but Stephen drove him out in 1140. The following year Hugh fought alongside Stephen at Lincoln. By 1143 he was back in conflict with the king and from 1148 he gave shelter to Theobald, Archbishop of Canterbury, who was in dispute with Stephen. (You can read more about Hugh Bigod's stronghold, Framlingham Castle, on pages 248–49.)

> 2 What does the career of Geoffrey of Mandeville reveal about the feudal system during the Anarchy?
>
> 3 Can you find any other examples of barons who rebelled against Stephen?
>
> 4 Would you say Stephen, Matilda or the barons was most responsible for the disruption?

How did Henry II re-establish control?

Stephen and Matilda finally reached a compromise, and Matilda's son was crowned as Henry II in 1154. Henry's efforts to re-establish royal control proved that the feudal system could work under the leadership of a strong king, and Henry's reign was a good example of balancing force with co-operation.

Through the 1150s, Henry seized over 40 castles from barons, keeping 30 of them and rewarding loyal barons with the others. He had the walls of Framlingham Castle pulled down. In the 1160s, he forced the barons to provide detailed information about the lands and other income they held. He taxed them on this basis, although he was careful not to over-tax them and cause discontent. He replaced two-thirds of the local sheriffs with officials he approved himself.

Henry was also wise enough to forgive barons once they accepted his authority. He was careful to consult them on important issues, such as his changes to the legal system. When Henry clashed with his Archbishop of Canterbury, Thomas Becket, most barons remained loyal to the king. When he died in 1189, the throne passed to his son Richard I (known as Richard the Lionheart).

> **1** Historians have criticised Stephen for being too forgiving. In what way was he different from Henry II?

Source 7 A photograph of Orford Castle. Henry II had Orford built as a warning to the Bigod family who were based at nearby Framingham Castle. Henry allowed the Bigods to rebuild Framingham after pulling down its walls. ▼

FOCUS TASK

Was the Anarchy caused by a failure in the feudal system or the failure of the monarch?

As a class or in small groups, hold an inquest into the Anarchy. Which of the following verdicts will you reach?

- War between Stephen and Matilda was the problem.
- Stephen's rule was the problem.
- The feudal system was the problem.
- The barons were the problem.

You should look at the events of Stephen's reign, but also at Henry II's actions afterwards.

Case study 2: King John and the barons

John is remembered as a particularly bad king, but he faced great difficulties during his reign. Many of his problems can be traced back to the issue of warfare, especially the cost of waging war.

Richard the Lionheart's expensive and on-going wars

John inherited major problems from his brother Richard the Lionheart. Richard spent most of his reign on crusade or defending his family lands in France against King Philip II of France. Richard was a skilled commander, but when he was killed in 1199 he bequeathed his brother unfinished wars and major financial problems.

John's taxes to pay for war

John might have been able to win support from the barons by giving up on his French lands and focusing on England. However, he spent the next ten years increasing taxes to raise the money needed for a large campaign to win back Normandy. In the process he fell out with the Church and the barons, who were unhappy about the increases in taxes (although some historians have argued that they could afford to pay and had been getting away with light taxes for years).

John's failings as a war leader

John tried to continue the wars, but in 1204 he lost Normandy (the most valuable of John's remaining French possessions) to King Philip. For a feudal lord, nothing was worse than defeat in war.

John's problems

Let down by the barons

John was not an outstanding commander, but his problems were heightened by the fact that he had little support from his barons. They sent smaller contingents of troops than were actually needed and were unwilling to risk their soldiers in big battles.

John's character and behaviour

John was a suspicious and treacherous man, and these were not good characteristics for a feudal war leader. He was cruel and mean in victory, where Richard had been generous. He harshly punished anyone who stood up to him. In 1211, for example, he imprisoned Matilda de Braose and demanded £25,000. When she refused to pay, he left her and her son to starve to death. He did not trust most of the barons, and refused to consult them on important issues. He forced the great barons to pay vast sums to inherit their estates or to marry. He also appointed many sheriffs (including Philip Mark, the infamous Sheriff of Nottingham who features in the Robin Hood stories) who were not from the areas they ran but were loyal to John. The barons felt that the king did not trust them to carry out the roles that they had traditionally performed.

ACTIVITY

Look at the Focus Task on page 36.
1 How many of the problems arising under John had also been a problem in the Anarchy?
2 Does this make you think that the problem was:
   a   the feudal system?
   b   the strains of war?
   c   King John?
   d   the barons?

The Barons' War and Magna Carta

The tensions between John and his barons reached a climax in 1215. John met with his opponents to see if a compromise could be reached. This failed and throughout April and May the rebels took up arms against him. They chose Robert Fitzwalter as their leader and were supported by the Archbishop of Canterbury, Stephen Langton.

As with previous wars, the main tactic was to build up a position of strength rather than fighting pitched battles. Both sides looked for allies. Both sides tried to control key lands, towns and castles. At first the rebels were more successful and the important cities of London, Lincoln and Exeter all declared for the barons. The barons also controlled key castles such as Rochester. However, John had powerful supporters, including the legendary knight William Marshal (see page 39), Earl of Pembroke, and Hubert de Burgh, Earl of Kent. Despite this, there is evidence that families were divided in the Barons' War – a baron might declare for the rebels, but his son or brother may have sided with the king. Historians think that many barons were hedging their bets, trying to ensure they were supporting the winning side. This may also have been a reason why John accepted MAGNA CARTA in July 1215.

Magna Carta has become a landmark document. It was important for two main reasons:

- It was written down. Kings had worked successfully with barons long before John, but Magna Carta put their agreements into formal contract, which would not be subject to the whims of the ruler in the future.
- It put the king under the law, not above it. Magna Carta effectively stated that even the king had to obey the law – a completely new idea at the time.

However, the document was not seen this way in 1215. At the time, it was regarded as a peace treaty between John and the barons, and most of its 61 clauses demanded an end to specific abuses that had developed in John's reign.

Not surprisingly, John overturned Magna Carta at the first opportunity, and by autumn 1215 war was raging again. The rebel barons invited the son of King Philip II of France to take the throne. Once again, a pattern of sieges rather than battles emerged. In July 1215, French forces besieged Dover Castle several times but, under the command of Hubert de Burgh, it held out.

Source 8 The tomb of William Marshal. ▼

Source 9 A reconstruction drawing of the siege of Dover Castle. It was attacked several times in the period 1215–17 but it did not fall. ▼

In October 1215, John besieged Rochester Castle to stop French forces joining up with rebel forces from London. The castle fell in November 1215 and John had to be persuaded by his commanders not to hang all the defenders. Alliances began to shift again, but within a year the king died. The majority of the rebels then pledged their loyalty to John's nine-year-old son, Henry III. In large part their loyalty to the boy king was because the regent ruling on his behalf was the hugely respected William Marshal (see Factfile on page 39).

FACTFILE

William Marshal – the greatest knight in history?

- Born in 1147, William was the fourth son of John Marshal. His father was a minor Norman noble and, as a younger son, William was even less important. He was unlikely to inherit land.
- When William was five, his father turned against King Stephen during the civil wars. Stephen took William hostage to make sure his father did not rebel any more, but his father continued to oppose the king. William was spared, trained as a squire and then became a knight.
- He turned out to be a superb fighter and a huge star in tournaments all over England and Europe. This earned him fame and fortune. He was invited to join the royal household and teach the young Henry II about chivalry and knighthood.
- He fell foul of court politics and was accused of an affair. He denied it, but was forced to leave the royal household anyway.
- In 1185, Henry II recalled him, as he wanted his help fighting in France against a rebellion led by his own son, Richard. Marshal fought Richard directly in battle; he killed the prince's horse but spared his life. Henry rewarded William with marriage to Isabel de Clare, which made William Earl of Pembroke and brought him wealth in the form of lands in Wales and Ireland.
- Richard I had so much respect for William that when he came to the throne in 1189, he invited William to be part of his household.
- In 1199, William was given care of King John's son, the future Henry III. Throughout the rebellions against John, William remained loyal. After John's death in 1216, William effectively ran the country as regent for Henry III.
- William died in 1219. He was the first person who was not a monarch to have a biography written about him. He has also been described by many as history's greatest knight.

ACTIVITY

Not many people got elaborate tombs like William Marshal's in Source 8. William Marshal was an extraordinary knight whose life spans the period you have just studied. Look through the information about him in the Factfile and find examples of ways in which he was both typical and untypical of a lord at the time.

FOCUS TASK

Why did feudalism fail in the period 1135–1216?

1 Why was there so much trouble in this period? Copy and complete the table to compare the two case studies.

	Case study 1: The Anarchy	Amount of responsibility for breakdown (%)	Case study 2: King John and the barons	Amount of responsibility for breakdown (%)
strain and cost of war				
quality of the monarch				
actions of the barons				
failings of the feudal system				
unfortunate circumstances				

2 Discuss this statement in pairs and make a list of evidence both supporting and opposing it:
'The Anarchy and the Barons' War were not similar at all.'

PRACTICE QUESTIONS

1 Describe two examples of feudal service. (2)
2 Describe two examples of disagreements between kings and barons in the period 1100–1215. (2)
3 Explain why kings and barons clashed in the early medieval period. (8)
4 Explain how kings and barons worked together in the medieval period. (8)

1.3B The significance of war in medieval society c1290–c1450

FOCUS

This part of the topic focuses on the reign of Edward I – one of England's most powerful and formidable rulers, and a great warrior king – and the period after his death. In this section you will look at:

● how Edward I's wars changed warfare and government
● how warfare continued to develop in the Hundred Years' War and how this affected England.

The age of chivalry?

The answer to whether this was an age of CHIVALRY is both yes and no. The literature of the period places great emphasis on chivalry, focusing particularly on the legendary King Arthur and the Knights of the Round Table. In the 1200s, the young Prince Edward was much influenced by these stories. When he came to the throne in 1272, he became obsessed with these stories. As king, he personally supervised the reburial of bones that were believed to be those of King Arthur at Glastonbury Abbey. He had a Round Table made for a tournament, just as King Arthur had done. Knights were initiated into their order pledging loyalty to one another and to the principles of chivalry.

Source 1 An image showing the legendary King Arthur and his wife Guinevere watching a tournament. Here the knights are fighting on foot with swords. They would also have jousted with lances and fought in a mock battle called the melee. ▼

1 Why did the artist in Source 1 show Arthur, rather than a real monarch, watching the tournament?
2 Read Source 2. Why might a monk write this kind of book?

Source 2 'The responsibilities that pertain to a knight' from *The Book of the Order of Chivalry* by Ramón Lull, a former crusader and monk, published in 1276.

The duty of a knight is to support and defend the Holy Catholic Faith.

The duty of a knight is to support and defend his earthly lord.

The duty of a knight is to support and defend women, widows and orphans, and sick or enfeebled men.

The duty of a knight is to have a castle and horse, to guard the highways and to protect those who work the land.

The duty of a knight is also to search for thieves, robbers and other wicked folk in order to punish them.

The age of professional warfare?

It might seem that Edward was a bit of a dreamer, but there was a lot more to him than this. As Source 3 shows, he was both a knight of chivalry and a clever politician. Edward was also a ruthless and successful warrior king – one of the most powerful in English history. His reign was a time of war, on a larger scale than ever before. In addition, these were wars between states – England against Wales and Scotland – not civil wars or rebellions. During his reign Edward fought wars not only with Wales and Scotland, but also with France. All this conflict demanded new solutions to the problem of warfare.

Source 3 Historian Marc Morris, writing in 2015.

[Edward] shared the longing of knights for feats of arms, adventure and the pursuit of noble causes. … He took care to involve his greatest magnates in the running of the realm, consulting them on matters of importance. … Smaller landowners, meanwhile, thanks to the development of parliament, were given a greater voice. … For the first time since the Norman Conquest, England had a government that was perceived to be working in the interests of the majority of its subjects.

FOCUS TASK

An age of chivalry or an age of professional warfare? (1)

On these two pages you have two possible titles for the period c1290–c1450:
● The age of chivalry
● The age of professional warfare

As you work through this topic, note down examples that you think support or undermine each title. You could record your findings in a table like this.

	Evidence to support title 'Age of chivalry'	Evidence to support title 'Age of professional warfare'
Sources 1–2		
Welsh wars		
Scottish wars		
Hundred Years' War		

Case study 1: **War and society under Edward I**

In his biography of Edward I, the historian Marc Morris uses the title 'A great and terrible king'. Morris felt that this summed Edward up. Edward was a powerful king, working with but also controlling his barons (see Source 3). Edward was also a mighty war leader and much of his reign was taken up with war.

> **Source 4** Extracts from the *Chronicle of London*, published c1480. This mainly described events in London, but it included information about occurrences elsewhere in the country.
>
> *1282 In this year was Llywelyn, Prince of Wales, taken and beheaded by King Edward, and his head sent to the Tower of London.*
>
> *1283 In this year was Dafydd, the brother of Llywelyn, drawn, hanged, and beheaded, and his head sent to the Tower of London.*
>
> *1292 In this year, the discord began between the King of England and Sir John le Balliol, who was then made King of Scotland.*
>
> *1295 At this time a war began between Sir John Balliol, King of Scotland, and the King of England. In the same year the King conquered the land of Wales and the land of Scotland and took Sir John Balliol and other barons and knights of Scotland, who were all sent to the Tower of London but later set free.*
>
> *1300 King Edward returned into Scotland, and came to the Castle of Stirling. The King swore a great oath that every person in the castle, whether earl, baron, or knight, high or low, in case they should not immediately surrender the castle, should be drawn and hanged without any mercy being shown him. And when those within heard this, they soon opened the gates, and surrendered to the King, and the King pardoned them. And then all the great men of Scotland made oath that they would each year come to Westminster, to his Parliament, and be at his bidding.*

FACTFILE

A map showing Edward I's Welsh castles.

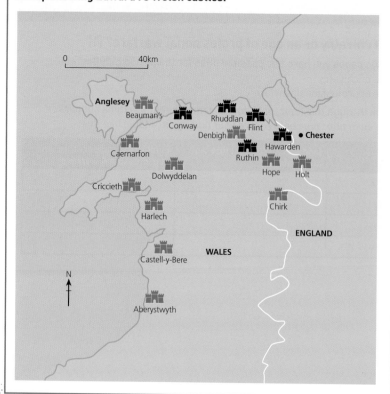

Edward I and the conquest of Wales 1276–94

English kings had never conquered Wales, although various princes of Wales had agreed to pay homage and money to English rulers. When Edward became king, Llywelyn refused to swear loyalty to Edward or to pay the money owed according to the terms of an earlier treaty. Edward immediately set out to show Llywelyn who was in charge. Historians are still debating whether it was always his intention to conquer Wales, but that is certainly what happened in the end.

The first campaign

Edward undertook several Welsh campaigns. In 1276, he recruited a huge army (1,000 knights and 15,000 infantry). In the face of this overwhelming strength most Welsh princes surrendered without a fight, and Llywelyn was no exception. He travelled to London to pay homage to Edward as his overlord in front of PARLIAMENT. As a further sign of English control, Edward also started to build a series of castles around Llywelyn's land (see Factfile).

The second and third campaigns

English rule, and English law in particular, was unpopular in Wales. In 1282, there was a series of co-ordinated attacks by Welsh rebels against Edward's royal castles, led by Llywelyn's brother Dafydd. Edward was furious and began to gather his forces to conquer Wales once and for all. He recruited a large army of soldiers and specialists, and transported many supplies by sea. However, as far as the Welsh were concerned this was now a national struggle that enjoyed wide support. For Edward it had become a war of conquest rather than just an expedition to punish the rebels.

The Welsh won some notable victories, but when Llywelyn was killed in battle Edward pressed on for total victory. Wars were normally fought in summer, but Edward decided on a winter campaign while he had the advantage. Parliament granted him a tax that enabled him to call up fresh troops, and he soon recaptured all the ground he had lost. One by one he hunted down and killed the rebels. Dafydd was captured, tried for treason then hung, drawn and quartered.

To recoup some of the cost of his campaign, Edward imposed a heavy tax on the Welsh, and this led to another rebellion in 1294. Once again Edward responded with overwhelming force and crushed the rebellion. After a 20-year campaign Edward was finally the ruler of Wales.

1 What evidence is there of chivalry (or lack of it) in the Welsh campaigns?
2 Study Source 5 carefully. What can you infer from this source about the purpose of Caernarfon Castle and town? You may find it helpful to look at pages 244–53 to help you interpret this image.

Source 5 An aerial photograph of Caernarfon Castle showing its position and some of the walls that encircled the town. ▼

FACTFILE

A map showing Edward I's Scottish campaigns.

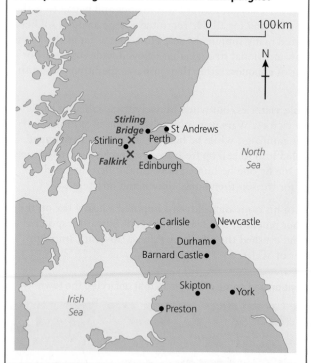

Source 6 John Balliol paying homage to Edward I. ▲

Edward's invasions of Scotland

In 1290, Edward was hoping to marry his son to Margaret, the heir to the Scottish throne, and so unite England and Scotland, but Margaret died before this could happen. The leading Scottish nobles asked Edward to judge which of the claimants should become king of Scotland. He chose John Balliol (probably because he thought he could control him) and demanded that Balliol offer him homage.

Edward had ambitions to control Scotland just as he did Wales. Some of the leading Scottish nobles responded by forming an alliance with France then launching an attack against England, advancing as far south as Carlisle. This threat won Edward the support he needed in parliament to raise a tax to pay for an invasion of Scotland.

In March 1296, Edward marched north with 1,000 cavalry and 20,000 infantry. He first besieged Scotland's main port, Berwick, but the town refused to surrender and set fire to some of Edward's ships. The king's response was to launch a violent full-scale attack. An estimated 7,000 people were killed or burned to death. Edward brought in English settlers to make Berwick an English town.

At Dunbar there was a similarly overwhelming victory for the English. The Scottish and English cavalry charged each other and the Scots were easily defeated and Dunbar Castle surrendered. This was the end of Scottish resistance to Edward's invasion. He took possession of Stirling Castle – regarded as the gateway to the north of Scotland – and carried off the symbolic Stone of Scone, on which Scottish kings were crowned. This was placed in Westminster Abbey in London.

Edward's victory had been quick and decisive. He went back to England, leaving English officials to run Scotland. Just as they had in Wales, they effectively turned Scotland into an English colony run for Edward's benefit. They imposed heavy taxes (to pay for the wars). Edward redistributed rebel lands to Scots who had supported him (in true feudal tradition). As in Wales, harsh rule led to further rebellion, but this rebellion turned into an effective movement led by William Wallace. Edward had to return to Scotland four times more, each time with a bigger and more expensive army. Edward died leading a final campaign towards Scotland.

1 Source 6 is an image from an English chronicle. Does this surprise you?
2 What might the Scottish reaction to this image have been?
3 What evidence is there of chivalry (or lack of it) in the Scottish campaigns?

FOCUS TASK

An age of chivalry or an age of professional warfare? (2)

Look back at the Focus Task on page 41 and add more examples and evidence to your table.

What were the consequences of Edward's wars?

Edward took the country to war on a completely new scale. The Factfile below shows exactly what was involved in carrying out campaigns like those in Wales and Scotland.

FACTFILE

How to raise and supply an army in the 1200s

Knights

Knights on horseback were the core of Edward's armies. Their main role was to charge the enemy and scatter them. Edward took nearly 1,000 knights with him to Scotland. He still used the feudal system to recruit his knights:

- **Feudal summons:** The king ordered all his VASSALS (those who held land from him) to serve for 40 days and to bring their promised number of knights. This was increasingly unreliable, as a campaign was likely to last much longer than 40 days. Many vassals simply did not turn up. We know of one knight who arrived at a battle, fired one arrow and then went home! Many vassals preferred to pay SCUTAGE instead of fighting (which the king did not mind, as he needed the money).
- **General summons:** The king appealed for volunteers. There was no payment but some knights responded out of loyalty or because they hoped to be rewarded by the king, or through ransom or PLUNDER. However, this method was also unreliable because it was impossible to predict how many knights would volunteer. Significantly, Edward got a better response to his general summons for the French wars (where financial gain was more likely) than for his wars against Scotland.
- **An indenture or a contract:** A knight agreed to provide military service to the king for a fixed period of time in return for wages. This made armies more reliable – the king knew who would turn up to fight. However, it all cost money. This was just getting started in Edward's time, but it became much more common in the fourteenth century.

Infantry

The infantry were the bulk of the army. They were not highly trained or well-armed. Edward took a staggering 20,000 infantry soldiers with him to Wales and Scotland. Under the feudal system, villages had been expected to provide a quota of soldiers but this was hopelessly inadequate for the size of armies Edward was using. The main way to get enough troops was to pay soldiers. For his Welsh campaign, Edward recruited thousands of Welsh and Irish men to his army, who were paid 2d per day.

Some of the infantry were archers. Their role was to launch a shower of arrows to stop the enemy from charging. As the medieval period wore on, archers became increasingly important to success in battle, and archery practice became compulsory for all young men. Laws were passed banning football because it was distracting young men from archery practice!

Specialists

For his Welsh campaigns, Edward employed thousands of woodcutters to chop down trees and make roads for his army. He also recruited carpenters (who were paid double what a foot soldier received), blacksmiths, engineers and miners to build and look after his siege equipment and weapons.

Sieges were the most common form of warfare, and Edward took with him battering rams, giant catapults and enormous siege towers to help scale the walls of besieged castles. He took three wooden bridges with him on his invasion of Scotland.

Supplies were brought by boat, which was both more reliable and cheaper than by land. But for this he needed a reliable fleet of ships – and the transport was an extra cost.

An army needs food. Traditionally armies had lived off the land (this was one reason why wars only happened in summer). They took what they needed from local people. Edward's armies did this, but he could not leave food to chance with such a big army – Edward knew that soldiers deserted if supplies ran out. So he took huge quantities of wheat, ale, wine and oats with him. When he captured Anglesey in 1277 he also employed 3,000 people to harvest the grain there to feed his army.

The impact – local level

Such a massive mobilisation of resources was bound to have significant consequences. At the local level, the effects of war could be immensely destructive and disruptive. One standard tactic adopted by Edward's armies in Scotland was a *chevauchée*. This was an aggressive march through enemy countryside, looting anything that might be useful and then setting fire to what that was left (see Source 7). Even 'friendly' armies could be disruptive. For example, when Edward I stopped at Lanercost on his way to fight the Scots in 1306, his personal household was made up of over 200 people, not including the military personnel coming to discuss the campaign with the king, or the merchants, beggars and others who tended to tag along with medieval armies. The cost of hosting the king was staggering, and new buildings had to be hastily built.

Source 7 An image of soldiers looting in a *chevauchée*. This example is from France, but the Scottish campaigns would have been similar. ▼

1 Imagine you are describing the scene in Source 7 for a modern radio or internet news service. What can you see?
2 In what ways is Source 7 similar to images of more recent conflicts you have come across?

The impact – national level

The strain at local level was replicated at the national level. As Source 8 reveals, the cost of war was beginning to affect the leading barons, encouraging them to challenge even a king as formidable as Edward.

> **Source 8** A royal proclamation issued by Edward I in 1297.
>
> *The earl of Hereford and the Earl Marshall have delivered a letter to the king, in which they refused to act upon an order of the king. The letter includes complaints about some of the burdens of tax that the king has placed on his kingdom. The king is well aware of these burdens. It grieves the king greatly. He asks them to be willing to consider his reasons. He has not used the money to buy lands, castles or towns, but on defending himself, his people, and all the realm.*
>
> *The council of barons who met with the king recently agreed a tax to be paid to the king. For this reason, the king begs all men who own property, and all the people of his realm, to honour their duty to pay the tax. And let everyone remember how there has been great misery in the past in this realm through dispute between the king and his people, and the harm that has resulted from them.*

3 How useful is Source 8 as evidence about the impact of war?
4 How useful is it as evidence of Edward I's political skill?

The impact – government level

As Edward's reign – and his wars – continued, he needed more money, and warfare increasingly became the job of professional fighters. The feudal system was starting to become too inflexible for large-scale, long-term wars. As a result, parliament became increasingly important. In 1295, he called what became known as the Model Parliament. This included the great barons and churchmen, of course (these were the Lords). Edward invited two knights from each county or shire, plus two representatives (burgesses) from the major towns in England. These knights and burgesses were the Commons. A pattern was emerging in which kings used parliament to listen to the concerns of their subjects; in return parliament would give the king the money he needed for wars or other matters. Edward accepted that those who would be affected by the taxes levied to raise that money should have their say in parliament. He even reissued Magna Carta in 1297 to show that he would abide by the law.

The impact – psychological level

You have already seen how wars can have a major impact on ideas about national identity. Edward's campaigns certainly had an effect in this way. However, his Welsh and Scottish campaigns actually increased the sense of national identity in those regions, rather than crushing it as Edward had hoped. The Welsh national identity was preserved in songs, stories and the Welsh language. In Scotland, Edward's invasions created a sense of suspicion and hostility between England and Scotland that would last for centuries.

An English identity was also emerging, finally overcoming the bitter memories of struggles between Anglo-Saxons and Normans. One factor that helped with this was that many of Edward's nobles no longer held French lands, or saw their English lands as more important. The Church also used PROPAGANDA to present Edward as a great chivalric hero and England's protector.

However, an emerging national identity also brings with it a sense of those who do not belong – people who start to be considered as 'others'. One group who paid the price in Edward's England were the Jews. This group had come over with William the Conqueror and were particularly prominent in the area of money-lending, which the Church claimed was a sin. Because they were rich and non-Christian, the Jews became an obvious target in times of difficulty. Edward expelled them from England in 1290 and confiscated most of their wealth.

◀ **Source 9** A record of a court case against two Jews from the reign of Edward I, 1277. The image in the margin shows the father of the accused Jews, Aaron, and the caption reads: 'Aaron son of the Devil.' On Aaron's coat you can see a badge called a tabula, which had to be worn by Jews.

FOCUS TASK

An age of chivalry or an age of professional warfare? (3)

Look back at the Focus Task on page 41 and add more examples and evidence to your table.

Case study 2: **The Hundred Years' War**

The Hundred Years' War is a modern name given to the long series of wars between England and France that occurred between 1337 and 1453. The essence of these campaigns was a succession of English monarchs attempting to win the French throne, or at least posing enough of a threat that the French would pay them off with lands and money. At different stages of the war, each side had the upper hand. There were some spectacular English victories, including the Battle of Crécy in 1346 and the Battle of Agincourt in 1415. However, ultimately the French proved too strong and the English were forced to withdraw permanently.

The changing nature of warfare

Throughout the period of the Hundred Years' War there were significant changes in the nature of warfare, which triggered changes elsewhere in society.

The decline of feudalism and the knight

The change in recruitment that had started in Edward I's time was now well established. The majority of nobles chose to pay scutage instead of enduring military service, and men–at–arms were increasingly employed under contracts or INDENTURES such as Source 10.

> **Source 10** The contract between Sir Thomas Tunstall and King Henry V, 1415.
>
> *This indenture … bears witness that the said Thomas is bound towards our lord the king to serve him for a whole year. … Thomas shall have with him in the expedition for the whole year six men-at-arms, himself included, and 18 mounted archers. He will take wages for himself at 2 shillings per day. … In the event that Thomas goes in the company of the king into the kingdom of France, he shall take as wages for each of the men-at-arms 12d per day, and for each of the archers 6d per day, during the year. If the expedition is to France then Thomas shall take the customary regard [a bonus payment common after the 1340s] for himself and his men-at-arms.*
>
> *Thomas shall be obliged to be ready at the sea coast with his men well mounted, armed and arrayed. … Thomas shall have shipping for himself and his retinue, their horses, harness and provisions, at the expense of the king, and also return shipping. …*
>
> *If it happens that the [king of] France, or any of his sons, nephews, uncles or cousins shall be captured in the expedition by Thomas or by any person of his retinue, the lord king of England shall have whoever are captured and shall make reasonable [payment] with Thomas or with the person who made the capture. With reference to other profits or gains of war the lord king shall have one third of the gains of Thomas as well as one third of a third part of the gains of the men of his retinue gained during the expedition, relating to gains of prisoners, booty, money, all gold, silver, and jewels worth more than 10 marks.*
>
> *In witness of these matters, Thomas has affixed his seal.*

1 What did Thomas agree to provide for the king?
2 What risks was he facing?
3 Explain how this type of contract was similar to or different from the feudal system you studied on pages 32–39.

Knights also became steadily less important as a weapon of war, certainly for English armies. To begin with, there were fewer knights to recruit. In 1200, there were around 5,000 traditional feudal knights in England. By 1350, there were only around 1,500. The extra numbers were made up with paid knights. Not surprisingly, English kings – struggling to fund their wars – began to rely more heavily on cheaper archers and foot soldiers. These troops and methods proved to be very effective, especially in the decisive victory over the French at Agincourt. Later still, the arrival of gunpowder, ARTILLERY and firearms also led to further changes in the conduct of warfare.

The business of war

For professional soldiers war became a way to make a living, or for professional knights to make serious profits. They fought for money, not out of loyalty or service, and looted goods or money from ransoms were considered part of the reward. Robert Knolles (see Profile) is an example of someone who grew very rich from war. Even foot soldiers could make a decent living in a professional army. However, the soldiers were not the only people who benefited from the business of war.

The bankers who lent money to Edward I to pursue his war with France also lent money to his enemies. Some nobles did very well out of loaning money to the king, but others lost out and were never repaid. Some noble families built castles with the proceeds of war (for example, Bodiam Castle in Sussex). Many people were involved in his campaigns, including merchants who provided or shipped the food to the armies; people who made, provided or stored weapons and armour; those who made and supplied the tents for the campaign; or who designed and built the castles. The whole process of waging war and maintaining control had become valuable business.

ACTIVITY

Compare the careers of Robert Knolles and William Marshal (see Factfile on page 39). Make a list of similarities and differences.

PROFILE

Robert Knolles (c1325–1407)

- Robert Knolles did not come from a noble family. He started his military career as a humble archer. However, he quickly did well enough to become a knight and used his plunder (stolen from his enemies) to buy extensive lands in Brittany.
- He was involved in the early decades of the Hundred Years' War.
- By 1356, Knolles was a leader in a great English *chevauchée* that devastated much of Normandy. He became well known for leaving a trail of burning villages, as well as for being an inspirational leader.
- Further success followed at the battles of Auray (1364) and Nájera in Spain (1367).
- In 1370 he was appointed to lead a *chevauchée* into northern France. However, he shared command with less effective knights and the expedition ended in failure. Knolles was blamed, but was eventually forgiven and continued fighting.
- He invested his loot and payments for fighting in property and loaning money. He bought extensive property in London, where he played a part in defeating the Peasants' Revolt of 1381.
- Towards the end of his life, Sir Robert gave a lot of money to religious charities, perhaps seeking forgiveness for his deeds in war.

How did the Hundred Years' War change England?

It finally dismantled the feudal system

The Hundred Years' War changed weapons and tactics so much that the idea of a feudal army gradually disintegrated. In the 1300s, heavily armoured knights on horseback were still considered the most powerful force on the battlefield. By the mid-1450s the longbow had changed this. At Agincourt, for example, English longbow men firing thousands of arrows per minute decimated the French cavalry. Heavily armoured knights were replaced with lightly armoured troops, called hobelars, who could ride through difficult terrain. They dismounted to engage the enemy. The days of the armoured knight were over, and with them the feudal system and nobility as the basis of the army.

It built a sense of national identity

As the war dragged on, it was no longer seen as purely a battle between the kings of England and France; it was also considered a conflict between their people – a national war. Rumours circulated in England that the French intended to invade the country and destroy the English language. Such rumours fuelled an increasingly nationalist feeling – 'us against them' – an attitude that we take for granted as a feature of modern war. It finally killed off the use of French in England, which had been the language of the nobility and trade merchants since the Norman Conquest. It also made foreigners in England a target for resentment, and equally a target for a king looking for an opportunity to win favour and make money. In 1440, Henry VI introduced a tax known as the Aliens' Subsidy to England. This was effectively a tax on foreigners living in the country. It was partly a measure to raise money and partly intended to gain favour in the climate of antagonism towards foreigners.

> **Source 11 A petition presented to Henry VI by the House of Commons, November 1439.**
>
> *Sire: great damage and losses come to you and your people daily as a result of the deals which alien merchants and other foreigners make with each other. They make agreements with each other whereby the alien merchants are greatly enriched, and your subject denizen merchants of your same realm are grievously impoverished. Great treasure is taken out of your realm by the same aliens, and the customs duties and taxes which they owe you are greatly lessened.*

1 Read Source 11. Do you think parliament is really concerned about the king losing taxes?
2 Why is the date of this petition significant?

It reduced the appetite for war

There was always an anti-war faction in English politics – particularly when it came to wars that cost a lot of money. The Hundred Years' War strengthened this faction. England's political elite showed less enthusiasm for conflicts that were not clearly in the national interest. Experience showed that such wars cost too much money and created too many casualties for no clear gain. However, some people argue that the shock of defeat in France and the loss of land and prestige was a factor in causing the civil wars between leading noble families in England known as the Wars of the Roses.

It weakened England's links with Europe

For centuries, the English rulers (kings and barons) had held lands in France. With the end of the Hundred Years' War, England was left an island nation on the edge of Europe, which affected English attitudes towards Europe for centuries to come. It also helped fuel a new interest. The age of European exploration was about to begin. England was well suited to take advantage of its location and seafaring abilities to explore, and later conquer, much of the world.

FOCUS TASK

An age of chivalry or an age of professional warfare? (4)
Look back at the Focus Task on page 41 and add more examples and evidence to your table.

The Wars of the Roses and the end of chivalry

The Hundred Years' War was followed by a bitter period of civil war that later became known as the Wars of the Roses. These were disruptive and damaging, and proved how knighthood had largely lost its glamour by this time (see Source 12). In 1485, a new ruling family, the Tudors, took the throne. They were determined to reduce the power of knights and noble families.

> **Source 12** Caxton's Epilogue to his reprinting of Ramón Lull's book in 1483 (see Source 2 on page 41)
>
> *O ye knights of England, where is now the practice of noble chivalry that was used in those days? What do you do now but go to the public baths and play at dice? Leave all of this and instead read the noble volumes of Sir Lancelot and the Holy Grail, of Sir Galahad, of Tristan, of Perceval, of Gawain and many others. There will you see manhood, courtesy and nobility. ... Alas! What do you do, by contrast, but sleep and take your ease and stray from true chivalry. I would ask a question if it would not displease you: 'How many knights are there now in England that actually practise knighthood; that is, that know their horses and are ready to perform deeds of valour?' ... Then let every man of noble blood who intends to enter that noble Order of Chivalry read this little book and follow its instructions, keeping the commandments comprised therein. If he does, I do not fear but that he shall attain to the Order of Chivalry.*

PRACTICE QUESTIONS

1   Describe two examples of how warfare changed in this period. (2)
2   Explain why monarchs found it increasingly difficult to pay for wars in the period 1290–1450. (4)
3   Explain how monarchs tried to fund wars. (4)

KEY QUESTION REVIEW

A Why was warfare such a significant element of medieval society?

You have been collecting evidence about the following features of the period:
- land
- wealth
- equipment
- civil wars
- national wars
- chivalry
- leadership
- homage
- religion and the Church
- national identity.

Now organise these features into three categories:
a   Little or no change
b   Some change
c   Significant change

B How and why did the business of war evolve during the medieval period?

Complete your chart from the Key Question task on page 31.

1.4 Review: War and society c AD790–1500

You have now looked at many different wars in the medieval period and considered how war affected society and how society adapted as a result of war. In this review, you will think about the big patterns and trends that run across the whole topic.

A What types of war were there in this period?

1   Historians often look at different types of wars, compare how they are fought and the effects they had. The list below shows some different types of wars:
   ● opportunism/ambition/plunder
   ● wars beween peoples, nations or states
   ● conquest/invasion
   ● defence
   ● rebellion
   ● religion
   ● civil war.

   Look back over your work and try to find two examples of each category. Some wars might fit more than one category.

B Attitudes and responses to war

2   The history of warfare inevitably tends to focus on warriors and battles and rulers. But these warriors and rulers would have not been able to achieve much without people to grow their food, make their weapons and armour, build their ships and pay their taxes. How exactly did this work? Look back over the conflicts you have studied and find evidence of the importance of each of the following factors in the different conflicts you have studied:
   ● taxes
   ● feudal service by knights
   ● tenant farmers and peasants producing food
   ● craftsmen (e.g. armourers)
   ● parliament
   ● popular support
   ● the Church.

   You could either record your findings in a table or label them in a copy of the diagram.

   As an extension task, you could decide whether particular roles were more important than others.

C The impacts of war on people

3   Look at these cards, which show some of the ways that wars affected people in the medieval period. Make your own set of cards. Look back at your work in this chapter, find at least one example of each of the types of impacts and write them on the cards.

Fear and horror

War weariness

Disruption in trade and economic prosperity

Resentment of foreigners

Increased taxes

Enslavement

Breakdown of law and order

Invasion by foreign armies

Shaping or attacking national identify

Intermarrying

Development of idea of chivalry

Death and destruction

Increased faith and devotion to the Church

Equipping armies with supplies

Development of language and literature

4   Now sort your cards into piles:
   ● Direct impact
   ● Indirect impact
   ● Psychological impact
   ● Social and cultural impact.

   You might find that other students in your class disagree with your categories, but that does not matter as long as you can justify your decision.

5   As an extension task, look back at Key Question A and see whether you think particular types of wars tended to have particular types of effects (e.g. did wars of conquest have a bigger effect on national identity)?

D War and government

6   You have probably noticed that in the medieval period the demands of war often led to changes in government. Copy the table below and note down examples of how and why this happened.

Conflict	Challenges to monarch(s)	How they responded	Impact/effectiveness	Comments
Anglo-Saxon campaigns against Vikings				
Norman Conquest				
the Anarchy				
the Barons' Wars				
wars against Wales and Scotland				
Hundred Years' War				

7   Historians ask several questions to decide whether events are significant:
    ● Did it matter to people at the time?
    ● Did it affect a large number of people?
    ● Did it affect a small but important group of people?
    ● Did it cause change, and if so how great was the change?
    ● Was the change long lasting or short term?
    ● Is it still seen as important today and if so, why?
    Look back at the events listed in the table below and decide how far you think they were significant.

Event	Arguments that this was significant	Arguments against	Rating
Viking attacks			
emergence of Wessex and English state			
Norman Conquest			
the Anarchy			
Magna Carta			
Edward I's wars			
Hundred Years' War			

8   A book publisher is planning to publish a book called *War and Government in the Medieval Period*. The publisher is finding it hard to decide how to divide up the book. They want a chapter on each conflict but they also want chapters to be in sections. For example, one possible idea is to have a section called 'Wars of Conquest', which include the Anglo-Saxon campaigns and the Norman Conquest. What would you advise them to do?

KEY TERMS

Make sure you know what these terms mean and can use them confidently in your writing.
● Anarchy
● baron
● Danegeld
● Danelaw
● feudalism
● knight

2.1 Elizabeth's wars 1585–1603

FOCUS

After the end of the Wars of the Roses, the Tudor dynasty came to power. The first Tudor king, Henry VII, was cautious and avoided wars because they were risky and expensive. However, his son Henry VIII was a war-maker. His dreams of regaining English lands in France put him deeply in debt. His religious changes – breaking away from the Catholic Church – also changed England's place in the world, making enemies of Catholic France and Spain. This in turn meant more expensive wars. Henry's daughter Elizabeth I claimed to be anti-war, but during her reign there were continuing conflicts with Ireland, France and Spain. In this topic you will examine:

● how Elizabeth managed her father's legacy of warfare
● how these Elizabethan wars changed society.

The big picture

What kind of wars were they?

Elizabethan wars were about religion, defence and – to some extent – ambition. They were complex conflicts with complex responses. For example, conflict with Spain arose for several reasons, including England's support for the Dutch revolt against Spain, religious differences (Catholic vs Protestant), the activities of English privateers who were raiding Spanish ships, and Spanish support for Catholic plots against Elizabeth. In many respects, the Anglo-Spanish war was a case of David (England) against Goliath (Spain). The Armada campaign was a defensive war to protect England from invasion. The English won this early engagement, but did not ultimately win the war. The war with Spain dragged on, indirectly leading to a bloody and expensive conflict in Ireland, and continued after Elizabeth's death.

What were the attitudes and responses to war?

Elizabeth was reluctant to wage war because of the cost and the risk. She had cleared her regime of debt by 1574, and ten years later she had a surplus of £300,000, helped by the activities of privateers. From the 1580s this changed, however. Elizabeth's advisers and courtiers took England into an escalating war. After the success over the Armada, Elizabeth gained great support and the Protestant majority celebrated. As the conflict wore on, war-weariness inevitably set in. But Elizabeth's government had an effective propaganda machine that helped boost support for Elizabeth's campaigns by increasing fear of Catholics.

What impact did the wars have on England?

From the 1580s, constant war led to high taxes which, coupled with high inflation, meant that poverty increased during Elizabeth's reign. War also hindered England's trade with Europe, which harmed both the merchants and traders, especially those involved in the cloth trade.

What impact did the wars have on the relationship between government and people?

Elizabeth depended on taxes. This gave MPs in parliament more power because they had to approve the taxes. Elizabeth had to accept that MPs would sometimes question her policies. Elizabeth needed the approval and support of the population, who would pay the taxes or serve in the armed forces. Elizabeth and her government tried to win support with extensive propaganda, including portraits, pamphlets, songs and stage plays.

KEY QUESTIONS

A Why did Elizabeth I fight so many wars when she was generally anti-war?

As you study the various wars fought during Eilzabeth's reign, decide how far each war was a war of religion, survival/defence or ambition.

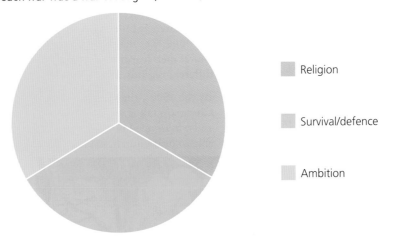

- Religion
- Survival/defence
- Ambition

B Why did Elizabeth fight the way she did?

At the time, England did not have the same resources in terms of wealth and people that great powers like France and Spain had. As a result Elizabeth had to use her resources carefully. As you work through this topic, note down examples of how she chose to fight various campaigns.

Methods	Examples	Why she chose this method
helping the enemies of her enemies		
direct involvement of troops on land		
privateering		
official war at sea		
attacking Spain itself		
attacking Spanish colonies		

C What impact did Elizabeth's wars have on England?

The table below lists some of the ways that the wars might have affected England. As you work through this topic, look for examples of the wars' impacts. Record this evidence in a copy of the table.

Impact of wars	Positive examples	Negative examples
financial		
economic		
political		
support of people		
recruitment of armed forces		

Background to Elizabeth I's wars

In order to fully understand the wars that took place during the reign of Elizabeth I, it is important to know something about the developments taking place in Europe at this time.

The Reformation and religious wars

In the medieval period, western Europe was almost entirely Christian – in fact it was known as CHRISTENDOM. The Catholic Church, based in Rome and led by the POPE, was the centre of religious life. The pope appointed the senior churchmen (cardinals, archbishops and bishops). They ran the Church in their different regions, appointing priests and maintaining church buildings.

By the 1500s, the Catholic Church was very powerful and very wealthy. Some Christians felt it was *too* powerful and *too* wealthy – that it had become corrupt and was in need of reform. These Christians wanted ordinary people to be able to hear church services and even read the Bible in their own language rather than in Latin. This idea of Church reform took hold, and as it gathered pace across Europe its followers became known as PROTESTANTS. The movement is known as the Reformation. The religious disputes took on a political dimension, as some European rulers saw advantages to supporting the Protestant Reformation while others continued to back the power and control of the Catholic Church.

Throughout the 1520s and 1530s, the religious disagreements erupted into wars in which atrocities were committed by both sides. The result was that by the 1550s, Europe was divided into Protestant states – mostly in the northern half of Europe – and Catholic states, mostly in the southern half (see Figure 3), in regular conflict with one another.

Source 1 A drawing called *Battlefield* by Urs Graf, 1521. Graf was a former soldier. ▼

1. In Source 1, the artist is trying to convey the horrors of war. Do you think he succeeds?
2. Does Source 2 have the same aim as Source 1 or a different aim? Explain your answer.

Source 2 A representation from 1562 of French Protestants (known as Huguenots) being massacred by the forces of the Catholic French ruler. ▼

The Reformation in England

Until the 1530s, the English king, Henry VIII, supported the Catholic cause. However, he quarrelled with the pope when the Catholic leader refused to ANNUL Henry's marriage to his first wife, Catherine of Aragon. As a result Henry broke away from the Catholic Church and later established himself as head of the Church of England. When Henry died, his son Edward VI continued to lead the Protestant Church of England. However, Edward died in 1553 and was succeeded by his sister Mary, who made England Catholic again. The country was greatly divided by this. Just as during Edward's reign many Catholics had refused to accept the Protestant changes, many Protestants under Mary refused to accept the return to Catholicism. Throughout this period, people on both sides were killed for their religious convictions.

Mary died in 1558 and was succeeded by her younger sister. Elizabeth was cautious by nature. She decided England would be a Protestant country, but she exercised some religious tolerance. Catholics faced some restrictions in the way they could worship, and they were sometimes made to pay fines, but they were not severely persecuted.

Figure 3 A map showing religious division in Europe in the 1550s. ▼

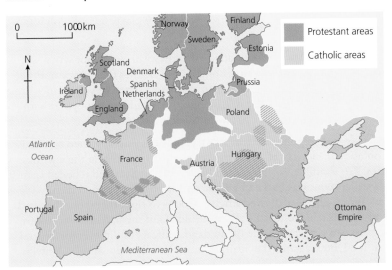

Despite this, Elizabeth faced a Catholic rebellion in 1569 and for many years afterwards there was a series of Catholic plots intending to kill Elizabeth. The pope sent priests to England to maintain the faith of the Catholics there. In 1582, a government proclamation made it treason for foreign Catholic priests to remain in England and for anyone to help conceal them. Condemned traitors were tortured and executed.

Elizabeth had hoped to stay out of Europe's religious wars, but she found herself drawn into them despite this. England was a relatively small, weak Protestant country with two wealthy and aggressive Catholic neighbours in France and Spain.

Figure 4 A map showing Portuguese and Spanish trade routes in the 1500s. ▼

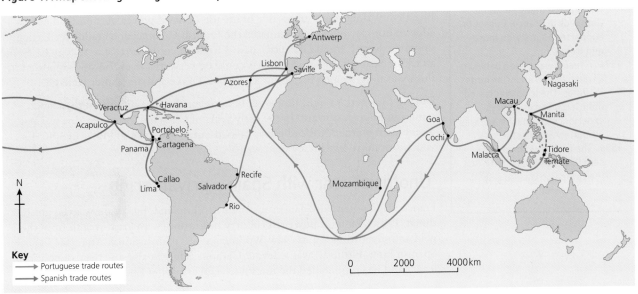

FACTFILE

Elizabeth I's wars

1559–60 Protestants in Scotland rebelled against their Catholic ruler. Elizabeth aided them secretly with money, arms and 'volunteer' troops.

1562–63 Elizabeth allied with French Protestants called Huguenots and tried to capture the French port of Le Havre. The campaign was a failure.

1560s onwards Privateers regularly attacked Spanish ships carrying gold from South America to Spain. These privateers were effectively pirates, but over time they were given royal approval.

1565–mid-1570s Series of campaigns in Ireland with very limited success.

1577–85 Elizabeth provided financial aid to the Protestants in the Netherlands who were rebelling against their Spanish rulers.

1585 Elizabeth sent troops to help the rebels in the Netherlands against the Spanish. England was effectively at war with Spain.

1588 Philip II of Spain sent an Armada to invade England and depose Elizabeth. The Armada was defeated.

1589 The Protestant Henry IV became king of France, but faced rebellion and civil war against many powerful Catholics in France. Elizabeth supported Henry with money and troops.

1594 A major war began between English forces and Irish lords in Ulster. The Irish War lasted until 1603. The campaign experienced setbacks, but was ultimately successful.

1596 The English Armada was sent to attack Spain, but the campaign was largely unsuccessful.

The nature of Elizabeth's wars

Elizabeth's wars are not easy to categorise:

- They were wars of religion – the main threats were Catholic France and Spain, although Ireland was also a worry as it could be a potential 'back door' through which Spain might attack England. At the same time, Elizabeth wanted to defend Protestantism, and she supported Protestants in Europe.
- They were wars of defence/survival – the Spanish actually attempted an invasion in 1588 and again in the mid-1590s.
- They were also wars of ambition – Elizabeth wanted to increase England's power and influence on the world stage.

A cautious approach to land war

Elizabeth had limited power and resources and she wanted to spend as little money as possible, so her strategy in war was usually defensive. However, many of her advisers disagreed with this. Some members of the PRIVY COUNCIL felt that England should be more involved in events unfolding on the European mainland – for example, by sending large armies to the Netherlands to help Dutch rebels fight the Spanish. This was in part due to a desire for military glory, but religion was a major factor

However, Elizabeth would not be persuaded. She knew she could not win a war on land against Spain or France, because England had neither the money nor the population to win such a campaign. Elizabeth was also a sensitive politician – she knew that sending men abroad to die in a foreign war would be unpopular with her people, as would imposing taxes to pay for such a war.

Elizabeth was prepared to go to war if necessary, but she generally tried to avoid direct confrontation. One way of doing this was by offering to help the enemies of her enemies. For example, in 1559 when Protestants in Scotland rebelled against their Catholic ruler (who was backed by France), Elizabeth supported them with money and weapons. She also allowed English troops to fight them, but they had to pretend to be volunteers so that Elizabeth could claim she had not sent troops. The same pattern was repeated in the Netherlands. Elizabeth did eventually send troops to help the Dutch against the Spanish, but officially they were 'volunteers', so again Elizabeth would not be directly at war with Spain.

A key role for sea power

Elizabeth was far more supportive of the use of naval power. As an island on the edge of Europe, England dominated the English Channel and could attack enemy shipping along Europe's Atlantic coast. Elizabeth could see that a strategy based on attacking Spanish ships and seaports could be very effective. She was supported in this by leading seamen including Sir Francis Drake and Sir Walter Raleigh.

During Elizabeth's reign, sea power became much more important than land armies in English warfare. In the early years of her reign, however, this was not direct naval warfare. Instead it was carried out in the form of PRIVATEERING – which was more like piracy than war.

'Unofficial' war with Spain – privateering

France was a potentially dangerous enemy to England, but Spain was the greatest threat. It was the most powerful country in Europe, with great wealth from the gold and silver mines in its New World colonies, mainly South America. The Spanish king, Philip II, was a devout Catholic. He was also an effective political leader and he commanded the most powerful armies in Europe at this time.

Relations between England and Spain had been good under Elizabeth's sister, the Catholic Mary, but they deteriorated when Elizabeth took the throne. The situation worsened as attacks by English privateers on Spanish ships increased. Francis Drake, for example, attacked Spanish ports in the Americas and captured Spanish ships on his voyage around the world (1577–80). Elizabeth pocketed £265,000 as a result of the voyage (equivalent to around £80 million today) and Drake earned a knighthood. Spanish support for Catholic plots against Elizabeth also caused friction between the two countries.

Source 5 Drake's ship the *Golden Hind* capturing the *Cacafuego*, Spain's richest treasure ship, in 1579. The picture was painted in the seventeenth century. ▼

Source 6 A portrait of Sir Francis Drake from 1580. It was created to mark when he was knighted by Queen Elizabeth. The painting was by Nicholas Hilliard, whose work was in great demand by nobles of the time. Drake is shown with red cheeks to represent the effect of the sea air on his face. ▶

1. What does Source 5 show about privateering activity in the late sixteenth century?
2. Study Source 6. Why is it useful to know who painted the portrait?
3. What does Source 6 reveal about Drake, his status and how England regarded seafarers?
4. Explain the connection between Source 5 and Source 6.

FACTFILE

Privateers

- Privateers were privately owned ships (or seamen) that had been given permission by the government to attack enemy shipping.
- Privateering began as a defence against piracy, but it turned into a form of piracy as privateers started abusing their right and attacking any ship that looked like it was carrying rich cargo, whether or not it was a pirate ship. The Spanish regarded the English privateers as pirates.
- Wealthy people (including the queen herself) invested in the privateers' expeditions by paying for their ships and supplies. Investors hoped for a profit by sharing in the wealth the privateers brought back. The potential rewards for investors were enormous. The crew also shared in the takings, which gave them a great incentive to capture Spanish ships.

- From the early 1560s, John Hawkins led three expeditions that mixed trading (including taking slaves from Africa to America) with privateering. The first two voyages made a lot of money for Hawkins and his investors. The third was almost destroyed by the Spanish, who did not want English ships taking part in the trade across the Atlantic.
- The next 20 years saw a series of similar voyages by English 'privateers'. The most famous was Francis Drake's voyage around the world from 1577 to 1580.
- Privateering brought immense wealth back to England but it helped Elizabeth in other ways too. It saved her the expense of building warships. She could also claim that these privateers were not acting officially with her approval.

Source 7 A portrait of Elizabeth I from the early 1580s, known as the 'Peace Portrait'. She holds an olive branch, a symbol of peace, in her right hand and the sword of war is sheathed and on the floor at her feet, showing she does not want conflict. The painter was a Protestant from the Netherlands who had fled to England. ▼

War in the Netherlands: war with Spain becomes 'official'

The Netherlands was part of the Spanish Empire, and in the 1570s Elizabeth helped a Protestant rebellion there against Spanish rule. However, at first she tried to avoid being officially drawn into war with Spain. In fact, she even claimed to be playing the part of peacemaker (see Source 7). As in Scotland, English 'volunteers' fought against Spain. Elizabeth claimed she had not sent or even given permission for these troops to fight, but it was clear that this was not true. In 1585, the Treaty of Nonsuch was signed, by which Elizabeth agreed to send help to the Netherlands. By this time, even the queen could no longer pretend that England was not involved in outright war with Spain.

1 Historians usually work with facts, but sometimes it is useful to speculate. What do you think King Philip II of Spain might have said on seeing the portrait in Source 7?
2 Explain the message of Source 8, referring to each of the labelled features.

Source 8 A painting from the 1630s called *The Dairy Cow*. It was an allegory (telling a story through symbolic images) of Elizabeth's wars in The Netherlands. ▼

Elizabeth is feeding the cow.

Philip of Spain is riding the cow.

The cow represents the Netherlands.

The Spanish commander is milking the cow.

The Spanish Armada

By the late 1580s, King Philip II decided it was time to fight back. He assembled a great fleet – an Armada – to invade England. The situation might have turned out very differently, but in 1587 Francis Drake attacked the Spanish port of Cadiz, which delayed the departure of the Spanish Armada, giving Elizabeth time to improve England's defences.

In 1588, the Armada, commanded by the Duke of Medina Sidonia, finally set sail. The duke's orders were to sail to the Netherlands first, meet up with the Duke of Parma and then transport his Spanish troops to England.

As the 127 ships of the Spanish Armada sailed up the English Channel in July 1588 they were tracked by the English fleet, led by Lord Howard of Effingham with Drake as second in command. The Spanish had more men, but the English had 197 ships and they carried better guns. English artillery proved crucial in the battle that followed; although the fleet failed to sink many Spanish ships, it easily outgunned them.

The Armada anchored at Calais, but when the English sent in fire-ships the Spanish ships put out to sea again in chaos. Instead of heading to the Netherlands to meet up with the Duke of Parma, the battered Armada headed north, intending to sail round Scotland and Ireland. Bad weather and rough seas inflicted even more damage than the English had, and King Philip's Armada was forced to return to Spain. Less than half the Armada returned, and 10,000 Spanish soldiers and sailors died.

The English victory showed off the technical superiority of Elizabeth's naval forces. However, hundreds of English sailors died of disease, and the English government refused to pay for their care or even pay their wages.

3 What was the Armada's plan?
4 Why did it fail?
5 In what ways was the English victory significant?

Continuing naval war with Spain 1588–1603

The defeat of the Armada in 1588 was not the end of the war with Spain, and Elizabeth feared that King Philip would attack again once his fleet had recovered. In 1589, therefore, she sent Drake on a naval expedition to Spain, with 130 ships carrying 13,600 troops. Elizabeth paid half the fleet's cost. She hoped it would destroy any Spanish ships that had survived the Armada, ending the threat once and for all. The merchants and privateers who provided most of the ships for the fleet hoped that the expedition would bring them rich profits. Despite these high hopes, the expedition failed and thousands more English sailors died.

After this, Elizabeth was reluctant to order further large-scale expeditions. Instead she relied mainly on privateers to keep the Spanish threat under control, attacking Spanish ships as well as Spanish settlements in the Americas. An expedition to Cadiz in 1596 captured the city and destroyed many Spanish ships. The Spanish tried to fight back, but two more armadas in 1596–97 were driven back by bad weather. England remained undefeated, but it had not defeated Spain.

FOCUS TASK

Was England becoming an important power?

When Elizabeth I came to the throne, England was not in the same league as great powers like France and Spain. Do you think this position had changed by the end of her reign? Study the various campaigns on pages 58–61. For each one, decide what it reveals about England. Use a table like the one below to help you.

Campaign	What is significant about this campaign in terms of England's importance?	If Spain is a 10, on the power scale, after this campaign I think England was ...
'volunteer' troops to Scotland and Netherlands sea power and privateering ...	Elizabeth had to pretend troops were volunteers, too afraid to face Spain directly	

War in Ireland

The war in Ireland during Elizabeth's reign was really an extension of the war with Spain. The English feared that the Spanish might use Ireland – a Catholic country – as a 'back door' through which to attack England. Earlier English monarchs had tried to control Ireland by imposing on the Irish the Protestant faith as well as the English language and customs. Part of this policy consisted of 'planting' English farmers, merchants and craftsman in Ireland by giving them land and incentives to settle there.

Despite these efforts, the Irish remained stubbornly Catholic. Many Irish lords opposed English rule and attempts at colonisation and there were numerous rebellions against English rule in the 1570s and 1580s. These were crushed by English forces but the Irish continued to reject English laws and customs, and the only way to enforce them was by keeping large numbers of troops in Ireland, which was very costly.

In 1595, a major revolt led by Hugh O'Neill, Earl of Tyrone, broke out in Ulster. Spain sent 3,500 troops to help the Irish and within three years the English had lost control of most of Ireland. Elizabeth decided to launch a full-scale conquest of Ireland and dedicated massive resources to the campaign. The tactic worked, and in 1603 Tyrone made peace. The Irish conflict cost Elizabeth about the same as the entire war with Spain – an estimated £1.9 billion (around £6 trillion today). Despite its defeat Ireland remained a troublesome territory for England, and the wars were deeply unpopular by the 1590s. They were costing huge amounts of money and lives, and they seemed to be gaining little.

FACTFILE

A map showing Elizabeth I's Irish campaigns.

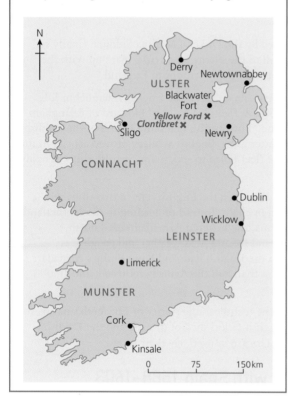

1. How can you tell that this is a Catholic propaganda print?
2. In what ways is this source similar to Source 2 on page 56?
3. Elizabeth's campaigns in Ireland have sometimes been called 'a disastrous success'. What do you think this means and do you agree?

Source 9 A Catholic propaganda print from the late sixteenth century, showing the treatment of Catholic priests in Ireland by the English. ▼

Impact of war 1: Recruitment

Before 1585, England had no large army or navy, so to fight these wars it needed to recruit thousands of soldiers and sailors. From 1585 to 1603, Elizabeth raised the largest forces yet seen in English history. Some 385,000 men were recruited at a time when the combined population of England and Wales was only 4 million.

The army

The militia

The organisation of the militia was improved. Better-off men were provided with arms and taught how to use them. Some 92,000 men served in the so-called 'trained bands'. These were mainly intended for defence in the invasion scares of 1588 and the mid-1590s.

Volunteers

Around 5,000 men joined up as voluntary soldiers overseas.

Officers

There was no shortage of nobles and gentlemen willing to serve as officers, although in 1585 few of them had much military experience.

How were Elizabeth's armies recruited?

Feudal recruitment

Around 16,000 men, mainly the servants of aristocrats, were recruited by semi-feudal means. The cavalry was made up almost entirely of the tenants of great landowners.

Overseas levies

Over 110,000 English soldiers fought abroad in Elizabeth's reign. The government raised most of these men by ordering LORD-LIEUTENANTS to levy a specific number of recruits from the local population. CLERGY, servants of the crown and nobility, and 'trained band' men were exempt. The choice of who to recruit was left to local officials, who usually selected men whose absence would have the least impact upon the community. Many were vagrants or criminals.

Traditionally, the northern counties were expected to defend England against the Scots, so they did not provide levies for overseas service from 1585 to 1603. Southern counties raised most of the men for wars in France and the Netherlands. Wales, Cheshire and Lancashire raised men for the war in Ireland.

The navy

Elizabeth's father, Henry VIII, had encouraged England's shipbuilding and cannon-making industries. Elizabeth continued this support with the result that English ships were among the best built and the best armed in Europe. The Royal Navy had 34 ships in 1585, most of which were well equipped with long-range guns. Elizabeth could also call upon the services of 1,500 armed merchantmen and privateers. Such ships made up the bulk of English naval expeditions over the next 18 years.

The Royal Navy had no permanent officers or sailors. Royal ships, auxiliary merchantmen and privateers were commanded by freelance captains and manned by crews who were temporarily taken into the queen's pay. Men in coastal regions could be forced to serve in the navy and aboard privateers. But many of Elizabeth's 50,000 sailors were volunteers who hoped to get rich by capturing Spanish ships.

Source 10 A contemporary drawing of musketeers of the London trained bands, 1587. ▼

4   According to Source 10, how well-armed were the trained bands?

FOCUS TASK

War in Tudor and medieval times

Make a list of the similarities and differences between the organisation of war in Elizabeth's time and in the medieval period in terms of:
- recruiting troops
- the role of nobles and gentlemen
- the numbers involved
- the importance of sailors.

Impact of war 2: **Taxes**

Even in the relatively quiet years of the 1560s, Elizabeth spent a lot on wars. Her campaigns in Scotland and France in the 1560s cost around £750,000 (about £2.4 billion today). The Spanish wars were far more expensive. During these conflicts Elizabeth spent around £500,000 every year, yet her normal income was only around £300,000. So how did she raise the extra money she needed?

Local taxes

Many costs of war were borne by towns and counties, which had to:

- train and equip the militia
- pay to build or maintain the queen's ships
- repair coastal forts
- equip troops for overseas service.

Local taxes increased as a result.

Selling Crown lands and borrowing

Elizabeth raised extra money by selling Crown lands (£608,000) and she borrowed a further £461,500 between 1589 and 1603, mainly from wealthy subjects.

Taxes approved by parliament

Elizabeth asked parliament to vote in taxes to pay for the war. While parliament passed increasing numbers of subsidies after 1585, this did not necessarily result in greater taxation because:

- taxpayers were assessed using traditional valuations
- there was widespread evasion.

The subsidy raised £140,000 in 1558, but by 1603 it was only £80,000. Most Englishmen, therefore, were taxed relatively lightly. Elizabeth used 3 per cent of England's national income for the war. In contrast, Philip II of Spain used 10 per cent of Spain's wealth.

How were Elizabeth's wars paid for?

Profits from privateers

The queen shared the profits from the hundreds of privateering raids. However, few captains declared the full extent of whatever wealth they captured.

Ship money

Traditionally in wartime the crown had REQUISITIONED merchant ships from coastal towns and counties to use in the navy. In the 1590s, Elizabeth demanded money *as well as* ships. When this tax was extended to inland areas it was bitterly opposed.

The situation in 1603

These various measures worked well for Elizabeth. In 1558, she had inherited a debt of £300,000. When she died in 1603, she left a debt of £365,000. This comparison shows the success of her policies and demonstrates Elizabeth's prudence. Philip II of Spain died in 1598 leaving a debt of 100 million gold ducats – a debt 136 times greater than Elizabeth's.

Impact of war 3: **Economic crisis**

In the 1590s England faced an economic crisis, with widespread unemployment and rampant inflation. As food prices soared, many people suffered and some even died of malnutrition. The war contributed to this, although it was not solely to blame.

Military recruitment probably had a detrimental effect on the economy. Men who might otherwise have worked on the land were no longer available to do so.

The war also led to disruption of trade – particularly the wool trade with the LOW COUNTRIES. At the same time, however, a host of English industries, particularly those supplying arms and essential supplies such as food or equipment for the army, profited from the wars.

There were major outbreaks of plague, and the disease was often carried back to England by soldiers returning from abroad. However, these could not all be blamed on war – plague was common in this period in times of peace as well as war.

There were serious food shortages. England's population was rising and there was a series of bad harvests in the mid-1590s. These factors were not connected to the wars, but they added to the hardships caused by war.

Despite the economic problems, signs of unrest were relatively rare. Elizabeth did not face serious protests or riots by ordinary people.

Impact of war 4: **Casualties**

There was no fighting on English soil, so there was no damage to property or civilian casualties. However, military casualties were very high. We have no accurate figures about casualties at sea or in the Netherlands, but historians estimate that around 30,000 English soldiers died in the wars in Ireland, mostly from disease. This was a huge figure when the population was only around 4 million.

FOCUS TASK

What was the impact of the wars?

Look at the pie chart below, which shows four effects of Elizabeth's wars that had an impact on the people: recruitment, taxation, economic crisis and casualties. At the moment it suggests that the effects of each factor were the same. Draw your own version of the pie chart to show what you think is the relative importance of these factors. Add labels to explain your decision.

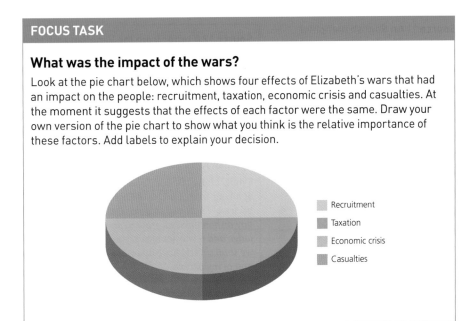

- Recruitment
- Taxation
- Economic crisis
- Casualties

Keeping the support of the people

The growing importance of parliament

For most of the medieval period, the monarch only really had to worry about the leading nobles. If they supported a war then the monarch could be confident of getting the troops, equipment and other resources they would need. By the end of the Middle Ages, however, parliament had become more important. Changes to the way the country was run meant that a ruler needed permission to impose taxes to raise the money necessary to pay and supply armies and navies.

This process of parliamentary approval for wars continued under Elizabeth I. By the 1590s, MEMBERS OF PARLIAMENT (MPs) even felt confident enough to criticise the queen's policies. In 1601, for example, MPs attacked the granting of licences and monopolies to particular individuals who were then able to corner the market in certain commodities, and raise prices. Elizabeth revoked several unpopular monopolies – an indication of parliament's growing influence.

Propaganda

Unlike most monarchs in medieval times, Elizabeth needed some degree of support from her own people. One way of achieving this was through the use of propaganda such as portraits. These created an image of Elizabeth as wise and successful, clever and caring, brave and loyal to her country. Leading nobles had copies of these portraits made and hung them in their own homes – and so the legend spread and strengthened.

The same propaganda effort was applied to Elizabeth's wars. They were portrayed as Protestant CRUSADES. If England was defeated, Catholicism would be reimposed. Elizabeth's subjects would lose their freedom in this life and the prospect of going to heaven in the next. Elizabeth's government used the printing press to good effect. Pamphlets, poems, songs, even playing cards and plays were used to emphasise the rightness of the English cause and the evil nature of Spain and of Catholicism generally. As Sources 11–15 show, the propaganda effort was in full swing during the Armada crisis, but it used the defeat of the Armada to its advantage for many years to come.

Source 11 An English pamphlet telling people about the orders issued by the commander of the Spanish Armada. ▼

ORDERS,
Set dovvne by the
Duke of Medina, Lord general
of the Kings Fleet, to be obferued in
the voyage toward England.

Tranflated out of Spanifh into Englifh by T.P.

Imprinted at London by Thomas Orwin for Thomas Gilbert, dwelling in Fleetftreete neere to the figne of the Caftle. 1588.

> **Source 12** A letter from the Venetian ambassador to Spain to his government, 1559.
>
> *The demonstrations and performance of plays by the London populace in the hostels and taverns were so spiteful and abominable that I was surprised they were tolerated. They brought upon the stage all personages whom they wished to revile, however exalted their station, and among the rest, in one play, they did this to King Philip of Spain and the late Queen Mary, saying whatever vile things they fancied about them.*

> **Source 13** Part of Elizabeth's speech to soldiers at Tilbury, August 1588, during the Spanish Armada.
>
> *I know I have the body of a weak and feeble woman, but I have the heart and stomach of a king, and of a king of England too, and think foul scorn that Parma or Spain or any prince of Europe should dare to invade the borders of my realm. To which, rather than any dishonour shall grow by me, I myself will take up arms, I myself will be your general, judge and rewarder of every one of your virtues in the field.... By your valour in the field, we shall shortly have a famous victory over these enemies of my God, of my kingdom, and of my people.*

1 Look at Source 13. What was the purpose of Elizabeth's speech?
2 Why was the speech good propaganda?
3 Source 11 was meant to be an English translation of the orders issued by the commander of the Spanish Armada. Do you think it was an accurate translation? Why might it not be accurate?

Source 14 An extract from a letter from the Privy Council to Sir Owen Hopton, lieutenant of the Tower of London, 26 July 1588.

Sir

Although Peter Pette had royal orders to purchase anchors, cables and planks for the fleet as a matter of urgency, certain people have refused to deliver these things because they did not think they would be paid. Sir Owen is to see that such people are put into prison and that Mr Pette obtains the things that he needs.

4 Why is Source 14 useful to historians studying Elizabeth's propaganda?

5 Explain the message of the 'Armada Portrait' in Source 15.

Source 15 The 'Armada Portrait', painted in 1588. Elizabeth's face is set in a look of commanding determination. She is dressed richly in jewels paid for by her successful, adventurous privateers. Her hand rests on a globe – covering the New World. Through the windows behind you can see the utter destruction of the Spanish Armada that had threatened to invade England. ▼

War-weariness

For the most part, the English people supported the war against Spain. There was a great outpouring of support when the Spanish Armada threatened to invade in 1588. A large army of volunteers assembled at Tilbury and heard the famous speech from the queen when she came to review them (see Source 13). Protestants regarded the conflict as part of the Protestant–Catholic struggle being waged across Europe. The victory over the Spanish was celebrated all over the country. Some people criticised the cost of the war and the way it was managed, but there was little open opposition.

However, by the 1590s, as the wars dragged on, war-weariness took over. Many Englishmen disliked the increased tax burden and the levying of troops. Large numbers of young men were sent to fight in the Netherlands, France and Ireland; many did not come back. Despite Elizabeth's efforts, expenditure on warfare soared and led to higher taxation. There was no decisive victory and this, together with a series of bad harvests, led to increasing dissatisfaction.

KEY QUESTION REVIEW

A Why did Elizabeth I fight so many wars when she was generally anti-war?

Make sure you have tackled this question for each of these conflicts:
- Scotland and the Netherlands
- privateering
- the Netherlands
- the Armada
- the naval war
- Ireland.

When you have considered each one, see if you can decide on one single graph that summarises all the campaigns.

B Why did Elizabeth fight the way she did?

Complete your table.

PRACTICE QUESTIONS

1 How effectively did England raise its armed forces between 1585 and 1603? (4)

2 How popular were the Spanish and Irish wars? (14)

2.2 A kingdom torn apart: Civil wars 1642–51

> **FOCUS**
>
> During Elizabeth's reign, England increased its capacity for fighting wars to a greater level than ever before. However, Elizabeth still left her successor James I (1603–25) with large debts. James's son, Charles I, inherited the throne in 1625. His financial troubles were even greater, but the real problem was that Charles was not a good politician. He alienated many of his subjects over campaigns against Spain, finance, the way he governed, the rights of parliament, relations with Scotland and Ireland and, above all, religion. The result was a civil war, which began in 1642. This was one of the most destructive conflicts that had ever taken place on British soil. You will learn more about the causes and politics of the English Civil War in the depth study. In this topic you will examine how the war was fought and how it affected the people of Britain.

The big picture

What kind of war was this?

The wars of 1642–51 were civil wars, between people in the same country. There had been civil wars in England before, but they had largely been between monarchs and barons or noble families competing for the throne. The wars of 1642–51 affected almost everyone. There were several great battles but also many local skirmishes. Towns were besieged. There were massacres and other atrocities. The causes of the wars were mainly religious and political ideologies, but racial issues also contributed.

What were the attitudes to war?

Two minorities dragged the rest of the country into conflict. The king and his allies had a vision of how he should rule and how religion should be practised. An equally determined minority was not prepared to accept Charles's religious views or his rule without parliament. Local communities and even families were divided by this war and both sides believed that God was on their side. The majority of ordinary people did not want a war, of course. They were forced to choose sides (or forced to accept the control of one side).

What was the impact of the wars?

The wars were devastating. Each side recruited troops, collected taxes (and food, clothing, horses, etc.) and controlled the population in much the same way Elizabeth I's wars had been organised and run. Both sides bombarded the population with propaganda. Historians estimate that 180,000 (3.6% of the entire population) died from fighting, accidents, starvation and disease caused by war – that would be around 2.3 million people today. In addition people were taxed more heavily and controlled more closely than ever before.

What was the response to the wars?

There is evidence from quite early on that people were suffering from war weariness. In 1643, one leading parliament supporter argued that the cause was not worth the terrible cost. Groups known as Clubmen tried to keep troops from both sides out of their local areas.

During the war, censorship lapsed, allowing groups with new religious and political ideas, such as the Levellers and the Quakers, to emerge. Many were attracted to these ideas but many more found them terrifying.

Most terrifying of all was the execution of the king in 1649, which made the country a republic run by parliament and the New Model Army. The new government had many enemies, and warfare and bloodshed continued until 1651.

KEY QUESTIONS

A Why did people fight and how did this affect the nature of the wars?

Make a copy of the table. As you work through this topic, use the table to record what you discover.

Reason	Explanation	How this affected the nature of the war
Religion		
Political beliefs		
Nationalism / race		

B Why were the Civil Wars of 1642–51 so devastating?

Here are some of the factors that made the English Civil Wars so disruptive and destructive. In this version of the chart they are shown as equally important. Redraw the chart so that the greater factors (in your view) are larger segments. Add labels to your diagram to explain your decisions.

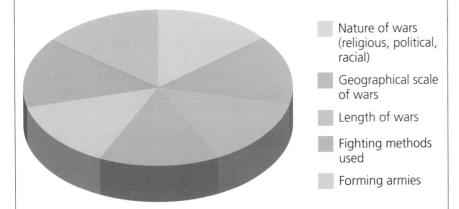

- Nature of wars (religious, political, racial)
- Geographical scale of wars
- Length of wars
- Fighting methods used
- Forming armies

C How did people react to the wars of 1642–51?

Here are some examples of reactions to the Civil Wars:
- neutrality
- war weariness
- fear.

1 Find examples of each of these reactions and explain them in a short paragraph.
2 Work with a partner and see if you can find other examples of how people reacted.

The nature of the English Civil Wars 1642–51: Why did Britain tear itself apart?

Most of the wars covered in this book are those in which the monarch or government *led* the country into conflict with a foreign enemy. In civil wars, however, opposing governments and people are from the same country. The 'enemy within' is often more frightening than a foreign enemy, and the bitterness that characterises civil wars can make them even more horrific. Source 1 demonstrates this attitude in the English Civil Wars that began in 1642. The pro-PARLIAMENTARIAN artist claims to have discovered a monster that threatens parliament, the Church, the city of London and the whole kingdom.

Religion: A war of beliefs

Religion was probably the biggest division between the two sides in the Civil Wars. Charles I had very clear views about religion. He wanted church services in England and Scotland to be the same, using the same prayer book and the same ceremonies. He wanted churches to be beautiful – decorated with works of art and stained-glass windows. He demanded obedience in these and other matters, and would not tolerate any dissent. Many people supported Charles's views and believed that religious life in the country would be improved as a result.

However, there were many others who disagreed. In particular a group of hard-line Protestants called PURITANS were appalled by the changes Charles introduced. They feared he was bringing back Catholicism. You have already looked at some religious propaganda from the time of Elizabeth I (see pages 66–67); such propaganda was even more extreme in the 1640s. Pamphlets issued by parliament reflected the fears that Charles was in league with the pope and that all good Protestants would be slaughtered. Many people believed that this war would bring about the end of the world, as described in the Bible's Book of Revelation. They thought Charles and the pope were the devil's allies, and believed that their souls were in danger. In these circumstances, it is not surprising that the fighting was often savage and desperate.

Political ideology – who rules and how?

Since the time of Henry VIII, parliament had become increasingly important. MPs never really challenged the monarch, but over time they came to expect that they would be consulted on important issues and that the monarch would listen to them. Charles would not accept this situation. As well as dictating religious policy, the king demanded that he be obeyed in all decisions regarding the running of the country. In 1628, MPs openly challenged him about this. In response, Charles dismissed parliament and did not call it again until 1640. Those who criticised the king could be arrested, imprisoned and tortured. During the Civil Wars, those who stood against the king believed they were fighting to preserve the rights of parliament, while those on Charles's side felt they were fighting for the traditional authority of the king and his right to rule without question.

As the war went on, new political ideas began to emerge that challenged the authority both of the king and of parliament.

Source 1 A pro-parliament print from 1643 called 'The Kingdom's Monster Uncloaked'.
The monster has three heads. Each head represents an enemy – Catholics, Royalists and the Irish. ▼

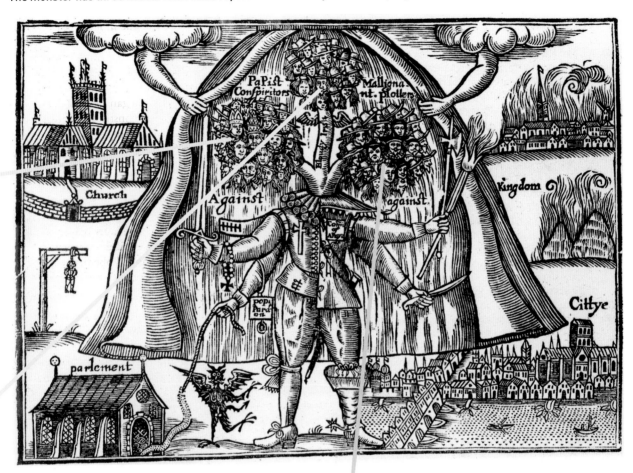

Three kingdoms ... and racial prejudice

The civil wars of the 1640s are often referred to as the English Civil War. Historians tend to refer to them as the British Civil Wars or the Wars of the Three Kingdoms (England, Scotland and Ireland). In the course of the war, Scottish and Irish troops fought in England, and English troops fought in Ireland and Scotland.

Supporters of parliament regarded the Irish with particular fear. Elizabeth I had fought wars in Ireland all through the later years of her reign. Propaganda in England had portrayed the Irish as savages and, as Catholics, they were believed to be in league with the pope (and the devil – see Source 1). In 1641, Catholic rebels massacred many Protestant settlers in Ireland (see page 77). Even so, Charles recruited large numbers of troops from Ireland to fight in his armies. Parliamentarian propaganda skilfully played on the fears of English Protestants that there was a deadly conspiracy against them. In the later 1640s, parliament sent troops to Ireland to crush the rebels, committing atrocities of their own and leaving a legacy of bitterness that would last for centuries.

FOCUS TASK

Why were the Civil Wars so savage?

1   Write a detailed caption to go with Source 1 for a museum exhibition on the Civil Wars. Explain why it is useful in explaining why they were so savage.
2   Source 1 is obviously biased. Explain why the bias is useful in explaining why the wars were so bitter.

FACTFILE

The course of the English Civil Wars 1642–51

1629–41 Personal Rule – Charles I ruled without calling parliament.

1641 Rebellions in Scotland and Ireland resulted in Charles I demanding money to establish new armies. Parliament feared that Charles would use the armies against MPs and refused. Trust broke down.

1642 Between spring and summer there were many clashes between supporters of parliament and those of the king as both sides tried to gain control of key towns or supplies of weapons and gunpowder. The war really began in August 1642, when Charles raised his STANDARD at Nottingham. The first really major battle was Edgehill in October, in which there was no clear winner. In November, Charles I tried to take London but his troops were beaten back. The king established his headquarters in Oxford for most of the rest of the war.

1643 For much of 1643, Charles and his supporters had the upper hand. They enjoyed successes in the north of England, captured Bristol and besieged the Parliamentarian city of Gloucester.

1644 The tide began to turn in favour of parliament. Parliament allied with the Scots and together they won a key victory at Marston Moor, which gave parliament control of northern England. Charles won important victories in the south-west, however.

1645 As the war went on, parliament became stronger. The areas it controlled had more money and a larger population, and parliament exploited these resources. Charles did the same in his areas, but he did not have the same resources to draw on. Parliament also reorganised its armies and created the New Model Army. This was well organised, well paid, well led and well equipped. It defeated Charles at Naseby in June.

1646 Parliament pressed home its advantages. By June, Charles and his supporters had surrendered.

1647 Despite long negotiations between Charles and his enemies (see page 183) no agreement could be reached. Charles exploited divisions between his enemies, escaped from prison and allied himself with the Scots, who had fallen out with parliament by this point.

1648 Charles's actions triggered the Second Civil War, which ended in another victory for parliament. It also saw the emergence of Oliver Cromwell as the leading figure in the army.

1649 In January, Charles I was put on trial and executed. England was now a republic. Scotland and Ireland refused to accept this and threw their support behind Charles I's son (also Charles). Under Cromwell, the New Model Army invaded Ireland and crushed Charles's supporters there in a brutal campaign.

1650–51 Cromwell led the army into Scotland and defeated the Scots at Dunbar in September 1650. Scottish and Royalist resistance continued until September 1651, but it was eventually crushed.

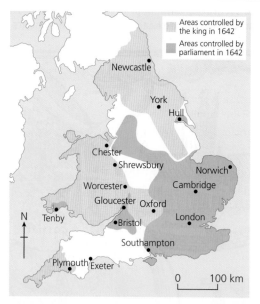

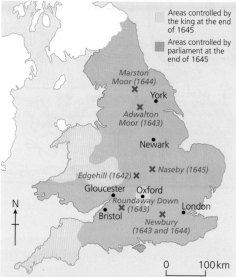

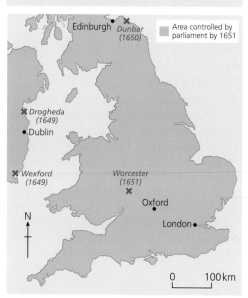

Source 2 A letter from the Countess of Denbigh to her son Basil, 1643. Basil supported parliament while his father William supported the king. William was wounded in the Royalist sacking of Birmingham in 1643 and later died.

I beg you, my son, to leave those who murdered your dear father. I believe you were misled into supporting parliament against the king. Let your dying father and your sorrowful mother make your heart relent and come back to us and ask forgiveness from the king.

Source 3 A petition sent to both the king and to parliament by the gentry of Somerset in 1642.

We continue to receive differing commands issued from the commanders of king and parliament, causing great terror of those of us who simply wish to obey all commands based on the laws of this kingdom.

We humbly ask to avoid the miseries that may befall us by means of contrary commands. We ask that his gracious Majesty would please suspend his orders to assemble the militia. We ask that the High Court of Parliament would likewise please suspend the carrying out of their order for the militia. We ask that his Majesty and the members of both Houses of Parliament would please assemble again and come to an arrangement about the militia of this kingdom according to the law. Or take some other good course to establish the peace and security of this kingdom. And we ask that in the meantime the militia of this county be controlled by the Justices of the Peace of this county according to the laws now in force.

Impact 1: **A divided nation**

Taking sides

As Charles and parliament clashed in 1642, people in the country chose their side – king, parliament or neither. The maps opposite give you some sense of the main areas of support for each side, but within these areas there was often bitter division. There were many Royalists in London, for example, but under parliament's control they were intimidated, forced to leave and sometimes imprisoned. Counties, towns, villages and even individual families were divided. It is likely that some of the fighting involved local feuds or settling old scores rather than big questions about religion or the right to rule. In many parts of the country there were effectively two governments – parliament and the king – and each tried to enforce its authority.

Raising armies

Both Charles and parliament tried to order the people of the country to join their armies. The system for raising troops was similar to that in Elizabeth's time (see page 63). Local GENTRY were ordered to call out the militia and trained bands and march to join their local Parliamentary or ROYALIST commanders. This could be complicated and even dangerous (see Sources 3 and 4).

Paying for the war effort

At a national level the money came from taxes. In the areas controlled by parliament, people had to pay two main taxes: the assessment and the excise. In Royalist areas, Charles imposed a tax called the contribution. In many counties, people received demands for taxes from both sides. Many people tried to avoid paying these. Parliament was more ruthless – and more successful – in collecting taxes. It set up County Committees in the areas it controlled, run by loyal Parliamentarians who worked hard to collect the taxes that parliament believed it was owed.

Source 4 An ordinance from parliament in 1643, which gave Parliamentarian commanders the power to impress (force) men into their armies. ▶

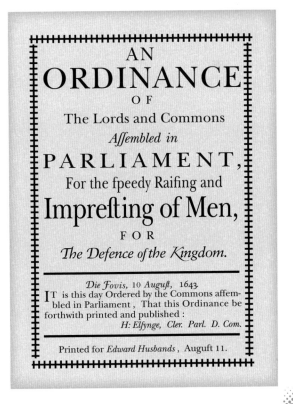

AN
ORDINANCE
OF
The Lords and Commons
Affembled in
PARLIAMENT,
For the fpeedy Raifing and
Imprefting of Men,
FOR
The Defence of the Kingdom.

Die Jovis, 10 *Auguft,* 1643.
IT is this day Ordered by the Commons affembled in Parliament, That this Ordinance be forthwith printed and published :
H: *Elfynge, Cler. Parl. D. Com.*

Printed for *Edward Husbands,* Auguft 11.

Impact 2: Fighting

Battles

Between 1642 and 1651, 22 battles were fought on English and Scottish soil. Some of the smaller battles involved around 5,000 troops, while major battles such as Marston Moor involved around 40,000 men (see Factfile on page 72). Warfare was evolving and these battles would have been terrifying. Guns were an increasingly important weapon, so there would have been a lot of cannon fire and musket fire. However, there were also cavalry charges and hand-to-hand fighting using pikes, swords, knives, clubs – or indeed anything with which a soldier chose to arm himself. Images such as Source 5 give us an idea of how the two sides lined up for a battle, but they do not capture the chaos of the battle itself. Historians estimate that 80,000 people were killed in these battles.

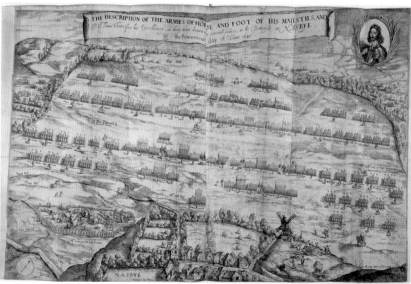

Source 5 A drawing made in 1647 of the Battle of Naseby in 1645. The Royalist army was defeated and suffered around 6,000 dead, wounded or captured. ▼

Figure 6 A map showing the main battles and sieges of the Civil Wars. ▼

Skirmishes

A major feature of the Civil Wars was the small-scale fighting between local Parliamentarian and Royalist forces. These skirmishes sometimes occurred because opposing forces simply ran into each other unexpectedly. Sometimes they were contests to take control of a key position such as a bridge or road junction, or to access resources such as food or arms. They took place all over the country and for the duration of the Civil Wars.

Sieges and sackings

In the 1640s, there were still many castles and fortified manor houses in England. There were also many walled towns (often surrounding a castle). These places usually controlled important roads or rivers, so they were obvious targets for both sides to try and capture. If they fell, they would be sacked, which meant that anything of value would be taken or destroyed, and the inhabitants would perhaps be killed or imprisoned. The siege and sacking of Colchester in the Second Civil War of 1648 was notorious for the savagery of the fighting and the high rate of civilian deaths.

Many castles, the towns around them and the people in them suffered during sieges. The siege of Basing House in Hampshire (see case study opposite) is one of the most famous, but it was not unique. Carlisle Castle was besieged several times during the Civil War. The garrison held out but the townspeople were reduced to eating rats and dogs because food was in such short supply.

Case study: The siege of Basing House

Basing House was situated on the main road between London and the West – a strongly Royalist area. Its owner, John Paulet, Marquis of Winchester, was a committed Royalist. He had a garrison of hundreds of troops. The struggle over the house lasted two years.

- **Stage 1, November 1643:** 7,000 Parliamentarians under Sir William Waller attempted a direct assault. After three failed attempts and heavy losses Waller retreated, believing his troops 'lacked the necessary resolve'.
- **Stage 2, early 1644:** The Parliamentarians secretly attempted to negotiate with the temporary commander (Lord Charles Paulet) to surrender, but the plot was discovered. Lord Charles was tried for treason.
- **Stage 3, June 1644:** The Parliamentarians set a siege to prevent Royalists getting into or out of the house, to try to starve them into submission. This was broken on 12 September 1644 when a Royalist army broke through parliamentary lines and resupplied the garrison. The Parliamentarians restarted the siege but by November, threatened by another Royalist army and with their troops suffering from disease, they withdrew.
- **Stage 4, October 1645:** With the war now going badly for the king, Oliver Cromwell joined a new parliamentary force besieging the house. He brought his own men and heavy guns. They quickly broke the defences and on the morning of 14 October 1645 successfully stormed the house. Because they had refused to surrender (and because they were presumed to be Catholics), the attackers killed about a quarter of the 400 members of the garrison, including ten priests. They looted and wrecked the house.
- **Aftermath:** During the assault the house caught fire and was badly damaged. What remained was 'totally slighted and demolished' by order of parliament, with the stones of the house offered free to anyone who would cart them away. Through the two years of siege, more than 2,000 Parliamentarians were killed. At least 100 Royalists were killed in the final assault and 300 taken prisoner, but we do not know how many were lost in the fighting that went before.

> 1   Source 7 is clearly a reconstruction and does not date from the time. Is it still a useful source? Explain your answer.

Source 7 A reconstruction of the siege of Basing House. There were actually two houses linked by a causeway. The Old House in the centre was built inside the remains of medieval fortifications. The New House was built outside the fortifications. ▼

Impact 3: **Physical destruction**

Another factor that made the Civil Wars so devastating was that they were fought on home soil. Most of Elizabeth I's wars had been fought at sea, in Europe or in the New World. They cost a lot of money but there was relatively little death and destruction at home. In contrast, civilian casualties during the Civil Wars were very high. Historians estimate that a total of 180,000 soldiers and civilians died as a result of fighting, accidents, hunger and disease. That is 3.6 per cent of the population at the time. During the First World War (1914–18), which is often seen as the deadliest war ever, 2.6 per cent of the British population were killed.

Free quarter

Look back at Sources 5 and 7. It is not difficult to imagine the effects of being in the war zone, but consider also the numbers of troops shown. Each of those men needed to be fed every day. They needed a place to sleep. They needed spare clothes and replacement equipment. They needed food for their horse. They may even have needed a new horse. And the soldiers all had to be paid. All this food, accommodation, equipment and money had to come from somewhere.

In many cases it was local towns, villages and communities that supplied what the armies needed as they marched through. Both sides frequently forced local civilians to provide 'free quarter'. This meant they had to feed and house troops with no payment, or with a promise of payment (which usually failed to materialise). Many soldiers were guilty of looting and pillaging as well.

Source 8 A pro-parliament print from 1642. Its title is 'The English Irish soldier'. Charles I recruited many Irish troops into his armies. This print is supposed to show the behaviour of the Irish troops in particular, but in reality almost all troops behaved in a similar way. ▼

> **ACTIVITY**
>
> Source 8 may look odd, even comical, to you. In fact it represents a deadly and very serious effect of war. For example, look at the man's shield. Is it really a shield? Where has he got it from? Do you think he bought it or was given it? Now look closely at the other details in the source and explain:
> - what it is saying about soldiers in the Civil War
> - what historians can infer about soldiers in the Civil War
> - what historians can infer about the effects of war on civilians
> - what it reveals about Parliamentarian propaganda at the time.

If local communities resisted or were suspected of supporting the opposite side, it was not unusual for property to be destroyed and houses set on fire. There were many complaints to the king and to parliament about the actions of troops. In south Wales and south-west England, groups of men called Clubmen were formed. They armed themselves and tried to keep both sides out of their areas.

Destruction in Scotland

Scotland escaped some of the disruption of the First Civil War, but it felt the full force of Cromwell's New Model Army in the Second Civil War. At the Battle of Dunbar in 1650, around 3,000 Scottish troops were killed and 10,000 taken prisoner. The following year saw Cromwell's army ruthlessly stamping out support for the Royalists and causing much destruction in the process.

Devastation in Ireland

The fighting in England and Scotland was bitter, but the savagery in Ireland was even greater. One of the triggers for the war in 1642 had been a rebellion in Ireland in 1641. Also, the Royalists had recruited many troops from Ireland for their forces. Prejudice and years of anti-Catholic and anti-Irish propaganda left many Protestants feeling that the Irish were an inferior race. When Cromwell led troops to crush the Irish rebellion in 1649, the fighting and the measures imposed afterwards were brutal. Some historians estimate that 40 per cent of the population of Ireland died in the war, hunger, disease and disruption of the 1640s. Cromwell threw thousands of people off their land and forced them to move to the barren western part of Ireland. Around 12,000 Irish – many of them children – were sold into slavery in the Caribbean.

Source 9 A propaganda print showing atrocities committed by Irish rebels, 1641. Such behaviour was heavily exaggerated in propaganda materials and created anti-Irish hysteria in England. ▼

1 Study Source 9. Why would this source and similar material have had such a dramatic impact on people's attitudes towards the Irish?

2 Compare these sources with some modern newspaper headline descriptions of recent war atrocities. Do you think they are similar in any way?

3 How far does Source 9 explain what happened in Source 10?

Source 10 An extract from a report by Oliver Cromwel, describing his attack on the Irish town of Wexford, 1649. The town was destroyed and almost the entire population killed or driven away.

As we came into the market place the enemy put up strong resistance but our forces broke them and we put all to the sword. Two boatfuls of the enemy attempted to escape but they all drowned. I believe two thousand of the enemy were killed while I believe we lost around twenty men. In His righteous judgement God has brought a just judgement on these Irish Catholic people, making them answer for the cruelties they brought upon many poor Protestants.

Source 11 A pamphlet called 'The World Turned Upside Down'. It was published and reprinted several times in the 1640s. ▼

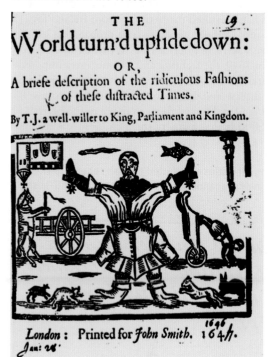

Impact 4: The social and psychological impact

Source 11 is a very famous image. It has appeared in many textbooks because it gives us a strong sense of how people in the 1640s must have felt. At different times they would have been angry, frustrated, confused, afraid, outraged and shocked.

A country without a king

For most people, the monarch was more than a human being, he or she was almost god-like. Even a poor ruler like Charles I was respected in this way. As a result, seeing him challenged in 1642 was deeply shocking. Parliament's war against him, and particularly the king's imprisonment from 1646 to 1648, would have been regarded by many as SACRILEGIOUS. His death in 1649 was traumatic to his supporters. Accounts exist describing how people fainted at his execution.

Despite his flaws Charles was still the king, and a country without a king was a terrifying prospect. Officially the country had no king until 1660, but in reality the army commander Oliver Cromwell carried out the role. After his death in 1658, no successor could be found and so Charles I's son was restored as Charles II in 1660. People could not imagine a stable country without a monarch, and the disruption and devastation of the Civil Wars only strengthened that belief.

New ideas

Before the Civil Wars, there had been strict censorship and harsh punishments for those who expressed political or religious ideas. Once war broke out, censorship collapsed. As men and women fought and faced the horrors of war, many began to question existing ideas. New political and religious groups emerged, including the following:

- The Levellers argued for a more equal society, including religious freedom and the vote for all men.
- The Diggers (or True Levellers) wanted to get rid of all forms of authority – including the Church and parliament – so that people could rule themselves.
- The Quakers rejected the need for churches, bishops or any other kind of religious authority.

At the time, many people found the emergence of these groups threatening and they were all eventually banned.

Rule by parliament

Before the Civil Wars, parliament had a certain amount of power, but it could not formally overrule the king. By 1651, parliament had executed Charles I and was the official ruler of England, Wales, Ireland and Scotland. However, the army had a significant say in what happened. For the majority of the people, rule by parliament meant heavy taxes and strict control of their lives. Many people longed for a return to the monarchy. Charles I's rule might have been harsh at times, but parliamentary rule was worse.

The rise of the army

In 1645, parliament passed the Self-Denying Ordinance. This meant that any MPs who were also commanders in the army had to resign from one position or the other – they could not do both. On one hand, this helped create a professional and effective army. On the other hand, these commanders saw themselves as the men who had won the war. They began to get more involved in political matters, and army leader Oliver Cromwell emerged as the most powerful figure. The Self-Denying Ordinance made an exception for him, and he and the army were more powerful than parliament. Cromwell himself was largely respected, but most people disliked the army's involvement in politics. It left a legacy of mistrust between parliament and the army that lasted for 200 years.

Social change and local authority

For most civilians, the people who held authority were the local vicar and the local landowner. Landowners were usually MAGISTRATES. They handled local law and order issues and collected taxes. In the Civil Wars, the Royalists and Parliamentarians both introduced County Committees, run by men whose first loyalty was to parliament or the king. This undermined the authority of the local landowners and was bitterly unpopular.

KEY QUESTION REVIEW

At the start of this topic, on page 69, you were asked to think about three key questions. Make sure you are confident about your ability to answer these questions and support what you say.

A Why did people fight and how did this affect the nature of the wars?

Check that you have a range of examples and explanatory points in your table.

B Why were the Civil Wars of 1642–51 so devastating?

Make sure you can write a paragraph on at least three of the factors set out in the diagram.

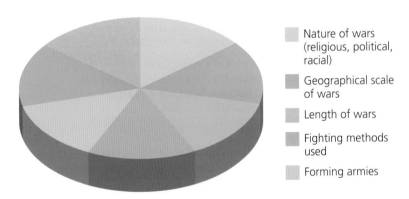

- Nature of wars (religious, political, racial)
- Geographical scale of wars
- Length of wars
- Fighting methods used
- Forming armies

C How did people react to the wars of 1642–51?

As a class, share your explanations and see what further types of reactions other students have found.

PRACTICE QUESTIONS

1 Describe two examples of divisions caused by the Civil War. (2)
2 Explain why the Civil Wars caused such heavy casualties. (8)
3 How significant an event was the establishment of the Commonwealth in 1649? (14)

2.3 Anglo-Scottish Wars 1500–1746

The big picture

What was the nature of the Anglo-Scottish conflict?

Anglo-Scottish relations varied considerably throughout this period. There was particular enmity in the early sixteenth century. This included invasions by large armies leading to major battles, but also small raids on neighbouring clans by reivers.

After 1603 both countries had the same monarch, which helped with the reiver problem. However, relations were not always amicable, especially during the Civil Wars and after 1714, when Highland clans joined the Jacobite rebellions and invaded England.

These wars need to be seen as part of a wider conflict. For example, England invaded Scotland in the sixteenth century not because it hated the Scots but because Scotland was an ally of Catholic France, with which England was at war.

What were the attitude and response of Britons to Anglo-Scottish conflict?

Anglo-Scottish conflict particularly affected people who lived near the frontier. Full-scale invasions passed through the borders. Scots were enlisted to fight on both sides. Throughout the sixteenth century, the borderlands were an area of lawlessness and reiver activity.

What impact did improved Anglo-Scottish relations have on Britain?

Improved Anglo-Scottish relations (especially after 1603) resulted in greater peace across the border area in the early seventeenth century. The Scottish Highlands were not fully integrated into Great Britain until after 1746.

What impact did unity have on Anglo-Scottish governments and people?

English governments sought to reduce Anglo-Scottish conflict by uniting the two countries. In 1603, James VI (I of England) became king of both countries. In 1707, the Act of Union led to the formation of Great Britain. There were further conflicts, most notably in 1715 and 1746, but the majority of Scots were prepared to accept the Union. Scottish soldiers, sailors, scientists, doctors and engineers went on to play important roles in the development of the United Kingdom and the British Empire.

What impact did the conflict have on emigration and empire?

One of the unplanned outcomes of conflict between England and Scotland was large-scale emigration from Scotland. A lot of this migration was relatively well organised and took the form of military service. Scottish troops served all over Europe in this period and, once England and Scotland were united, they served all over the British Empire. They had a particularly powerful and long-lasting influence in Canada.

KEY QUESTIONS

A Why was there so much conflict between England and Scotland c1500–c1750?

The table below lists some of the reasons why England and Scotland fought in this period. Make your own copy and complete it as you work through the chapter.

Reasons for conflict	Specific examples	Importance
religion		
local feuds		
wealth/plunder		
national interest of England/Scotland		
international dimension		

B What impact did the Anglo-Scottish wars have on Britain?

Copy the table below, which lists some ways in which the conflict between England and Scotland may have affected Britain. As you work through this topic, look for evidence of how the wars affected Britain. Record this evidence in the second column. In the third column, give a mark between 1 and 4 for each piece of evidence, where 1 means the evidence is unimportant and 4 means it is very important.

Feature	Evidence of impact	Importance of impact
military impact		
financial impact		
impact on the borders		
political impact		
British unity		
empire/migration		

FACTFILE

A map of Scotland showing the main battlefields.

Background: Anglo-Scottish conflict 1485–1750

For most of their history, England and Scotland were separate nations. Even when James VI of Scotland was invited to succeed Elizabeth I in 1603, the two kingdoms remained technically separate. Scotland and England continued to share the same monarch after the Restoration of Charles II in 1660 (see page 204), but they were not officially united as one kingdom until 1707.

Relations between England and Scotland had been relatively peaceful until the reign of Edward I in England. He effectively tried to control Scotland – and Scotland resisted (see page 44). This led to long periods of conflict, interspersed with intervals of tense peace. Anglo-Scottish hostility sometimes led to war. However it was often events in Europe that influenced England's relations with Scotland.

2.3A Anglo-Scottish conflict: Border warfare c1500–c1600

FOCUS

From 1500 to 1600, the border between England and Scotland was a wild and dangerous place. In many areas, the law barely operated and the only real power was that of gun and sword. In this section you will examine how this situation came about and how it affected the people in the region.

'Official' warfare

Source 1 A modern photograph of Carlisle Castle. The castle was built in 1092 and then upgraded many times. It was besieged by Scottish forces seven times between 1173 and 1461. The semicircle at the front of the castle was added by Henry VIII in 1542 as a battery for modern cannon – just one part of his upgrading of the castle. ▼

1   Look at Source 1. How can you tell that Carlisle Castle was important to English rulers?

The nature of official warfare

England and Scotland came into conflict many times in the period c1500–c1750. Sometimes this was a consequence of border disputes; at other times it was due to wider European conflicts. Scotland and France had a long tradition of friendship, and each found in the other a useful political and military ally against their common enemy, England.

In 1513, Henry VIII of England went to war against France. France was allied with Scotland and so the Scottish king, James IV, invaded. After initial successes in northeastern England, James was decisively defeated in the Battle of Flodden Field in 1513. In 1542, James V of Scotland renewed his country's alliance with France and attacked England. English forces defeated the Scots at Solway Moss near Carlisle. Despite his victory, Henry VIII ordered a programme of improvements to strengthen the key stronghold of Carlisle Castle (see Source 1).

James V died soon after this. His daughter, Mary Queen of Scots, was only a child at the time, so Scotland's nobles ran the kingdom. However, they were divided over whether to ally with France or England. When they showed signs of making an alliance with France in 1544–45, Henry VIII sent an army led by the Earl of Hertford to ravage southern Scotland and intimidate the Scots (see Source 2). This caused a great deal of damage but was eventually repelled by Scottish forces.

Impact of official warfare

Official warfare could be devastating. Armies lived off the surrounding countryside, often simply taking what they needed. English tactics in Scotland also involved deliberate destruction. For example, the Earl of Hertford's campaign in 1545 destroyed seven monasteries, 16 fortified towers, five towns, 243 villages, 13 mills and three hospitals. Many parts of the border region, like most war zones, were plagued by poverty, disease and under-development in this period.

Henry VIII died in 1547 and England faced its own political, religious and financial problems. As a result, official war with Scotland became less frequent. By Elizabeth I's reign, both sides were keen to avoid further expensive and destructive wars so peace reigned for the most part. It was, however, an uneasy peace, and visitors to the border regions might not think it at all peaceful…

'Unofficial' warfare

During this period of uncertain peace, the English and Scottish rulers remained suspicious of each other. One result was that the border region became a sort of no-man's land for the rival monarchs – a place where their authority was relatively weak. In a strange way this worked for them both: if neither monarch built up strong forces on their side of the border there was less danger of full-scale invasion. However, this weak royal authority had serious consequences for the people who lived in the border regions.

The reivers

In these border areas, bands of raiders from different clans – REIVERS – paid little heed to distant governments in London or Edinburgh. Local communities owed loyalty to their blood relatives or clans, which sometimes straddled the border. Relationships between the clans ranged from uneasy alliance to deadly feud. Feuds could continue for decades and might only be set aside in the face of invasion or when new feuds caused alliances to shift.

FOCUS TASK

Evidence of official warfare

What types of reasons have you found for the 'official' warfare between England and Scotland in this section? Record what you have found in your table for Key Question A on page 81.

FACTFILE

Border clans and reivers
This map shows the border region and the families and clans associated with cross-border reiving. Each side of the border was divided into three Marches. In theory these were run by royal officials called March wardens (see page 85).

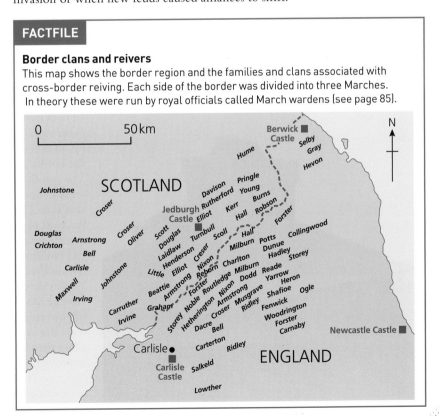

Reiver loyalties

Border clans sought to improve their livelihood at their enemies' expense. They did this by launching raids (usually involving a few dozen men), stealing cattle, sheep or other goods. They also took hostages for ransom. Raids by one clan would lead to retaliatory raids. While reivers saw themselves as English or Scottish, most were loyal first and foremost to their clan. Scottish and English reivers thus raided on both sides of the border.

Reiving became an accepted way of life. English and Scottish governments rarely took action against their own border clans because it was in their interests to keep it lawless. The borders, with the reivers, were seen as the first line of defence in the event of invasion. Henry VIII had been quite happy to use this strategy, storing up rivalries in the border lands to help win his wars with Scotland.

> **Source 2** A retelling of a story from a sixteenth-century ballad called 'Jamie Telfer of the Fair Dodhead'.
>
> *Jamie Telfer lived in Fair Dodhead in Ettrickdale, with his wife and bairns [children] in an isolated location – far from neighbours. The family had few possessions, ten cattle and their smallholding of land. The Captain of Bewcastle [just on the English side of the border] wanted to teach the Scots a lesson for the many Scots raids on his land, so set off with his marauding band. When they came to Dodhead they laughed as they saw easy pickings. They stole the cows, and ransacked the house. The parents were left face down in the mud as their children looked, crying in distress.*
>
> *Jamie ran ten miles to Branxholme, home of Scott, the Laird of Buccleuch and Branxholme. Jamie had paid protection money to Scott. Scott duly called out all his clan and they rode after the raiders who were making slow going because of taking the cows with them. They attacked the raiders and retrieved Jamie's cattle.*
>
> *But why stop there? The Scotts decided to try their luck at the Captain of Bewcastle's home. They broke down the door of his home, outfought the English garrison and made away with some of the captain's cattle.*
>
> *Meanwhile back at Fair Dodhead Jamie was lost in wretched thought. Imagine his relief when the Scotts returned with his beasts. The relief turned to delight when Jamie counted not just ten but thirty-three cows, twenty-three of which had formerly been pastured at the home of the Captain of Bewcastle.*

1 Read Source 2. Does Jamie appear to be an innocent victim in the events of this story? Explain your answer.

Source 3 A reconstruction drawing of a pele tower. The lower floors would have housed animals and the upper floors the people and their possessions. This is a particularly strongly defended pele – many were smaller and had no outer walls. ▼

The impact of border warfare

If you travel around the border regions today you cannot go far without seeing a pele tower. These were defensive positions designed to protect cattle, people and possessions. One research project has found 600 of these towers on the English side of the border alone, and there may have been more. The fact that there are so many of them gives us a sense of how dangerous and violent activity in the area was. There is other evidence to support this. Records of the West March wardens for a five-month period in 1543 reveal that reivers destroyed 192 buildings (including churches, pele towers and farmhouses). They also stole over 10,000 cows, 12,500 sheep and 1,300 horses. The historian George Macdonald Fraser researched the activities of one reiver family, the Elliots. Over ten years from the early 1580s, they made over 40 raids. More than 3,000 cattle were stolen, 66 buildings destroyed, 14 men murdered and 146 prisoners captured. They also stole household goods such as clothing, sheets and a cooking cauldron.

The wardens of the Marches

The border zone was not completely lawless and there were attempts to control reiver activity. On both sides of the border, the land was divided into three MARCHES – East, West and Middle – each with an appointed warden. A March wardens' duty was to deter raiders from the other kingdom. However, they did little to maintain law and order.

Scottish wardens were usually chosen from among border families in the hope that they could exercise some control over the reiver families. However, they often joined in raiding activity and the favour they showed to their own kindred caused jealousy among other border families.

English wardens often came from southern England and were specifically chosen so that they would not be biased in favour of any group. But most failed to command the loyalty and respect of the locals. A warden's salary was inadequate and many were as corrupt as their Scottish counterparts. All wardens made many enemies because of their role, whether they were honest or not. Several of them were murdered.

The end of the reivers

The reivers prospered because it suited the English and Scottish rulers for the border to be turbulent. This all changed swiftly with the death of Elizabeth in 1603 and the accession of James VI of Scotland as James I of England. With the two thrones united, there was no longer any advantage to be gained from a lawless border region. English and Scottish forces combined to bring it under the same justice systems as England and Scotland, and this was achieved by the end of the decade.

Source 4 Yanwath Hall in Cumbria. The left end is an old pele tower. The lower part of the building to its right was built towards the end of the reiver period. ▼

Reivers were dealt with savagely. Many were executed, often without trial; others were conscripted to fight in the Netherlands or sent to Ireland as unwilling farmers. Although some border families retained power and influence, their military role soon became less important and they began to convert their homes into impressive houses rather than military bases.

> 2 How are Sources 3 and 4 similar or different?
>
> 3 How could you explain any differences?

ACTIVITY

Write captions for Sources 1, 3 and 4, explaining how each one helps historians understand the differences between types of border warfare and the changing situation from c1500 to c1600.

FOCUS TASK

How similar was official and unofficial border warfare in the period c1500–c1600?

Study the two different types of warfare. Use a table like the one below to record the similarities and differences.

	Reasons	Type of warfare	Effects	How similar on a scale of 1–10
official warfare				
unofficial warfare				

Anglo-Scottish relations 1603–1707: A changing scene

The accession of James as ruler of Scotland and England effectively ended the border tensions and the reivers. For a while there was peace between England and Scotland. The two countries shared both a monarch and a religion.

In fact the main tensions were not between England and Scotland but within the two countries. You have already seen how religion was a source of tension in England. This was also true in Scotland. The Scottish Lowlands favoured a Protestant Presbyterian Church, characterised by plain churches, an emphasis on reading the Bible and parishes run by local elders. In the Highlands, there was greater support for the Catholic Church. James I was wise enough to compromise and avoid religious strife in England and Scotland. However, his son Charles I was not. He tried to impose his Anglican form of Protestantism on the Scots. In 1639, the Scots rebelled against Charles to preserve their Presbyterian Church. This rebellion is often referred to as the Bishops' War.

The Civil Wars

The Bishops' War was a trigger for the Civil Wars of 1642–51, in which Scottish forces played an important role. In the First Civil War (1642–45) they fought with parliament against Charles, but in the Second Civil War they switched sides. After Charles I's execution, his son Charles led his Royalist followers and the Scots in a Third Civil War (1650–51). Under Cromwell, the English defeated the Scots at Dunbar in September 1650 and the Scottish army retreated northwards, holding Cromwell at bay. In August 1651, the Scots invaded England. The two armies met at Worcester the following month. Cromwell's forces won a resounding victory, killing or capturing some 16,000 Royalists (mainly Scots).

Restoration to Union

At the Restoration in 1660, Charles II was established as king of England and Scotland. For the duration of his reign, relations remained quite peaceful between the two countries. However, Charles's successor, his brother James, proved a poor ruler. When he tried to restore Catholicism in England, he was overthrown by leading English nobles, who invited James's daughter Mary and her husband William of Orange to take the throne in 1688. A substantial minority in Scotland, known as JACOBITES, were angered by this, believing that James should still be king. However, when the English and Scottish crowns were united in the Act of Union in 1707 (see Factfile) their cause seemed lost.

ACTIVITY

1   The title for this page is 'A changing scene'. Do you think it is a good title? In pairs or small groups debate the merits of this title and also of these possible titles:
    a   A time of peace
    b   A time of conflict
    c   Religious strife
    d   A hated union
2   Add your own ideas.
3   Try to agree on the best title, then compare your views with the rest of the class.

FACTFILE

The Act of Union 1707
- The English government wanted union with Scotland because it was at war with France and it wanted to ensure that its two enemies did not form an alliance.
- Scotland wanted union with England for economic reasons. In 1698, Scotland had attempted to set up a colony in Darien, on the Isthmus of Panama. The scheme was a disaster and resulted in the Scottish government going bankrupt.
- In 1707, the Act of Union abolished the Scottish parliament. Scots were given a proportion of seats in the London parliament.
- England and Scotland became one country – Great Britain.
- Not all Scots supported the union: some wished to restore Scotland's independence. However, most Scots benefited economically from the union so accepted it. They played an important role in all aspects of British life – economically, politically, culturally, militarily and imperially.

2.3B New Anglo-Scottish conflict: The Jacobite Wars 1715 and 1745

The Highland military tradition
- Highland clans effectively made their living from the land, but they could also be mobilised into small armies quickly and efficiently.
- They had a long tradition of fighting and feuding with each other, much like the reivers (see page 84).
- Between 1500 and 1700, the Highland clans turned fighting into an export industry. The Highlands were overpopulated and there grew to be a strong tradition of young Highlander men serving as mercenaries in the armies of European states, particularly France. They would then earn money to buy land of their own after several years' service.
- They were formidable soldiers – disciplined and organised. They made effective use of a range of weapons including rifles, pistols, swords, shields and dirks (knives).
- This was a large-scale enterprise and tens of thousands of young Highland men served abroad in places such as France, Russia and Poland.
- From 1707, Highlanders were allowed to join the British army and many did so. This number steadily increased throughout the 1700s.

---

1 How can you tell that Lord Argyll regards the Jacobites as a serious threat in Source 1?
2 Use the information on this page to add a paragraph to Source 1 explaining why the Jacobites are still a threat.

FOCUS

The Act of Union joined England and Scotland politically. However, many Scots were still bitterly opposed to it. In this section, you will examine how they tried to restore the old Stuart monarchs to the throne, and the short- and long-term effects of those attempts.

When James II was overthrown in 1688 he was replaced by his daughter Mary and her husband William. They were succeeded by Queen Anne. Anne died in 1714 with no surviving children. Legally the most obvious person to take the throne was James Stuart, son of the DEPOSED King James II. However, he was a Catholic and the English nobility was not prepared to accept this. Instead, the Act of Settlement was agreed, by which the crown went to the Protestant Prince George of Hanover.

The 1715 rebellion

The Jacobite cause was particularly strong in the Scottish Highlands, where many clans remained Catholic. The Highland clans were also highly militarised (see Factfile). A Jacobite rebellion, centred on the Highlands, occurred in 1715. The rebels, who supported the claims of James Stuart, were supported by England's old enemy, France. With its rising population and a small but growing overseas empire, France saw England as a real threat and was keen to help England's enemies.

The Jacobites had initial success. By October 1715 they had 20,000 troops in the field and had taken control of much of Scotland. However, the Jacobite leaders grew cautious. They knew the English would recover and they also knew that they had little support from Lowland Scotland, which they would need to maintain control of their country. A small Jacobite force invaded England, but it surrendered at Preston in November 1715. James Stuart, who came to Scotland, quickly returned to France, while Jacobite leaders retreated to the Highlands.

The British government did not see this rebellion as a major threat and showed leniency to the Jacobites. They were partly encouraged in this reaction by the fact that pursuing the Highlanders into their own territory would be difficult and dangerous. However, they built several forts and nearly 400 kilometres of roads to ensure that government troops could move quickly to crush any further risings.

The failure of another attempted rebellion in 1719 seemed to prove the effectiveness of this policy. Yet for all the seeming success in uniting Scotland under HANOVERIAN rule, there was underlying conflict. While many Scots supported the Hanoverian succession for political, religious and economic reasons, others – especially in the Highlands – still favoured the return of the Stuarts and the Catholic religion.

Source 1 Part of a letter from Lord Argyll to King George I, 1715. Argyll was the commander of the royal forces against the Jacobites.

This Victory we have got is owing to God's favour. Our officers and soldiers deserve your Majesty's favour. My Lord if I may advise you, I would humbly beg of his Majesty not to put the kingdom in a position of risk. If these people reassemble, depend upon it my Lord, we cannot hope always to beat them.

The 1745 rebellion

A second, more serious, Jacobite rebellion broke out in 1745. This was led by Charles Edward Stuart, known as Bonnie Prince Charlie or the 'Young Pretender' – the son of James Stuart. At the time Britain was once again embroiled in war with France. With most of the 62,000-strong British army fighting in Europe, Charles saw an opportunity. He landed in Scotland in August 1745 and began to rally support. He had received a promise of French backing and hoped that the Highland clans would come to his aid in this attempt to win back the throne for his father.

Initial success

Several clans supported Charles's cause and he was eventually able to march south with 2,500 men. He arrived in Edinburgh in September 1745 and there proclaimed his father as James VIII of Scotland. On 21 September, his Highland army defeated a small British force at Prestonpans, ensuring Charles controlled much of Scotland.

Into England ... and back

Charles's next target was England. In November his forces captured Carlisle and its castle. By 4 December, his 5,000 men had reached Derby, causing panic in London. However, the Young Pretender was also worried. He had expected Jacobite sympathisers in the north to support him, but only 300 English Catholics had joined his army and he had received no extra help from France. Surrounded by pro-government forces, he decided to return to Scotland. After winning a minor victory at Falkirk, he retreated to the Highlands.

He had caused enough alarm for the British government to recall large numbers of troops from fighting in the Netherlands. The government also used the invasion to stir up national sentiment. Most English people supported their Protestant German king. Noblemen raised regiments of volunteers to defend the monarch (it was at this time that the song 'God Save the King' was adopted as the national anthem). Lowland Scots – and many Highlanders who served in the British army – were also eager to fight back against the Jacobites. In fact, more Scots fought against Charles Stuart than fought for him.

Source 2 'The Highland Visitors' – a British government propaganda print published in 1746, showing Jacobites 'visiting' a peaceful English village. ▼

THE HIGHLAND VISITORS.

1   Examine Source 2. What exactly is happening?
2   What does the print suggest was the main concern of Scottish invaders?
3   Why do you think the print was made?

The Battle of Culloden

In late December 1745 an English army, led by the Duke of Cumberland, headed north, seeking battle. Carlisle was recaptured on 30 December. Jacobite prisoners were thrown into the dungeons with little or no food or water – they are rumoured to have survived by licking the damp walls. On 16 April 1746, Charles tried and failed to take Cumberland by surprise at Culloden. His 5,000 Highlanders were defeated in one hour by Cumberland's 9,000-strong army. Charles escaped from the battlefield and fled to France.

Source 3 *Incident in the Battle of Culloden* by David Morier, 1746. Jacobite prisoners from the rebellion were used to pose for the painting. ▼

4   What impression do you get of the Highlanders in Source 3?
5   How does it compare to the portrayal of the British troops?

Source 4 An extract from *The Butcher, The Duke of Cumberland and the Suppression of the 45* by W. A. Speck.

The Forty-Five had not seriously threatened to remove George from the throne. Instead of revealing that the dynasty was essentially unstable, it demonstrated as nothing else could have done just how firmly established the Hanoverian regime was.

6   In what ways do Sources 4 and 5 disagree?
7   Which source do you find more convincing? Explain your answer.

Source 5 Historian Linda Colley, writing in 1992.

The romantic aura that still hovers around Bonnie Prince Charlie's memory should not obscure the seriousness of his invasion. That it had achieved so much with such minimal resources was a testament to the Jacobite army's mettle and leadership, and to the ineptitude of much of the formal machinery of the British state.

Impact of the rebellion

Short term

Wounded Jacobites were killed where they lay. Across the Highlands precious livestock – vital for survival – were rounded up and sold. Hundreds of Jacobite supporters were hunted down and imprisoned, although most were later released. Over 100 were executed, with another 1,000 being transported to the British colonies in North America. Several high-ranking Jacobite leaders were publicly executed at the Tower of London. Charles Stuart was not one of them. Despite a huge reward being offered for his capture, no one betrayed him and he eventually escaped to France. However, his cause was ended. It was clear that there was very little real support for it.

Medium term: Breaking the power of the clans

To make sure this remained the case, the British government passed a series of laws intended to demilitarise the Highland clans. All swords had to be surrendered. Even the wearing of tartan by anyone except soldiers in the British army was banned by an Act of Parliament. The government also ended the right of Highland chieftains to make law in their domains. Pro-government chieftains were compensated while those who had supported Prince Charles had their lands confiscated. Many went into exile.

Source 6 A painting of Highland troops at the Plains of Abraham in Canada, 1759. The painting is from the later nineteenth century. This was a time of increasing Scottish nationalism and the successes of Highland troops were a source of great pride. ▼

Longer term: Scotland and the union

The defeat of the rebellion in 1745 marked the end of the Jacobite threat. From this point, Scotland was dominated by Lowland Scots who supported the government, backed by the British army. Englishmen were not sent to rule Scotland – loyal Scots did that effectively enough. In time, Jacobite sympathies faded and the Highlands became more integrated into Great Britain.

Longer term: Scotland and the wider world

Technically the Highlanders were demilitarised, but their fighting expertise would still be called upon. By the 1750s, Britain's rivalry with France was more intense than ever, and it was a global rivalry, with each state trying to build empires, particularly in North America and India. Britain could not afford to ignore the potential of a large group of effective soldiers like the Highlanders. Thousands of Highlanders joined the British army and played a key role in the expansion of the British Empire. For example, Highland troops who had fought against each other at Culloden fought together against the French at the Battle of the Plains of Abraham at Quebec in 1759. This decisive battle led to the conquest of Canada by the British. In the years that followed, many Scottish soldiers settled in Canada, marrying into the local population or bringing relatives from Scotland to settle.

FOCUS TASK

How similar were the Jacobite Wars of 1715 and 1745?

Use a table like the one below to compare and contrast the Jacobite Wars.

	1715	1745
type of conflict/reasons		
impact on relationship between England and Scotland		
impact on Scotland		
significance		

KEY QUESTION REVIEW

At the start of this topic on page 81 you were asked to think about two key questions. Make sure you are confident about your ability to answer these questions and support what you say.

A Why was there so much conflict between England and Scotland c1500–c1750?

Make sure your table is complete, then compare it with those of other students in your class.

Reasons for conflict	Specific examples	Importance
religion		
local feuds		
wealth/plunder		
national interest of England/Scotland		
international dimension		

B What impact did the Anglo-Scottish wars have on Britain?

Make sure your table from this task is complete, then see whether the rest of the class agrees with your rank order.

Feature	Evidence of impact	Importance of impact
military impact		
financial impact		
impact on the borders		
political impact		
British unity		
empire/migration		

PRACTICE QUESTIONS

1   Describe two examples of border warfare in the sixteenth century. (2)
2   The Jacobite rebellions failed because they lacked popular support. Do you agree? (8)
3   Why was there so much lawlessness on the English–Scottish borders in the sixteenth century? (8)
4   How signifciant were the Jacobite campaigns? (14)

2.4 Review: War and society c1500–c1750

PERIOD REVIEW TASKS

A What types of war were there in this period?

1 Historians often look at different types of wars, compare how they are fought and the effects they had. The list below shows some different types of wars.
- opportunism/ambition/plunder
- wars beween peoples, nations or states
- conquest/invasion
- defence
- rebellion
- religion
- civil war

Look back over your work and try to find two examples of each category. Some wars might fit more than one category.

B War and people: Attitudes and responses to war

2 War and its impact in the early modern period is quite complex because of the different types of wars that were fought. The following statements are designed to help you consider some of the main issues and questions surrounding this period. Draw your own version of the table and use Sections 2.1–2.3 to complete it.

In the early modern period ...	Events/developments I would use as evidence to agree with this	Events/developments I would use as evidence to disagree with this	Overall I agree/ disagree/in between	This is similar to/a change from the medieval period because ...
people supported the monarch when they went to war				
war made parliament more important				
rulers needed the support of their populations to fight wars effectively				
governments tried to influence people's attitudes towards war with propaganda				
people were enthusiastic about war				
religion influenced people's attitudes to war				

KEY TERMS

Make sure you know what these terms mean and can use them confidently in your writing.
- Hanoverian
- Jacobites
- privateering
- Puritans
- reivers

C The impacts of war on people

3 Look at the cards below, which show some of the ways that wars affected people in the early modern period. Make your own set of cards. Look back at your work in this chapter and find at least one example of each of the types of impacts and write them on the cards.

4 Now sort your cards into piles:
- direct impact
- indirect impact
- psychological impact
- social and cultural impact

You might find that other students in your class disagree with your categories, but that does not matter as long as you can justify your decision.

5 As an extension task, look back at your work for Question 1 and decide whether you think particular types of wars tended to have particular types of effects (e.g. did wars of conquest do more to create a sense of national identity?).

Death and destruction

Fear and horror

Increased faith and devotion to the Church

Breakdown of law and order

New religious ideas

War weariness

Disruption in trade and economic prosperity

New political ideas

Increased taxes

Invasion by foreign armies

Equipping armies with supplies

Resentment of foreigners

Shaping or attacking national identity

D War and government

6 You have probably noticed that in the early period, the demands of war often led to changes in government. Use the table below to note down examples of how and why this happened.

Conflicts	Challenges to monarch(s)	How they responded	Impact/ effectiveness
Elizabeth's involvement in Scotland			
Elizabeth's wars in Netherlands			
wars against Spain			
privateering			
First Civil War			
Second Civil War			
Third Civil War			
Anglo-Scottish border wars (official)			
Anglo-Scottish border wars (unofficial)			
Jacobite rebellion 1715			
Jacobite rebellion 1745			

7 A publisher is planning to publish a book called *War and Government in the Early Modern Period*. They are trying to decide how to divide up the book. They want a chapter on each conflict but they also want chapters to be in sections. For example, one possible idea is to have a section called 'Wars of Survival', which might include Elizabeth I's wars against Spain. What would you advise them to do?

3.1 Wars of empire 1756–1902: How did war change British society?

FOCUS

Britain emerged from the early modern period as a rising power on the world stage. The country was no longer fighting 'wars of survival' as it had under Elizabeth I. Under the Georgian kings, Britain became a genuine rival to France, the other leading power of the time. Throughout this period, Britain continued to grow in importance, fighting wars to acquire territory, influence and wealth all over the world, then fighting wars to maintain or protect this empire. In this topic you will examine four of these wars of empire:

- The Seven Years' War 1756–63
- The Revolutionary and Napoleonic Wars with France 1792–1815
- The Crimean War 1854–56
- The Boer Wars 1880–81 and 1899–1902.

The big picture

What was the nature of Britain's wars?

These were mostly wars of empire and ambition as well as deadly rivalry with France. Underpinning most of Britain's wars was the issue of trade. Trade made Britain massively wealthy and it emerged as the first industrial economy. Traders brought in raw materials including cotton and rubber, and Britain's factories turned them into clothes, pots and pans, and countless other goods. The Seven Years' War, waged against France and its allies, secured these supplies of materials. There was fighting in Europe, the Caribbean, Africa, India and America. The war ended successfully for Britain and turned the country into a superpower with a vast empire. For the next 150 years, Britain focused on maintaining and expanding this empire, as well as keeping ahead of rival states (first France, then Russia, then Germany).

How did the British respond to these wars?

Most British people supported the government in its wars, although there were doubts at times. Historians still disagree about how far British people were interested in wars and empire-building. Many people probably did not think about it. We know that most did not really consider the terrible cost of the luxuries they enjoyed, such as tea or sugar – which were produced by enslaved Africans or Indian labourers.

How did the wars change the relationship between government and the people?

Britain changed rapidly in the period 1750–1900. War was one factor, but others contributed to this change. Industrialisation, a rising population and growing towns all brought about social change. War often generated controversy and public opinion was divided on the effects of war, whether it was justified and how effectively it was being fought.

What was the impact of these wars on Britain?

This is a very mixed picture. Wars of empire brought tremendous wealth and prosperity into Britain. At the same time, wars were expensive and the government needed to raise taxes to pay for them. This led to some economic hardship and protest. There was a real fear that the wars with France in particular would lead to revolution. As Britain became more democratic through the nineteenth century, another factor became more important – public opinion. This played a particularly important role in the Crimean War and the Boer War.

KEY QUESTIONS

A What was Britain fighting for in its wars of empire 1756–1902?

The table lists some reasons why Britain was involved in wars in this period. Complete your own copy at the end of each section, to analyse Britain's motives in each war. Add other reasons if you wish.

Reason for fighting	Seven Years' War	French Wars	Crimean War	Boer Wars
to make money				
to develop trade				
to challenge a political rival				
to prevent invasion				
to gain or protect territory				
to win prestige				
by accident				

B How did the population react to Britain's wars of empire in the period 1756–1902?

It is difficult to gauge public opinion in the past. However, one way to get some idea of what people thought is to look at what was said in books at the time. In recent years, Google has digitised many books and produced a tool call the Ngram viewer that allows you to search these books. When we searched for mentions of 'war' in books or journals written at the time, we got the following results.

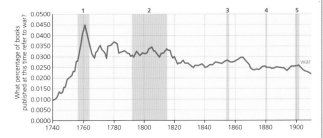

Unfortunately, Google Ngram does not tell us exactly what is being said about war in these books and journals. In this task, therefore, you are going to use your understanding of the period to label the graph.

First, think about what wars was Britain involved in through each of the peaks and troughs. After you have labelled these, you need to infer from your study of the period what the key issues would have been at various moments. There are no right answers (actually there are, but you will only know them if you read *all* these books!). Instead you should speculate intelligently, using your understanding of the period. To get you started here are ten 'labels'. When do think these issues would dominate?

- new territory
- increased wealth
- recruitment of armed forces
- mismanagement of war effort
- economic impact of war
- luxury goods
- improved medicine and health
- military defeat

FACTFILE

A map showing the British Empire c1750–c1914

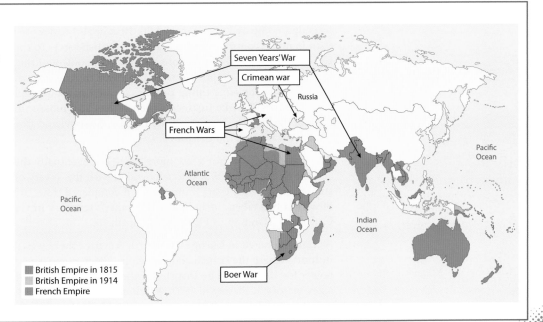

3.1A

Wars with France 1: The Seven Years' War

FOCUS

The Seven Years' War could be described as the first world war. It was fought by many countries in Europe, in India and in North America. It was a key stepping stone on Britain's rise to becoming a great imperial power and a leader on the world stage.

Causes of the Seven Years' War

Britain and France were traditional enemies. Britain wanted to stop France becoming too powerful in Europe, while France regarded Britain as a growing threat to its own ambitions. Both countries believed that a key way to increase their strength was to take over parts of the world outside Europe as COLONIES. These would provide raw materials for growing industries at home but would also serve as markets for the manufactured goods. As each country's trade grew, it would take money and power from the other. Britain and France competed in the search for territories to colonise, particularly in North America, India, the Caribbean and Africa.

Why did Britain win the Seven Years' War?

At first, France seemed to have all the advantages. It was a bigger country with a larger population, a larger army and greater wealth. It also had Spain as an ally. Despite this, Britain won the war decisively. How did this happen?

On land, Britain sent some of its own troops to fight against France, but it also paid its ally Prussia to send soldiers to stand against the French. Combined British and Prussian forces won a decisive victory at Minden in 1759. British forces also captured Quebec, destroying French power in Canada and most of North America (see Source 1).

At sea, the British navy had the upper hand from the start. It boasted 105 large warships, compared with France's 70. Britain also had more smaller warships than France. Control of the seas allowed British forces to capture most of France's colonies in the Caribbean. More importantly, control of the seas allowed Britain to send troops and supplies to fight land wars in America while preventing the French doing the same thing. Britain's greatest naval triumph also came in 1759, when Admiral Hawke smashed a French fleet at Quiberon Bay. This destroyed most of the French shipping in the English Channel and stopped any possible French invasion of the British Isles.

The war dragged on for a few more years, but eventually the French gave up hope and the Seven Years' War officially ended with the Treaty of Paris in 1763. France and Spain returned everything they had conquered from Britain. Britain kept most of what it had taken, including all of France's territory in Canada, many of its Caribbean islands, plus Florida from Spain.

As fighting raged in Europe and North America there was also intense conflict in India, where the British and French had been competing for trade and political power for 100 years. The British and their Indian allies (led by Robert Clive) won a key victory at Plassey in 1757, which drove the French out of India. Clive went on to secure Britain's control over much of India by 1765, through a combination of political manoeuvres and military force.

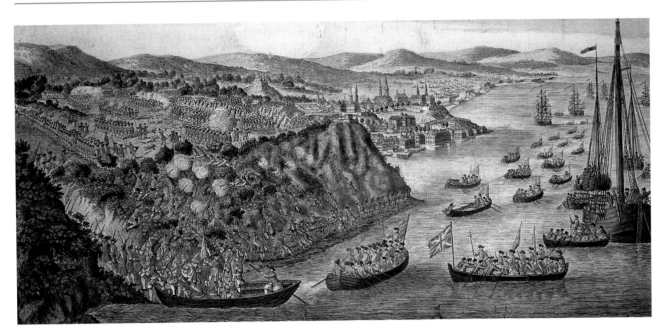

Source 1 An engraving from the time showing General Wolfe's attack on Quebec in September 1759. ▲

1 What do you think the artist was trying to show in Source 1?
2 What does Source 1 suggest about the nature of warfare in 1759?

The impact of the Seven Years' War

In the short term...

The most obvious impact on ordinary people was in **recruitment**. Both the army and navy were desperate for recruits. The navy was allowed to IMPRESS men into service, and 'press gangs' were sent out to round up suitable men. Although most people in Britain opposed conscription to the army, naval impressment was grudgingly accepted because the navy was regarded as vital for the nation's security. The army used financial incentives and appeals to patriotism to recruit young men.

Another significant impact was the **higher taxes** that resulted from this costly war. The government covered some of the costs by borrowing money (so there was a huge rise in the NATIONAL DEBT), but it also increased taxes. There was no system of income tax at this time, but the government put taxes on goods such as tea and sugar, which affected everyone, as well as on glass and on large properties, which particularly affected the upper classes.

In the longer term...

The longer-term economic consequences were significant. Military success turned Britain into an imperial power, with interests and responsibilities all over the world. This affected life in Britain itself in complex ways (see Factfile on page 99).

Being a global power was expensive. The navy and army were both rapidly reduced after the war, but they remained larger than before and were stationed across several continents. Paying for troops to protect and control the expanded empire proved a major problem, especially in the American colonies.

Impact on trade and industry

Because of the Seven Years' War, Britain dominated global trade – and with that came great wealth. The country had access to the riches of India, including luxury goods such as tea, spices and precious stones. India also provided huge manpower, and Indian troops became the backbone of many British campaigns. Control of the Atlantic, Caribbean and North America gave Britain control of the trans-Atlantic slave trade, as well as the sugar, the tobacco and, later, the cotton trades. Britain also controlled much of Canada, which produced valuable goods such as furs and timber. All this trade went hand in hand with Britain's Industrial Revolution, and set it on the path to becoming the world's first industrial nation.

Attitudes and responses to the Seven Years' War

Most people in Britain – of all classes and regions – supported the Seven Years' War, although there were differing reasons for this support. Many people regarded France as Britain's national enemy. To fight France was always right! Others saw the war as a religious conflict that must be fought – Catholic France and Spain against Protestant Britain.

Britain's great successes in the war, of course, encouraged people's support. It turned Britain into a global superpower, which brought great economic benefits and encouraged a strong sense of national pride. It also helped that, despite estimated casualties on all sides of around 1 million, British casualties were relatively light.

Culture

This enthusiasm and support for the war was reflected in the culture of the time. Newspapers and journals supported the war and helped mobilise public opinion in its favour (see Source 2), especially through stories of popular heroes. One of the greatest of these was James Wolfe, who commanded the British forces at Quebec (see Source 3).

> **Source 2** An extract from a British journal called the *Critical Review*, published in 1756.
>
> *Every Briton ought to know about the ambitious views of France, her eternal thirst after world domination, and her continual attacks on the property of her neighbours. Our trade, our liberty, our country, and all the rest of Europe, are in a constant danger from the common Enemy, France, that would, if possible, swallow up the whole world.*

> **Source 3a** A scene painted by Benjamin West in 1770, showing Wolfe's death at Quebec. This painting became very famous. ▼
>
>
>
> **Source 3b** Wolfe also has a memorial in Westminster Abbey. The inscription reads:
>
> *To the memory of James Wolfe Major-General and Commander in Chief of the British land forces on the expedition against Quebec, who after surmounting by ability and valour all obstacles of art and nature was slain in the moment of victory on the XIII of September MDCCLIX. The king and the parliament of Great Britain dedicate this monument.*

1 Is Source 3a an attempt to record what happened like a photograph or is it more of a propaganda piece? Explain your answer.
2 How does this source help historians understand the value of the empire to Britain?
3 'Source 3 would have gained more attention but Source 4 tells a more important story.' Do you agree?

Source 4 Broad Quay, Bristol, painted around 1785 by the Dutch artist Philip Vandyke. The painting shows the range of goods being imported through the city's docks and the ships from all over the world that carried those goods. The artist was struck by how busy the port of Bristol was through trade with the empire. ▶

FACTFILE

The impact of Britain's imperial power after 1763

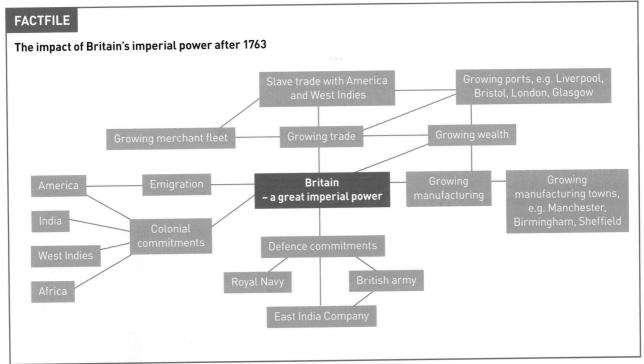

FOCUS TASK

A forgotten war

The Seven Years' War is not well known to most people in Britain now; it is much better known in the USA and Canada (where it is often called the French-Indian War).

Write a proposal to a British museum suggesting that it runs an exhibition about the Seven Years' War. Your proposal should mention:
● a very brief outline of events
● the effects of the war
● the war and public opinion
● why the war should be remembered
● suggestions on documents, paintings, maps or other items that could be included in the exhibition.

3.1B

Wars with France 2: The Revolutionary and Napoleonic Wars 1792–1815

FOCUS

The years after the Seven Years' War saw steady growth of Britain's economy and empire. However, this did not end Britain's rivalry with France. The two countries were soon at war again.

Source 1 A foreign observer in Paris, writing in 1793.

A force appeared that beggared all imagination. Suddenly war became the business of the entire people – a people of thirty millions, all of whom considered themselves to be citizens. The people became a participant in war; instead of governments and armies as before, the full weight of the nation was thrown into the war effort. The resources now available surpassed all previous limits. Nothing could impede the energy with which war could be waged.

Source 2 A reconstruction drawing of a Martello tower. These towers were built all along the British coastline in the late eighteenth and early nineteenth centuries. ▼

1 Read Source 1. Do you get the impression that the French war effort is something new? Explain your answer.

2 Explain why Source 2 is good evidence that Britain was concerned about possible invasion during the Napoleonic Wars.

The War of American Independence 1776–83

In 1776, Britain's American colonies rebelled against it. In the war that followed, France backed the Americans. At first this guaranteed that the British public would support the war, but Britain – already at war with the Netherlands – was overstretched, and a series of defeats by American and French forces turned public opinion against the war.

Britain's surrender in 1783 was not just a humiliation, it also threatened to become an economic disaster because Britain relied so heavily on Atlantic trade. However, trade with the colonies quickly recovered and, as Britain no longer had to pay for troops and ships to protect them, there were economic advantages too.

The French Revolution 1789

Meanwhile, France had problems of its own. The American war cost more than France could afford. It had an unfair tax system. Poverty was rising and there were deep class divisions. These factors combined to cause revolution in 1789. The French monarchy was overthrown and the aristocracy lost its power.

At first there was some sympathy in Britain for the revolution. However, as it became more radical and violent, the British government – and other major European powers – grew increasingly alarmed at the events unfolding in France. In 1793, Britain, Prussia and Austria formed a coalition against France, intending to crush the new French government and reinstall the old one. What resulted was a war that would tear Europe apart for the next 20 years.

The revolutionary government reorganised its armed forces and mobilised the French people in a way that gave a glimpse of the future of warfare (see Source 1).

Britain's military war effort

In the early years, there was a real fear of French invasion. However, Britain's navy proved to be a decisive factor once again. In addition to fighting sea battles, it blockaded French ports, protected British merchant ships so they could continue trading across the world, and transported British armies to fight. Britain's main naval hero was Admiral Horatio Nelson.

At the start, British troops were not much involved in the land battles in mainland Europe. However, in the later years of the Napoleonic Wars British troops became more involved, particularly against Napoleon's forces in Spain and Portugal in 1808–14. The British commander Arthur Wellesley (later made Duke of Wellington) emerged as a hero to match Nelson, winning a famous victory at Waterloo in 1815 that finally ended the long war.

FACTFILE

British wars with France 1792–1815

1792–97 First Revolutionary War

The coalition invaded France in **1792**. By **1794** the tide had turned. The French introduced mass conscription, drove back their attackers then went on the offensive themselves. In **1795**, Napoleon Bonaparte emerged as commander. By **1797** he led French forces to victory over the Austrian Empire. Austria surrendered. Only Britain remained.

1798–1802 Second Revolutionary War

In **1798** Britain, Austria and Russia formed a new coalition against France. They attacked again and had initial successes. However, in **1799** Napoleon took charge of ruling France as well as leading its armies. Once again he defeated his enemies and forced them to sign a treaty in **1802**.

1803–15 Napoleonic Wars

Britain was wary of fighting France alone in a land battle. Instead there were seven coalitions against Napoleon in **1803–15**. Napoleon defeated most of them. A stalemate emerged. Then in **1812** Napoleon invaded Russia. He over-stretched his forces and suffered disastrous losses. This was his first major defeat. Even so it was not until **1815** that he was finally defeated at the Battle of Waterloo.

Map key:
- French Empire
- Areas controlled by Napoleon
- French allies in 1810
- ★ Major battles
- ◆ French defeats

Britain's economic war effort

Britain provided its allies with money to help pay for their campaigns. Napoleon hoped to prevent this by damaging British trade. In 1806, he introduced the CONTINENTAL SYSTEM, which banned French territories – which by this time included most of western Europe – from trading with Britain. Napoleon also used smugglers to try to drain Britain's gold reserves. Despite the ban on trade with Britain, French smugglers were allowed to take French goods into Britain (to be paid for in gold). However, the Continental System damaged Europe more than it did Britain. For four years Britain flourished as it supplied new markets that France could not.

Industrial growth
- Cotton production increased threefold.
- Iron and steel output increased fourfold.
- Steam power began to replace water power.

Weapons
- Private and state-controlled armament manufacturers produced the ships, cannon and weapons needed by Britain's military forces.

Canal development
- The Grand Junction Canal, for example, joining the Midlands to London, was built between 1793 and 1805.

Britain's war economy

Expanding government
- Thousands more civil servants were recruited to oversee government contracts, make sure troops were paid, collect taxes, etc.
- This made government more efficient and also less corrupt
- It also made government more expensive. Increasing the army, navy, government spending and the number of civil servants inevitably meant higher taxes.

Money
- Much government income came from customs duties. Increased trade was vital to funding the war effort.
- The government also raised loans from bankers in the City of London.
- An income tax was introduced in 1799, which was paid mainly by the rich.
- Many other new taxes were imposed, for example on salt, beer, windows, carriages, servants, dogs and newspapers.

Farming improvements
- High food prices encouraged landowners to invest in farming.
- The government promoted new farming methods.

Trade boom
- Cotton textiles led the export drive. By 1815, their value was six times greater than in 1793.
- Britain's merchant fleet increased from 14,500 ships in 1793 to 22,000 in 1815.

Draw a simple diagram to sum up who contributed most to the British war effort of 1792–1815. Include the following key figures: Napoleon, Nelson, Wellington, a farmer, an industrial worker, a soldier, a sailor. Decide:

- how big each contribution should be
- how they should be related to each other.

Carry out further research on these people if necessary. Be imaginative. Write some notes to explain your finished diagram.

Britain's attitude and response to the French war: propaganda and patriotism

The war against France was generally supported by Britain's ruling classes. They were aware that in 1793–94 French revolutionaries had executed the French king, Louis XVI, and thousands of French nobles. Government records from the time show that there was a genuine fear that similar revolutionary ideas might spread to Britain, especially if war began to cause economic strain.

The government had learned from the French the importance of mobilising the entire population and keeping the public on-side. To help with this, it launched a powerful propaganda campaign, which lasted throughout the wars. Although newspapers were restricted in what they could print, they covered the war in detail. The government actually subsidised some newspapers to ensure that the right message was disseminated. Both newspapers and theatre shows encouraged British patriotism by celebrating the heroics of British forces and their commanders and by vilifying the French enemy.

It is difficult to measure the effectiveness of propaganda, but historians think that it worked well during this period of war in Britain. This was partly because the government disguised it well – for example, by encouraging and supporting shows such as the one in Source 5 but not actually taking part in organising them.

Source 3 A song published in 1797 called 'The British War Song'. It appeared in a government-backed newspaper.

Let France in savage accents sing her bloody revolution;
We prize our Country; love our King, adore our Constitution;
For these we'll every danger face and quit our rustic labours;
Our ploughs to muskets shall give place, our scythes be changed to sabres.
And clad in arms our Song shall be, 'O give us Death – or Victory!'

Source 4 An extract from the *Weekly Register*, by the journalist William Cobbett – a critic of the government.

The country people in England, and a great many townspeople, never know anything of the defeats in the wars. The London newspapers, which have a very wide circulation, are employed in the spreading of falsehood and the suppressing of the truth.

Source 5 An advertisement from 1804 for a show at the Sadler's Wells Theatre about Nelson's success at the Battle of the Nile in 1802. ▼

Sadler's Wells.

Battle of the **Nile**
ON
Real Water

Every Evening.

1 Would you say that Source 3 or Source 5 is more accurate in judging popular opinion on Britain's wars with France?

2 Source 4 is by a critic of the government. Does that mean it is not useful? Explain your answer.

Source 6 Philip Taylor, a historian specialising in propaganda, writing in 1995.

In the 19th century Britain emerged as the unrivalled leader in the field of political propaganda. This will be a surprising claim to those (mainly British, it must be said) who believe that, of all the nations, Britain is and always was the most reluctant to use propaganda. In Britain, propaganda is something that other countries do, an 'un-British' activity which undermines free speech and thought. Yet in the 19th century Britain developed a system of media manipulation both at home and abroad that would serve it very well.

Source 7 A cartoon by James Gillray, 1818. Gillray was a famous cartoonist and critic of the government. He supported the campaigns of the time to give the vote to a much wider section of the population. It is significant that this source dates from 1818, three years *after* the war, and is complaining about the fact that taxes were still high. ▼

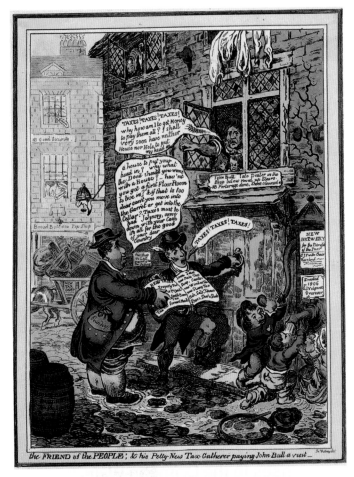

the FRIEND of the PEOPLE; & his Petty New Tax-Gatherer paying John Bull a visit

The impact of the French wars on the relationship between people and government

During times of war it is often the poorest people in society who feel the greatest strain. The longer wars last, the more distress they cause. At the same time, wars can generate economic growth. All these factors were true of the wars with France. The diagram on page 101 sums up the ways in which the war boosted the economy. Now we will consider the other side of the coin.

Protests and reaction …

Despite the fact that this was a period of economic growth for Britain, 23 years of war led to serious problems for poorer people. High food prices resulted in disturbances in 1794–95. In 1795, soldiers had to rescue King George III from a threatening crowd.

The government was worried enough about the general level of unrest in the country to suspend the Habeas Corpus Act in 1794. This meant that people could be imprisoned without a trial. Then, in 1799 and 1800, parliament passed the Combination Acts. These were designed to prevent revolutionary activity, and made it illegal for workers to unite to campaign for better wages and conditions.

In the latter stages of the wars there was high unemployment in the Midlands and northern England. In 1811–12 this led to unrest, particularly among skilled weavers who were losing their jobs due to the introduction of power looms. Groups known as Luddites (after their leader, Ned Ludd) smashed the new looms and threatened factory owners. Such protests were put down firmly by government troops. Sixty Luddite leaders were put on trial. Many accusations turned out to be false and half of them were acquitted; the rest were imprisoned or transported.

… but no revolution

The government clearly took these protests seriously, but there was no major revolution in Britain. This is even more significant when you consider that the end of the war brought a serious economic recession that worsened the situation for many ordinary Britons. Many soldiers became unemployed and industries that had made war supplies such as cannon and uniforms no longer had a market.

On the other hand, there *was* a major campaign for political reform to give the vote (which at the time was restricted to wealthy landowners) to a wider section of the population. This campaign started during the wars and was fuelled by some of the wartime hardships, but it really took off *after* the end of the wars in 1815.

3.1C

Changing times, new rivalries 1: The Great Game and the Crimean War 1854–56

> **FOCUS**
>
> After defeating France in 1815, Britain took its place as one of the world's major powers. By the 1850s, however, Britain had settled into an uneasy alliance in the face of a potential new rival: Russia. Britain and Russia became involved in a diplomatic, military and political struggle similar to the Cold War between the USA and Soviet Union that emerged over a century later. The struggle was known by politicians and military leaders of the time as the 'Great Game'.

FACTFILE

Rivalry with Russia: the Great Game

- Russia worried Britain because its ruler, Tsar Nicholas I, was trying to modernise Russia and expand its territory. He had already taken the **Caucasus region** from the Ottoman (Turkish) Empire.
- The most valuable part of Britain's empire was **India**. Britain feared that Russia planned to take over India.
- Russia and Britain both wanted to control **Afghanistan**: Russia to gain access to India and Britain to stop Russia. The Afghan tribesmen fought to keep both sides out.
- The Mediterranean was one of the main routes for Britain to get to India. The eastern half of the Mediterranean (including the **Dardanelles**) was controlled by the Ottoman Empire. Russia wanted to control the Dardanelles so it could send its ships from the Black Sea into the Mediterranean. Britain was anxious to prevent this, so the British supported the Ottomans.
- France had many colonies in **North Africa** so France also wanted to keep Russia out of the Mediterranean.

Background to the Crimean War

Tsar Nicholas spent heavily on the Russian army. He hoped to take territory from the Ottoman Empire, which was in decline. In October 1853 Russian troops invaded Ottoman territory. The Ottomans fought back but the Russian army was huge. Britain and France were worried that their ally might collapse, so in June 1854 they sent forces to help the Ottomans.

In September that year, the British, French and Turks attacked Russian territory in the Crimea. They besieged the city of Sevastopol and fought off a Russian counter-attack at the Battle of Balaclava in October. It became clear that Russia was not as powerful as Britain and France had feared – it had a large army, but its forces were poorly trained and its technology was old-fashioned. It could not compete on a modern battlefield.

In March 1856, the new tsar, Alexander II, asked for peace and the Treaty of Paris formalised the end of the war. As part of this treaty, Russia agreed not to place any warships in the Black Sea – effectively keeping them away from the Mediterranean.

Attitudes and responses to the Crimean War

The Crimean War was not on the same scale as the Napoleonic Wars so there was no need for mass recruitment. Britain relied on its navy and its small but professional army, as well as its allies. The country was at the height of its economic power at the time, so covering the cost of the war was also not a problem. All these things meant that the war had minimal impact on civilian life.

The British public was generally behind the war. People understood the political reasons for supporting the Ottoman Empire. They recognised that the tsar was an AUTOCRAT with absolute power, who never consulted his people. By contrast, Britain prided itself on being increasingly democratic. Despite this, the Crimean War is not remembered as a great victory for Britain in its pursuit of an expanding empire. In fact, it turned out to be a disaster for the government.

Changing Britain

The underlying reason for this was that Britain itself was changing. It was becoming:

- more **urban** (by 1851 more people lived in towns and cities than in the country)
- more **literate** (more people could read)
- more **questioning** (traditional sources of authority such as the landowners and the Church were being challenged)

1 Why was Source 1 critical of Lord Raglan?
2 Why was Source 2 critical of Lord Raglan?
3 What impression does Source 3 give of the war?

- more **democratic** (the Great Reform Act of 1832 had started this process, and more and more people were campaigning for the right to vote)
- more **connected** (the rapid growth of railway systems made travel from place to place much quicker and cheaper).

All these trends were connected and they reinforced one another.

Increased importance of newspapers and war reporting

One of the most obvious signs of these changes was the staggering growth of the British newspaper industry. At the start of the French wars in 1792 there had been 76 newspapers in Britain. They were heavily taxed (to ensure they were expensive), and the content was controlled or influenced by government. In 1836, the government reduced taxes on newspapers and, by 1851, there were 563 newspapers and journals published in Britain. Advances in printing made newspapers cheaper; the invention of the telegraph meant news was more up to date; and railways meant they could reach a huge readership much more quickly.

Of course, there were many people in Britain who could not afford a newspaper, and many working people still could not read. But the fact remains that in the 1850s more people read more newspapers than ever before in British history. *The Times* alone was read by 40,000 people each day.

Widening newspaper readership directly affected attitudes to war. In the French wars, newspapers had sometimes been banned from reporting news from the front, and stories of military and naval battles often took weeks to reach Britain. By contrast, there was extensive newspaper coverage of the Crimean War. Britons were now able to read about military events almost as soon as they occurred.

The most influential reporter was William Howard Russell of *The Times*. Russell invariably praised the courage of British troops. However, when he saw problems, he wrote about them. Stirred by Russell's reports of the army's plight in 1854, the newspaper's editor John Delane accused the army commander Lord Raglan and the army's aristocratic leadership of incompetence. There was probably no greater inefficiency in the Crimea than there had been in past wars, but thanks to newspaper correspondents it appeared that there was. The government did not try to censor the newspapers. It feared that if it did so, it would seem as though it was trying to hide its responsibility for what was happening in the Crimea.

Source 3 A war picture from the *Illustrated London News*. Newspapers in the 1850s were unable to print photographs; however, the *Illustrated London News* (which supported the war) sent artists to the Crimea. The paper was highly innovative in having so much space for images. Its primary aim was to tell exciting and interesting stories for a new readership, many of whom had low literacy levels (or could not read at all). ▶

Unexpected heroes: The troops

In previous wars, newspaper reports had tended to praise leaders such as Nelson and Wellington. However, in the Crimean War the ordinary soldier emerged as the hero – brave and determined, putting up with terrible hardships and often misled by incompetent commanders.

Source 4 A photograph by the war photographer Roger Fenton. He titled this 'The Valley of Death'. The objects on the ground are mostly cannon balls fired by the Russians at British troops travelling down this road. ▼

British military incompetence – and bravery – was summed up in the Charge of the Light Brigade in October 1854. In this infamous event, the Earl of Cardigan misunderstood an order and led 664 cavalrymen in an attack against almost the entire Russian army. Of the men who charged, 110 were killed, 130 wounded and 58 captured.

The public was also horrified to learn of the terrible conditions in which the soldiers had to live, including the poor arrangements for supplying troops with clothing and basic medical supplies. By the end of the war, some 20,000 British soldiers had died, mainly from disease. This change in perception – viewing the soldiers as heroes – brought about a change at home as war memorials were built honouring dead soldiers for the first time.

1 At this time, cameras could not capture action shots. Do you think that Source 4 is useful in understanding the experience of warfare? Why, or why not?

2 Why do you think Fenton titled this photograph 'The Valley of Death'?

Unexpected heroes: The nurses

Florence Nightingale

Florence Nightingale devoted her life to nursing. Her decision to do so was remarkable partly because she came from a rich family, and women with wealthy backgrounds had never become nurses before. Nightingale took up the cause when reports reached Britain about horrific hospital conditions at the battlefront. In October 1854, she and 38 female volunteers set out for the Crimea. Arriving at Scutari (in present-day Istanbul), they found sick and wounded soldiers being badly cared for by overworked, all-male staff.

In the army there was deep prejudice against women nurses. However, Nightingale had influential supporters, including the secretary of state for war, Sidney Herbert. She also managed to raise £30,000 to help the soldiers, which enabled her to purchase some of the necessities so badly needed. Her nurses ensured that wards were cleaned, fresh bed linen was available and that special diets were prepared for the wounded men.

Source 5 An extract a report by John MacDonald, published in *The Times*, February 1855. At the time, MacDonald was in the Crimea administering money collected by the newspaper to support sick soldiers.

Wherever there is disease in its most dangerous form ... there is that incomparable woman [Nightingale] sure to be seen; her benign presence is an influence for good comfort even amid the struggles of expiring nature. She is a 'ministering angel' without any exaggeration in these hospitals, and as her slender form glides quietly along each corridor, every poor fellow's face softens with gratitude at the sight of her. When all the medical officers have retired for the night and silence and darkness have settled down upon these miles of prostrate sick, she may be observed alone, with a little lamp in her hand, making her solitary rounds.

Source 6 Florence Nightingale doing her rounds in the hospital at Scutari – a painting by Henrietta Rae, created after 1879. ▼

Despite the efforts of Nightingale and her team, over 4,000 soldiers died at Scutari over the winter of 1854–55. Nevertheless, she became a national heroine, remembered as the compassionate 'Lady with the Lamp' – although in reality she was more a tough-minded administrator. At first she had believed that the high death rates in the war were due to poor nutrition and supplies rather than a lack of hygiene. Once she realised her mistake, she worked to improve matters, and through her efforts a Royal Commission on the Health of the Army was appointed in 1857. This led to improvements in army hospitals and barracks.

Back in England, Nightingale used her reputation from the Crimea to good effect. She wrote an influential book called *Notes for Nursing*, set up the first training college for nurses and midwives, and recommended major improvements to hospital design. She inspired many women to become nurses.

Mary Seacole

Mary Seacole, the daughter of a Scottish army officer and a Jamaican woman, has become almost as well known as Florence Nightingale for her work in the Crimea. Hearing that they needed nurses there, she applied but was turned down. She decided to go anyway, and she built a makeshift hospital at Balaclava, where she nursed sick soldiers. Seacole did not have Nightingale's wealth or connections, so her nursing achievements had less impact and received less attention than Nightingale's. However, she certainly helped many soldiers and she is also remembered and respected today for refusing to be beaten by the racial and gender prejudices of society at the time.

> **3** How useful are Sources 5 and 6 as information about Nightingale and her actions?
>
> **4** Are Sources 5 and 6 more useful about her reputation with the public?

Source 7 T. H. Qualter, a historian specialising in the history of propaganda, writing in 1991.

In the mid-19th century even politicians who despised public opinion found that they had to learn the mechanics of peaceful persuasion by propaganda. With an extended franchise [the number of people who could vote] and an increasing population it was becoming impossible to do anything else. In the past voters could be bought or bullied. Now they had to be persuaded.

Impact of the Crimean War on the relationship between government and people

The key effect was that the government realised how important public opinion was in fighting a war and in attitudes towards government more generally (see Source 7). In response to the criticisms, the new prime minister, Lord Palmerston, made some modest changes to the war effort:

- A Sanitary Commission helped improve hospital conditions.
- Military administration was reformed.
- Appointment to some posts in the civil service now depended on examination success.

FOCUS TASK

How did newspapers affect Britain's war effort in the Crimean War?

A key element of this section on the Crimean War has been the importance of the newspapers and popular opinion. Write a report for Lord Palmerston's government, explaining what lessons have been learnt about:

- running a war
- making sure the newspapers are on your side.

3.1D

Changing times, new rivalries 2: The Boer Wars

FOCUS

Throughout the late nineteenth century, Britain competed with other European powers to seize land in Africa. This became known as the 'Scramble for Africa' and it resulted in almost every country in Africa coming under the control of a European colonial power. This rapid expansion of empire caused many wars. In this section you will examine two of the most costly and destructive for Britain – the Boer Wars of 1880–81 and 1899–1902, which were fought in southern Africa.

Background to the Boer Wars

In the 1600s, European settlers arrived in southern Africa and seized lands from the native Africans. These settlers became known as 'Boers', which means 'farmers'.

In 1806, the British took control of the Cape region on the coast of southern Africa, which was a vital staging point on the important trade route from Britain to India. The Boers disliked being controlled by the British, and many moved further inland to get away from it. In doing so, they themselves took land from the Africans and created the new territories of the Transvaal and the Orange Free State.

An uneasy peace was established between these different groups, but this changed in 1867, when diamonds were discovered in the Transvaal. Ten years later the British took control of the territory. The Boers rebelled and the conflict that became known as the First Boer War broke out in 1880. At the time, Britain was facing problems in other parts of its empire, too, so it re-established peace in southern Africa, allowing the Boers to continue ruling the Transvaal and the Orange Free State.

In 1886, however, more diamonds were discovered in the Transvaal, and a flood of migrants (called *Uitlanders* by the Boers) rushed into the area. The British tried to increase their influence over these Boer regions, and the result was the Second Boer War in 1899.

FACTFILE

Britain and the Boers
A map of southern Africa, showing British territories (purple) and Boer territories (orange).

The main developments: Phase 1 – 1899 to mid-1900

Most people in Britain were confident of success against the Boers. Britain was the world's leading military power and could draw on the resources of its empire – a population of millions if necessary. The entire population of the two Boer republics was only 300,000. Moreover, the Boers had no regular army. However, they were excellent horsemen and MARKSMEN and were more familiar with the terrain than British soldiers and officers.

In the early months of the Second Boer War, Britain suffered a series of humiliating defeats (see Source 1) and the Boers laid

Source 1 A photograph showing some of the 243 British soldiers who died in the battle at Spion Kop, 24 January 1900. ▼

1 Look at Source 1. Why could this photograph not have been taken and published during the Crimean War?
2 What impact might this picture have had on public opinion?
3 Many football and rugby league grounds in Britain have steep terraces which are still referred to as the Spion Kop. (The most famous is probably the Kop at Liverpool's ground.) Do you think this is just a useless piece of trivia, or can we infer something from this about the impact of the Boer War on the British public?

Source 2 British and foreign war correspondents photographed in southern Africa in 1899. In the middle row, second from left, is Winston Churchill. He was a soldier and a correspondent. He became famous for his writings during the war – and for his adventures (he was captured by the Boers but escaped). ▼

4 How is Source 2 helpful in explaining the profile of the Boer War in public opinion?
5 Do you think that the Boer War was more or less unpopular in Britain than the Crimean War? Give reasons for your answer.

siege to the cities of Ladysmith, Kimberley and Mafeking. Britain sent more troops and better generals, notably Lord Roberts and Lord Kitchener. By January 1900, 180,000 British and COLONIAL TROOPS were in southern Africa – the largest force Britain had ever sent to fight overseas. The increased force and new leaders turned the tide, and by mid-1900 British forces had captured the main Boer towns. Victory seemed assured.

Attitudes and responses: Phase 1 – 1899 to mid-1900

When the war broke out, a significant minority of the British population opposed it. However, the majority supported it and 500,000 people cheered the First Army Corps as it left Southampton for southern Africa in 1899. Britons rushed to volunteer to fight. There were scenes of national jubilation when Mafeking was retaken after a 217-day siege in May 1900. The table below shows some of the reasons people in Britain opposed or supported the war.

Reasons people opposed the war	Reasons people supported the war
Little Englanders insisted that Britain's empire distracted attention (and money) away from solving social problems at home.	It was seen as a just cause. The newspapers portrayed the conflict as the British trying to protect the rights of the oppressed Uitlanders from the backward-looking Boers.
The newly formed Independent Labour Party argued that the war was about making money for the rich, not about a threat to the empire.	Early British defeats, especially those in December 1899 (which came to be known as 'Black Week') led to a desire for revenge back home.
The war was condemned by radical Liberal David Lloyd George in 1900 as 'a crime and a blunder, committed at the instigation of irresponsible capitalists'.	Many people saw the war as a threat to Britain's empire. There was a lot of rivalry between European powers over empires, and Britain did not want to lose prestige. An added factor was that the German ruler Kaiser Wilhelm II – a rival of Britain – expressed support for the Boers.

The role of the press

Once again newspapers played a huge role in shaping attitudes to the war. By 1899, there were around 150 daily newspapers in Britain, as well as hundreds of weekly and monthly periodicals. These were the main way for politicians to put their views to the people and for the people to keep themselves informed about events.

The trend that had begun with the Crimean War was now established: war sells newspapers! Many papers therefore sent their own war correspondents to southern Africa to report on the conflict. The British commander General Roberts went out of his way to befriend these reporters and keep them supplied with good news. He kept them away from unpleasant scenes such as the typhoid epidemic in mid-1900.

The press was overwhelmingly patriotic, encouraging support for the Boer War. This was particularly true of the *Daily Mail*. Launched in 1896, the *Mail* sold for a halfpenny when most papers cost a penny. By 1900, it had a circulation of nearly a million – far more than its rivals.

Source 3 Women cleaning at a camp in Pretoria during the Boer War. ▼

The main developments: Phase 2 – late 1900 to 1902

From around September 1900, this positive attitude to the war began to weaken. There were two main reasons for this: the nature of Boer warfare and the establishment of concentration camps.

Guerrilla war

Despite a series of British victories, the Boers did not surrender; instead they began using guerrilla tactics. They attacked British weak points such as small garrisons and supply convoys. If they faced a large British force they rode off into the VELDT, where they could ambush British troops if they tried to follow them.

In response to this, Lord Kitchener divided Boer territory into zones, sectioning them off with barbed wire. He also adopted a SCORCHED-EARTH POLICY: anyone who might support the Boer guerrillas was forced off the land and anything that the Boers might be able to use was destroyed. People suspected of assisting the Boers had their farms burnt down and livestock taken away or killed.

Concentration camps

With the young Boer men driven away or fighting the guerrilla war, old men, women and children were left. In order to prevent them supporting the campaign against them, the British removed these people from their farms and put them into camps. These were called 'concentration camps' because they concentrated the population into a small area. Inadequate food, poor shelter, bad sanitation, a shortage of medical facilities and overcrowding led to epidemics of diseases such as measles and dysentery. Over 20,000 Boer women and children died in the 40 camps – about one in four of the inmates. Around 12,000 black inmates, placed in separate camps, also died.

This high death rate was not a deliberate policy of extermination, but the result of incompetence on the part of British military authorities. Civil authorities later took over the running of the camps and by early 1902 the death rate for white inmates dropped to 2 per cent – a lower rate than that in many British cities. By this point, however, the damage had been done to Britain's reputation. People back home were horrified at the establishment of these camps and what happened in them.

Source 4 A letter by Emily Hobhouse to a family member in 1901. She is writing about her visit to a camp at Bloemfontein in January 1901.

The authorities are at their wits' end and have no more idea how to cope with the difficulty of providing clothes for the people than the man in the moon. Crass male ignorance, stupidity, helplessness and muddling. I rub as much salt into the sore places of the minds as I possibly can, because it is good for them; but I can't help melting a little when they are very humble and confess that the whole thing is a grievous mistake and gigantic blunder and presents an almost insoluble problem and they don't know how to face it.

1 Sources 3 and 4 are both about the concentration camp in Bloemfontein. How and why are they so different?

Source 5 Unveiling a war memorial to those killed in the Boer War, Haverfordwest, south Wales, 21 October 1904. ▼

The impact of the Boer Wars on Britain

Military reputation

The Boer War shattered national complacency about the quality of the British army: 450,000 troops from Britain and the empire had struggled to defeat a far smaller enemy force. Another shock was that many of the men who volunteered to join the army were rejected as medically unfit. After 1900, there was much talk of 'national efficiency'. There were calls for health and welfare reforms similar to the systems in Germany (this was one factor behind the welfare reforms introduced by the Liberal government from 1905 onwards).

Feelings about empire

The war had exposed both the costs and the contradictions of having an empire. There is some evidence that anti-empire feeling increased. However, we should not overstate this. There is also plenty of evidence to suggest that imperial sentiment (love of empire) remained strong after 1902. The empire was still celebrated in newspapers, in advertising and in movements such as the Boy Scouts and Girl Guides, which were set up as a direct result of the Boer War.

Impact of the Boer Wars

Casualties and memorials

22,000 British soldiers died in the war (more from disease than fighting). 100,000 were wounded or incapacitated. Death and injury were part of any war, but the Boer War marked a further change in attitude to the war dead. The practice of setting up war memorials to ordinary soldiers had started in the Crimean War, but after the Boer War memorials appeared all over the country.

Financial impact

The Boer War cost Britain £217 million. Only a third of this was met by increased taxation. Instead the government borrowed money, which increased the National Debt.

Political impact

The poor leadership, the poor quality of troops and the horror of the concentration camps which erupted into a national scandal all helped weaken the government.

---

2 Review your answer to Question 5 on page 109, comparing the popularity of the Boer and Crimean Wars. Do you want to change your answer?

FOCUS TASK

What impact did the Crimean and Boer Wars have on Britain?

The government is planning a new History curriculum. There is only space to cover one of these two wars. Write a paragraph arguing that the Boer War should be included rather than the Crimean War. You could refer to:
- the nature of the war
- the impact of the war
- the consequences of the war.

PRACTICE QUESTIONS

1 Describe two examples of imperial wars. (4)
2 Describe two effects of the Seven Years' War on Britain. (4)
3 Explain how public opinion affected the Boer War/ Crimean War. (8)
4 'The most significant impact of the wars of empire was to make Britain rich.' Do you agree? (14)

KEY QUESTION REVIEW

A What was Britain fighting for in its wars of empire 1756–1902?

Review your table from page 95. Use what you have found out to prepare an answer to the following practice question:
Explain why Britain became involved in wars of empire in the period 1756–1902.

B How did the population react to Britain's wars of empire in the period 1756–1902?

Use your completed graph from page 95 to plan answers to the following practice questions:
Why did some of the wars of the period 1756–1902 anger many British people?
Which of the wars of the period 1756–1902 had the greatest impact on the people of Britain?

3.2 The World Wars: How did total war affect British society 1914–49?

FOCUS

You have studied how the relationship between government and people began to change in the later nineteenth century. As war became more demanding, the government needed the public on-side. In the twentieth century, this trend escalated dramatically into what historians now call 'total war'. In previous centuries, Britain's traders, farms and factories had continued 'business as usual' while its soldiers were at war. But the First World War (1914–18) was different – it was a war that involved or affected all of society. It disrupted trade, threatened food supplies and demanded that everything and everyone be focused on winning the war. When Britain once again faced total war in 1939, the government was ready to turn society and economy into a war machine. In this section you will investigate the reasons for and the results of this massive increase in government control.

The big picture

What was the nature of the two World Wars?

Like some of the other wars you have studied, the World Wars were fought between great powers and they ranged over a large area of the world. However, they were also different in several important ways. First and foremost was the scale. The First World War lasted four years and the total killed and wounded from both sides numbered more than 37 million. The Second World War lasted six years and resulted in an estimated 80 million casualties. 'Total war' meant that it was not just front-line troops who were involved; civilians also found themselves in the firing line. These wars required the total mobilisation of the population and the economy to supply the armed forces with the weapons and equipment they needed.

How did the British respond to these wars?

For the most part, the British people supported the war effort. There were exceptions, of course – some people with strong beliefs, particularly pacifists, refused to support the war effort or to serve in the forces. Others had strong political beliefs, particularly socialists, who argued that it was wrong for ordinary people to fight and die while businesses made money out of war. In the First World War, there was a great deal of enthusiasm at first, but this drained away as the death toll rose. Nevertheless, there was no serious protest against the war. The Second World War was not greeted with enthusiasm, but the majority of the British population supported the war effort out of a sense of self-preservation and also because they found the ideology of Nazi Germany appalling.

What was the impact of these wars on Britain?

The impact of the World Wars was both direct and indirect. In the First World War, Britain suffered heavy military casualties but also some civilian casualties from bombing. In the Second World War, military casualties were smaller but the civilian death toll was higher. In both wars, people had to endure shortages of food and other essentials.

How did these wars change the relationship between government and the people?

During both World Wars, the government controlled the lives of the population to an extent never seen before. It kept control over information, food supplies, weapons production, coal and many other areas of life. People were bombarded with propaganda. Men and women were conscripted into the armed forces or into key industries, whether they liked it or not. In each of the wars, the contribution of the people and their willingness to support the government led to a change in the political landscape after the war. Women won the vote in 1918 and after the Second World War a new government brought in the welfare state and the National Health Service.

KEY QUESTIONS

A What was Britain fighting for in the World Wars?

1 In Topic 3.1, you completed this table for the wars of empire 1756–1902. As you read through this section, look for examples of the same reasons for Britain's involvement in the World Wars and note them down.

Reason for fighting	First World War	Second World War
accident		
financial (money)		
commercial (trade)		
political		
fear of invasion		
growth or protection of empire		
prestige		

2 When you have completed the table, decide which of the wars of empire of 1756–1902 most closely resembles the World Wars.

B What was the most significant impact of the World Wars on ordinary people?

The World Wars affected the lives of ordinary people in different ways. Four categories of impact are listed in the table below. Complete columns 2 and 3 as you work through the chapter. Add rows for other types of impact if you wish. At the end you will rank each impact by significance during and after each war.

Type of impact	Examples from the First World War	Examples from the Second World War
bombing		
shortages		
restrictions on freedom		
expectations of government help		

Source 1 A war memorial in Sheffield. Memorials were built all over the country after the First World War, to help communities grieve and remember. The majority of soldiers killed were buried in France. ▼

What was Britain fighting for in the First World War?

To challenge an increasingly powerful Germany

After decades of being the most powerful nation in Europe, Britain found itself facing a rival for that title. In the 1860s, Germany had been a collection of small independent states. In 1871, the largest state, Prussia, united them all into a single German Empire. France went to war with Prussia to try to stop this happening but was defeated in 1871. The Prussian king became Kaiser (emperor) of the new, unified Germany.

At first Britain had positive views on this new state. It was a potential ally against its traditional enemy, France, and Germany's large and growing population might be a profitable market for British businesses. However, in the 1890s Britain became increasingly concerned about Germany under the influence of its new Kaiser, Wilhelm II. He was obsessed with increasing Germany's armed forces. He ignored his parliament and ran the country with just a few advisers who were almost all army or navy officers.

The Kaiser felt that Germany was not respected in the world because it lacked an overseas empire like other European powers. This alarmed the British government, but this alarm increased when Wilhelm II made clear his intention of building a great German naval fleet. This triggered an arms race, and from 1900 Britain and Germany both dramatically increased their programmes for building warships.

To support its allies

Relations between the European powers grew tense. Britain, France and Russia formed a military alliance called the Triple Entente, by which they pledged to help one another in the event that any of them was attacked. Germany, Austria and Italy did the same, forming the Triple Alliance.

Source 2 A *Punch* cartoon from 26 August 1914. The figure on the ground represents Belgium. ▼

THE TRIUMPH OF "CULTURE."

The establishment of these two groups had dangerous implications: one small conflict might escalate into a full-scale war between these heavily armed powers. This is exactly what happened in 1914. A minor dispute between Austria and the small state of Serbia triggered a chain reaction that led to global war.

The propaganda version

So, in one respect the First World War was similar to the wars of empire you studied in Topic 3.1 – it was a war between great powers for supremacy in Europe and around the world. Once the war started, however, British propaganda told a different story. Newspapers portrayed it as a war of British civilisation against German barbarism. Another common theme was that Britain was standing up for the rights of small nations, particularly Serbia and Belgium (which was invaded by Germany in 1914). Germany was accused of planning to take over Europe and the rest of the world. As the war progressed, propaganda pointed to the disparity between military-dominated Germany and democratic Britain.

> **1** What is the cartoonist saying in Source 2?

What type of war was the First World War?

A global war

During the First World War, most fighting took place in Europe, but there were also many battles in Africa and in the Middle East, as well as at sea. Britain had fought global wars before, but never on this scale – and not with large armies taking on enemy forces on land. The resources of the whole empire were drawn into the conflict. Around 5.7 million British troops served alongside over 1 million from South Africa, Canada, Australia and New Zealand. But these contributions were dwarfed by India, which supplied around 1.4 million soldiers (including Hindus, Sikhs and Muslims) serving in all campaigns of the war.

Source 3 A photograph of Indian troops arriving in Britain, 1914. The woman is pinning a flower on one of the soldiers. At the time, people in Britain were very aware of the role of Indian troops, although it is much less known today. ▼

> **2** The newspapers published many photographs like Source 3 in 1914. What caption or headline might a newspaper have added to this photograph?

A total war

Millions of ordinary Britons were recruited as soldiers, but the war also brought greater control over civilian life than previous wars and, for the first time, people on the home front were directly affected by the fighting.

Attack from the air

The first air raids came in January 1915 from giant airships called Zeppelins. These raids continued until 1917, when the Zeppelins were replaced by aircraft, notably the giant Gotha bomber. There were 50 air raids throughout the war, which killed around 500 people and injured 1300.

Civilians in the firing line: First World War

Shortages

The Royal Navy blockaded Germany to prevent supplies reaching German ports. From 1915, Germany tried to do the same to Britain using submarines (U-boats) to sink supply ships. At the height of the U-boat campaign in 1917, the government estimated that Britain had only six weeks' supply of wheat left.

Attack from the sea

In November 1914, German ships shelled Great Yarmouth. In December the same year, they shelled the coastal towns of Whitby, Hartlepool and Scarborough, damaging houses and killing around 200 people.

Spies

Under the Defence of the Realm Act (DORA) the authorities could restrict people's movement and arrest suspected spies or saboteurs. They depended on civilians to report suspicious activity.

Source 4 A poster issued by the War Office in 1914, published in a local newspaper in Sussex. ▼

Daddy, what did YOU do in the Great War?

How did British people respond to the First World War?

In 1914, most British people were enthusiastic about fighting Germany and defending other countries against German aggression. Huge numbers of young men volunteered to join the army. Many people expected a quick war. Newspaper headlines claimed the conflict would be 'over by Christmas'. Instead the war turned into a desperate WAR OF ATTRITION, with massive casualties on both sides. The initial enthusiasm changed into something else: a determination to keep supporting those who were fighting.

The Battle of the Somme in 1916 was a turning point. As the death toll mounted, people expressed shock, anger and criticism of the government and the military. Still no one suggested that Britain should withdraw from the fighting. Even in 1917 – one of the toughest years of the war – people still believed that war against Germany should be pursued to a final victory.

ACTIVITY

Imagine you work for a museum that is putting on an exhibition about the First World War. You have to decide which of these sections Source 3 belongs in:
- Threat of invasion
- Propaganda
- Popular opinion about the war

Unfortunately you are finding this difficult. Write a short email to your boss explaining why.

What was Britain fighting for in the Second World War?

FOCUS TASK

How was the Second World War different from the First World War?

As you work through this section, give a 'similarity rating' of 1–5 between the wars in terms of:
- reasons for fighting
- scale of threat
- global nature of the wars
- total nature of the wars.

Source 5 British government instructions from 1940, detailing what to cover in propaganda films about 'What Britain is fighting for'.

British life and character, showing our independence, toughness of fibre, sympathy with the underdog, etc. …

British ideas and institutions: Ideals such as freedom and institutions such as parliamentary government can be made the main subject of a drama or treated historically. It might be possible to do a great film on the history of British liberty and its repercussions in the world.

A war of ideology

In the First World War, the warring countries shared many similar beliefs. However, in the Second World War this was not the case and the two sides were driven by very different IDEOLOGIES.

Germany's Nazi war leaders were FASCISTS. They believed in:

- total obedience to authority and contempt for democracy
- the superiority of the German people over other races, such as Jews and other minorities and the people of Eastern Europe
- the positive value of war and conquest in building a nation.

The German leader, Adolf Hitler, was also strongly anti-COMMUNIST. His long-term plan was to conquer a huge empire in Eastern Europe and destroy the USSR. Hitler's allies Japan and Italy, collectively known as the AXIS POWERS, were also fascist and had similar beliefs.

Britain fought for ideological reasons as well. One of these was simply that they abhorred what the Nazis stood for. Churchill described Nazism as 'perverted science'. Britain was also fighting to defend its way of life, particularly its democratic system of government and the institutions and values that supported it (see Source 5). Of course, Britain was also fighting for its survival.

A war of defence

In the First World War, Britain had suffered greatly but never faced a realistic threat of invasion. In the Second World War, however, German armies swept through much of Western Europe, then launched a massive air assault on Britain to prepare for a planned land invasion. The Royal Air Force (RAF) fought off this air attack through the summer of 1941, in what became known as the Battle of Britain. However, the government still planned for a possible invasion. The threat only finally receded in the summer of 1941, when Hitler turned his attention away from Britain and invaded the USSR.

What type of war was the Second World War?

A truly global war

The Second World War affected more countries than the First World War. Fighting raged across Europe, North Africa, Asia and the Pacific (see Factfile on page 118). The First World War had been a war of attrition fought, for the most part, by vast armies on land. In the Second World War, naval and air power played a much greater role.

Source 6 An extract from a government report, March 1941.

The chiefs of staff are anxious that a voluntary flow of evacuation from the coastal areas should begin from about the 1st of April, as weather conditions after this are favourable for invasion. They recommend that the public should have been made 'invasion conscious' by this date and that they should also be made to realise that the danger period for invasion may well last throughout the summer months.

> **FACTFILE**
>
> **The main areas of conflict in the Second World War**
> - **Western Europe:** Germany controlled most of Western Europe in 1940–44. The Germans were pushed back steadily after the D-Day landings in June 1944. Germany finally surrendered in May 1945.
> - **Eastern Europe:** Hitler invaded the USSR in 1941. This became the most significant battleground of the war and more than 90 per cent of German casualties occurred here. In 1944–45, Soviet forces pushed the Germans back and they captured Berlin in May 1945.
> - **Atlantic:** Sea warfare took place between German U-boats and Allied convoys and their escort ships and planes. Hundreds of thousands of troops, along with millions of tonnes of food and equipment, crossed the Atlantic to Britain.
> - **North Africa:** Allied forces gained their first real successes against German and Italian forces in North Africa in 1942; they then went on to invade Italy in 1943.
> - **Asia:** Japanese forces had invaded China before war began. From 1939, they quickly invaded much of east Asia, threatening India. British and Empire forces fought a brutal war in Burma against them.
> - **Pacific:** Japanese forces took control of the main Pacific islands, invaded Borneo and threatened Australia. The Japanese attack on the US territory of Hawaii in 1941 brought the USA into the war. From 1945, British Empire and US forces gradually drove out the Japanese, island by island, suffering very heavy casualties. The Pacific war ended with the USA dropping nuclear bombs on two Japanese cities in 1945.

A truly 'total' war

The Second World War was even more a total war than the First World War. Compulsory military service was in place even before the war started. The government controlled the economy tightly, along with most other aspects of life (see page 121). And for civilians in Britain the threat was much greater than in the First World War.

Attack from the air

This was much more damaging than in the First World War. In 1940, the Germans started bombing British cities. In the first few months, up to 50,000 people lost their homes each week. In November, 4,500 people were killed and thousands more injured. In December, 12,500 people were killed in London. In Liverpool the biggest raid, on 3 May 1941, involved 500 bombers. There was some respite in 1942–43 but in 1944 a new threat emerged – V-1 missiles, which could reach Britain from launch sites in Europe, removing the need for aircraft to drop bombs. Six thousand V-1s hit targets in Britain, causing 20,000 casualties and considerable damage to houses (which were already in short supply). Its successor, the V-2, was even more fearsome. It was so fast that it could not be shot down or even seen. Around 500 V-2s hit London between September 1944 and March 1945, causing 9,000 casualties.

Civilians in the firing line: Second World War

Shortages

German U-boats attacked ships carrying food and other essentials to Britain. In 1940, they sank 25 per cent of all Britain's merchant ships. In 1943, Britain was only able to import a third of what it needed. There were shortages, but Britain was well organised with a good rationing system.

Spies

In the Second World War the government was even more concerned about spies and saboteurs than it had been in the previous war. Everyone had to carry identity papers and these were regularly checked. There was a huge poster campaign encouraging people to be vigilant and urging them not to talk about anything that a spy might overhear and find useful. Around 8,000 people of German or Italian origin were interned in camps, mostly on the Isle of Man.

How did people respond to the Second World War?

There were sometimes protests about hardships and the efficiency of the government in dealing with them, but despite this the population generally supported the war effort. There were important reasons for this:

- patriotism – people remained loyal to their country
- an enemy that the majority of the population believed should be resisted
- a bargain between parliament and the people that their loyalty would be rewarded with benefits after the war.

A phrase often used for the British attitude to the Second World War is BLITZ SPIRIT, whch describes the way people rallied around, helped each other, put on a brave face and supported the war effort in whatever ways they could. There is much truth in this. However, historians are cautious about accepting this view without question. They point out that Britain was very effective in its use of propaganda, which convinced the British people that everyone else supported the war and so made it uncomfortable to voice any doubts

ACTIVITY

Imagine you are working on a museum exhibition about the Second World War. In which sections of the exhibition would you use Sources 7 and 8?

Source 8 St Paul's Cathedral during the London Blitz, December 1940. This is one of the most famous pictures of the war. ▼

Government control in the two World Wars

In a total war, civilians are an essential part of the war effort. In both World Wars, the government took unprecedented control of many aspects of day-to-day life to ensure that civilians played their part. The governments were backed by massive propaganda campaigns to make these measures work and to maintain morale and support for the war.

In the First World War

FOCUS TASK

The extent of government control

Copy the table below. Complete it as you read through the section below.

Government control of ...	Examples from the First World War	Examples from the Second World War	Ways in which they were similar or different
recruitment			
industry			
food production			
information			

Recruitment

The war required a massive army. At the start, the government tried to raise the soldiers it needed by persuading men to volunteer, and this initial recruitment campaign was incredibly successful. Half a million people signed up in the first month! By 1916, over 2 million had been enlisted.

As the war dragged on and casualties mounted, however, the army found itself short of troops. In 1916 the government, with great reluctance, took the decision to introduce CONSCRIPTION – any man aged 18–41 could be called up to serve in the armed forces. This represented a massive increase in government control.

Some Britons were opposed to war for religious or political reasons (reasons of conscience). CONSCIENTIOUS OBJECTORS (known as 'conchies') had to appear before a tribunal to prove they had a genuine reason for objecting to war and were not just cowards. Some lost their appeals but still refused to serve. They were sent to prison, where they were often badly treated. Others actually went to the front but in a non-combat role – for example, to work in a hospital or as a stretcher bearer.

Conchies get lots of attention but they were only a small group. The vast majority (95 per cent) of appeals to be excused from military service were from men who had businesses or families to look after, or who faced other practical difficulties.

You can tell that conscription was largely accepted by the country from that fact that only 16,000 out of a possible 8 million affected by conscription actually refused to enlist. The vast majority of Britons welcomed conscription because it was fairer than voluntary recruitment, treating all social groups equally.

Information

News was strictly controlled. Journalists on national newspapers had to have their articles approved by the censor. Newspapers that did not back the war effort were closed down (including the PACIFIST newspaper *The Tribune*). However, the press largely censored itself. Newspapers were in favour of the war and did not need the government to tell them what they could or should not say. On the other hand, local newspapers were not as closely controlled and provided more uncensored information to the public – for example, about casualty figures.

Food supply

The British people needed food. The government worked with local councils and organisations to increase food production, including measures such as ploughing up school playing fields to grow crops. Even so, Britain relied on food from the USA and Canada to see it through. German U-boats sank so many supply ships that in 1917 the government estimated Britain had only six weeks' supply of wheat. It launched a system of voluntary rationing and a propaganda campaign to get people to eat less bread. When this proved inadequate, the government introduced compulsory rationing (covering sugar, butter, meat and beer) in early 1918.

Industry

The war effort needed massive supplies of weapons and raw materials. The government took control of the coal industry and set up its own arms factories.

There were clashes with trade unions when the government tried to stop workers moving from industries where they were needed (such as coal mining) to better-paid or safer jobs (such as in the shipyards). There were many strikes over pay and conditions.

To replace men serving in the armed forces, women worked in war industries and many other jobs. Trade unions forced the government to pay women equal wages (so men's wages did not fall) and also demanded that women would not be kept on in 'men's' jobs once the war was over. Thousands of women replaced male farm workers by serving in the Women's Land Army.

In the Second World War

In the Second World War, the government learnt from past experiences. It was better prepared for what total war involved. From 1940 there was a coalition government, led by Winston Churchill, involving ministers from the three main political parties – Conservative, Liberal and Labour – to avoid partisan politics detracting from the war effort.

At the outbreak of war, the government quickly took control of all areas of life. Military historians claim that only the USSR was more fully mobilised than Britain in the Second World War. This is remarkable when you consider that the USSR was a dictatorship that could imprison or even kill people who did not comply. As a democracy, Britain's war effort depended on people *choosing* to support the war effort. The vast majority did.

Industry

The technology of war had advanced in the 20 years since 1918. One of the biggest challenges was to produce the necessary aircraft, ships, tanks and weapons on which success depended.

Trade unions were more involved in the war effort from the start. Many Labour ministers in the wartime government came from a trade union background, including Ernest Bevin – the minister of labour. They worked *with* the unions not against them, as far as possible. One of the most significant examples of co-operation between government and trade unions was the conscription of men as young as 16 into the coal mines. Wages were controlled, but so were prices.

By the middle of 1941 over half the British men of working age were employed by the government, but this was still not enough and women were conscripted in late 1941. Eight times more women were involved in war work than in the First World War. This included women from all groups of society, whereas in the First World War it had been mostly young, working-class women. Flexible working and childcare facilities were introduced to help women juggle work and family commitments.

Food supply

The threat to food supplies was similar to that in the First World War, with German U-boats attacking convoys bringing supplies to Britain.

Rationing was introduced from the start of the war. This time it covered items such as fuel and clothing as well as food. There was a flourishing black market of luxury goods for those who could afford them, but most historians believe that the rationing system was relatively fair and that the health of the population actually improved as a result of rationing (as it had in the First World War).

By 1943, more than 80,000 women were working in the Land Army. They were nicknamed Land Girls, and they did the work that farm labourers had traditionally done. This included looking after animals and heavy manual work such as harvesting crops, digging ditches or repairing fences.

Recruitment

The government introduced conscription in 1938, before the war even began, so the armed forces got the troops they needed. Large numbers of women joined the armed services and many served overseas. By 1943, over 443,000 women were in the auxiliary branches of the armed forces (the ATS, WAAF and WRNS). They were involved in a huge range of military activities, including anti-aircraft work.

Information

As in the First World War, newspapers, books and films were censored. In 1941, the *Daily Worker* newspaper was closed down for suggesting that industry bosses were benefiting from war while workers made all the sacrifices.

However the most significant new medium was radio. The government had set up the BBC in 1925 and by the time of the Second World War most people had a radio set in their home. People relied on it for information and entertainment in the way they rely on the internet today. Radio content was not controlled by the government, but the BBC effectively censored itself and played a key role in informing the public and keeping up morale.

Evacuation

As soon as war was declared in September 1939, around 1.5 million people, mainly school children, were moved from areas at high risk of bombing: big cities, industrial areas, ports, and villages and towns near to airfields. The evacuation programme was well planned but such a huge migration was complicated and brought with it several problems. Many evacuees found it hard to adjust to life in the countryside and were brought home. Those who stayed effectively grew up with strangers rather than their own families for five years. There were also clashes between evacuees and local children. Despite this, the majority of evacuees were treated well and were kept safe.

FOCUS TASK

Did the British people support the war effort?

Part 1

Source 9 A government poster from the First World War. ▼

Are **YOU** in this?

Source 10 A government poster from the Second World War. The term 'combined operations' usually referred to actions involving different branches of the military (such as the army working with the navy to land an invasion force). ▼

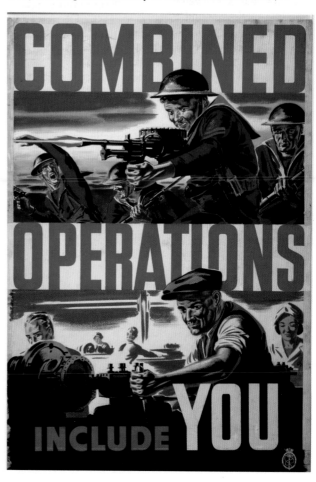

COMBINED OPERATIONS INCLUDE **YOU**

1 The aim of both Sources 9 and 10 was to get people involved in the war effort. Select three details from each source and explain how these details help the poster achieve its purpose.
2 Sources 9 and 10 are both examples of propaganda, but does that mean we should dismiss them as evidence about the war effort in the First and Second World Wars? Copy the table below, then read through pages 124–25 and make your own decision.

After reading this section I think …	Sources 9 and 10 are complete fantasy	Sources 9 and 10 are propaganda but they are realistic about people's involvement in the wars	Sources 9 and 10 are completely accurate

Part 2

Source 11 A poster from 1919 advertising Victory Bonds. Bonds were effectively loans to the government and in return for people received interest. Millions bought War Bonds during the war and Victory Bonds were introduced to help pay for the continuing costs of rebuilding the country after the war. ▼

Source 12 A British government poster from 1939. The ATS was the Auxiliary Territorial Service. One of its main roles was to watch for approaching enemy aircraft and to direct anti-aircraft fire. ▼

3   Now look at Sources 11 and 12. What do these tell you about support for the war effort that Sources 9 and 10 do not? Think about:
   ● the role of women
   ● the role of workers
   ● the role of the press.

Part 3

4   Using your work from Part 1, decide on a scale of 0–5 how far you agree with each of these statements:
   ● The British people supported the war effort equally in both World Wars.
   ● Britain could not have fought total wars without the support of the people.
   ● People did not support the wars – they were pressured into not opposing them.

How did the World Wars affect the relationship between government and people?

The First World War and after

Through the nineteenth century, most people believed that governments should not interfere in the lives of ordinary people. They felt that everyone should take responsibility for themselves. By the early 1900s, however, this attitude was changing and the government brought in welfare reforms, including measures to protect children, old people and the unemployed. A general feeling began to emerge that government involvement made things better for the majority of the population. So when war broke out in 1914, people were more ready to accept government control of other aspects of their lives and work than they would have been 20 years earlier.

As the war progressed, it became clear that even more government control was needed. Under DORA (see page 115) the government introduced restrictions on daily life. For example, people could not buy rounds of drinks, give bread to dogs, ring church bells or light bonfires. These changes only lasted through wartime, but others proved so helpful that they are still in place today, such as putting the clocks forward in summer to lengthen the working day (British Summer Time) and limiting pub opening hours.

In return for their support and sacrifice in the war, the government recognised that all people should have a say in government and be rewarded for their efforts. The first sign that this agreement would be honoured was the 1918 Representation of the People Act, which gave the vote to all men over 21 and to women over 30. Women over 21 gained the vote in 1928.

However, the path to these rewards was not always easy. In 1918, the prime minister, David Lloyd George, made a memorable speech in which he said the government's post-war task was 'to make Britain a fit country for heroes to live in', but throughout the 1920s and 1930s this proved difficult to implement and there was high unemployment in many areas of Britain. For most of the period there was a Conservative government, which clashed with trade unions. There were many strikes, including the massive General Strike of May 1926.

The government introduced some measures to help the unemployed, but anyone claiming such help had to take a means test to reveal how much money they really had in case they were trying to cheat the system. To many it felt as if the workers who had fought in the war were no longer needed or valued. The working classes in Britain's industrial areas were left feeling particularly bitter and betrayed.

Source 13 A photograph of the Jarrow March in 1936. Jarrow's shipyards closed in the 1930s, leading workers to march 480 km to London. Parliament refused to meet the marchers and they were monitored closely by the Police Special Branch, which feared they were political agitators. The woman at the front in this picture is the Labour MP Ellen Wilkinson. ▼

1 How might critics of the Conservative government in the 1930s make use of photographs like Source 13?

The Second World War and after

Government control of everyday life reached new extremes in the Second World War, as did civilian deaths and homelessness. There was a strong sense that, this time, the government really needed to deliver on its promise to make Britain a better country, to reward the people for their support in the war and to recognise the great sacrifices made by both civilians and soldiers. The war had also exposed some of the great inequalities between the lives of the urban poor and the wealthier people in the suburbs and rural areas. Evacuation of children from towns to the country had particularly helped open the eyes of the upper classes to the desperate problems facing many ordinary Britons.

The Beveridge Report

The government set a senior civil servant, Sir William Beveridge, to research the problems and to suggest solutions. In 1942 he published an influential report

Source 14 A cartoon from a Labour Party election leaflet 1945. ▼

2 Is Source 14 more useful as evidence of Labour campaign methods or as evidence of why Labour won in 1945? Explain your answer.

in which he identified five 'giant evils' affecting society: want (poverty), disease, ignorance, squalor and idleness. Beveridge set out a series of recommendations to tackle these problems. In simple terms he recommended the creation of the 'Welfare State'. This meant government-funded health care, benefits to protect the unemployed and family allowances to protect children. The Labour Party enthusiastically supported Beveridge's ideas. Although the Conservatives were traditionally suspicious of too much government involvement and spending (because that would mean increasing taxes), they also accepted many of Beveridge's ideas. So both parties went into the election of July 1945 promising to build a better Britain.

The 1945 General Election – the Labour landslide

Prime Minister Winston Churchill hoped that his outstanding record as war leader would win him the support of the people. However, while he had the respect of the population, the vast majority did not see him as the right leader for a new era in peacetime Britain. The Labour Party won a landslide victory and brought in the reforms Beveridge recommended. These included the National Health Service, a programme of house-building and slum clearance, and a programme to provide full employment for all workers.

FOCUS TASK

How did the World Wars change the relationship between government and people?

1 Complete a table like the one below to record evidence of these changing views.

Changing views	Evidence of this in the First World War and after	Evidence of this in the Second World War and after
The British people believed the government needed to increase its involvement in people's lives.		
The British people believed the government should reward the sacrifice of the war years.		

2 Now decide whether you think governments kept their side of the bargain.

Changing views	Evidence of this in the First World War and after	Evidence of this in the Second World War and after
The government did increase its involvement in people's lives.		
The government did reward the sacrifices of the war years.		

PRACTICE QUESTIONS

1 Describe four ways in which government control increased during the World Wars. (4)
2 Describe the results of the General Election in 1945. (4)
3 Explain why introducing conscription made it easier for governments to organise the economy, as well as provide enough men for the army. (14)
4 Which was more significant in changing attitudes towards the role of government in Britain: the First World War or the Second World War? (14)

KEY QUESTION REVIEW

1 Using your completed table from page 113, rank the types of impact for their significance *during each war*.
2 Rank them again for their significance *after each war*.
3 Compare the rank orders, then try to reach an overall judgement about the impact of the two World Wars. What type of impact was most significant overall and why?
4 Use your work on this chapter to plan and write an answer to this question: *'The World Wars were completely different from any previous wars.'* Do you agree with this view?

3.3 Conflicts since 1945: How did they affect British society and how did people respond?

FOCUS

Although in some respects Britain has been at peace for most of the period since the Second World War, it might be more accurate to say that the country has not been involved in any major or total wars. Since 1945, Britain has been involved in many conflicts, but these have been of a different type. The Cold War was possibly the most serious – a war of ideas and propaganda and political alliances. Britain also faced conflicts ranging from the invasion of Iraq to the battle against terrorism at home. In this section you will examine four important case studies and investigate:

- how Britain became involved in each conflict
- how governments responded to them
- how these conflicts affected the people of Britain.

The big picture

What kind of conflicts did Britain face in the post-war years?

By 1945, Britain was no longer a global power and the USA and USSR were the world's two superpowers. These two rivals were locked in a Cold War in which Britain had only a supporting role, as an ally of the USA. Even so, the conflict had a significant impact on life in Britain.

The closest conflict to home was the so-called 'Troubles' in Northern Ireland – part independence movement, part civil war and part intelligence war. It mixed nationalism, religion and politics.

In the 2000s, Britain became involved in the controversial invasion of Iraq as an ally of the USA. Some saw this as a war of defence against a dangerous dictator, Saddam Hussein; others regarded it as a war of empire, with the invaders most interested in Iraq's oil. At the same time, a new type of conflict was emerging – the battle against Islamist terrorism. This was a conflict of ideologies, religious beliefs and values.

What was the impact of these conflicts?

Britain's post-war conflicts did not have a direct impact on Britain in the way that the World Wars had, but their effects were still felt. The Cold War put Britain into a mental state of war, ideologically and politically. 'The Troubles' saw bombings and shootings in Northern Ireland and in mainland Britain. The Iraq War contributed to Islamist extremists' hatred for Britain, and the country became a target for terrorist attack.

How did the conflicts affect the relationship between government and people?

During the Cold War, the British public largely supported the government, although there was more dissent than in the World Wars and it was easier to express that dissent. The IRA campaigns generally united the people of mainland Britain behind the government, although Northern Ireland was of course deeply divided. By contrast, the Iraq War of 2003 was the cause of bitter division and damaged the reputation of the government in the eyes of many British people. However, it was not until the war started to go wrong that the majority of people expressed disagreement with it. The War on Terror has brought a mixed picture. The majority of the population support the government's plans and actions. However, a small minority have supported and even carried out terrorist acts. This has had a profound impact on the Muslim community in particular.

How did people react to these conflicts?

Most people supported the government in its response to these various conflicts. However, this generalisation hides significant areas of disagreement about each one. For example, in the Cold War, many people criticised the government for its close alliance with the USA. Others protested against Britain developing and maintaining nuclear weapons. In the Northern Ireland conflict, some people argued that Britain should try to reach a political settlement with the IRA rather than simply trying to defeat it militarily. Britain's role in the Iraq War was just as controversial and there was widespread opposition to the invasion.

KEY QUESTIONS

A What kinds of conflicts did Britain fight in the years after 1945?

As you read about each example and complete the Focus Tasks for each case study, fill out a table like the one below to summarise the key conclusions. Use the final column to record similarities and trends.

Factors in conflict	Cold War	IRA campaigns	Iraq War 2003	War on Terror	Increasing or decreasing significance 1945–2010
international politics					
politics at home					
ideology					
nationalist/independence movements					
religion					increasing

B How did post-war conflicts affect Britain and how did people respond?

Britain's conflicts after 1945 were probably more divisive than the two World Wars. As you work through this section, use a copy of the table below to record how the conflicts in the case studies caused controversy.

Question	Cold War	IRA campaigns	Iraq War 2003	War on Terror	Trend?
How did the conflict impact British people?					
How did the majority of Britons respond to the conflict?					
What dissent was there and why?					
What war was similar (in terms of public response or opinion)?					

C How similar were wars in the period after the Second World War?

As you look at the wars in the following section, use a table like the one opposite to record similarities between the wars. These could include the type of war, its aims, the way it was fought, its impact on Britain and British people, the reaction of the public, its impact on government.

Modern wars	Cold War	IRA campaigns	Iraq War 2003	War on Terror
Cold War				
IRA campaigns				
Iraq War 2003				
War on Terror				

FACTFILE

Britain's post-1945 conflicts

- **Cold War 1946–89:** As the USA's ally, Britain sent forces all over the world, particularly the navy. The main commitment of British troops was in Germany, to defend against a possible Soviet invasion.
- **Palestine 1948:** An insurgency led by Zionists. Britain withdrew and the state of Israel was founded.
- **Malaya 1948–60:** Part independence movement, part attempt by communists to take control. Malaya gained independence from Britain and remained non-communist.
- **Korean War 1950–53:** British forces fought alongside the USA and other allies against North Korea and China.
- **Kenya 1952–60:** Kenyan independence movement (the Mau Mau) fought a guerrilla campaign to end British rule. Britain responded brutally. Kenya achieved independence in 1960.
- **Suez Crisis 1956:** Britain, France and Israel took control of the Suez Canal from Egypt but were forced to withdraw after coming under pressure from the USA.

- **Northern Ireland 1968–98:** Struggle between Irish Republican Army and British forces.
- **Iceland 1970s:** Disputes over fishing rights in the North Atlantic.
- **Falkland Islands 1982:** Argentina invaded the British territory of the Falkland Islands, claiming SOVEREIGNTY. Britain sent a force to retake the islands. The campaign succeeded but with significant casualties on both sides.
- **First Gulf War 1991:** Iraq invaded Kuwait. Britain joined a coalition of 34 countries to drive out Iraqi troops.
- **Afghanistan 2001:** Al-Qaeda attacked New York in September 2001. British forces joined the USA and other countries to attack al-Qaeda and the Taliban in Afghanistan.
- **Iraq 2003:** British forces joined US forces to invade Iraq and overthrow its leader Saddam Hussein.
- **Islamist extremism c1990–present:** A consistent threat with numerous attempts and some successful attacks on British civilians, notably the London bombings of 7 July 2005.

Case study 1: Britain and the Cold War in the 1950s and 1960s

By 1945, Britain was no longer a great world power. To maintain influence around the world, it adopted a policy of allying closely with the USA through NATO. For example:

- Britain usually supported US resolutions in the United Nations.
- It shared intelligence gathered by British spies.
- The British government allowed the US air force to use bases in Britain, particularly in the south and east of England. British forces were also stationed in Germany, alongside US forces, for most of the Cold War to defend against a Soviet attack.

Britain's nuclear deterrent

Another important way in which Britain contributed to the Cold War was its nuclear deterrent. Both the superpowers, the USA and the USSR, had nuclear weapons – enough to destroy each other many times over. Deterrence worked on the idea of Mutually Assured Destruction (MAD) – each side knew that if it launched a nuclear attack, the other side would retaliate immediately and both would be wiped out. Having nuclear weapons therefore deterred the enemy.

Britain was one of the few states other than the superpowers to have its own nuclear weapons. In the 1950s, Britain had created a fleet of Victor and Vulcan bombers (known as 'V bombers') armed with nuclear missiles. In the 1960s, it switched to submarine-based Polaris nuclear missiles. As well as its own weapons, the British government allowed the USA to station nuclear weapons at the Greenham Common Air Base in Berkshire – and possibly other secret locations as well. This became a very controversial issue in Britain.

The impact of the Cold War in Britain

Cold War tensions formed a background to people's daily lives. The 1950s and the 1960s had a strong Cold War 'flavour' – for example, cinema and TV schedules included dramas about the Cold War and most news programmes featured Cold War confrontations around the world. Many people were anxious about the threat of nuclear war.

Responses to the nuclear threat

The government was aware of the potential damage a nuclear attack might cause (see Source 1). It organised training for fire, health and police services, as well as thousands of volunteers in CIVIL DEFENCE. It made information films and distributed pamphlets describing what might happen in an attack and how people should prepare for it.

The government also made detailed plans to keep the country running if an attack did take place. This included giving emergency powers to the army and building underground bunkers to protect top government and military officials who would govern the country after an attack.

Some people actively opposed nuclear weapons (see page 131), but more British people agreed with the government's policy of nuclear deterrence – believing that the only thing keeping them safe was the threat of retaliation in the face of a nuclear attack.

Source 1 An extract from a secret British intelligence report, 1955.

We are advised that 10 H bombs delivered on the western half of the UK or in the waters close off the western seaboard, with normal winds, would effectively disrupt the life of the country and make normal activity completely impossible. Government could no longer function, with the mass of the people becoming preoccupied with their own survival rather than the country's war effort and prepared to run the risk of being shot rather than to obey orders.

1 Why do you think reports such as Source 1 or bunkers such as those shown in Source 2 were kept secret?

Source 2 This house is a fake, built to disguise the entrance to a nuclear bunker. The bunker was built in 1952 in Essex, England. It was one of a number of bunkers for the use of the Air Ministry. If there was a nuclear strike it would allow 600 personnel to work underground for up to three months. The first picture shows the house from outside; the second shows what lies below ground. ▼

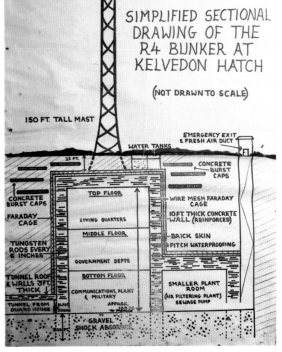

Source 3 A British government poster that was regularly published in the 1950s and 1960s. ▼

somebody isn't using his intelligence...

KEEP OUR SECRETS SECRET

Espionage

The government was also anxious about Soviet spies, especially as the USSR had first gained access to knowledge of how to build nuclear weapons through their spies. It was also known that the Soviets had detailed maps of Britain, which they used to plan possible attacks. As in the Second World War, people were urged to be on their guard at all times and to be careful about mentioning anything that might be helpful to an enemy (see Source 3).

Support for Britain's Cold War policies

The two main political parties in Britain – Labour and Conservative – were both hostile to communism. So were organisations like the Trades Union Congress, which represented Britain's working classes, and most of the MASS MEDIA. They all actively supported the government's Cold War policies. One good source of information on this issue is the Mass Observation Project, which ran from 1937 to the mid-1960s and was then revived in the 1980s. It was designed to provide a picture of public opinion. Around 500 volunteers were asked to keep diaries and respond to questionnaires. Other observers actually recorded conversations in public places. There were many different opinions of course, but the general picture that emerged from MO data was that the majority of the population shared the government's fears and concerns about communism and supported the government's policies in the Cold War.

In the years 1945–50, newspapers fed the public stories of communist atrocities (such as the murder of political opponents in Czechoslovakia and East Germany) and the threat posed by communist agents. They emphasised how awful life was under communism and how much better people had it in non-communist Britain. The historian Tony Shaw has studied British newspapers in this period in great detail and concluded that they helped build a consensus among the population that communism must be resisted. This helped ensure solid support for government policies through the rest of the Cold War. It was not only newspapers that reinforced these attitudes. In the 1940s and 1950s in particular, cinemas were full of US films, many of which carried anti-communist messages.

Some argue that the government used even more resources than it did in the World Wars to win the support of the British public. It used censorship laws to control theatre, books, radio, TV and films. These laws had been established to prevent offensive or obscene materials being shown, but they were often used to ban any works that were sympathetic to communism or the USSR.

The government also had a strong influence over the BBC. For example, in 1965 a film with a strong anti-nuclear weapons message called *The War Game* was banned from being broadcast by the director of the BBC. The government even produced its own documentary films about the horrors of life under communism (see Source 4).

> **Source 4** Part of the script for a film about East Berlin, produced by the Ministry of Information in 1962. This was shortly after the communist government in East Germany put up the Berlin Wall. The title of the film was *Berlin: Outpost of Freedom*.
>
> *Germany today. Barbed wire running like a scar across the land, dividing East from West. These East German watch towers are not watching the West – they are watching for East Germans who would flee their country.*
>
> *What kind of people are they, these refugees who come to this camp, bringing their world with them in a suitcase? These are not refugees from hunger or poverty – they are reasonably well fed and clothed. They are fleeing from oppression of the mind. They long to say what they think; to vote freely. Most are young. Nearly three million have left East Germany for the West in the last twelve years – and the great majority come through the gateway to freedom in West Berlin first to this camp, then to the airport, and then to West Germany and a new life.*

Opposition to Britain's Cold War policies

Although the feeling in Britain was overwhelmingly anti-communist, there were still communists in the country, and those who sympathised with communist ideas. Files released since the end of the Cold War show that the intelligence services were monitoring the activities of prominent people such as the singer Ewan McColl and his wife Joan Littlewood. McColl criticised inequalities in British society and praised the virtues of Stalin and the communist system. He wrote songs criticising US policy in the Vietnam War in particular. Another critic was Eric Hobsbawm, an academic historian. Hobsbawm was a member of the Communist Party and wrote history books that emphasised the role of the working classes in history, which was unusual at the time. He also criticised the repression and violence in the USSR, but nonetheless MI5 watched him closely. Many other artists, writers and academics also came under scrutiny.

In times of crisis

A more widespread form of dissent came in times of crisis, when people criticised the government for being too closely allied to the foreign policy of the USA. For example:

- **The Suez Crisis 1956:** The Egyptian leader Gamal Abdel Nasser took control of the Suez Canal. Although the canal is in Egypt, it was built and owned by Britain and France, who sent troops to regain control. The USA challenged

Source 5 An anti-Soviet cartoon by Vicky (Victor Weisz) from the *London Evening Standard*, 24 October 1962. The caption reads: 'Intolerable having your rockets on my doorstep!' ▼

"INTOLERABLE HAVING YOUR ROCKETS ON MY DOORSTEP!"

Source 6 From an article in the *Manchester Guardian*, 25 October 1962, at the height of the Cuban Missile Crisis.

THE YOUNG ONES IN REVOLT – school strikes in protest at actions of superpowers

The two Ks – Kennedy and Khrushchev – will get a cable [telegram] from Britain's young ones in revolt today.

The sender: Robin Mariner, 18-year-old head boy at Midhurst, Sussex, grammar school, and leader of a strike by 40 of the school's sixth formers yesterday. The strikers told their headmaster, Mr Norman Lucas, after morning assembly that they would not attend classes for two days.

Source 7 Marchers on the 1963 Aldermaston March, organised by CND, from the government's Atomic Weapons Research Establishment at Aldermaston, Berkshire, to the centre of government in London. Aldermaston was used as a US airbase in the Second World War and had been used for atomic weapon research since 1950. ▼

1 Which of Sources 5 and 6 do you think would cause greater concern to the British government or the US government?
2 Source 7 shows citizens protesting against government military policy. Have you come across such protests in earlier periods? If so, how is this one different?

this move and pressured Britain to pull out, which it did. The USA's response and the fact that the British had to give in to pressure from this stronger nation generated ill-feeling towards the USA. Many saw this as a humiliation.

● **The Cuban Missile Crisis 1962:** In 1962, the USSR placed nuclear missiles in Cuba, a communist ally of the USSR. The Americans reacted furiously and a dangerous stand-off followed. Many historians believe this was the closest the world has ever come to a nuclear war. In Britain, people believed that the USA's actions were unreasonable and protested against them. Even strong supporters of the British government and the USA criticised US actions and encouraged the British government to try to restrain US President John F. Kennedy.

● **The Vietnam War 1968:** There were even more violent protests against the Vietnam War. US involvement in Vietnam had turned the conflict into a brutal – and to many people, unjustifiable – killing match. The use of chemical weapons, which caused devastation to the land and people in Vietnam, was particularly controversial. In 1968, large demonstrations were held in London, which ended in violence between police and protesters outside the US Embassy.

The Campaign for Nuclear Disarmament

The most organised form of protest was against nuclear weapons. The Campaign for Nuclear Disarmament (CND) began in 1958. CND supported UNILATERAL DISARMAMENT, which was not a strategy that military leaders would ever support. However, CND hoped that if Britain led the way, other countries would follow.

All sorts of people joined CND – scientists, religious leaders, politicians and students. There were many different reasons why people opposed nuclear weapons. Some believed that this form of weapon was immoral; others felt that nuclear weapons were simply too expensive. There was also a real fear of a nuclear accident or of one side mistakenly thinking they were under attack and retaliating.

The CND symbol became a famous logo (it was designed by a man who had been a conscientious objector in the Second World War) and was very popular with the 1960s anti-war 'counterculture' in the USA, where it symbolised peace and love. In 1962, 150,000 people marched in support of CND and an opinion poll in the early 1960s suggested that 20–30 per cent of British people supported unilateral disarmament. However, support for CND declined throughout the rest of the 1960s (although it re-emerged in the 1980s).

FOCUS TASK

Did the British people support the government during the Cold War?

Record one example of each of the following responses to the Cold War and the reasons for it.
● active support
● passive support
● opposition.

Source 8 British troops searching civilians, 1971. ▼

Case study 2: 'The Troubles' – Northern Ireland and the IRA campaigns 1969–94

In the 1920s Ireland was partitioned; the largest part was independent of British rule and became the Republic of Ireland in 1949. The six counties of Northern Ireland remained part of the UK. They sent MPs to Westminster but also had their own government in Stormont, near Belfast.

Northern Ireland was a divided region (see Factfile), but despite these divisions the different communities co-existed without serious conflict for several decades. That changed in 1969 with the onset of 'The Troubles'.

What kind of conflict was 'The Troubles'?

In the late 1960s, there was a series of marches by the Northern Ireland Civil Rights Association to challenge discrimination against Catholics. Marchers were attacked by Loyalist mobs. The police (the Royal Ulster Constabulary, RUC) did little to protect the marchers. Violence soon spread. Loyalist mobs attacked Catholic areas and burnt Catholic homes. Some Catholics fought back and by 1969 SECTARIAN VIOLENCE had become so serious that the British government sent troops to restore peace.

The emergence of the Provisional IRA

The first British soldiers were warmly welcomed by many Catholics, but some hard-line Republicans were deeply opposed to British rule in Northern Ireland and saw these troops as a symbol of British domination. They set up a PARAMILITARY group called the Provisional IRA (also called the 'Provos'), supposedly to defend Catholic communities. They bought arms and trained young men in how to use them.

In July 1970, four Protestants were killed in a gun battle with IRA activists. In response, 3,000 British troops were ordered into the Catholic area of the Falls Road in Belfast to search for IRA weapons and suspects. As they searched, the troops wrecked people's homes and used tear gas against them. This was a decisive moment in turning Catholic opinion against the British army. It boosted the IRA's image as defender of the Catholic community and gave them an excuse to turn their fire on British troops. However, most historians agree that even without these events the IRA would have started attacking British soldiers, simply because it did not want them in Ireland.

The conflict escalates

There followed 30 years of guerrilla warfare (although opponents of the IRA regarded its actions as terrorism). The IRA's strategy was to kill so many British troops that people in Britain would force the government to withdraw and surrender control. IRA campaigns also targeted RUC members, Loyalist paramilitaries and Protestant businesses in Northern Ireland. From 1973, the IRA also attacked targets on the British mainland. For example:

● In 1974, it killed 28 and wounded 200 people in a series of pub bombings.
● In 1984, it almost succeeded in killing the prime minister, Margaret Thatcher (see Source 9).
● In 1991, it launched mortar bombs on 10 Downing Street while prime minister John Major was meeting with officials.

Source 9 The Grand Hotel in Brighton after an IRA bomb attack that almost killed Prime Minister Margaret Thatcher in 1984. ▼

The IRA was not the only paramilitary group in Northern Ireland. Loyalist violence echoed IRA violence, in sporadic attacks throughout 1969–70 but steadily increasing in pace with the IRA from 1971 onwards.

The government responds to the IRA threat

The government was determined not to give in to IRA violence. In August 1971 it introduced internment: suspected terrorists could be arrested and kept in prison (interned) without trial. This was regarded as a controversial measure both in Northern Ireland and mainland Britain and it boosted sympathy for the IRA overseas.

The government also sent more troops to Northern Ireland. This kept control but also increased support for the IRA, as Catholics saw the British soldiers as an occupying force. Incidents like Bloody Sunday in 1972 – when British troops shot dead 13 unarmed demonstrators – also helped the IRA. As the conflict escalated, the government set up the first branch of the Security Service, with undivided responsibility for counter-terrorism. The media was banned from airing interviews with IRA members.

None of these measures defeated the IRA. It had great support in the Catholic communities in Northern Ireland and also received money and weapons from supporters in Irish communities in the USA. IRA activists could plan attacks in safety in the Irish Republic and escape back there after an attack. However, the IRA did not succeed. The British government did not bow to pressure and withdraw its troops.

Changing tactics early 1980s to mid-1990s

By the mid-1980s the British government, the Irish government and the IRA all began to change tactics.

- The IRA began to build up its political wing, Sinn Fein, under the leadership of Gerry Adams. This political wing was legal, could speak openly and make use of the media.
- At the same time, the British government began co-operating with the Irish government on security matters, such as making it harder for IRA activists to escape across the border into the Republic to try to restrict IRA operations.
- In return, the Irish government demanded more say in affairs in Northern Ireland. Unionists protested but the British government carried on anyway.

Gradually, British government officials began to make contact – in secret at first – with IRA leaders and the Irish government. In 1993, the British and Irish governments jointly announced the Downing Street Declaration. The British government said that it had no interest in Northern Ireland other than the welfare of the Unionist community. It would not oppose a united Ireland if the majority of people in Northern Ireland voted for it democratically. This was an important concession. It won support in Britain and the Republic and in the Irish American community in the USA. It is no coincidence that the following year the IRA announced a ceasefire, as did the Loyalist paramilitaries. Although there were more violent incidents and a lot of negotiation, the ceasefire mostly held. Despite on-going tensions, this ceasefire is still in place today.

ACTIVITY

In conflicts like 'The Troubles' propaganda often plays an important role. Work in pairs and study Sources 8 and 9. One of you decide how they might be used as propaganda by the IRA. The other work out how the British government might have used these images.

What was the impact of 'The Troubles'?

... in Northern Ireland

Random violence: For ordinary civilians there was always the possibility of a bomb attack, usually in a public place such as a high street. The death toll in 'The Troubles' was around 3,500. Over half of those killed in Northern Ireland were civilians who had no connection with or role in the conflict.

Sectarian attack: For Catholics, there was the additional risk of Loyalist paramilitaries. Loyalists used different tactics from the IRA, targeting Catholics simply because they were Catholics. This caused around 30 per cent of the deaths in 'The Troubles'.

Punishment attacks: In working-class areas, both the IRA and Loyalist paramilitaries exercised strict control. Anyone speaking up against them ran the risk of a beating or even being killed.

Disruption: Roads all over Northern Ireland were regularly blocked by security checkpoints. People in the region learned to carry identity papers, driving licences and other documents at all times. Some roads that crossed the border between Northern Ireland and the Republic were destroyed.

Discrimination by security forces: Security forces regarded Catholic communities as a greater threat. When internment was introduced, it was almost entirely Catholic Nationalists who were arrested. Many were mistreated or even tortured.

Divisions between government and people: The British government disbanded the Northern Ireland government in 1972 and replaced it with DIRECT RULE from London. This was meant to ease tensions, but actions like internment led many in the Nationalist community to feel that the British government was not *their* government. At the same time, many Unionists worried that the British government would not continue to look after their interests. Although the majority of the population did not support violence, they had little love for the government either.

... in mainland Britain

Britain was not affected to the same extent by the IRA campaigns, but the government continued to urge people to be vigilant for suspicious objects or activity. In 1993, after two boys were killed by a bomb left in a litter bin in the main shopping centre in Warrington, local authorities removed the majority of public bins. Security became much tighter at airports, railway stations and sea ports, although not to the same extent as in Northern Ireland.

How did people react to 'The Troubles'?

... in Northern Ireland

Many Nationalists felt that the security forces were biased against them, and treated Catholic communities with suspicion. They accused the government of double standards: it interned IRA activists but when they went on hunger strike to demand political status (which would mean being treated like prisoners of war) Margaret Thatcher refused, saying that members of the IRA were just criminals.

In Britain, most people approved of this attitude and supported Thatcher. However, in Northern Ireland the hunger strikers gained a great deal of support, even from moderate Nationalists. They even got one hunger striker, Bobby Sands, elected to parliament. This did not mean that the majority of Nationalists supported the IRA – far from it. Despite the support for Sands and the rise of Sinn Fein, the majority still voted for the Social and Democratic Labour Party, which was the moderate Nationalist political party.

Source 10 A photograph of a mural in Belfast from 1994. ▼

Source 11 The BBC Northern Ireland reporter, Richard Frances, speaking in the early 1990s.

In Northern Ireland, our extensive coverage of sport, our sponsorship of musicians, writers and actors, the daily advertising of events and discussion of household matters in regional programmes such as Good Morning Ulster, Taste of Hunni, and our access and community programmes are all apparent. More than 80 per cent of Radio Ulster's output is concerned with normality.

FOCUS TASK

What was the impact of 'The Troubles'?

Here is a list of statements about 'The Troubles'. Study each one. Decide how far you agree with it and find some examples to support your decision.
- 'The Troubles' increased prejudice against Irish people.
- 'The Troubles' only really affected Northern Ireland.
- The majority of people just wanted peace.
- The IRA proved very hard to defeat.
- Politicians could ignore public opinion during 'The Troubles'.

Many Unionists saw themselves as a community under threat. It was not just the threat of violence that they felt; they were also concerned that their national identity and way of life were being threatened. They regarded the police as being on 'their' side, and the majority of police officers did come from a Unionist background (partly because the IRA intimidated Catholics who wanted to join the police). Like the Nationalist community, the majority of Unionists were moderates, with no involvement in paramilitary activity. Also like the Nationalists, most Unionists voted for the moderate Ulster Unionist Party, although many also supported the more Loyalist Democratic Unionist Party.

However, in both Republican and Loyalist areas, most people just tried to get on with their lives. They adapted to the challenge of living in a war zone surrounded by soldiers on patrol, fortress-like police stations and the ever-present threat of paramilitary violence.

Others went further and actively worked for peace. Political parties, trade unions, churches and other organisations tried in different ways to build bridges between the communities and to challenge the power of the paramilitaries. For example, in the late 1970s a movement called The Peace People emerged after an IRA getaway car killed three children. The movement grew rapidly at the time, but faded in the early 1980s in the face of paramilitary threats and criticism by politicians, who saw it as a threat to their own interests. In 1987, Gordon Wilson's daughter was killed by an IRA bomb. Wilson influenced many people by publicly refusing to hate the IRA and calling for the various sides in the conflict to talk.

... in mainland Britain

At the start of the conflict there was mostly confusion and indifference, but the IRA bombing campaign on mainland Britain had a dramatic effect on attitudes. The overwhelming majority of the British public supported government policies and were extremely hostile to all paramilitary groups, but to the IRA in particular. Successive governments talked tough on the IRA and insisted they would not negotiate with terrorists.

As in Northern Ireland, however, some people did think and speak differently. The most high-profile example was Ken Livingstone, the leader of the Greater London Council. Livingstone was a controversial politician and openly sympathised with the IRA. He was attacked bitterly in the media.

However, while there was little sympathy for the IRA in Britain, most people and politicians recognised that the conflict had reached a stalemate that needed a political settlement. The British public largely approved of government talks with the Irish Republic over the future of Northern Ireland. They also supported the paramilitary ceasefires in 1994 and were positive about the Good Friday Agreement of 1998.

◀ **Source 12** A cartoon from a British newspaper in 1982. The groups named at the bottom were all Republican or Loyalist paramilitary groups.

Background to the Iraq War

- From 1979, Saddam Hussein ruled Iraq as a dictator. He planned to make Iraq the leading power in the Arab world, and began by declaring war on Iraq's neighbour Iran in 1980.
- Iran had just been through a revolution, led by the Muslim cleric Ayatollah Khomeini, which deposed Iran's shah (king) and created a new Shi'ah Islamic Republic.
- The shah had been an ally of the USA but the new Iran was its bitter enemy. The USA gave Saddam Hussein financial support and weapons, including chemical weapons. He also got support from Britain, France and Saudi Arabia, which all feared Iran.
- The war was a disaster for Saddam. It turned into a bloody stalemate that lasted until 1988. Iraq was left weakened and in debt.
- Saddam tried to improve his position by invading his rich neighbour Kuwait in 1990. This also proved to be a disastrous mistake.
- Kuwait was an ally of the USA and Saudi Arabia. In 1991, a coalition of forces led by the USA and including Britain attacked Saddam and easily drove his troops out of Kuwait in what is now known as the First Gulf War.

Case Study 3: **The Iraq War 2003**

Causes of the Iraq War

Saddam Hussein was the ruler of Iraq, but as the Factfile shows, he had a lot of enemies. By 2000, his days seemed numbered.

A new mood in the USA

US president George W. Bush was hostile to Iraq. His hard-line advisers wanted to topple Saddam and establish a pro-USA democracy in the country. They wanted an extra ally in the region, as well as favourable access to Iraq's oil.

Saddam's actions

The USA tried to weaken Saddam by funding his enemies, but he held tightly to power. He used chemical weapons against the Kurds in the north of Iraq who opposed his rule. He used air strikes and his armed forces to savagely crush Shi'a Muslims in southern Iraq who also opposed him (Saddam was a Sunni Muslim, as were the majority of Iraqis). In 1998, he expelled United Nations weapons inspectors who had been monitoring Iraq. Intelligence reports suggested that Saddam was building many weapons of mass destruction (WMDs), including missiles armed with chemical weapons. With hindsight we know that Saddam had no WMDs. However, Saddam did not want to admit this and appear weak, so he refused to deny the claims or allow inspectors to conduct any checks.

Al-Qaeda, the Taliban and Afghanistan

On 11 September 2001, the Islamist extremist group al-Qaeda attacked New York and other targets in the USA, killing thousands of people. This convinced Bush and many other Americans that something had to be done about Afghanistan, where al-Qaeda was based. They called this the 'War on Terror'. The USA (with support from Britain and many other countries) destroyed al-Qaeda's bases in Afghanistan and defeated the group's ally the Taliban, which ruled Afghanistan at the time. The victories were swift. US attention then turned to Saddam Hussein. They assumed he could be removed just as quickly and easily. There were also strong suspicions that Saddam was somehow connected with the 9/11 attacks (although this was not true).

UN Resolution 1441

In 2002, the United Nations passed Resolution 1441. This accused Iraq of making WMDs and demanded that Saddam either allow inspectors in or 'face serious consequences'. Saddam refused. President Bush claimed that Resolution 1441 gave him authority to attack Iraq, but leaders in many other countries disagreed, arguing that an attack would be illegal unless there was a second UN resolution *specifically authorising* an attack.

Support from Britain

The British prime minister, Tony Blair, had shown consistent support for US policies, and he backed Bush's view of Resolution 1441. Britain's political and military support was an important factor for the USA because it helped to avoid the impression that Bush was making unilateral decisions.

ACTIVITY

Carry out a survey of your class. Based on the information here, who do you think would have supported Britain joining a war against Saddam in 2003?

British public opinion: March 2003

Unlike the World Wars, the Iraq War did not require mass mobilisation. Britain's professional army had the necessary troops and equipment to carry out the task. However, Blair did need parliament's approval to commit those troops to war, and gaining that approval was not a simple matter:

Source 13 A photograph showing demonstrations against the Iraq War in London in February 2003. ▼

- Blair's critics attacked him for being submissive to Bush.
- They argued that war against Iraq was illegal because the United Nations had not sanctioned it.
- Blair claimed that Iraq could launch WMDs in 45 minutes, but his critics doubted the evidence.
- They worried that the USA and Britain had no clear plan for Iraq after the war.

Blair was undeterred. In one of his most powerful speeches, the prime minister urged parliament to approve an attack on Iraq (see Source 14). He compared refusing to attack Iraq with the government's policy of appeasement towards Hitler in the 1930s. He argued that it would encourage terrorists around the world to think that Britain was weak and unwilling to act. He claimed that Saddam's weapons threatened Britain both directly and indirectly, because Saddam might give these weapons to terrorists. Blair made it clear that he and several other senior members of the government would resign if parliament did not support him.

Despite the controversy, Blair won the vote by 412 to 149. According to a survey, he had the support of the British population (see Source 15).

Source 14 An extract from Tony Blair's speech to parliament in March 2003

To step back now, I believe, would put at hazard all that we hold dearest, turn the UN back into a talking shop, stifle the first steps of progress in the Middle East, leave the Iraqi people to the mercy of Saddam. To step back now would tell our allies that at the very moment of action, at the very moment when they need our determination, that Britain faltered. I will not be party to such a course. This is not the time to falter. This is the time for this house, not just this government or indeed this prime minister, but for this house to give a lead, to show that we will stand up for what we know to be right, to show that we will confront the tyrannies and dictatorships and terrorists who put our way of life at risk, to show at the moment of decision that we have the courage to do the right thing.

1 Is Source 13 or Source 15 more useful in informing us about public opinion on the Iraq War in the period February to May 2003?

2 Look back at your polling results from the Activity on page 136. How similar or different were they from Source 15? Explain any differences.

Figure 15 The results of public opinion polls March to May 2003. People were asked: 'Do you think the USA and Britain are/were right or wrong to take military action against Iraq?'

Date	Right [%]	Wrong [%]	Don't know [%]
March	53	39	8
April	54	40	6
May	57	34	9

What happened in the Iraq War?

The invasion took place in March 2003. Iraqi forces quickly collapsed and the country suffered heavy military and civilian casualties. It seemed like a great victory for the USA and its allies, but the situation soon began to unravel. The US commanders and their allies made a series of incorrect assumptions and mistakes. They had assumed that the Iraqis would welcome their intervention, but this was not the case. They also did not have enough troops to properly control a collapsing Iraq. In addition:

● Cities were devastated by looting and riots. Impoverished Iraqis looted government buildings, hospitals, museums and anywhere else they might find items of value.
● The invading forces did nothing to restore law and order. They focused their efforts on setting up their own headquarters and searching for the WMDs. It was soon clear that there were none.

With Saddam gone, traditional clan leaders began to establish local power bases. They were happy to see the end of Saddam, but they did not want to live in an Iraq dominated by the USA. Many decided to fight the US and British forces in an INSURGENCY.

Source 16 A cartoon from the *Independent* newspaper, published in Britain in July 2003. The main figures are Tony Blair, his press secretary Alistair Campbell and the foreign secretary Jack Straw. ▼

The insurgents used classic hit-and-run guerrilla tactics. Between 2003 and 2007, they inflicted around 4,000 casualties on US and allied forces. Insurgents suffered around 18,000 casualties. However, by the far the hardest hit were civilians. Hundreds of thousands were killed, millions of lives were disrupted and millions of Iraqis became refugees to escape the fighting.

Responses to the Iraq War

British public opinion: July 2003

As it became clear that the main justification for the invasion – weapons of mass destruction – did not exist, public opinion turned dramatically. Criticism increased as people realised that the USA and Britain had no plan for controlling Iraq and that the invasion had made the situation much worse for the Iraqi people. You can see the effect on popular support in Source 17.

1 How can you tell the cartoonist of Source 16 is an opponent of the war?
2 Would the government be more concerned about critics like Source 16 or the opinion polls in Figure 17?

Figure 17 The results of opinion polls on the Iraq War 2003–15. The question was the same as in Source 15. ▼

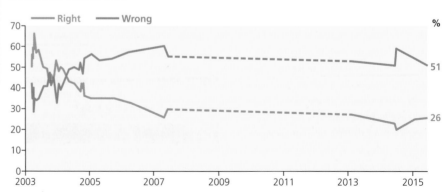

British public opinion: 2011

As the extent of the chaos in Iraq became clear, disapproval over the war rose and it seems that people even began to alter their own memories! Across 21 surveys in 2003, on average 54 per cent had said it was right, yet ten years later only 37 per cent of the public said they had thought it right at the time.

> **Source 18** Journalist Patrick Cockburn, writing in 2015.
>
> *Tony Blair is still pilloried for ... going to war in Iraq in 2003. The lead-up to the invasion has become a national obsession in which Blair is a scapegoat, as if most of the British establishment and popular opinion did not support him at the time. Admittedly this support was partly the result of concocted evidence about Saddam Hussein's non-existent WMD, but there is something absurd about the fact that it is almost impossible these days to meet a diplomat or a general who does not claim to have been deeply, if silently, opposed to the whole venture at the time.*

The impact of the Iraq War on Britain

British troops eventually pulled out of Iraq in 2011. In comparison with earlier conflicts, British casualties were light. Official figures record that 179 British servicemen and women had died, although many more had been injured by snipers, bombs and other attacks.

However, the war had a significant and lasting political effect on Britain. Many historians believe that the Iraq War seriously damaged the relationship between the government and the British people. Tony Blair's popularity declined significantly. It also made the public and even MPs suspicious of intelligence reports and any military action taken based on such reports. A powerful example of this came in 2013 when the Conservative prime minister David Cameron tried to get parliament to authorise British air strikes against the regime of President Assad of Syria, who was using chemical weapons against his own people. Parliament refused to authorise this action.

Another key reason the Iraq War was unpopular and controversial was that in many people's eyes it made Britain more of a target for Islamist extremist attacks. You will look at this in more detail in the next case study.

FOCUS TASK

Why was the Iraq War so controversial?

The chart below suggests four reasons why the Iraq War was controversial and suggests they were all equally important. Draw your own version, but:
- add labels explaining each factor
- resize the columns if you disagree they were all equally important
- add more columns if necessary.

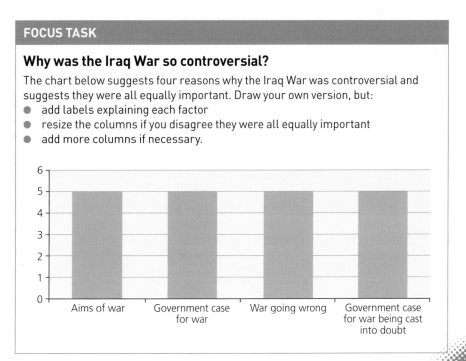

Case study 4: **Terrorist threats and counter-measures since 2003**

From the 1990s a radical ISLAMIST movement called al-Qaeda (led by Osama bin Laden) carried out regular terrorist attacks on the USA and its allies. Al-Qaeda believed that Islam was under threat from enemies everywhere, and that it was the responsibility of every Muslim to resist these attacks by taking part in jihad ('struggle' or 'holy war') against Islam's enemies, particularly:

- Western democratic countries and values
- communism
- Jews and the state of Israel
- Muslim governments that were not strict enough or co-operated in any way with al-Qaeda's enemies.

Al-Qaeda regarded the USA as its greatest enemy. Throughout the 1990s and early 2000s al-Qaeda attacked targets connected with the USA specifically and the West in general. The group's trademark was the use of suicide bombers and its highest-profile action was the 9/11 attack on the World Trade Center, in 2001. As well as these attacks, al-Qaeda provided finance, training and support to other like-minded groups or individuals.

In October 2001, the US government put together a coalition of forces to attack al-Qaeda and its Taliban allies in Afghanistan. This destroyed al-Qaeda as a single organisation, but the group's aims, influence and expertise continued to filter down and support or motivate countless small organisations and individuals.

From 2006 onwards, a movement called Islamic State (also known as IS, ISIS or ISIL) emerged in Iraq and Syria. This group seized control of large sections of those countries and set up a CALIPHATE. It took on a similar role to al-Qaeda in training and supporting groups and individuals in attacks on the USA and its allies.

Why did Britain become a target for terrorist attack?

Mainland Britain had been a target for IRA bombings in the 1970 and 1980s (see pages 132–35). Britons had grown used to living with the threat of terrorist attack and accepted the security measures needed to counter such attacks. However, IRA attacks had declined and Britain had faced no terrorist attacks on home soil since 1997.

FACTFILE

Some known terrorist plots against Britain 2003–11

Date	Codename used by police	Details	Outcome
2003	Operation Crevice	British-born activists created bombs made from fertiliser and planned to attack civilians in places such as shops, bars, nightclubs.	Stopped
2005	Operation Theseus	British-born activists detonated bombs on London Underground on 7 July (often referred to as the 7/7 attacks). Over 700 injured and 52 killed.	Succeeded
2005	Operation Vivace	British- and foreign-born activists attempted suicide bombings on the London Underground.	Stopped
2006	Operation Overt	Plot to bring down aircraft by arming suicide bomber passengers with liquid explosives.	Stopped
2007	Operation Gamble	Plan to kidnap and murder a British soldier.	Stopped
2007	Operation Seagram	Attempted suicide car-bomb attack on Glasgow Airport.	Failed
2008	No codename	Bombs placed in restaurants in Exeter.	Failed
2011	Operation Pitsford	British-born activists planned to pose as charity collectors and set off bombs in crowded public places.	Stopped

Britain's close involvement in the Afghanistan campaigns and then the Iraq War in 2003, and its consistent loyalty to the USA, put it on the frontline for potential attack by Islamist terrorists. Between 2003 and 2011, there were at least eight major terrorist plots known to the police (see Factfile). They involved at least 50 activists, many of whom were born in Britain, although there were probably many more plots and plotters whom the security services did not know about (or did not tell the public about). Civilians were the main target of these attacks, and their aim was to spread fear and anxiety, to disrupt transport, work and daily life. Most plots during this period were foiled. One succeeded.

The London bombings July 2005

On the morning of 7 July 2005, people listened in shock to reports of a series of co-ordinated terrorist attacks on the London Underground and a bus in central London. Four Islamist militants carried explosives and detonated them in suicide attacks. Their aim was to cause terror and confusion – and they succeeded. Over 700 people were injured in the attacks and 52 were killed. Many more were traumatised by what they saw.

Source 19 A photograph showing the aftermath of the London bomb attack of 7 July 2005. ▼

Source 20 Supporters of Islamic State demonstrating in London. ▼

1 Look at Sources 19 and 20. Is one of them more useful in telling us about terrorism in Britain since 2003? Explain your answer.

2 Study Source 20 carefully. Do you think it would be effective? Explain your answer.

The government response

The attacks of July 2005 showed that the threat was serious. They also demonstrated how difficult it was to combat: this was not an organisation with a leader. There was no one to negotiate with – it was a loose network of RADICALISED individuals.

● **Recruits:** There were plenty of willing recruits, mostly young men. At first they were believed to have been recruited by the preaching of radical IMAMS in British mosques. However, it soon became clear that online contact was more influential. In fact, most extremists avoided mosques and were not welcome there.

● **Training:** Some young British Muslims went to training camps in Afghanistan, and later in Syria and Iraq, to receive instruction and to gain experience of combat and jihad.

● **Support:** As well as those who took part in plots or attacks, there were others who supported them practically, providing vehicles, transporting equipment, researching targets.

● **Anonymity:** The vast majority of Muslims did not (and do not) support terrorism. But Britain had (and still has) many towns and cities with large Muslim communities where it was relatively easy for an activist to live and blend in. They were trained in how to keep a low profile and hide their activities even from their own families.

Government departments, the police and the intelligence agencies developed different ways to deal with the terrorist threat, as Source 21 shows.

> **Source 21** Extracts from *Countering International Terrorism: The United Kingdom's Strategy*, July 2006 published by the British government.
>
> *THE THREAT*
>
> *The principal current terrorist threat is from radicalised individuals who are using a distorted and unrepresentative version of the Islamic faith to justify violence. They are, however, a tiny minority within the Muslim communities here and abroad. Muslim communities themselves do not threaten our security; indeed they make a great contribution to our country. The Government is therefore working in partnership with Muslim communities to help them prevent extremists gaining influence there.*
>
> *THE RESPONSE*
>
> *Tackling the radicalisation of individuals by:*
>
> *Tackling disadvantage*
>
> *Deterring those who facilitate terrorism*
>
> *Engaging in the battle of ideas – challenging the ideologies that extremists believe can justify the use of violence, primarily by helping Muslims who wish to dispute these ideas to do so.*
>
> *Pursuing terrorists and those that sponsor them through:*
>
> *Gathering intelligence*
>
> *Disrupting terrorist activity*
>
> *Working with partners and allies overseas*
>
> *Protecting the UK and UK interests overseas. This covers a range of issues including;*
>
> *Strengthening border security*
>
> *Protecting key utilities*
>
> *Transport – reducing the risk and impact of attacks*
>
> *Crowded places – protecting people going about their daily lives.*

1 Do you think Source 21 is an effective strategy?
2 How do you think the press would have reported Source 21? What might the newspaper headlines be?

Detention without trial

One of the most controversial measures introduced by the government was to increase the time a suspect could be held by the police. According to the ancient law of Habeas Corpus, a person in Britain cannot be held for longer than two days without being charged with a crime. In 2003, this was increased to 14 days for terrorism suspects. The Terrorism Act took it to 28 days. Tony Blair tried to extend it to 90 days, but parliament would not accept this.

Source 22 Increased security at Heathrow airport in February 2003. Intelligence reports indicated an attack on the airport, while other reports suggested that terrorists had managed to acquire hand-held anti-aircraft missiles. ▼

Source 23 An extract from a BBC news report in February 2003 on the Heathrow threat.

BBC political editor Andrew Marr underlined what he described as an 'appalling dilemma' for ministers who – with a mountain of intelligence to sift through – were caught between overreacting to threats or not doing enough to prevent an attack. He said: 'We have a political blame culture and an unquantifiable threat. No wonder ministers are jittery.'

Threat level

In 2006, the security services introduced a system of 'threat levels' designed to tell the public the likelihood of a terrorist attack. For much of the decade 2006–16 the threat in Britain was 'substantial' (meaning an attack is a strong possibility) or 'severe' (highly likely). During this period it was twice 'critical' (expected imminently).

The popular response

At first, people were sceptical about the supposed threat posed by terrorists. For example, when Blair sent troops to guard Heathrow Airport in 2003 (see Source 22), many saw it as a stunt to generate support for the war against Iraq. However, over time the population took the threat more seriously, especially after the attacks in July 2005. Most people accepted the inconvenience caused by extra security checks at airports, stations and sea ports. When the government proposed introducing national identity cards in 2004, around 80 per cent of the population were prepared to accept the idea. There were limits, however. A 2007 survey showed that the great majority opposed using evidence against terror suspects if it had been gained by torture. They also thought it was unacceptable to ban public demonstrations or rallies, irrespective of what the rally was about.

Islamist terrorism negatively affected attitudes towards Muslims. Research in 2006 found that 91 per cent of press coverage about Muslims was negative and represented them as a possible threat to the safety of the country. These headlines made Muslim communities feel threatened, a fact that radicalised activists could then exploit. However, this was only true in a minority of cases. Research evidence, rather than hysterical media headlines, reveals that the values held by British Muslims were actually very similar to the values of most British people.

PRACTICE QUESTIONS

1 Describe two examples of governments trying to win support for wars in the years after 1945. (4)
2 Describe two examples of asymmetric warfare (where the resources or tactics of the two sides are vastly different) in the years after 1945. (4)
3 Explain why the public mostly supported the government's policies in the Cold War. (8)
4 How significant was the threat of terrorism in Britain from 1969 onwards? (14)

FOCUS TASK

The impact of Islamist terrorism

Here is a list of statements about the terrorist threat. Study each one. Decide how far you agree with it and find some examples to support your decision.
● The terrorists succeeded in dividing the population.
● The media made the war against terrorism more difficult.
● The media was largely ignored by the population.
● Islamist terrorism failed in Britain.

KEY QUESTION REVIEW

Look back and make sure you have completed your notes and tables from Key Questions A–C on page 127. When you have done this, prepare an answer to the following question:

'Wars after 1945 affected civilians more than any previous wars.' How far do you agree with this view?

3.4 Review: War and society c1750–c2010

PERIOD REVIEW TASKS

A What types of war were there in this period?

1 Historians often look at different types of wars, compare how they are fought and the effects they had. The list below shows some different types of wars.

- opportunism/ambition/plunder
- wars beween peoples, nations or states
- conquest/invasion
- defence
- rebellion
- religion
- civil war

Look back over your work and try to find two examples of each category. Some wars might fit more than one category.

B Attitudes and responses to war

2 In the modern period, attitudes and responses to war become even more complex than in earlier periods. Read the statements in the first column of the table and decide how far they apply to the wars you have studied from the modern period. Record evidence for and against each statement in columns 2 and 4. Use columns 3 and 5 to draw some conclusions and to make comparisons with other periods.

In the modern period …	Examples/events/ developments I would use as evidence to agree with this statement	Similar examples in the early modern period	Events/ developments I would use as evidence to disagree with this statement	Similar examples in the early modern period
People supported the government when it went to war.	In 1939, most British people did not want to go to war with Germany but they felt it was necessary to fight Nazism, so they supported the government.	When the Spanish Armada was threatening England, most people supported Elizabeth's campaign against Spain and the Armada.	When Britain went to war against France in 1793, many people who supported the French Revolution opposed the war.	When war broke out between Charles I and parliament in the 1640s, many people, and even whole counties, tried to stay neutral.
Governments needed the support of their populations to fight wars effectively.				
Governments tried to influence people's attitudes towards war with propaganda.				
People were enthusiastic about war.				
Religion influenced people's attitudes to war.				
Ideology influenced people's attitude to war.				
People's views on identity influenced their attitude towards wars.				

C The impacts of war on people

3   Look at these cards, which show some of the ways that wars affected people in the modern period. Make your own set of cards. Look back at your work in this chapter and find at least one example of each of the types of impacts and write them on the cards.

4   Now sort your cards into piles:
   ● direct impact
   ● indirect impact
   ● psychological impact
   ● social and cultural impact
   You might find that other students in your class disagree with your categories, but that does not matter as long as you can justify your decision.

5   As an extension task, look back at your work on Questions 1 and 2 and decide whether you think particular types of wars tended to have particular types of effects (e.g. did modern wars do more to create a sense of national identity?).

D War and government – the rise of public opinion

6   You will have noticed that in the modern period, governments had to pay more attention to public opinion in order to fight wars. Use a copy of the table below to note down examples of how and why this happened.

Conflicts	Challenges to government(s)	Role of public opinion in conflict	How government(s) responded	Impact/effectiveness
Seven Years' War				
French wars				
Crimean War				
Boer Wars				
First World War				
Second World War				
Cold War				
Northern Ireland				
Iraq War				
War on Terror				

PERIOD REVIEW TASKS

7 A book publisher is planning to publish a book about war and society in the modern period. They are finding it hard to come up with a suitable title. Some of the suggestions include:

- *A Time of Misery*
- *People's Wars*
- *The Rise of Popular Opinion*
- *The Business of War*
- *The Rise of Government Control*

Choose one of these book titles and write a short paragraph explaining your choice. Or come up with a better title!

The publisher also wants you to recommend an image for the front cover. It could be a single image or a montage. Make your recommendations in an email, explaining your choice.

E How similar were wars in the modern period to early modern wars?

8 Look at the two lists below of early modern and modern wars you studied in Chapters 2 and 3. Choose two wars (one from each period) that you think are *similar* in some ways and explain their similarities. This could include: type of war, aims, ways they were fought, impact on Britain, reaction of the British people, impact on government, and other points of your own.

Then choose two wars (again one from each period) which you think are *different* in some ways and explain how they are different. This could include: types of war, aims, ways they were fought, impact on Britain, reaction of the British people, impact on government, and other points of your own.

Early modern wars
- Elizabeth's involvement in Scotland
- Elizabeth's wars in the Netherlands
- Wars against Spain
- Elizabeth's privateering
- First Civil War
- Second Civil War
- Third Civil War
- Anglo-Scottish border wars (official)
- Anglo-Scottish border wars (unofficial)
- Jacobite War 1715
- Jacobite War 1745

Modern wars
- Seven Years' War
- French wars
- Crimean War
- Boer Wars
- First World War
- Second World War
- Cold War
- Northern Ireland
- Iraq War

PRACTICE QUESTIONS

1 'In the period 1450–2010, the main impact of warfare was economic.' How far do you agree with this view? (24)
2 'For most of the period 1450–2010, monarchs and governments did not need popular support for wars.' How far do you agree with this view? (24)
3 'War generally brought the people and the monarchs or governments closer together in the period 1450–2010.' How far do you agree with this view? (24)
4 'In the period 1450–2010 it was civil wars rather than wars between states that caused the greatest disruption.' How far do you agree with this view? (24)

ASSESSMENT FOCUS

How the thematic study will be assessed

The thematic study will be examined in Paper 2. It is worth 25 per cent of the overall marks for your GCSE. There will be four questions, which test the first two assessment objectives:

- AO1: Knowledge and understanding
- AO2: Explanation and analysis.

The questions could be on any part of the content, but that does not mean you have to try to remember every event! Above all, the paper is assessing your ability to think and work like a historian. In the introduction, you looked at how historians work (page 4). There we set out some steps that historians take:

1 focus
2 ask questions
3 select
4 organise
5 fine tune.

If you have tackled all the Key Question Review tasks you will be fine. In fact, our advice is not to take lots of notes and try to remember them. Revise your work from the Focus Tasks and Key Question Review tasks. That will prepare you more effectively.

Question 1

Question 1 will usually ask you to describe an event or development in the story of war and British society c790–c2010. It is a simple knowledge question, probably requiring a description of two examples of a type of event. For example:

> **Describe two examples of wars between medieval monarchs and their barons. (4 marks)**

Aim of the question

There are no tricks to this question – it is simply testing your knowledge. There will not be anything obscure. The examiner wants to see that you can describe important events accurately without simply writing down everything you know.

Advice

Select: The question asks you to select two examples of conflicts between monarchs and barons in the medieval period. Do not 'over-answer'. There are many examples, but the question requires *two*. You will not gain anything by selecting more than two examples. In fact you may lose marks. The examiner is looking for a description of these conflicts, so you do not need to go into detail about how serious the conflict was, for example.

Organise: The important thing is to use your knowledge in a relevant way. In this question a good way to organise your answer might be: 'Monarchs and barons often clashed about X, for example.'

Fine tune: Make sure that your spellings and dates are correct and that your answer is clear – in the pressure of an exam it is easy to accidentally say something you do not mean.

Example answer

> There were numerous examples of conflicts between monarchs and barons in the medieval period. Monarchs and barons sometimes clashed over who should be on the throne. This happened in the reign of King Stephen. Stephen took the throne but many barons supported the claim of Matilda, the daughter of the previous king Henry I. A bitter civil war resulted. Another reason why monarchs and barons clashed was the amount of tax the king wanted them to pay. A good example of this was in the reign of King John. To pay for his wars, John increased taxes and eventually a large number of barons rebelled against him. This eventually led to Magna Carta in 1215. Another reason why barons sometimes rebelled was ...

Comments

This answer has lots of good points and would definitely get 4 marks. The opening statement is good. It is not absolutely essential, but it is a nice example of fine tuning – it shows that the candidate understands that they are only selecting two examples of conflict. The description of each conflict is effective and the answer clearly sets out what the conflict was about. It would have been just as good to describe the actual conflicts themselves and their outcomes but it would be necessary to describe the cause of the conflict and the fighting, battles and the outcome.

Practice

There are plenty of practice questions at the end of each topic. Go back and try a couple of the 4-mark 'Describe...' questions.

General advice on Questions 2–4

Questions 2–4 ask you to do more than simply describe. You have to explain things and reach judgements. You need to answer the question and explain why you think what you think. A useful way to think about Questions 2, 3 and 4 is to assess your answers yourself. Examiners use mark schemes but you do not need anything that complicated. Think of it like an Olympic medal ceremony. Read some of your practice answers and ask yourself which of these medals your answer deserves.

GOLD
(up to 100% of marks)

SILVER
(up to 60% of marks)

BRONZE
(up to 25% of marks)

Bronze: You describe something you know (which is good) but it is not really relevant to the question (which is a shame). Or you assert something (which is good) but you provide no supporting evidence (which is a shame).

Silver: You describe relevant events or developments (which is good) but you do not connect them to the question or explain why they are important in answering the question (which is a shame).

Gold: You make it really clear what you think the answer to the question is. You support your answer with at least one event or development and you explain how that event or development supports your answer.

Even a Gold answer can be improved by ensuring you have:

- a clear conclusion that rounds off your argument
- a balanced answer that shows you understand that there might be more than one view about the question or explains how the different elements are connected
- supporting evidence: using relevant knowledge and a good range of examples to support each point you make.

Question 2

Question 2 will usually be an 'explain' question. This might ask you to explain why something happened, or to explain what the effects of something were, or it might ask you to explain how something happened. For example:

> **Explain why there was popular support for the Cold War in Britain in the 1950s and 1960s. (8 marks)**

Advice

Select: It is sensible to think in terms of at least two reasons, or effects, or whatever the question is asking for. This will show the examiner what you know without spending too much time on the question.

Organise: The important thing is to use your knowledge in a relevant way. In this question, a good way to organise your answer might be: 'One reason why there was support for the Cold War was .... This increased support because .... Another reason was .... This created support because ...'.

Fine tune: Do all the usual checking, but when answering an 'explain' question it can also be a good idea to say which of your reasons you think is more important.

Example answer

One important reason why there was support for the Cold War was that communism was viewed in Britain with suspicion. Almost all the major institutions opposed it, including the Church, the Conservative and Labour parties and the Trades Union Congress. These organisations had a lot of influence. This ensured that people mostly supported the government. In addition, the British media was opposed to communism and supported government policy. The British historian Tony Shaw did a study of British newspapers from 1945–50. He found that they produced thousands of negative articles about the USSR and communism. This had a huge influence on how most British people thought. There is other evidence available too. From the 1930s onwards, Britain carried out the Mass Observation Project, which tried to measure the views and opinions of the people. Evidence from these projects also suggested that most people were anti-communist.

The aim of the question

This type of question is designed to stretch you a bit further. When examiners ask you to explain they want you to show that you know the events but also that you can explain why those events were important in affecting people or making something happen. In a 'describe' question you might say: 'The media supported the government in the Cold War.' In an 'explain' question you might say: 'The media supported the government in the Cold War. They did X, which helped influence public opinion because ...'.

Comments

This is a top-level answer. There are two clear reasons. More importantly the answer explains how the reasons helped create or increase support for the Cold War. This is what takes it into the top level. The reference to the British historian Tony Shaw is impressive, but examiners don't really expect you to have this level of detail at your fingertips!

To improve this answer: It might have been useful to add a sentence on what communism was or give some examples of some of the actions of the USSR which had alarmed people. An answer like this does not need the evidence from Tony Shaw's work or the Mass Observation Project. It is not wrong to include both but the candidate would need to be careful not to get into trouble over time.

Question 3

Question 3 will usually be about how significant or important something was. It can come in a number of forms. For example:

- How significant a change was X?
- How important was X in causing Y?
- How significant was X in how Y worked?

Remember that an event or development can be significant in many different ways. It may be significant because of its effect at a particular time, but it may be more significant in the longer term. Events may affect some groups more than others and so may be more significant to them. Events can also have moral or psychological significance as well as (or instead of) practical impacts.

This is probably the most important type of question for you to practise. If you can master this, then you will master all the techniques needed for the other question types. Here is an example:

> **How significant were the wars against Spain in the reign of Elizabeth I? (14 marks)**

Advice

Select: You need to select facts, events and developments that show some of the ways in which the wars against Spain affected England. It is important to explain how and why those effects were significant.

Organise: A possible way to tackle this question is to put together three paragraphs. Each paragraph should address the question in some way. You might choose to look at three different effects of the wars, one for each paragraph. Alternatively, you could devote one paragraph to arguing that the wars were not significant (this is generally more difficult).

Fine tune: Do all the usual checking, but here it is worth making sure you have said what you think about the question. In questions like this, a conclusion usually helps.

Example answer

From the 1560s to the 1590s, Elizabeth I was involved in a series of wars against Spain and these wars had a significant effect on England.

One way in which the wars were significant is that they raised England's profile in the world. When Elizabeth became queen, England was still seen as a second-rate power by countries such as France and Spain. By the end of Elizabeth's reign, and as a result of her wars, England was more respected. When Elizabeth first fought against Spain she was so nervous about it that she made her troops pretend to be volunteers who were not fighting on her orders. She also relied on privateers to attack Spanish ships, again pretending that these were not official actions. But in 1588 Elizabeth's ships defeated the Spanish Armada and it was clear that England was a serious power. On the other hand, even though England resisted Spain it could not defeat it, and was still not in the same league.

Another way in which the wars were significant was that they had a major impact on the majority of ordinary people. For most of Elizabeth's reign people supported the wars, but they did take a heavy toll. For the majority of the population, the wars were not seen as successful or glorious by the end of her reign. They were associated with heavy taxes and being forced to provide troops, animals and other supplies. Elizabeth's wars cost around £500,000 every year and around 1 in 10 of the population had to serve in the army or navy. So, in the short term the wars were significant in causing poverty in England and turning people against the wars.

One final effect of the wars was the impact on the way Elizabeth ruled. Because the wars cost so much money she had to raise taxes constantly. The only way to do this was to get parliament to approve taxes, so over her reign parliament became much more important. This was significant in the short term and in the longer term it would become even more significant.

The aim of the question

This question is asking you to assess the ways that the wars affected England and its people, but you need to do a little more than that. When you describe the changes you need to consider how great the change or impact was, who was affected, etc.

Comments

This is a very thorough answer. It gives three relevant ways in which the wars were significant for England. The answer does a particularly good job in explaining the significance of the impact in each paragraph. It is difficult to see how this might be improved. It certainly does not need more information or detail. It would probably achieve top marks with just two of these three paragraphs.

Practice

There are plenty of practice questions at the end of each topic. Go back and try a couple of the 14-mark 'How significant...' questions.

Question 4

Question 4 will usually be a big overview question. it will ask you to compare two eras – medieval and early modern or early modern and modern. It will give you a statement and ask you how far you agree with it. For example:

> *'Between 1500 and 2010, wars were supported by the population.' How far do you agree with this statement? (24 marks)*

The aim of the question

This type of question is designed to stretch you a bit further. When examiners ask you to explain they want you to show that you know the events but also that you can explain why those events were important in affecting people or making something happen. In a 'describe' question you might say: 'The media supported the government in the Cold War.' In an 'explain' question you might say: 'The media supported the government in the Cold War. They did X, which helped influence public opinion because...'.

Advice

Select: Selection is extremely important in this question. You do not need to cover the whole early modern and modern periods in your answer. The fact that there are 24 marks does not mean you have to write a lot – it means you have to think a lot! Select examples that support the view in the statement and examples that oppose it. Do this for the early modern and for the modern period, so think in terms of four examples.

Organise: A good way to tackle this question might be to put together an introduction, two paragraphs (the 'yes' paragraph and the 'no' paragraph), and then a conclusion.

Fine tune: Do all the usual checking, but here it is worth making sure you have said what you think about the question. In questions like this, a conclusion usually means:
- you agree *or* you disagree *or*
- the statement is true at some points in time but not in others.

Example answer

Comments

This is a good answer, probably borderline between Gold and Silver. The first paragraph is very much focused on the question of whether people supported the war and uses the Mass Observation archive as supporting evidence. This pattern is repeated – point about support, backed up by evidence – in the next two paragraphs. It is important to recognise that different approaches could have been taken.

To improve this answer it needs an overall judgement. There is no single right answer to this type of question. As long as there is supporting evidence in this particular question it would be reasonable to argue that overall: wars were supported more strongly in one period or the other; that support for wars depended on individual wars, leaders, circumstances; that different sections of the population were more or less supportive of wars in general or particular wars.

The statement is only partially correct. The Second World War was well supported by the population. It has been argued that Britain was second only to the USSR in terms of how completely mobilised the population was in the war. We know from the Mass Observation Project that the war had the support of the population, not least because the enemy being fought, Nazi Germany, was seen as utterly wrong and evil.

It was a similar picture in the 16th century, when Elizabeth I was fighting wars against Spain. Spain was the leading power in the world at this time and was also a Catholic power. England was a Protestant country after 1559. On the whole the country was united behind Elizabeth because England was threatened, most notably by the Armada in 1588, and also to defend the Protestant religion.

On the other hand other wars were very unpopular. For example, in 2003 British Prime Minister Tony Blair led Britain into a war in coalition with the USA against Iraq. There were massive demonstrations across the country to protest against the war because many people felt it was illegal. As the war progressed it became even more unpopular as Iraq disintegrated into chaos and British forces were attacked by an underground insurgency...

Practice

First of all, have a go at this question using our structure. Do not use our example, though. Pick others from Chapters 2 and 3. There are practice questions at the end of these chapters. Try a couple of the 24-mark 'period comparison' questions.

Part 2
British depth study:
**Personal Rule to Restoration
1629–60**

Introduction to the depth study

In this part of the book you will be studying British history from 1629 to 1660.

Why study the period 1629–60?

This is an interesting and action-packed period of history. It starts with King Charles I effectively trying to rule like an absolute monarch and ignoring parliament. It then takes us through civil war, the execution of the king, a republic and then back to a monarchy. It is an incredibly significant period for several reasons:

- It is the only period in which Britain has been a republic.
- The Civil Wars were perhaps the greatest trauma ever to affect Britain. The percentage of the population that died was greater than the proportion of deaths in the First World War.
- It was also psychologically traumatic. It saw the execution of the king, the destruction of many churches and the emergence of radical groups, with news ideas that inspired some and frightened others.
- It marked a massive change in the importance of parliament and it established many of the laws and practices that are the basis of today's democracy.
- It highlighted key ideas such as liberty, conscience and religious toleration. These ideas would be the basis of many later revolutions around the world.

The focus of the study

The big questions you will focus on in this period are:

- Why did Charles I try to rule without parliament?
- Why did he meet such fierce resistance?

- Why were England and the rest of Britain so bitterly divided during this period?
- Despite the upheavals, was there really significant change?

Sources and mindsets

One of the biggest challenges you will face in this study is understanding why so many people felt so strongly about particular issues. To help tackle this challenge:

- Put aside your modern views. Whatever your ideas, it is important to accept that in this period people held views about religion, how society should be organised, political power, taxes and many other issues that may seem unfamiliar or wrong to you. It is not your job to criticise, judge or approve these views. You just need to *understand* them.

- Study the documents, letters, images and other sources that people at the time were reading, writing and looking at. We cannot talk to these people, but we can use our ability as historians to get a glimpse into their world.

- Understand how historians use sources. Sources are not like textbooks, divided neatly into chapters. They are messy and complicated – just like people! Historians often use sources that may not at first appear to be about the thing they are investigating. A tax record can sometimes reveal a lot about religion, for example. And of course historians can often tell a great deal about an issue or about people by reading between the lines of a source.

Example 1

Here is the supposed reason for the proclamation. Apparently there is a problem with false cards and dice. How concerned do you think people were? Could there be something else going on?

At first sight you might think 'What am I going to learn from a proclamation about dice?'

> **A proclamation by Charles I on playing cards and dice, 1638.**
>
> By the King.
>
> An announcement about the making of playing cards and dice.
>
> To prevent the common abuses caused by the use of false cards and dice, deceiving and damaging his subjects, His Majesty has appointed an officer for finding and giving the seal of approval to all cards and dice made in this realm. All makers of cards and dice within the realm, and merchants or others who import them from foreign parts, should now bring these cards and dice to His Majesty's officer to be viewed, examined and given the seal of approval if they are good and saleable. For this seal they will pay His Majesty's officer or his deputies the fees set out in His Majesty's official document.

Is the king really bothered about dice? Bothered enough to appoint an officer?

So all card and dice makers have to have their dice and cards approved. That is likely to increase the cost.

So it it definitely is going to increase the cost – and cards and dice were among the most popular games of the time.

And we are left with the sneaking suspicion that the king is not really worried about the quality of cards and dice, he has just found a way to raise money. And it is probably fair to assume most people at the time thought that way.

Before we look at any details of *Eikon Basilike*, we can learn a lot from the story of the source (rather than the story being told *in* the source).

First of all, it was published ten days after the execution of King Charles I on 30 January 1649. It was said to be Charles's life story written by the king himself, although it is not clear whether this is the case. It does reveal Charles's state of mind, though. He saw his death coming and he wanted this book to be in people's hands in order to shape the way they thought about him.

There is a wider point here, which is the use of visual imagery. This was a period when literacy was increasing, but the majority of people could still not read and write. That did not stop them being interested in major events, and those who wanted to influence public opinion knew that images like this one had a powerful impact. The *Eikon Basilike* sold thousands of copies, including miniature copies that were easier to keep hidden.

Example 2

The cover page of *Eikon Basilike*. ▼

If we look at the image, we can note some important features. Charles is at the centre, of course. The crown is on the ground, symbolising his death but also that this earthly symbol of power is not as important as all the religious images that follow. From the window above, there is a heavenly crown labelled 'Blessed and Eternal'. The ray from Charles's eye says 'I look to Heaven'. The other ray of light shows light piercing the dark clouds to shine on Charles. In his hand is the crown of thorns, worn by Jesus at the Crucifixion and showing Charles as a Christ-like figure.

Perhaps the most important point we can learn from the *Eikon Basilike* is that religion and power were inextricable. The king is shown as a saint here, and kings were regarded as sacred, appointed by God. This is vital to understanding how people felt at this time and how they reacted to events.

4.1 What kind of king was Charles I?

FOCUS

Charles Stuart became king of England, Scotland and Ireland in 1625. He was never meant to be king – his older brother Henry was James's heir. But Henry died in 1612, and so it was Charles who inherited the throne. This topic looks at how well prepared Charles was for the role, and the relationship he developed with parliament.

How did Charles I think England should be governed?

In 1610, Charles's father James gave a speech to parliament in which he declared that the king was the most important person on Earth. James wrote down his beliefs for his children and published them as a book. He explained that God had entrusted the king with the power to rule – a belief known as the 'Divine Right of Kings' (see Source 1).

Charles listened carefully to his father's advice and shared his beliefs. Some years later, in 1636, Charles I installed a new ceiling in the Banqueting House in Whitehall, London (see Source 2). Each of its panels celebrated a key moment from his father's reign. The centre panel, which was designed to be seen by guests entering the throne room, showed James I being raised up to Heaven to sit at God's side after his death.

Source 2 tells us a lot more about Charles than it does about James. He completely believed his father's ideas about kings being divine. Charles believed his coronation oath was sacred – an oath made before God. He swore to uphold the laws of the kingdom and in return Charles expected total loyalty from his subjects. Some historians and art experts believe that Charles felt the painting in Source 2 was an ALLEGORY of his own birth as a divine king.

Social hierarchy in England

Charles was not alone in believing that there was a divinely established hierarchy. At the time, many people also felt that there was a strict social order, as outlined in the diagram below.

Source 1 An extract from the *Basilikon Doron*, a book written by James I for his son Prince Henry in 1598, telling him how to be a king. It was republished for the 16-year-old Charles in 1616.

The state of monarchy is the supremest thing upon earth, for kings are not only God's lieutenants upon earth and sit upon God's throne, but even by God himself they are called gods. ... In the Scriptures kings are called gods, and so their power after a certain relation compared to the Divine power. Kings are also compared to fathers of families; for a king is truly parent of the country, the political father of his people.

The king

The nobility
(old families with titles)

The gentry
(land-owning families)

The middling sort
(merchants and skilled producers)

The people
(largely agricultural workers, farm labourers, unskilled workers)

PROFILE

Charles I (1600–49)

- Charles's father James was James VI of Scotland, who also became James I of England.
- Charles was born in Scotland in 1600. He became king in 1625.
- He adored his athletic older brother, Henry, but Henry did little to return his affection.
- Henry died in 1612, making 12-year-old Charles heir to the throne.
- Charles had a Scottish accent. He spoke slowly in an attempt to overcome a stammer. As a result, he often avoided making long speeches in public.
- Charles was studious and hard-working. He also valued order and beauty. He and his wife spent extravagantly on paintings, clothing and other luxuries.
- Like his father, Charles believed in the 'Divine Right of Kings' – the idea that God had created an ordered society in which everyone should know their place. The king was at the top of this hierarchy. Charles did not feel he needed to explain his actions, and regarded criticism as an insult to his dignity and authority. He was stubborn and would rarely change his mind once he had made a decision.
- He took his role as king seriously. For Charles, kingship was a religious as well as a political duty.
- He was utterly loyal to his friends. On a number of occasions he even dissolved parliament to prevent his adviser, the Duke of Buckingham, being arrested.
- Charles was a Protestant, but in 1625 he married a Catholic, Henrietta Maria of France.

1 Find the following in Source 2:
  a James carried on the wings of a huge eagle
  b God seated on his throne
  c Piety and Religion accompanying him
  d the triumphal crown, carried by the goddess Minerva and a woman representing Victory.
2 What is the message of Source 2?

Few ordinary people questioned the right of the gentry and nobility to rule over them as landlords and employers. Church services reinforced this social hierarchy, with the local gentry sitting in pews towards the front of the church, or in galleries above the rest of the congregation. People depended on their social superiors for work and help in times of need, and they treated them with loyalty and respect.

Source 2 *The Apotheosis of James I* by Peter Paul Rubens. This painting was installed by Charles I in the Banqueting House, Whitehall, in 1636. 'Apotheosis' means someone being made into a god. ▼

Source 3 Historian Barry Coward, writing in 1997 about Charles I's father, James I.

One of James' greatest qualities was his ability to recognise what was politically possible and what was not. He realised that his dream to unite England and Scotland was not acceptable so he dropped it and remained king of England and king of Scotland separately. His religious policies show the same politically astute mix of idealism and realism. He was often the peacemaker between different religious factions. He learned that it was important for his court to be open to a wide variety of different people and opinions. Under James the court and parliament remained an important point of contact between the king and his most important subjects. As a result, before 1625 political tensions never really erupted into crises in the way that they did soon after his son took the throne.

How did parliament think England should be governed?

Parliament also had definite views about how England should be governed. After Magna Carta in 1215, it was generally accepted that monarchs had to obey the law just like everyone else. This contrasted with most other countries, particularly France, which was an ABSOLUTIST MONARCHY.

In practice, the rule of law meant that the monarch had to respect certain rights. For example, they could not simply arrest and imprison someone – people accused of a crime had to be given a fair trial. Monarchs also had to have parliament's approval to raise taxes. This was particularly important in times of war, because maintaining an army and navy was expensive. The king or queen was also required to call parliament regularly in order to listen to the concerns of the POLITICAL NATION.

Above all, the monarch and parliament had to show a certain amount of compromise. On the whole, members of parliament (MPs) were prepared to give the king the taxes and other measures he wanted if they felt he was listening to their concerns. James I had managed this relationship with parliament carefully and had compromised when necessary. Unfortunately, Charles proved to be less astute.

1   What lessons could Charles I have learnt from his father about avoiding crises?

FACTFILE

The roles of king and parliament in Stuart Britain

King	Parliament
The king's court helped him govern.	Parliament was made up of two houses.
The king chose his own advisers and ministers (usually from the nobility).	MPs in the **HOUSE OF COMMONS** (around 500 members) represented the views of land-owning people (the gentry) and wealthy merchants in the towns.
Some of these advisers were also members of parliament, but they did not have to be.	The **HOUSE OF LORDS** (around 90 members) represented those who held noble title (lords, dukes, bishops, etc.).
	New Acts of Parliament needed to be passed by both houses before receiving **ROYAL ASSENT** and becoming law.

Royal Prerogatives	Parliamentary Privileges
The king had the power to make decisions on:	Parliament had the right to:
· foreign policy (including war, peace, alliances and royal marriages)	· grant subsidies (taxes) to the king
· the army and navy (the king was commander-in-chief)	· discuss issues that affected the commonwealth (the common good) of the nation (this included things such as taxation, Poor Law, highways and crime)
· religion (the king was the supreme governor of the Church of England).	· free speech – while parliament was sitting it had freedom of speech and immunity from arrest
He could call and dissolve parliament whenever he wished.	· present petitions and **REMONSTRANCES** to the king in order to explain their views or concerns
He could raise **ORDINARY REVENUE** (money from customs duties, Crown lands and fines) without parliament's consent.	· **IMPEACH** royal advisers – accuse people of wrongdoing so they would face trial in parliament not in a regular court.
In emergencies, the king could collect **SHIP MONEY** from coastal counties to help pay for defence.	
He appointed members of **PREROGATIVE COURTS** (e.g. members of the Court of Star Chamber).	

Source 4 A portrait of Charles I, representing the fact that he was king of England, Ireland and Scotland. ▼

2 Look at Source 4 and its caption. Do you think we should have added the word 'separately' at the end after the word Scotland? Explain your answer.

Other key players

England, Ireland, Scotland

Charles ruled over three kingdoms – England, Scotland and Ireland – and the people of these kingdoms had no wish to be united. Events in one kingdom could affect the others.

The Political Nation

The nobility made up a tiny minority of the population but, apart from the king, this small group owned the land and held all the political power. The really important nobles owned huge estates and had enormous wealth. They sat in the House of Lords in parliament. The gentry were also wealthy, but not quite in the same league as the noble aristocracy. They had estates and were responsible for the people who worked on them. The gentry were the local justices of the peace, and they commanded the local militia in times of war. They would usually pay a lot towards the upkeep of the local church and have a strong say (along with the local bishop) in the appointment of the local priest. They elected the MP to represent their local area, and of course they chose one of their own. Local power and influence was very important to members of the gentry. In the towns, the leading merchants, lawyers and other successful men held a similar status to the gentry. If they owned enough property, this included electing and serving as MPs. Monarchs relied on this group of people to keep order, maintain the law, raise troops in time of war and collect taxes approved by parliament in their local area. This is why they are sometimes referred to as the 'Political Nation' – the section of the nation that has power and influence. They were generally proud of this position and responsibility.

Religion and the Church

The Church of England was organised in a clear structure (see diagram left). The vast majority of the population belonged to the Church of England. There were some Catholics, who were generally regarded with suspicion. During the reigns of Elizabeth I and James I, events such as the Gunpowder Plot had led to Catholics being feared, and people regarded the pope (the head of the Catholic Church) as the Antichrist – the servant of the Devil.

Then there were the Puritans. They were generally from the lower ranks of the gentry. Most of them were to be found in the south and east of England. Puritans were Protestants. Technically they belonged to the Church of England. However, they felt that it needed reforming. They disliked being under the authority of bishops. They felt that local communities should run their church. They liked sermons, because these taught what the Bible meant, which helped people with reading it. They disliked sacramental forms of worship and believed that churches should be plain, with no paintings, statues or stained glass. They were a minority, but they were generally well educated and highly committed to their beliefs.

The Monarch
Supreme Govenor of the Church appointed...

2 **archbishops** and 25 **bishops**, who made sure that...

the 9,000+ **parish priests** preached official church services to...

the people

Charles I's early reign 1625–29: the making of a tyrant?

Source 5 An extract from the diary of William Laud, describing an early meeting with Charles the year before he became king, 1624. Charles later made Laud Archbishop of Canterbury – the most important post in the Church of England.

Sunday [1 February 1624] I stood by the most illustrious Prince Charles at dinner. He was then very merry. … Among other things he said that if he had to take any particular profession of life, he could not be a lawyer; adding his reasons. 'I cannot' saith he, 'defend a bad, nor yield in a good cause.'

Source 6 Charles I on his throne in the House of Lords. The Lords take their seats while the MPs from the House of Commons assemble at the doorway in the foreground to listen to the king's speech. ▼

1 Look back at the profile of Charles on page 155. He clearly valued order and the idea of people knowing their place. How does Source 6 show this?

Within three years of becoming king, Charles had proved how badly he lacked the tact and political skills of his father. To begin with, he wanted to raise the wealth and status of the Church, so he tried to take back all the Church land that had been given to nobles in Scotland since 1540. The Scottish nobles were appalled, and open rebellion almost broke out before Charles backed down.

Charles was not a Catholic, but he was soon accused of having Catholic sympathies. His wife was Catholic and he seemed to favour Catholic-style religious ceremonies and decoration in churches. He suspended the RECUSANCY laws, which fined people for not attending Protestant services. He allowed bishops to use their powers more fully. After decades of anti-Catholic propaganda, Charles's pro-Catholic views were alarming, especially to hard-line Protestants like the Puritans.

Charles went to war with Spain in 1625. Although a popular move to begin with, as the war began to go badly MPs started to disagree not only with the cost but also with the way the war was run by Charles's closest adviser, the Duke of Buckingham.

All these concerns resulted in criticism from MPs – and Charles could not stand criticism. When MPs threatened to put Buckingham on trial in 1626, Charles simply dissolved parliament. The following year, the king found himself in need of money, but instead of calling parliament to approve a tax, he tried to raise money through a forced loan (in reality a tax not a loan). There was widespread discontent at this action and some MPs, landowners and even lords refused to pay. In one court case, five such 'refusers' (who became known as the 'Five Knights') were held in prison without trial.

Even with the forced loan, Charles was still short of money, and in 1628 he was forced to reconvene parliament. The case of the Five Knights had angered MPs, and the Lords – who usually sided with the king – and the Commons joined together to force Charles to agree to the Petition of Right. This meant that the king could not take any steps to raise money without parliament's approval. The Petition of Right did not really heal the divisions, however, and Charles dissolved parliament again in March 1629.

---

2 Create a list of all the problems that arose in the early years of Charles's reign.

ACTIVITY

Work in pairs. One of you is Charles I, the other is the ghost of his father James I, who has visited him one dark night. How do you think the conversation would go? Would James approve of Charles? Would he warn him of the dangers of exerting his authority like this? How might Charles react? Make sure you can bring real historical examples into this conversation so that it is more than just an imaginative exercise.

PRACTICE QUESTIONS

1 Explain why Charles I sometimes clashed with parliament in the period 1625–29. (10)
2 'Charles I was well suited to the challenge of ruling England.' How far do the sources in this section convince you that this statement is correct? (20)

TOPIC SUMMARY

What kind of king was Charles I?

1 Charles shared his father's belief that he was divinely appointed and ruled on behalf of God. In fact, he was even more committed to this idea than James had been, and would not accept anyone contradicting his decisions.
2 Charles was studious and hard-working. He paid close attention to detail and took his role as king seriously. This attitude was reinforced by his strong religious beliefs.
3 Parliament believed that England's ancient constitution balanced the power of the monarch with the rights of the people. One important aspect of this was the rule of law – the idea that the king should uphold the law and rule according to it. He should also call regular parliaments.
4 The king's powers (Royal Prerogatives) included foreign policy, the armed forces, religion and raising small amounts of money.
5 Parliament's rights (Parliamentary Privileges) included approving taxes, freedom of speech, petitions to the king and impeachment of wrongdoers.
6 Charles clashed with parliament from the start, particularly over his adviser Buckingham, who parliament thought was incompetent. They also disagreed over Charles's method of raising taxes without parliament's agreement, and his mistreatment of some MPs.
7 Parliament presented its Petition of Right in 1628, which Charles agreed to, but a year later he dissolved parliament again.

4.2

The period of Personal Rule 1629–40

FOCUS

The period 1629–40 is known as the 'Personal Rule' because, for 11 years, Charles I ruled without parliament. That was not unprecedented – earlier monarchs had ruled for long periods without parliament – but Charles's Personal Rule led to deep and bitter divisions. In this topic you will examine why this was the case.

The impact of Charles I's Personal Rule

The period of Personal Rule poisoned relations between the king and a large section of the people he ruled, represented by parliament. He only recalled parliament in 1640 because he had no other choice, but even then he expected MPs to simply give him what he wanted. However, instead he faced a barrage of grievances. The main reasons for these are outlined below.

Hostility towards the 'evil advisers'

To understand what the MPs were complaining about, it is necessary to look at the actions of Charles's three closest advisers during the Personal Rule:

- Richard Weston, the Lord Treasurer, who found ways of raising money that did not require parliamentary approval.
- Thomas Wentworth, whom Charles appointed to run the COUNCIL OF THE NORTH in York. In 1632, he was promoted to the position Lord Deputy of Ireland.
- William Laud, Archbishop of Canterbury.

The actions of these advisers, and the fact that the king listened only to a narrow range of advice, angered MPs, who felt they were being excluded from the decision-making process. It is also important to consider the role played by Charles I's wife, Queen Henrietta Maria. Charles and Henrietta Maria were devoted to each other, and many MPs felt that the Catholic queen had too much influence on the king.

At first, grievances were aimed at Charles's advisers rather than the king himself. This was partly out of respect for the king and partly out of fear – it was not a good idea to criticise the king directly. Parliament refused to grant him any taxes until their concerns had been addressed. In parliament's view, Charles had been misled by 'evil advisers' and MPs hoped he would soon right the wrongs. Charles, however, did not see it this way. He believed that these complaints were a personal attack on him and his royal authority.

Concerns about 'the liberties of freeborn Englishmen'

To fully understand why the actions of these advisers caused trouble during the 1630s, it is necessary to understand the values and beliefs that Englishmen held in this period.

Protecting the Protestant Church of England

For thirty years, England had been torn apart by the differences between Catholics and Protestants. The ELIZABETHAN SETTLEMENT of 1559 brought this turmoil to an end and made England officially a Protestant country. Catholics were fined if they did not go to Church of England services and they were regarded with deep suspicion as possible spies or agents of the great Catholic powers, France and Spain.

Defending the rule of law

Englishmen were proud of their legal system. Unlike other European countries, the COMMON LAW in England meant that people were guaranteed a fair trial before a judge and jury. They could not be imprisoned or held without a trial. Kings of England swore to uphold the law in their coronation oath and were bound by the law.

Local power and accountability

The Political Nation was mostly made up of the landowners, ranging from the great aristocrats to local gentry. They elected and served as MPs. They were also local justices. They led local militia forces in times of war. These people were proud of their power and influence, and the role they played in maintaining peace and order in the kingdom. They resented it when the king and his officials attempted to bypass them.

Not being taxed without parliament's agreement

In England, most taxes that a king raised had to be agreed by parliament first. If a king raised a tax without first consulting parliament, then he would be accused of breaking his coronation oath. People would suspect him of trying to rule as an absolute monarch – a term used to describe a king who did not rule with the consent of or for the good of his people.

ACTIVITY

Study the 'liberties of freeborn Englishman' above. In pairs, devise three measures that you think would upset people who held these values. Then read on and see if you were close.

Sir Richard Weston, Lord Treasurer

As Lord Treasurer, Weston was responsible for raising money so the kingdom could be run effectively. In normal circumstances he would have called on MPs to grant the king the right to raise taxes. However, since parliament had been dissolved in 1629 he was forced to be more inventive with his tax-raising methods. He fell back on old ways of taxing people that did not need parliament's consent.

Ship Money

This was a one-off tax that the king could levy in emergencies. It was traditionally paid by people living in coastal towns and was intended to help pay for the navy. Charles first raised this in 1634. In 1635, he levied it again, but this time extended it to inland counties. In 1636, he repeated the tax again and it was clear that this was going to become an annual tax. On average it raised £170,000 per year.

Sale of monopolies

Weston sold monopolies to merchants or companies, and this gave them the exclusive right to import and sell particular items (such as soap or wine). This usually meant that prices rose, because no other merchant could sell that item. Elizabeth I and James had restricted monopolies, but Weston restarted them. They were extremely valuable – for example, the monopoly on soap alone brought in around £30,000 a year.

THE KING'S FINANCES

£

Distraint of Knighthood

This was a fine for gentlemen who owned £40 worth of property but who had not presented themselves at the king's coronation to receive a knighthood. This fine raised up to £174,000 per year.

Tonnage and Poundage

This was a tax on goods that were imported or exported. Parliament normally granted the king the right to raise this for life. However, in 1625 parliament only granted it to Charles I for a year. The king felt this was an insult and a break from tradition, so he raised it whenever he wanted to anyway. It brought him a massive £270,000 per year.

Forced loans

These were not really loans at all, but rather a tax on wealthy property owners or merchants. These people were required to pay a contribution to the forced loan or face an even greater fine, or even imprisonment. Forced loans could raise the king £200,000 per year.

Forest Fines

This was an ancient fine that the king could impose on people who lived or worked within the boundaries of the old royal forests. Over the centuries, many of these forests had shrunk and people had started to farm the land or build homes on it. They were, however, still inside the boundaries of the old royal forest and so were liable to pay the fine. It was highly unpopular with landowners, but raised an extra £39,000 per year for the king.

The problem of Weston's taxes

Although it was perfectly legal for Charles to raise these taxes, one of the problems was that many of the methods had fallen into disuse because society had changed. For example, the Distraint of Knighthood was based on a custom from the thirteenth century, and people saw such measures as a cynical way to get money.

Another problem was the ruthless efficiency with which Weston gathered these taxes. It soon felt as though the burden placed on the people was much more than they were used to. Most importantly, none of these measures had been agreed by parliament. Many people believed that the king was taking his personal powers too far. They feared that if the king could successfully raise money without a parliament, then he would have no reason to call a parliament ever again. There would no longer be a balance against the absolute power of the monarchy.

The John Hampden Case 1637

The most famous challenge to the king's financial policies was that of John Hampden in 1637. Hampden, from Buckinghamshire, was tried by the COURT OF EXCHEQUER for refusing to pay Ship Money. Despite the fact that the judges were all appointed by the king, they were split seven to five in Charles's favour.

1 Do you think the king was really concerned about his subjects playing with poor-quality cards and dice? If not, what do you think his real concerns were?

2 Explain why Source 1 is useful as evidence of the ways Charles tried to raise money during the period of Personal Rule.

3 Read Source 2. Do you think Richard Strode's main concern was his cow? Explain your answer.

Source 1 A proclamation by Charles I about playing cards and dice, 1638.

By the King.

An announcement about the making of playing cards and dice.

To prevent the common abuses caused by the use of false cards and dice, deceiving and damaging his subjects, His Majesty has appointed an officer for finding and giving the seal of approval to all cards and dice made in this realm. All makers of cards and dice within the realm, and merchants or others who import them from foreign parts, should now bring these cards and dice to His Majesty's officer to be viewed, examined and given the seal of approval if they are good and saleable. For this seal they will pay His Majesty's officer or his deputies the fees set out in His Majesty's official document.

Source 2 A legal complaint made by Sir Richard Strode about Ship Money, August 1639. Strode was a Puritan and a critic of Charles I. A constable was a local official who collected taxes and generally enforced the law.

Laws were passed in the reign of Edward I that no tax shall be taken by the king or his heirs without the good will and agreement of the Lords and Commons. In the reign of Edward III another law said that no one shall be forced to make any loans to the king against his will. Yet contrary to these laws and freedoms, one cow worth £4 10 shillings, belonging to Sir Richard Strode of Plimton St Mary in the county of Kent was taken by Constable Thomas Row and sold for the king's service on 23rd March at Newingham to raise money for shipping, without the consent of parliament.

Source 3 An extract from a book by Sir George Croke about the 'Ship Money Trial' in 1637. Croke was one of five judges who ruled in favour of John Hampden in the trial. The book was based on notes taken at the time.

We are not here to give judgements which support what the king wants as his policy. We are judging according to the law of England. We find it in our books, records and statutes. The law respects the property, goods and estates of the king's subjects. Without their consent (either their private actual consent or implicitly by agreeing to taxes in parliament) their property cannot be taken from them by the king or anyone else.

Hampden may have been defeated, but his case revealed that many people opposed Charles raising finance without parliament's consent. Many people claimed that Hampden had won a moral victory. One judge even supported Hampden and claimed that 'the people of England are subjects, not slaves … [they] are not to be taxed … at will, but according to the laws of this kingdom'. Charles's methods of raising money were clearly proving divisive.

FOCUS TASK

Why were Richard Weston's financial methods unpopular?

Use the following table to help you analyse Richard Weston's financial measures using the text and sources here and on the previous page.

Method of raising finance	How much did it raise?	Who opposed it?	Why was it unpopular? (Refer to concerns about liberties on page 161)
Ship Money	£170,000	local gentry in many areas (e.g. Richard Strode, John Hampden)	not agreed by parliament

Sir Thomas Wentworth (later Earl of Strafford)

President of the Council of the North

Sir Thomas Wentworth had been an MP in the early parliaments of Charles I's reign. He had regularly criticised the king's ministers, especially the Duke of Buckingham, and had been a leading critic of the Crown. In 1627, he had even refused to pay a forced loan (see page 162).

However, in 1628 Wentworth seemed to change sides. He was appointed president of the Council of the North and in this role he showed himself to be a powerful enforcer of order, efficiency and the king's will. He sacked many local officials he regarded as incompetent. In 1631, the new *Book of Orders* gave Wentworth the power to make local officials send regular reports to the king's government in London. There had never been this kind of centralised control over local officials before, and they deeply resented it. It became known as the POLICY OF THOROUGH.

Lord Deputy of Ireland

Wentworth did such a good job whipping the North into line that in 1632 Charles promoted him to Lord Deputy of Ireland. For decades, Ireland had been a problem for English kings. There were deep divisions between the Catholic Irish and Protestant settlers in the region. There were regular rebellions, law and order was hard to impose, and it was a drain on English finances. Wentworth acted with ruthless efficiency. He essentially bypassed the law and acted as ruler of Ireland, enforcing his actions with his own army. He even managed to persuade the Irish parliament to pay taxes to Charles.

Of all of Charles's ministers, Wentworth was considered the most dangerous by the king's opponents. His energy, his ability and his loyalty to Charles made him a powerful ally and a dangerous enemy. It is not surprising that when his opponents got their chance in 1640, they did all they could to bring him down (see page 173).

1 Look back at the concerns about liberties on page 161. How do you think the Policy of Thorough was viewed?

2 Is the author of Source 4 an admirer of Wentworth or a critic? Explain your answer.

3 Why might Wentworth's actions in Ireland create mixed feelings back in England?

Source 4 An extract from a letter to a friend written by Sir Thomas Roe, a diplomat who served Charles I.

The Lord Deputy of Ireland does great wonders, and governs like a king. He has taught that kingdom to behave so well that they have given the king six subsidies [the right to collect six taxes] ... he is a ruthless judge and a strong enemy; a servant violently zealous in his master's ends ... he will either be the greatest man in England or the least.

FOCUS TASK

Why did Thomas Wentworth's actions cause concern?

Complete a table like the one below to summarise Wentworth's actions and the reasons they were unpopular.

Role	Main actions	Cause of concern because...
President of the Council of the North		
Lord Deputy of Ireland		

William Laud, Archbishop of Canterbury

In 1633, Charles made William Laud the Archbishop of Canterbury. Laud believed that the English Church was beginning to collapse. The Elizabethan Settlement had prevented religious arguments by giving people a degree of freedom in the way they conducted their church services, but by the 1630s Laud had come to believe that this had resulted in divisions in the Church of England. Above all, it meant that the king (who was the supreme governor of the Church of England) was losing control of what was going on in his own Church.

The Puritans worried Laud most. These extreme Protestants hated ceremony and any decoration in their churches. They preferred their worship to be 'pure', in churches with whitewashed walls and simple services. Puritans placed great emphasis on the Bible, so preaching sermons and lessons from the Bible formed the most important part of their services. Puritans allowed anyone to preach – not just the priest. Laud disliked this, as it stopped him controlling what was going on in churches all over the country. He also felt that the Puritans were not showing the churches sufficient respect, particularly when they moved the ALTAR to the centre of the church building (there are even examples of altars being used as a place to put people's hats during services). Worst of all – in Laud's eyes – Puritans believed that they could, through prayer and Bible study, speak directly to God. This meant they had no need of priests or churches. Laud was convinced that the Puritans were corrupting the Church of England and undermining the king's control.

> 4 Look at Source 5. Explain why this source is useful to a historian studying Laud's reforms.
>
> 5 Why would the altar in Source 5 anger Puritans?

Source 5 A modern photograph of four-sided Laudian altar rail. The walls behind the altar would probably have been plastered and painted at the time. ▼

FACTFILE

Laud's religious reforms

Laud introduced a wide range of reforms, including:

- moving the altar to the east end of a church
- the erection of altar rails to keep the congregation (and their dogs) away from the holiest part of the church; only priests were allowed behind it
- priests were the only people allowed to preach a sermon
- all priests had conduct their services according to the Book of Common Prayer; this prevented Puritans from simply preaching what they thought was important
- more elaborate decoration and ceremony in church services, such as bowing at the name of Christ and making the sign of the cross during baptisms
- reissuing the *Book of Sports*, which gave a list of sporting activities that people could do after they left church on a Sunday; this angered the Puritans, who believed that the whole day should be spent reading the Bible and praying
- scholarships at the universities of Oxford and Cambridge for training Arminian priests.

1 Source 6 is from William Laud's own diary, so it will be biased. But does that mean it has no value? How might historians find this source useful and/or reliable as evidence about this period? Make sure you can explain your answer.

Laud's religious reforms

Laud was keen to reform areas such as training for priests. He was also influenced by the ideas of the Arminian movement about faith and salvation, and ways in which people could come closer to God. His reforms were sometimes called Arminian reforms, but in practice they involved more than ideas and religious debate (see Factfile).

He initiated a series of reforms to combat the Puritans' changes. They were strictly enforced on local churches, many of which had developed their own forms of church service. Laud appointed other Arminians as bishops. They carried out 'visitations' to inspect the churches in their areas and ensure that the reforms were being enforced. Charles I – who believed in the 'beauty of religion' and liked order and ceremony – wholeheartedly backed Laud's actions. When people criticised these reforms, they were accused of breaking England's strict censorship laws, which forbade criticism of the Church or the king. Offenders faced the risk of being betrayed by informers and enduring savage punishments.

Source 6 Extracts from the diary of Archbishop Laud in 1637. ▼

Junii 14. This day, Jo. Bastwick, Dr. of Physic; Hen. Burton, Batch. of Divinity; and Wi. Prynne, Barrister at Law, were censured for their libels against the Hierarchy of the Church, &c.[s]

Junii 26[t]. The speech I then spake in the Star Chamber, was commanded by the King to be printed. And it came out Junii the 25.

Junii 26. This day, Monday, the Prince Elector, and his brother Prince Rupert, began their journey toward the sea-side, to return for Holland.

Junii 30. Friday, The above-named three libellers lost their ears.

Julii 7. Friday, A note was brought to me of a short libel pasted on the cross in Cheapside : That the Arch-Wolf of Cant. had his hand in persecuting the saints and shedding the blood of the martyrs. Memento for the last of June[1].

The trial and punishment of Burton, Bastwick and Prynne 1637

In 1637, three leading Puritans, Henry Burton, John Bastwick and William Prynne, were arrested for publishing pamphlets that criticised Laud's religious reforms. They were tried before the Court of Star Chamber, which was made up of judges appointed directly by the king. The three men were imprisoned, fined £5000 each and had their ears 'clipped' (cut off).

Source 7 A Puritan pamphlet criticising Laud's reforms. The priest on the right wears the elaborate gowns brought in by Laud and his bishops, and bears a resemblance to Laud himself. ▼

Source 8 A Puritan cartoon showing Laud having Prynne's ears served up on his table. The two bishops on the right-hand side are shown carrying muskets. ▼

2 What do you think Sources 7 and 8 are trying to say about Laud?

3 Explain why these sources are useful to historians as evidence about Puritans.

Reactions to Charles I's and Laud's religious policies

It is important to remember that a large proportion of the population either did not feel strongly about the reforms or simply followed them because they had always done what the Church told them. It is difficult to be sure what other people thought, because those who did not strongly oppose reform did not produce pamphlets or similar materials to share their ideas. However, from diaries and letters historians have concluded that many people, particularly among the gentry, did approve of Laud's reforms. Many of them shared his dislike of the Puritans. They also felt that the reforms strengthened the authority of the Church, which in turn strengthened their own authority and helped them keep good order.

However, in some sections of society there was great unease over Laud's reforms. Many of the measures seemed intended to return England to Catholicism. In fact, this was not the king's intention – Charles was a devout Protestant and Laud actually turned down an offer from the pope to join the Catholic Church and become a cardinal. Their biggest mistake may have been refusing to explain their actions or answer any concerns in this regard. They simply demanded obedience. As the Personal Rule continued, the queen became a focus for leading English Catholics (including Sir Richard Weston), who accompanied her at court and publicly attended her chapel on Sundays. This created great unease among the Protestant majority.

FOCUS TASK

Why did Laud's reforms face opposition?

Complete a table like the one below to summarise Laud's actions and the reasons they were unpopular.

Policy	Main actions	Cause of concern because...
church decoration		
Prayer Book and services		
preaching		
censorship		
scholarship and training		

The Scottish crisis and the end of the Personal Rule

By 1637, discontent with Charles's Personal Rule was simmering but there was no end in sight. Without parliament in session, there was no way for people to express their concerns, complaints and grievances. This frustration led some Puritans to emigrate to America to start a new, godly life in the New World. Within three years, however, parliament had been reconvened and grievances against Charles's advisers were pouring forth. So what changed, and what led Charles to recall an angry and hostile parliament?

The answer lies in Scotland. Charles was keen to bring unity to his kingdoms, but this was easier said than done, particularly as Scotland had a separate Church (or Kirk) to England (see Factfile opposite).

In 1637, Charles decided that the spirit of Laud's religious reforms needed to be spread to Scotland. However, when Charles introduced his new BOOK OF COMMON PRAYER, riots broke out (see Source 9).

Source 9 An engraving produced in 1642 showing rioting in Edinburgh Cathedral, 1637. It was created by Wenceslaus Hollar, a Czech artist living in England at the time. Hollar fought on the Royalist side in the Civil Wars. ▼

> 1 Look at Source 9. Do you think the artist's intention was to criticise the rioters, support them or simply record events? Explain your thinking. (Note: we do not know the answer to this question but Source 10 might help you formulate your own view.)

Source 10 The text of the Scottish National Covenant of 1638. The document was made in 1643, when parliament also accepted and promised to uphold the Covenant. The top two sections set out why, in the view of those who support the Covenant, the kingdom is in a terrible state. Section I then attacks the Laudian reforms of the Church. Section II urges all people to completely reject anything to do with the Catholic Church. Section III asserts the rights of parliament and criticises the attacks on personal rights and liberties that have been happening. Section IV promises to root out opponents of the Covenant (which means supporters of Charles I). Section V promises that there will be peace and harmony between the kingdoms of England, Scotland and Ireland. Section VI sets out a promise that all supporters of the Covenant will stick together and not betray their comrades. ▶

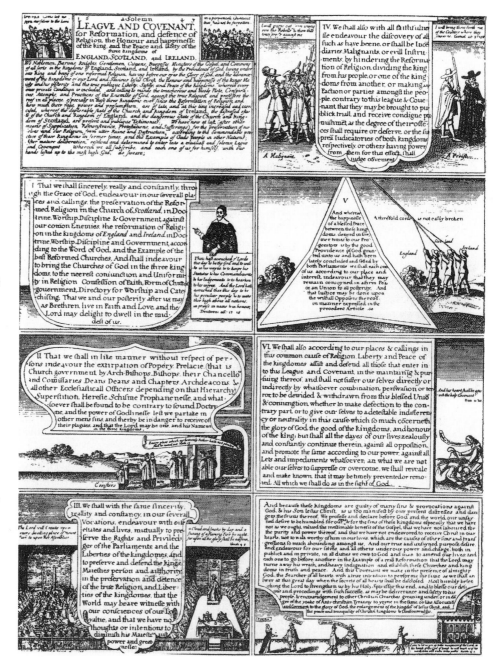

The National Covenant

Afterwards, Scottish Presbyterians who opposed the reforms sat in a General Assembly, without the king's permission, and drew up what became known as the National Covenant. The Covenant effectively rejected the authority of Charles and the bishops in Scotland, and accused the king and Laud of trying to introduce 'papistry', or Catholicism. Charles responded furiously to the defiance of the Scots. He raised an army of English militia (part-time soldiers) to fight them, triggering what became known as the First Bishops' War (1639). Charles was confident that the Covenanters would flee in the face of his army. He also believed that the majority of Scots would rise up in support of him. He soon discovered his mistake. After the two sides met near Kelso, the king was forced to retreat. He agreed to withdraw the Book of Common Prayer and abolish bishops in Scotland.

The Short Parliament

In September 1639, Charles recalled Wentworth from Ireland to help him deal with the Scots, giving him the title Earl of Strafford. Strafford advised the king to call a parliament, in the hope that anti-Scottish feeling would lead MPs to grant the king funds for an army. Parliament first met in April 1640, but refused to grant Charles the funds he needed to raise a fresh army unless he first dealt with their grievances. Charles dissolved parliament almost immediately, so this session came to be known as the Short Parliament.

1. According to Source 11, who was more responsible for the tensions between king and parliament in the Short Parliament?
2. Explain why Source 11 is useful as evidence about the tensions at this time.

> **Source 11 A letter from the Duke of Northumberland, a member of Charles I's Privy Council, to his friend Viscount Conway in May 1640. He was writing about the Short Parliament.**
>
> *The king yesterday offered to give up Ship Money if the House of Commons would supply him with 12 subsidies [grants of money]. They were not happy with this. They also protested a lot about changes in religion. They brought up other complaints, but these were the main ones they complained of. And had they been well advised, I think they might in time have got what they wanted. But they went on with their business in a noisy and confused way, which offended His Majesty so much that this morning he ended the parliament.*

Charles was still facing a crisis, however. In the Second Bishops' War, the Scots invaded England and captured Newcastle. Charles was so desperate for money he had to recall parliament once again.

> **Source 12 The MP Edward Hyde writing about the dissolution of the Short Parliament in 1640. Hyde remained loyal to Charles I in the Civil War and later served Charles II in government and was given the title Lord Clarendon. He was writing in the 1670s.**
>
> *Nothing could have more depressed the spirits of the nation than the dissolution of the Short Parliament. All members of parliament feared there would be great misery. They lost hope that they would ever be able to meet again and they could not understand how they had offended His Majesty. In such time of confusion only the wise men of parliament could have found a remedy. They feared matters would now become worse before they could ever get better.*

The Long Parliament meets

On 3 November 1640, the Long Parliament assembled in London. Many MPs felt that they would finally have a chance to air their grievances. Speech after speech from MPs attacked the policies imposed by Weston, Wentworth and Laud during the Personal Rule. All MPs hoped that the king would listen and reverse the abuses that his 'evil advisers' had forced on the nation. The word on everyone's lips was 'reconciliation' – but would the two sides be able to achieve it?

> **FOCUS TASK**
>
> ### Why was the Long Parliament so hostile to Charles I in 1640?
>
> It is now time to draw some conclusions.
>
> Look back over the three Focus Tasks in this topic and summarise the key points in a table like the one below.
>
> | How did the king's financial measures cause problems? | How did Wentworth's actions cause problems? | How did Laud's religious reforms cause problems? | How were Charles's opponents responsible for any problems? |
> |---|---|---|---|
> | | | | |

ACTIVITY

The events you have studied are very important, and are hotly debated by historians. Join the debate by discussing or writing an answer to one of the following questions.

1 Evidence shows that English Puritan MPs were in touch with the Scottish Covenanters during the Bishops' Wars. They urged the Scots to keep applying military pressure on Charles. Why do you think they did this, and risked being accused of treason if found out?

2 The historian John Morrill has described the mood in England during the Personal Rule as being like a 'coiled spring'.
   a What evidence is there to support this idea?
   b What effect did the Scottish crisis have on this 'coiled spring'?

3 Traditionally, historians have talked of the English Civil War beginning in 1642. More recently, historians have begun to speak of the 'British Civil Wars' beginning in 1639. Based on what you have learnt in this chapter, why do you think this shift has taken place?

PRACTICE QUESTIONS

1 Explain why the Long Parliament was so critical of Charles I. (10)
2 'Opposition to Charles's religious reforms was the biggest concern by 1640.' How far do the sources in this topic convince you that this statement is correct? (20)

TOPIC SUMMARY

The period of Personal Rule 1629–40

1 From 1629 to 1640 Charles ruled without parliament. Other monarchs had done this in the past, but in this case personal rule led to bitter divisions between the king and MPs.

2 MPs believed their role was to keep England Protestant, to approve taxes, and to exercise local power and influence as intermediary between king and people. They were alarmed by Charles's so called 'evil advisers', who seemed to ignore these 'Liberties of Freeborn Englishmen'.

3 To avoid having to ask parliament to approve taxes, the Lord Treasurer, Richard Weston, revived many old taxes such as Ship Money and Forest Fines. This was legal, but many felt he went too far and that not consulting parliament set a dangerous precedent.

4 John Hampden challenged the king's right to raise Ship Money and was taken to court. He lost, but his high-profile trial highlighted how people mistrusted the king.

5 Sir Thomas Wentworth had been a critic of the king, but when Charles gave him a major role running the North of England then subduing Ireland, he became the king's most loyal and effective minister. He removed local officials and ruled efficiently but ruthlessly. He earned himself many enemies.

6 William Laud, Archbishop of Canterbury, tried to make the English Church more Catholic. He reversed changes made under the Tudors (e.g. the altar was moved back to the east end of a church; only priests were allowed to preach). Opponents of these reforms were punished (e.g. Puritans Burton, Bastwick and Prynne had their ears cut off in 1637 for criticising them).

7 In 1639, Charles tried to extend Laud's reforms to Scotland. When the Scots refused he sent an army to enforce them. He was so out of touch he thought the Scots would give in, but instead they fought back and he had to withdraw his reforms.

8 Charles faced a large bill for this war, so he recalled parliament to ask MPs to approve taxes to pay for it. Instead, they issued a long list of grievances.

4.3 Events leading to civil war

FOCUS

When considering the period 1640–42 it is important to remember that we have the benefit of hindsight. Because we know that the Civil War happened, it is tempting to think that it was inevitable. But in 1640, nobody was expecting war, and even in 1642 most people wanted to avoid it. So why did it happen? This topic explores the series of disastrous events that took place between November 1640 and January 1642, when parliament and the nation divided and two sides emerged.

The opening of the Long Parliament – hopes of reconciliation, November 1640

PROFILE

John Pym (1584–1643)

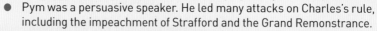

- Pym was a Somerset MP.
- He had served in the parliaments of the 1620s and had criticised the growing power of the king.
- Pym was a leading member of the increasing number of Puritans in both the Commons and House of Lords. They became known as 'Pym's Junto', and Pym himself as 'King Pym' due to the prominent part he played in parliament.
- Pym was a persuasive speaker. He led many attacks on Charles's rule, including the impeachment of Strafford and the Grand Remonstrance.
- His connections in London also allowed him to whip up large mobs in the city when he needed to add the threat of force to his actions.
- When war finally began in 1642 he held MPs together, arranged taxes and negotiated an alliance with the Scots.
- He died in December 1643.

1 Read Sources 1 and 2. What are the main concerns expressed in them?
2 Do you think Source 1 might have been influenced by Pym? Explain your answer by referring to the Profile.

Source 1 A petition from the Citizens of London to King Charles I September 1640.

Most gracious Sovereign,

Because of the duty and obedience which we owe to your sacred Majesty, we humbly present to your princely wisdom the following complaints:

The demanding and unusual taxes upon goods, importing and exporting, and the taking of ship money.

The many monopolies, patents and warrants, causing trade in the city and other parts of the kingdom to decline.

The many changes in matters of religion and the removal of many of our priests.

The great crowd of Catholics living in London plotting against the established religion.

The seldom calling and sudden ending of parliaments, without sorting out your subjects' complaints.

The imprisonment of various citizens.

Source 2 An extract from the 'Root and Branch' Petition in December 1640. This was presented to parliament, but MPs could not agree on it.

We ask parliament that the government of the Church of England by bishops with all its dependencies, roots and branches, may be abolished. Bishops have been responsible for many evils, including the publishing of Popish, Arminian, and other dangerous books, the turning of the Communion-table altar-wise, setting images, and crucifixes over them.

When Charles travelled to Westminster to open the Long Parliament in November 1640, he hoped that members of parliament would fall into line and grant him the funds he needed to raise troops to crush the troublesome Scots. However, MPs had other ideas, especially the Puritans led by John Pym (see Profile). The king could not fight the Scots without taxes granted by parliament, so they decided to use this as a bargaining tool. They made many speeches and statements criticising the Personal Rule. Rather than openly attacking Charles, they criticised his chief advisers, in particular Laud and Wentworth (by this time the Earl of Strafford).

While most MPs were angry about many aspects of the Personal Rule, not all of them shared the extreme views of Pym and the Puritans. Many genuinely believed that Laud, Strafford and the other 'evil advisers' had misled the king and that as soon as they were removed, Charles would happily resolve the MPs' grievances. Pym, however, had less faith in the king. He and his Junto effectively committed TREASON by communicating secretly with the Scots, urging them to keep the pressure up on Charles.

The king makes concessions 1640–41

In the first months of the Long Parliament, the majority of MPs were united in their opposition to Charles's religious and financial policies, and his perceived misuse of the law. The only way to get this hostile parliament to give him the money he needed was to make concessions.

First, Charles had to accept the impeachment of several of his leading advisers and supporters. In the past he had prevented this by dissolving parliament, but now he did not have that option. In December 1640, Laud was impeached and imprisoned in the Tower of London. In the same month, the judges involved in the Hampden Ship Money case (see page 163) were also impeached. They fled abroad.

In February 1641, Charles agreed to the Triennial Act, which ensured that parliament would sit at least every three years.

Pym also tried to get Strafford impeached for treason. When this failed due to a lack of reliable evidence, MPs resorted to an Act of Attainder. This meant they could simply declare him guilty without presenting evidence. Charles reluctantly agreed to accept the verdict. London was full of angry mobs stirred up by Pym, and the king feared that his family was not safe. His supporters also advised him to accept. In a noble act, Strafford himself urged Charles to accept the verdict in the hope that it would appease Pym and the other MPs. So Charles signed Strafford's death warrant and he was executed in May 1641.

Other measures quickly followed Strafford's execution. In May 1641, Charles was forced to accept the Own Consent Act, which meant that parliament could not be dissolved unless it consented to do so. In July, the Royal Prerogative Courts (where Charles had tried many of his opponents) were abolished. In August, Ship Money and knighthood fines were declared illegal.

Charles also appointed several leading Parliamentarians to important government posts, including Oliver St John as Solicitor-General and the Earl of Essex as Lord Chamberlain. It was now harder to argue that the king was being misled by evil advisers.

Source 4 An image of the execution of Thomas Wentworth, Earl of Strafford, in May 1641, by the artist Wenceslaus Hollar (see Source 9 on page 168). ▼

ACTIVITY

Make a list of the concessions Charles I made in the first months of the Long Parliament in chronological order. Test yourself to see if you can explain each one without referring to the book. Then rearrange the concessions in what you think is their order of importance:
- to Charles
- to parliament
- to the relationship between Charles and parliament.

Source 3 An extract from Pym's impeachment charges against William Laud in December 1640

Laud has traitorously endeavoured to undermine the Fundamental Laws and Government of this Kingdom ... to introduce an arbitrary and tyrannical Government against Law; and to that end hath wickedly and traitorously advised his Majesty, that he might ... levy and take Money of his Subjects, without their Consent in parliament: and this he affirmed was warrantable by the Law of God. ... He hath traitorously endeavoured to alter and subvert God's true Religion and instead has [introduced] Popish and Superstitious Ceremonies without any warrant of Law, and hath cruelly persecuted those who have opposed them.

---

3 Does Source 3 tell you more about the actions of Laud or the views of Laud's opponents? Explain your answer.

4 Does Source 4 suggest that Strafford's execution was popular? Explain your answer.

Moderate MPs in the Long Parliament

Many MPs in parliament were not Puritans and had more moderate views:

- They believed that England should return to normality as soon as possible.
- They wanted the balance between the king and parliament maintained.
- They were unwilling to see any radical changes to the way the country was ruled.
- They were anxious about Puritan religious ideas and many were probably closer to Laud than Pym in their religious views.

Divisions emerge among MPs 1641

By summer 1641, all the key elements of the Personal Rule had been dismantled. The question now was whether these concessions would win Charles the money he wanted. Many moderate MPs, including Sir Edward Hyde, believed that MPs had gained the concessions they wanted and MPs should give Charles something in return. However, radicals like Pym believed that now was the time to continue to press the king. Pym had already put forward the Root and Branch Petition in February 1641, which effectively tried to make the Church of England more Puritan, including the abolition of bishops. This measure had divided MPs and had not become law. However, in September 1641 Pym and the Puritans abolished Laudian changes to churches. The atmosphere in parliament was beginning to shift. While moderates like Hyde had opposed the king at first, they did not much care for Puritans like Pym either, particularly when it came to their views on religion. It became clear that parliament was less united than it had been.

Two of the most prominent moderates were Viscount Falkland and Edward Hyde. Historians know a lot about these two men because their papers have survived. In 1641, Charles offered both of them government posts. Both men eventually fought on Charles's side in the Civil War.

Rebellion in Ireland 1641

By the autumn of 1641, a tense stalemate had been reached. Pym did not trust Charles to stick to the concessions he had made. The Puritans still dominated parliament and demanded further restrictions on royal power. However, Charles was unwilling to grant any more concessions, and cleverly promoted moderates to his government – a move that gradually increased his support in parliament, particularly in the House of Lords.

This stalemate was broken in the most shocking and fashion. In November 1641, news reached England of a massive Catholic uprising in Ireland. English control in Ireland was overthrown and Protestant propaganda sheets circulated stories and pictures of massacres and atrocities carried out against Protestants in Ireland.

Source 5 A report on the rebellion in Ireland in 1641. The majority of the Irish were Catholics and they rose up against Protestant settlers loyal to England. Atrocities were committed and propaganda like this exaggerated them further, which alarmed and angered Protestants in England. ▶

> Driuinge Men Women & children by hund:
> reds vpon Briges & cafting them into Riuers,
> who drowned not were killed with poles &
> fhot with mufkets.
>
> G

1. Why would images like Source 5 have been so shocking in 1641?
2. Explain how the Irish Rebellion indirectly led to the creation of a Royalist party in parliament.

Parliament pushes: the Grand Remonstrance 1641

It was obvious that an army was needed to deal with the rebellion. Pym and the other radicals feared that Charles might use this army against them. At the same time, the Puritans also saw an opportunity – Charles needed funds for an army so perhaps he could be pressured into accepting even more restrictions on his power.

In an effort to achieve this, Pym drew up a document called the Grand Remonstrance and asked parliament to vote on it. This was a hugely controversial measure (see Factfile) and it only passed by a narrow margin (159 votes to 148). Nearly 200 MPs abstained or did not attend the debate. Many historians regard the Grand Remonstrance as a turning point because it alienated so many moderate MPs. Charles flatly refused to accept it, and 119 MPs, including Edward Hyde and Viscount Falkland, supported Charles. Hyde and Falkland began to represent Charles's views to ordinary MPs, winning many of them over. A Royalist party had now emerged in parliament.

FACTFILE

The Grand Remonstrance
The Grand Remonstrance was published in December 1641, but Pym had been working on it for much of the year. It contained two main elements: a summary of the abuses of the Personal Rule and a series of recommendations. The main recommendations were:
- Parliament to control the king's ministers.
- Bishops and Catholic lords to be banned from the House of Lords.
- Fundamental reform of the Church (to make it more Puritan).

It was extremely unusual and radical because:
- it directly criticised the king and was much less respectful than previous documents
- it was published for the ordinary people to read before it was discussed in parliament, which caused opponents to suspect Pym of trying to stir up trouble among the London mobs in particular.

Source 6 The views of MP Oliver Cromwell, reported by moderate MP Viscount Falkland. Cromwell was a strong Protestant who sympathised with the Puritans. At this stage he was not a prominent figure, but he would later become extremely important.

When I spoke to Cromwell he told me that if the Grand Remonstrance had not been passed he would have sold all he had the next morning, left England and never returned. He said he knew that there were many other honest men of the same view.

Source 7 The reaction of a supporter of Charles, written in 1642 and published in a book in 1701.

A blacker insult against the king's person or government could never be imagined than this Grand Remonstrance. When parliament approved it, I thought we were all sat in the valley of the shadow of death, for we English men had all but stabbed each other with our swords with this Remonstrance.

Source 8 The reaction of Sir Edward Dering, MP for Kent and a moderate, to the Grand Remonstrance.

The Remonstrance is now passing through the House. I must vote on it one way or the other and my conscience tells me to vote against. This Remonstrance will cause such bitterness and division that we shall never be able to undo it. I do not know one soul in my county who wishes parliament to pass measures such as this. They thank parliament for its good laws and statutes but not for this. When I heard about a Remonstrance I imagined we would present our concerns to the king as faithful servants. I did not dream that we should remonstrate against the king's dignity, nor spread such stories to the ordinary people.

3   Why are the reactions of Sources 6–8 to the Grand Remonstrance so different?

4   Do Sources 6–8 convince you that the Grand Remonstrance was the turning point on the road to civil war? Explain your answer.

Charles strikes: The Attempt on Five Members 1642

The situation hung in the balance, but in January 1642 Charles made a disastrous error of judgement – an act that has become known as the Attempt on the Five Members. By this time, Charles suspected (correctly) that Pym and other leading Puritans were communicating with the Scots. He also feared that they were stirring up the London mobs to attack him and his family. On the afternoon of 4 January 1642, the king and 200 men-at-arms marched through the streets of London to parliament. The king carried a warrant for the arrest of five MPs (Pym, John Hampden, Denzil Holles, Sir Arthur Hesilrige and William Strode) and one of the Lords (Edward Montagu, Earl of Manchester) on charges of high treason. The SPEAKER OF THE HOUSE knelt before Charles but refused to speak when asked to deliver the MPs. In fact, by the time Charles arrived, the five MPs and Montagu had escaped.

Source 9 A nineteenth-century painting of the attempt to arrest the five MPs. ▼

1 We could not find any visual sources from the time showing this event. Can you think of any reasons why?
2 Source 9 is not from 1642 but it is proof that the event was significant. Do you agree?

In taking this action, Charles had broken parliamentary privilege, and his use of armed force made him seem more than ever like a tyrant king. He undid much of the good work done by Hyde and Falkland in convincing MPs that the king could be trusted. In the days that followed, Charles tried to persuade the authorities to surrender the MPs to him, but they refused. With the London mob getting out of control the king once again began to fear for his family's safety. He left London.

Source 10 A letter written in 1642 by Thomas Wiseman, a Royalist, to Sir John Penington, a supporter and close ally of Charles I.

His Majesty yesterday came into the city and made a gracious speech to the Lord Mayor and city officials asking them to surrender the five MPs to him. They cried out to his Majesty to maintain the privilege of parliament. He gently replied to them that it was his wish to do so. But they must allow him to distinguish between the parliament and some discontented members in it who have tried by acts of treason to hurt him and to take away the loyalty of his people.

Afterwards his Majesty was pleased to go to dinner at Sheriff Garrett's, where his Majesty stayed till 3 o'clock. Then, returning to Whitehall, the rude crowd followed him crying again: 'Privileges of Parliament! Privileges of Parliament!' The good king was somewhat disturbed and I believe was glad when he was at home.

What these disorders will produce God only knows, but it is feared they must end in blood. The Puritan groups are too many, both in city and countryside, so that if the king and parliament should disagree, no man can tell which party would be strongest.

3   If you did not know that Thomas Wiseman was a Royalist, would you be able to work that out from the text of Source 10? Explain your answer.
4   Do Sources 10 and 11 agree on anything?
5   Why are the two sources so different?

Source 11 An official parliamentary account of Charles I's attempted arrest of the five MPs, January 1642.

Many soldiers, papists and others, to the number of about 500, came with his Majesty ... armed with swords, pistols and other weapons. Some held up their pistols ready cocked near the said door and said 'I am a good marksman; I can hit you, I warrant you.' Some of the said soldiers answered, 'A pox of God confound them', and others said 'A pox take the House of Commons, let them come and be hanged.' Some of them, when asked what they thought the said company intended to do, answered that, if the word had been given, they should have fallen upon the House of Commons and have cut all their throats.

The slide to war 1642

Once Charles fled, parliament began to divide, with Royalist MPs leaving the capital in support of the king. Trust had broken down completely. Fearing that Charles would use force, what was left of parliament passed the Militia Ordinance in March 1642. This order stated that parliament, not the king, had control of the militia and in particular the London trained bands (the militia in London). These part-time soldiers who could be called up in times of emergency were the closest thing the country had to an army. Charles would not tolerate this.

In April, he tried unsuccessfully to seize the armoury of weapons at Hull. In June, he issued a royal order called the Commissions of Array. This stated that the king controlled the militia and ordered local commanders to support him. The commanders were placed in an impossible position, receiving orders from both king and parliament. Fear of the other side starting a war effectively drove each side into war.

Source 12 An engraving showing the commander of the garrison at Hull refusing Charles entry into the town to take control of the armoury there. ▼

In June 1642, parliament presented the king with a peace deal entitled the Nineteen Propositions (see Factfile). However, the terms were so harsh that Charles felt he had no option but to reject them. The majority of men on both sides were unwilling to go to war with their countrymen, but they were also unable to reach a compromise. Charles raised his standard at Nottingham in 1642 and the Civil War began.

FACTFILE

The Nineteen Propositions June 1642
- Parliament should appoint all ministers.
- Parliament should discuss and approve all government policy.
- Parliament to arrange the education and marriages of the king's children.
- Anti-Catholic laws to be strictly enforced.
- Reform of the Church of England along Puritan lines.
- The king had to approve parliament's control of the militia (the Militia Ordinance) and hand over all forts and castles to the control of parliament.

FOCUS TASK

The steps to war

Impeachment of Laud

Charles's concessions
(e.g. advisers, Ship Money)

Execution of Strafford

Irish Rebellion

Grand Remonstrance

Attempted arrest of the five MPs

Nineteen Propositions

War

1 The diagram shows the key steps to war in the period 1640–42. Make your own copy and add notes and labels explaining why each event made war more or less likely.
2 The events are in chronological order. How would the diagram look if you rearranged the events in order of importance?
3 The diagram gives the impression that war was inevitable. Do you think that is correct, or is it misleading? Is there a better form of diagram, such as a roller-coaster ride? If so, draw your own version.

PRACTICE QUESTIONS

1 Explain why relations between Charles I and parliament were generally poor between November 1640 and August 1642. (10)
2 'The Civil War was the result of Pym's actions.' How far do the sources in this section convince you that this statement is correct? (20)

TOPIC SUMMARY

Events leading to Civil War

1 In November 1640, Charles asked parliament for money for an army to crush the Scots. Instead MPs used this opportunity to bargain with the king, presenting their grievances about the Personal Rule and Charles's ministers (although they avoided criticising the king overtly). Despite this, everyone hoped for and expected reconciliation.
2 Quite quickly, the radical Puritan MPs – stern critics of the king – emerged as the most powerful group in parliament and John Pym emerged as their leader. Pym was a powerful speaker. He also had popular support in London, where he could organise a large mob to support him. He had little faith that the king would do what parliament wanted without a show of force.
3 Charles realised he needed to make concessions. He agreed to the impeachment of his leading advisers. Laud was imprisoned and Strafford was executed. Ship Money and knighthood fines were declared illegal. Leading MPs were appointed as advisers. By summer 1641, all key elements of Personal Rule had been dismantled.
4 The more moderate MPs now believed that parliament had gained the concessions needed. However, radicals like Pym pressed for more, particularly on religious issues.
5 This stalemate was broken in November 1641 by a Catholic uprising in Ireland. Propaganda told of atrocities carried out against Protestants.
6 An army had to be raised to deal with the rebellion. Pym and the other radicals feared that Charles might use this army against them, but they also saw a chance to push their agenda further. The Grand Remonstrance – a proposal to severely limit royal power – was narrowly approved by MPs. It was a turning point because it alienated so many moderate MPs. A strong Royalist party emerged in parliament.
7 In January 1642, Charles made a serious error of judgement by sending soldiers to arrest leading Puritan MPs.
8 Trust broke down completely. Fearing that Charles would use force, what was left of parliament passed the Militia Ordinance in March 1642, giving parliament control of the armed forces.
9 With civil war looking likely, in June 1642 parliament presented the king with a peace deal entitled the Nineteen Propositions. However, the terms were so harsh that the king could not accept them. War soon followed.

5.1 The search for a settlement – the mood of the country in 1646

FOCUS

The Civil War began in 1642 and ended with Charles's defeat and capture in 1646. By this time, the country was sick of the conflict and wanted parliament and the king to reach a settlement. In this topic you will look at the issues that concerned people at the end of the war in 1646, and how these affected attempts to establish peace.

The public mood in 1646

By the end of the war in 1646, the vast majority of people in England were eager for peace. The war had brought hardship, chaos and misery.

> **Source 1** A letter from George Manley of Cheshire to his brother in London, 1646. George was looking after his brother's estates while he was involved in the wars.
>
> *A poor and miserable country we live in, and it is likely to be worse before long. The taxes are so many, and the payments laid upon us are more than our land is worth. Our stocks are all gone and we are in a way of ruin, not easily to be recovered except by great care and length of time. The lord look down in mercy upon his poor distressed people. It is a great grief to men to be reduced to so low an ebb. I cannot meet your needs with your own money, for your land this year will not give you £20. Your tenants are so burdened, the rent will hardly be gotten from them. And so with a troubled and grieved heart, I bid you farewell and assure you that I will ever be your loving brother.*

With his armies defeated, people hoped that the king would be prepared to discuss a settlement with parliament. This included reaching a compromise over the following issues:

- The future of the Church of England: this included deciding whether there would be a system of bishops (episcopacy), a Book of Common Prayer that all priests had to follow, the decoration and layout of churches and, above all, whether England would adopt the Scottish system of Presbyterianism.
- Parliament's powers: this involved taking on powers that had once belonged to the king, such as control of the army and the appointment of advisers.
- Punishment of Royalists: a decision needed to be made whether those who had fought as supporters of the king were 'traitors'.

There was little desire to remove the king or end the monarchy, which most people felt was the natural form of government. Charles was officially a prisoner, held under house arrest, but he felt confident that he could agree a settlement that preserved much of his royal power. A great proportion of the population shared Charles's views, and many were prepared to accept a settlement that put Charles back on the throne with few or no restrictions on him. In the 1630s and 1640s, people had accepted the social order with the king at the head of the hierarchy and the people below him (see page 154).

The impact of the Civil War

The war seemed to turn this ordered society upside down. The scale of death and destruction had never been seen before, and the majority of people wanted a settlement that would bring an end to war, taxes and armies. Many who had questioned Charles's Personal Rule had come to believe that rule by parliament and the army would be worse.

The rise of the New Model Army

In the course of the Civil War, parliament had reorganised its forces and created the disciplined, well-organised New Model Army. Under the Self-Denying Ordinance, MPs had to choose whether to be an MP or serve in the army. The New Model Army helped to win the Civil War. However, by 1646 many were unsure about it. To begin with, it was expensive to pay and properly equip – that meant more taxes. Secondly, English people had always been suspicious of standing armies, fearing that rulers might use the army against them or that army commanders might become too powerful. This is exactly what seemed to be happening. The army commander Oliver Cromwell had become particularly influential. There were also worrying signs that troops were developing their own political and religious ideas – the idea of turning England into a republic.

Religious turmoil

While the Puritans in parliament and in the army had grown more powerful, they were still an unpopular minority. During the war, they had destroyed many churches that had been reordered under Laud's authority. The Puritans also wanted local parishes to run their own affairs, effectively getting rid of a national Church of England. Most people feared this would lead to a breakdown in society. They wanted to keep a Church of England to which everyone belonged. Some might even accept a Presbyterian Church similar to that in Scotland. Although it had no bishops, this would maintain authority and control through the parish elders – usually the gentry and better-off members of the parish.

Impact of the Civil War

The local social order

In the Civil War, neighbours became enemies, and the gentry and nobility split between the two sides. During the war, both Royalists and Parliamentarians sent their own officials (County Committees) to many areas to collect taxes, bypassing the local gentry who would normally have carried out this role. The gentry were keen to see an end to these County Committees and they thought Charles would abolish them.

Source 2 Civil War woodcuts, showing the removal of religious decorations and monuments by parliament forces. ▼

The Levellers

Along with these disruptions, the Civil War also resulted in the emergence of new radical groups that challenged the old ways – both religious traditions and social hierarchy. In 1646, the group causing most concern were the Levellers. The Levellers believed that society should be 'levelled': property should be distributed equally and that all men should have the right to vote, not just the land-owning gentry. The key figures in the movement were John Lilburne, Richard Overton and William Walwyn. Each of these men published pamphlets and books demanding a more equal society. Many soldiers in parliament's New Model Army were Levellers – or at least were impressed by what the Levellers had to say.

Source 3 The title page of William Walwyn's pamphlet *England's Lamentable Slavery*, published in 1645.

England's Lamentable Slavery, the result of arbitrary desires, injustice and severity of kings, the negligence and corruption of parliament and the wickedness of others, can be put right through:

1 *Observing the Magna Carta*

2 *The Petition of Right of 1628*

3 *The abolition of the Star Chamber*

4 *The Solemn Protestation of the Kingdom*

5 *The Great Covenant of Scotland.*

1 Explain why each of Sources 2–4 would alarm many people.
2 Which one would be of greatest concern to the gentry? Explain your answer.

Source 4 An extract from *The Free Man's Freedom Vindicated*, a pamphlet published by John Lilburne in 1646.

Every man and woman is by nature equal and alike in power, dignity, authority and majesty. No person is born with any power or authority over any other. It is wicked, sinful and unjust for any servant of parliament, County Commissioner, clergyman, lawyer or gentleman to hold any power over another except with that person's consent.

When faced with these frightening forces, the people of England began to feel that society was collapsing. In light of these new circumstances, the order and discipline of Charles's Personal Rule seemed to be an attractive option. People began to encourage a settlement that effectively turned the clock back to 1640.

FOCUS TASK

Why did most people want Charles restored to the throne by 1646?

Write two short paragraphs:
- A paragraph explaining why someone who does not understand this period would find it surprising that most people wanted power to be restored to Charles by 1646 (you might mention opposition to the Personal Rule, lack of trust and the Civil War itself).
- A paragraph explaining why, if you look at events from the viewpoint of people at the time, it was *not* surprising that many people wanted Charles's power restored.

PRACTICE QUESTIONS

1 Explain why many people in England in 1646 felt that society was under threat of collapse. (10)
2 'Radical ideas were a serious threat to the established order in society at the end of the First Civil War.' How far do the sources in this topic convince you that this statement is correct? (20)

TOPIC SUMMARY

The mood of the country in 1646

1 By 1646, people in England wanted peace. Parliament expect the defeated king would reach a settlement with them on religion, the power of parliament and punishment of Royalist leaders.
2 There was little desire to end the monarchy. Most saw it as the natural form of government. After the trauma of war, many who had once questioned the king's rule now thought that government by parliament or the army alone would be worse. They were prepared for Charles to return with few restrictions.
3 Although Charles was officially held prisoner, he felt confident that he could argue for a settlement that preserved his royal power.
4 However, war had changed England in significant ways. The old belief in natural order and hierarchy, with the king at the top and everyone treating their social superiors with respect and loyalty, had been challenged.
5 War had weakened this social order. Neighbours became enemies. Gentry and nobility were split between those loyal to the king and those who supported parliament. Both sides had imposed their own officials to collect taxes, bypassing the local gentry.
6 The New Model Army was now the most powerful force in England. It was professional, disciplined and well-organised, and army commanders were determined to have a say in religious and political issues. Oliver Cromwell was particularly powerful.
7 Some people (including some soldiers) had radical ideas about religion and government. The Levellers believed that society should be 'levelled', giving people greater property and voting rights.

5.2 Why did it prove so difficult to reach a settlement 1646–48?

FOCUS

Despite the fact that most people were desperate for a settlement in 1646, by late 1647 Charles and parliament were still locked in negotiations. In this topic, you will see why it proved impossible to reach an agreement.

Charles was determined to win the peace

The key stumbling block in the negotiations was Charles himself. The king might have lost the war, but he thought he could win the peace. He was being held captive by the Scots in Newcastle, but despite this he had a number of advantages. He truly believed he had been appointed by God, and this meant he could justify any behaviour or action that secured his position as king. This included making promises he had no intention of keeping.

Charles's opponents were divided. MPs were split between two groups: the Presbyterians and the Independents. The army and the Scots also each wanted a say in the settlement.

The main factions and what they wanted to happen

Presbyterian MPs

The Presbyterians, led by Denzil Holles, were the largest group in parliament and they were closely allied to the Scots. They were:

- concerned by the fears outlined on pages 179–81
- hoping to settle with the king as soon as possible, and were prepared to accept few or no limits on his power
- worried that Puritans and the growing number of radical religious sects threatened to destroy the Church of England
- opposed to restoring the pre-war Church; most wanted the Church to become Presbyterian (similar to the Scottish Church) rather than risk it disappearing altogether
- (most importantly) unwilling to deal with the New Model Army's concerns regarding pay and religious freedom.

Independent MPs

The Independents included Oliver Cromwell and his son-in-law Henry Ireton, who were both MPs and army commanders. The Independents were:

- sympathetic to the concerns of the New Model Army
- not prepared to accept restoring the pre-war Church of England
- opposed to introducing Scottish Presbyterianism to England; they preferred to give congregations the freedom to worship in whatever way they wished (as long as it was Protestant)
- willing to use force to make the king accept their views.

The Scots

In the Solemn League and Covenant of 1643, the Scots fought alongside parliament. In return, parliament agreed that it would introduce Scottish Presbyterianism to the Church of England, but parliament had dragged its feet when it came to introducing Presbyterianism into England.

The New Model Army

The leaders of the New Model Army believed that God had granted them victory and that they were his 'instrument' on Earth. When the Civil War ended, MPs tried to disband the army and so avoid paying the soldiers the wages they were owed. The army responded by refusing to go. Instead, army members elected 'agitators' to represent their views in the Army Council. Many of these agitators were Levellers with radical views. The army began to express its own views on the settlement.

Source 1 A political pamphlet published in June 1646 by civilian radicals. It was widely distributed among the New Model Army, as well as on the streets of London.

It is against the law and will of God that the lives, property and freedoms of millions should be at the mercy of one man. It is against the law of nature, reason and human justice, for if the king has such power in his hand, he may overthrow us all as he pleases. The Bible says that kings should be the servants of their people not their masters.

Source 2 An extract from a pamphlet by Thomas Edwards, a supporter of the Presbyterian MPs, published in December 1646.

I acknowledge that the New Model Army did great service against the enemy. My aim is not to cast insult on the Army, but to point out errors and wrongdoing by some sections of it. A godly young man in Somerset told me of a lieutenant in the Army who believed 1) That women may preach 2) That if a woman's husband was absent she might lie with another 3) That it was unlawful to kneel in prayer.

1. What are the main claims of Source 1? How would they be viewed by each of the four main factions?
2. How reliable is Source 2 as a source about the New Model Army?
3. How reliable are Sources 1 and 2 as evidence about the divisions in England in 1646?
4. What does Source 3 tell us about Charles's attitude towards the negotiations?

Charles negotiates, tensions rise

Charles knew his opponents were divided. He believed that the longer he held out, the more divided they would become. He was sure that eventually they would accept that the only way for England to become stable again was to restore him as king, with full authority and powers. Charles's tactics were simple: he listened to the views and proposals of all the different factions but refused to make a deal with any of them.

While he was being held by the Scots, Charles discussed several issues. The Scots' priority was to preserve their Presbyterian Church. They thought it would be stronger if England had a Presbyterian Church as well. Charles hinted that they might get this, but he made no formal agreement.

In July 1646, parliament presented peace terms, known as the Newcastle Propositions (see Factfile on page 184). Charles rejected these terms.

Source 3 An extract from a letter by Charles I to his wife, July 1646.

Today I received a copy of Parliament's Propositions. I cannot accept them without loss of my principles, crown and honour. I can in no way accept them. I believe I will delay my reply as long as I can, and I need to think of an answer denying the terms which is as handsome as possible.

In January 1647, the Scots agreed to hand the king over to Denzil Holles and the Presbyterians, and he was moved to Northampton. Having access to the king strengthened the hand of the Presbyterians.

This move alarmed the army. In June 1647, soldiers seized the king and took him to their headquarters near Cambridge (then later to Hampton Court near London). Now it was the army's turn to negotiate with Charles.

In July 1647, they presented him with their Heads of Proposals (see Factfile on page 184). These terms were actually more generous to Charles than parliament's proposals had been. Even so, Charles continued to negotiate and would not sign a formal agreement.

As Cromwell and Ireton tried to negotiate with the king, the army became more restless. Support for the Levellers continued to grow among army members.

In October 1647, troops presented a set of demands to army commanders and parliament, called the Agreement of the People (see Source 4). Fairfax, Cromwell and Ireton, and the Army Council met with some of the key Levellers. They had a series of discussions now known as the Putney Debates. These debates revealed how divided the army was. Cromwell and the Army Council were firmly against the more radical Leveller demands, particularly the demand that all men should have the vote.

FACTFILE

The Newcastle Propositions and the Heads of Proposals

Parliament's offer Newcastle Propositions (July 1646)	The army's offer Heads of Proposals (1647)
Parliament to be called at least every three years.	Parliament to be called at least every two years.
Parliament to nominate 13 government ministers/advisers for top posts for ever.	Parliament to nominate government ministers/advisers for only 10 years.
Parliament to nominate commanders of the army.	Parliament to control army for 10 years.
Church of England reformed along Presbyterian lines for three years; bishops abolished.	No Presbyterian reforms for the Church; bishops to remain but with limited powers.
Anti-Catholic laws to be enforced.	Anti-Catholic laws to be abolished and new ones made.
58 leading Royalists to be punished.	Seven leading Royalists to be punished.
48 leading Royalists to be excluded from holding office for life.	Parliament's enemies to be excluded from holding office for five years.

Source 4 An extract from the Agreement of the People, published in 1647. It was put together by Levellers in the army working with some civilian Leveller leaders, particularly William Walwyn.

In matters of religion men should not be instructed about God but should follow their conscience.

Impressing and forcing men to serve in the armed forces is against our freedom. Men can be found to fight for any cause which is just.

In all laws made every person shall be bound by those laws in exactly the same way. No title, estate, wealth or position should give any exemption from the laws.

As the laws are equal, so they should be good and do no harm to the people.

Source 5 An extract adapted from discussions between the army Leveller leader Colonel Rainsborough and army commander Henry Ireton in the Putney Debates.

Rainsborough: The poorest man has a life to live just as the greatest man. And therefore sir I think it is clear that every man who has to live under a government should first consent to that government.

Ireton: I think that no person has a right to an interest or share in running the kingdom, which includes the vote, if he does not have a permanent interest in the kingdom, such as owning land. Those are the proper persons to be represented in parliament and to represent the kingdom as members of parliament.

1 Look back at the information given. What are the main areas of disagreement between the Levellers and the Army Council?

The Second Civil War

By November 1647, Charles's opponents were divided among themselves, both in parliament and in the army. At this point, Charles made a decisive move and escaped from captivity. Although he was successful, he was soon recaptured and imprisoned again on the Isle of Wight by parliamentary troops. However, his escape gave Charles the chance to secretly negotiate with the Scots. In December, he signed an agreement with the Scots called the Engagement. In it, the Scots said they would help Charles if the king agreed to a Scottish-style Presbyterian Church in England.

All his opponents were appalled. Parliament passed the Vote of No Addresses in January 1648 – all sides agreed they would no longer negotiate with the king. In March 1648, Royalist supporters of Charles I in South Wales rose up against parliament's rule. They were followed in May by Royalists in Kent and Essex. In July, the Scottish army invaded England.

This Second Civil War was brief but bloody (see page 72), and by August 1648 it was over in England. The Royalists and the invading Scottish army were crushed by Cromwell and the New Model Army.

Charles remained imprisoned on the Isle of Wight throughout the war, but he still had a lot of support or, perhaps more accurately, many still saw him as the country's rightful leader. For a short while it looked as though settlement talks would start again. However, it soon became clear that the situation in England had changed.

2 Explain how the creator of Source 6 is trying to express his support for Charles I in 1648.

Source 6 A pamphlet urging all people to be faithful subjects to the king, printed in 1648. At this time Charles was imprisoned on the Isle of Wight. ▼

FOCUS TASK

Who was responsible for the failure to reach a settlement 1646–48?

The diagram below suggests that all these groups were equally responsible. Redraw the diagram, showing how responsible you think each group was. Add notes and labels to explain your judgement.

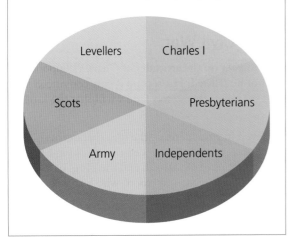

PRACTICE QUESTIONS

1 Explain why Charles I's opponents were so divided at the end of the First Civil War. (10)
2 'The main source of tension in the period 1646–48 was religion.' How far do the sources in this section convince you that this statement is correct? (20)

TOPIC SUMMARY

Why did it prove so difficult to reach a settlement 1646–48?

1 After the trauma of war, most people were desperate for a settlement in 1646. However, agreement could not be reached, mainly because Charles's opponents were divided and the king exploited these divisions.
2 As well as king and parliament, the army became a serious political force. Most army commanders wanted limits on the king's power and greater religious freedom.
3 Many soldiers in the army had more radical ideas, including changes to the way England was governed – even the idea of 'one man, one vote'.
4 Others, such as the Presbyterians, wanted the king back and saw the army and the emerging radical groups as a bigger problem than the king.
5 The Independents, including Cromwell, were caught in the middle. They had some sympathy for the army radicals but they also worried where this might lead.

6 Each group put proposals to Charles. He played for time, realising they could never agree. He considered each proposal in turn but did not accept any of them.
7 Although he was held prisoner, Charles still believed he had the divine right to rule England. In December 1647, he signed a secret agreement with the Scots that they would help him regain power. In return, Charles agreed to a Scottish-style Presbyterian Church in England.
8 This triggered the Second Civil War, in which the Royalists and the Scots were crushed by Cromwell and the New Model Army.
9 Even at the end of the war, Charles still had much support. Many still saw him as the rightful ruler of the nation.

5.3

The execution of the king 1649

FOCUS

The period 1646–48 showed how powerful the king was, even though he had lost in war. In 1646, there had been no question of removing the king, but by the end of 1648 the situation had changed, and Charles was eventually executed. In this topic you will look at the effect the Second Civil War had on the country and how the people reacted to regicide.

The impact of the Second Civil War

The Second Civil War had a major impact on the attitudes of Charles's opponents. Many now believed that he could not be trusted. His second defeat convinced key figures, particularly Cromwell and his allies, that it was God's will that the king should be removed.

Like many Puritans Cromwell believed in Providence – the idea that events reflected God's will. By late 1648, Cromwell was convinced that the king had lost God's favour. The army was the instrument of God's will and the king, or Charles Stuart as the army now referred to him, was a 'man of blood' who had waged war on his own people.

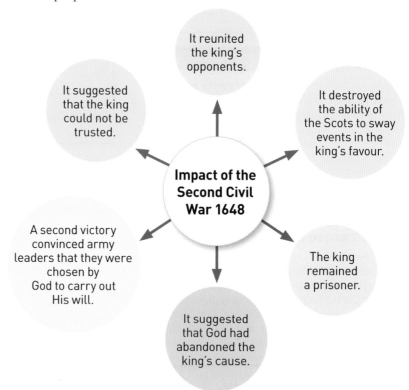

1 Study the impact of the Second Civil War in the diagram. Which do you think was the most important? Explain your answer.

Source 1 In April 1648, officers of the New Model Army met at Windsor Castle for a prayer meeting. At this meeting they resolved that:

It was our duty if ever the Lord brought us back again in peace, to call Charles Stuart, that man of blood, to an account for that blood he had shed, and mischief he had done to his utmost, against the Lord's cause and people in these poor nations.

Source 2 A description of Pride's Purge, from the diary of Edmund Ludlow, an army officer and committed opponent of the king, 1648.

Officers of the army went into a private room, to consider the best way to get the result we aimed for. We agreed that the army should be brought up the next morning, and guards placed in parliament. None would be permitted to pass into the House, except those who had been faithful to the public interest. To this end, we went over the names of all the members one by one, giving the truest estimate we could of their viewpoints. Commissary-General Ireton went to Sir Thomas Fairfax [head of the army], and told him about the need for this extraordinary action. He took care to have the army brought up the next morning by seven o'clock. Colonel Pride commanded the guard that waited at the parliament doors, with a list of those members who were to be excluded. He prevented them from entering the House, and secured some of the most suspected under a guard provided for that reason.

2 Explain why Sources 1 and 2 are so useful to historians about the views and the motives of the army in 1648.

Pride's Purge

In September 1648, parliament began to discuss yet another settlement with the king. Presbyterian MPs still felt a deal was possible, but the more radical elements in the army were outraged that MPs were still negotiating. In December 1648, Colonel Pride and his regiment surrounded parliament and arrested all those MPs who supported negotiations with the king. This event – essentially a military coup – became known as Pride's Purge.

There is no evidence connecting Cromwell to Pride's Purge, but it seems likely that he approved it. Out of 470 MPs, around 180 were excluded from parliament and around 100 more fled from London or simply stayed away. The day after the purge, Cromwell arrived in London. It was clear that the army was now in control.

As people realised that the king would be put on trial, more MPs left until eventually only around 80 remained – those willing to support the trial of the king. They were nicknamed the Rump Parliament.

The trial

Putting the king on trial was a huge step. Everyone knew that if it happened, the only possible verdict was 'guilty'. On 6 January 1649, the Rump Parliament established a High Court to sit in judgement on the king. It comprised MPs, civilians and army officers, and was headed by a well-known republican named John Bradshaw.

The whole idea of trying the king was so shocking that some of those called to sit as judges refused to do so. The charges drawn up against the king accused him of being 'a tyrant, traitor, and murderer, and a public and implacable enemy to the Commonwealth of England'. When these charges were read out at the start of the trial, the king laughed out loud – the trial, he claimed, was illegal. In one of the finest performances of his life, the king refused to plead on the grounds that the High Court had no LEGITIMATE authority to sit in judgement on him. Arguing that the trial undermined the freedom and liberties of all Englishmen, the king claimed the court was nothing more than a representation of the army's illegal power. The court refused to accept Charles's arguments. He was found guilty and sentenced to death.

Source 3 The charges made against Charles I at his trial in 1649.

Charles ... out of a wicked design to erect and uphold in himself an unlimited and tyrannical power to rule according to his will, and to overthrow the rights and liberties of the people, yea, to take away and make void the foundations thereof ... hath traitorously and maliciously levied war against the present parliament, and the people therein represented.

The execution

Charles was executed outside the Palace of Whitehall on 30 January 1649. He faced his fate with dignity. When the axe fell, a loud gasp was heard from the crowd; people fainted in shock, while others scrambled to dip handkerchiefs in the royal blood. Many saw Charles as a saint and a martyr.

The action proved divisive. There was no disguising the fact that the execution had been the act of the army supported by a small group of MPs in the Rump Parliament. These men felt they had dealt out justice 'in the face of God, and of all men'. The REGICIDE was a highly unpopular act. Many felt it was a step too far and threatened to plunge Britain into even deeper turmoil.

England no longer had a monarch. The Rump Parliament declared that the country was now a republic, but it was not at all clear what this would mean. All the fears and divisions of the 1640s remained, and the execution of the king created even greater tension.

> **Source 4** Historian Mark Goldie, speaking on a radio programme in 2001.
>
> *The execution of Charles I was very unpopular indeed. It was carried out by a small clique within the army. I think they had very good reasons for doing it, the main reason being that Charles I was simply a man you could not do business with. You could never trust anything he said. He would agree to things but his secret letters to his wife or friends made it clear he had no intention of honouring his word. The officers felt that they had no choice other than to remove him, but the country was horrified. Next to executing God it is hard to see what could be more horrifying – after all most people thought of the king as God's representative on Earth.*

Source 5 A Dutch drawing from the time of the execution of the king. ▼

Source 6 A playing card produced in the 1660s. It claims that Cromwell was a hypocrite, praying while he had the king murdered. ▼

Oliver seeking God while the K. is murthered by his order.

1. What evidence is there in Source 5 to support the views of Mark Goldie in Source 4?
2. Source 6 is trying to portray Charles as a saint. How does it do this?
3. Sources 4 and 6 are about the same event. Why are they so different?

PRACTICE QUESTIONS

1. Explain why there was no question of removing the king in 1646 and why this situation had changed by the end of 1648. (10)
2. 'The army was the main reason Charles stood trial in 1649.' How far do the sources in this topic convince you that this statement is correct? (20)

TOPIC SUMMARY

The execution of the king

1. The Second Civil War hardened attitudes. Charles's opponents in parliament and the army, particularly Oliver Cromwell, were now convinced that the king could not be trusted and that God wanted him removed as ruler. Cromwell believed that the army was the instrument of God's will.
2. In December 1648, Colonel Pride led his regiment to oust all MPs who wanted to negotiate with the king. This so-called 'Pride's Purge' was essentially a military coup.
3. The next day Cromwell arrived in London and the army took control. More MPs left London, leaving a 'Rump' of 80 MPs who were willing to put the king on trial.
4. The Rump Parliament established a court to try the king – led by a well-known republican named John Bradshaw – on the charge that he was 'a tyrant, traitor, and murderer' who had made war on his own people.
5. Charles refused to plead on the grounds that the court had no authority to judge him. He argued that the court was simply a representation of the army's illegal power.
6. The court did not accept Charles's arguments. He was found guilty, sentenced to death and executed outside the Palace of Whitehall on 30 January 1649.
7. Charles's execution was divisive. The Rump MPs felt they had dealt out justice 'in the face of God, and of all men'. For others, it was a highly unpopular. Others felt that Charles was a religious martyr.
8. The Rump Parliament declared that England a republic, but it was not at all clear what this would mean.

6.1 Britain without a king: The Commonwealth 1649–53

FOCUS

After the execution of the king, England became a Commonwealth rather than a kingdom. This meant it was a republic ruled by the Rump Parliament. There were many serious challenges facing the new regime: political and religious divisions; war with Scotland and Ireland; radical political and religious groups. In this topic you will examine how far the country coped with these challenges.

Challenges facing the Rump Parliament

Radical groups

The established views on religion and society were being challenged by radical groups (see Factfile on page 190). Members of the Rump Parliament feared these groups, as did the gentry they represented.

Source 1 The cover page of *Eikon Basilike*, a book that effectively portrayed Charles as a saint and a martyr. There were also many powerful images designed to appeal to those who could not read. Thousands of copies were sold, including miniature copies that were easy to hide. ▼

1 Explain what Source 1 is trying to say about Charles I.
2 How does the imagery in Source 1 help get the message across?

Scotland and Ireland

Within days of the execution, Scotland declared the king's eldest son, Prince Charles, King of Great Britain. Although England was now officially a republic, the young Charles had managed to escape to the continent, where many hoped he would gather support for an invasion to take back the throne. In Ireland, the rebels who had overthrown English rule in 1641 had formed the Irish Catholic Confederation and were still controlling the country. A Catholic-controlled state on England's border was seen as a threat to the Protestant religion and a potential ally for England's Catholic enemies, particularly France.

Political tensions

Many people viewed the new regime with suspicion. Many people felt the execution of the king was sacrilege (see Source 1). More worrying, however, was the power that the army seemed to have achieved – even many of the Rump MPs were concerned about this.

Religious divisions

The disputes of the period 1646–48 had not gone away. Tensions remained between those who wanted a compulsory national Church of England and those who sought greater religious freedom.

FACTFILE

Radical groups

Before the Civil War, England had strict censorship laws and there could be severe penalties for those who expressed views or printed material that the government disliked (see the example of William Prynne on page 166). During the Civil War, this system of censorship collapsed. Traditional authority figures like the local gentry were weakened. There was an explosion of discussion, debate and new ideas about politics and religion. Many new groups with radical ideas emerged, which the government regarded as a threat.

● **The Levellers:** You have already come across the Levellers on page 180. After the execution of the king, the civilian Levellers continued to argue for their ideals. In March 1649, the Rump Parliament had the Leveller leaders Lilburne, Overton and Walwyn arrested and imprisoned in the Tower of London. In April 1649, Levellers in the army in London mutinied over unpaid wages and being forced to fight in Ireland. Sir Thomas Fairfax and Oliver Cromwell persuaded them to surrender, and the ringleader Robert Lockyer was executed. In May, another mutiny broke out in Oxfordshire. Cromwell led troops against this and most of the mutineers were pardoned. Three of the leaders – Cornet James Thompson, Corporal Perkins and John Church – were executed. Lilburne was later tried but found not guilty. Walwyn and Overton were released in autumn 1649 because the movement was no longer seen as a danger.

● **Diggers:** The Diggers (or True Levellers as they called themselves) were led by Gerrard Winstanley. They believed that all land and property should be shared equally – they referred to the earth as 'a common treasury for all'. They set up small communities to work the land and share the produce. They despised landlords and the old social hierarchy. Wherever the Diggers set up their communes they faced harassment and sometimes even violence from local landlords. Eventually, the movement faded.

● **Quakers:** The key figure in this movement was George Fox. Quakers emphasised a close study of the Bible and believed that everyone had a personal relationship with God. This meant there was no need for an organised Church or for priests. Quakers refused to show respect to social superiors – for example they would refuse to doff their hats. The Quaker movement was generally stronger in the north of England. In the 1650s, the 'Valiant Sixty' – 60 Quaker preachers – travelled across the country gathering support. Historians estimate that by 1660 there may have been as many as 55,000 Quakers. Fox and other Quaker preachers were often arrested or imprisoned, usually for short periods of time. In 1660, the government launched a major campaign to destroy the movement.

Source 2 A news sheet published by parliament in 1650. ▼

A Perfect Table of one hundred forty and Five Victories obtained by the Lord Lieutenant of Ireland, and the Parliaments Forces under his Command, since his Excellency was made Governour Generall by the Parliament of England. From Wednesday August 1. 1649. to March the last, 1650. With a briefe Chronicle of the chiefe matters of the Irish Warres, from that time to this present.

1. Is Source 3 more useful as evidence of the events of 1649–51 or about attitudes at the time? Explain your answer.

2. What impression do you get of Oliver Cromwell from Source 3?

3. How far is Source 2 similar to or different from Source 3 in its view of Oliver Cromwell? Explain your answer.

Scotland and Ireland: The continuing rise of Oliver Cromwell

For Cromwell and the army, the most pressing threat was that posed by Ireland and Scotland. Throughout April and May 1649, Cromwell strengthened his standing in the army further by crushing mutinies led by Levellers within the army. Cromwell led the campaign in Ireland in August 1649. In a bloody and brutal conflict he defeated the Irish rebels. This campaign included the massacre of the populations of Drogheda (September 1649) and Wexford (October 1649). By 1652, the Irish Confederation had been defeated. By this time Cromwell himself had left Ireland to lead other forces against the Scots, taking part in bloody battles at Dunbar in 1650. He then defeated a joint force of Royalist supporters and Scots at Worcester in September 1651. This brought an end to the threat to the republic and secured Cromwell's reputation as a skilful commander. This was to prove significant: Cromwell had the respect (and perhaps fear) of the Rump Parliament as well as the support and loyalty of the army.

Source 3 An extract from the memoirs of Colonel John Hutchinson, one of the men who signed Charles I's death warrant.

After the king's death almost every man favoured a particular form of government, and was angry if his own ideas didn't take place. Among these, John Lilburne, a wild, spirited man, who never was quiet in anything, published criticisms. The Levellers made a disturbance with a kind of rebellion, which Cromwell soon calmed, the Levellers being betrayed by their own leaders. Cromwell finished the conquest of Ireland. Then in 1650 the angry Presbyterians spit fire out of their pulpits and tried to stir up the people against the parliament. They entered into a plot of treason with Scotland, which had now received and crowned the son of the late king. He led them here in a great army, but God upset their plans.

The rule of the Rump Parliament

With Cromwell off battling the enemies of the new republic, the running of the Commonwealth fell to the Rump Parliament. Some of the MPs who had refused to agree to Charles's trial were allowed back, bringing the number of those sitting in parliament to about 200.

In February 1641, the Rump created a council of state consisting of 41 members who were elected annually. This council effectively took the place of the king. It put forward many laws that the Rump Parliament then discussed and voted on. Some were radical reforms, others designed to be measures taken for the good of the people. These included:

- **March 1649:** Monarchy and the House of Lords officially abolished.
- **April 1649:** Sale of royal lands to help to pay wages owed to the army.
- **May 1649:** England declared to be a Commonwealth ruled by parliament.
- **September 1650:** Compulsory church attendance abolished.
- **December 1650:** The use of English rather than Laton in courts of law.
- **October 1651:** The Navigation Act introduced, which helped British merchants and increased their trade and also ensured Britain had plenty of experienced sailors in case of a war.

Source 5 A set of accounts reporting the cost of the war in Ireland to parliament, 1651. The portrait is of Oliver Cromwell. The coat of arms at the top of the document is the arms of the Commonwealth, with the symbols of England, Ireland and Scotland. ▼

Source 4 The Great Seal of the Commonwealth 1651. ▲

4 Which measures taken by the Rump Parliament were radical reforms?

5 Which measures were for the good of the people?

6 Look back at the great seal of William the Conqueror on page 21. How is the seal in Source 4 different?

7 Does it strike you as odd that Source 5 should have a portrait of Cromwell? What does this suggest about where power lay at this time?

Cromwell vs Commonwealth – clashes with the Rump Parliament

Cromwell was occupied with wars for most of the period 1649–51. However, he was also an MP and followed what was happening in parliament. While he approved of many measures, he felt that some actions showed that members of the Rump were more concerned with keeping themselves in power, crushing radical groups and enforcing their order and authority on the country than anything else:

- **March 1649:** Arrest of the civilian Leveller leaders.
- **September 1649:** Censorship reintroduced, mainly as a response to the activities of radical groups.
- **January 1650:** All adult males ordered to take the Engagement – an oath of loyalty to the Rump Parliament.
- **April 1650:** Observing the Sabbath made compulsory.
- **June 1650:** A new government newspaper launched, the *Mercurius Politicus*.
- **August 1650:** Blasphemy Act passed, aimed at undermining and restraining the activities of extreme Puritans.

Cromwell was not worried by the crushing of the Levellers and other groups. What mattered most to him was the Rump's lack of religious reform. Cromwell believed that England could become a truly godly nation and hoped that parliament would reform the Church of England. As a Puritan himself, Cromwell wanted greater religious toleration – freedom for people to find God through Bible study, prayer or discussion. He did not want people to be forced to worship God in strictly controlled ways. However, religious freedom frightened many of the Rump MPs and the gentry they represented. They thought that a strong Church with strict authority would help to keep order in society.

To encourage religious reform, Cromwell reached an agreement with the Rump MPs on 19 April 1653. The Rump Parliament would dissolve itself and hold fresh elections, supervised by the army. Cromwell and his troops planned to select MPs who would be willing to reform religion. The next morning, news reached Cromwell that MPs were about to break the agreement. They planned to hold free elections outside the army's control. Cromwell hurried into parliament. He insulted the MPs, saying: 'Whoremasters! Drunkards! You have sat here too long for the good that you have been doing. Depart I say and let us have done with you. In the name of God go!' Then he called in soldiers to clear out the MPs. He dissolved the Rump by force. The army was once again in control.

1. Cromwell was greatly admired in the nineteenth century. Do you think Source 6 demonstrates this?

Source 6 A nineteenth-century drawing of Cromwell dissolving the Rump Parliament. ▶

Source 7 The views of Clement Walker on the Rump Parliament. Walker was one of the MPs excluded in Pride's Purge.

This fag end, this veritable Rump of a Parliament with corrupt maggots in it. … There is an endless list of fathers and sons and brothers who fill this house. They come in couples like unclean beasts to Noah's Ark.

Source 8 The memories of Rump MP Bulstrode Whitelocke of a private conversation with Oliver Cromwell about parliament in 1652. Whitelocke suspected Cromwell of wanting to become king.

Really their pride and ambition and self-seeking, taking all places of honour for themselves and their friends ... their delay in parliament business and constant divisions into factions against each other ... and the scandalous lives of some of the most senior of them ... gives too much reason for people to criticise them. There will be ruin unless some authority takes control and keeps matters in better order.

Source 9 Edmund Ludlow's account of Cromwell's speech when dissolving the Rump Parliament in April 1653. Ludlow was an MP and had served with Cromwell in Ireland.

Cromwell attacked the parliament with the vilest reproaches, accusing them of having no desire to serve the public good, to have been no better than the corrupt Presbyterians and lawyers who supported tyranny and oppression, accusing them of wanting only to maintain their own power and privilege.

Source 10 Historian Barry Coward, writing in 1994.

The Rump Parliament was a victim of the dilemma facing England as a Republic. It was too conservative and timid for the army and the Puritans and religious reformers. At the same time it was not conservative enough to heal the wounds and the mistrust which Pride's Purge and the king's execution had opened up, particularly for the gentry.

FOCUS TASK

The Rump's reforms

Read Source 10. Write two paragraphs adding some examples to support Coward's main points:
- Examples that the Rump was too conservative.
- Examples that the Rump was not conservative enough.

EXTENSION: Add a third paragraph explaining the importance of Cromwell's role.

PRACTICE QUESTIONS

1   Explain why Cromwell became more powerful in the period 1649–53. (10)
2   'Cromwell seized power because he felt he was guided by God.' How far do the sources in this section convince you that this statement is correct? (20)

TOPIC SUMMARY

Britain without a king: The Commonwealth 1649–53

1   After the execution of Charles I, England was a Commonwealth ruled by the Rump Parliament.
2   Parliament appointed a council of state to replace the king. This council put forward laws for the approval of MPs. Some were radical reforms (e.g. the abolition of the House of Lords), some were practical (e.g. replacing Latin with English in courts of law).
3   During the Civil War, the Irish Catholic Confederation ruled Ireland. The Rump feared Catholic enemies in Europe might invade via Ireland and Cromwell led a brutal campaign that crushed the Irish.
4   When Charles was executed, Scotland declared his eldest son to be king of Great Britain. Cromwell defeated the Scots in a bloody battle at Dunbar. A Scottish army invaded, with Royalist support in England. Cromwell defeated them at Worcester.
5   Radical groups flourished after the Civil Wars. The Rump Parliament imprisoned the leaders of these groups and restricted their freedom. A Leveller-led mutiny in the army was crushed by Cromwell.
6   Cromwell's leadership earned him both respect and fear. He was the most powerful person in England.
7   Cromwell was unhappy with the Rump, particularly its lack of religious reform. He believed that England could become more godly if the people were given greater religious freedom. However, this frightened many Rump MPs. They favoured a Church that imposed conformity in areas such as services and prayer books, because they believed this strengthened order and authority in society.
8   Cromwell was determined to get the reforms he wanted. In April 1653, he persuaded the Rump MPs to hold fresh elections, supervised by the army. When he found they were about to break the agreement, Cromwell and his soldiers expelled the Rump MPs and dissolved parliament. The army was once again in control of England.

6.2 Parliament and the Protector 1653–58

FOCUS

Cromwell dissolved the Rump Parliament in April 1653. He was now without question the most powerful man in Britain. Cromwell had a vision of a godly country and was determined to bring this about. However, despite his power and influence, Cromwell faced many challenges and a great deal of opposition. The country was still deeply divided, and the question was whether Cromwell could truly bring peace.

Cromwell's aims

Cromwell had two key aims – to build a godly society and to heal the country after the trauma of the Civil Wars. To a great extent, these aims conflicted with each other.

Building a godly society

Cromwell believed in religious toleration. He felt that a strict, centrally organised Church of England, with the clergy telling people what to do, prevented people finding God. With religious freedom, people would be able to study the Bible and discuss their faith with others. In this way they would become more 'godly' of their own free will.

The army and the Puritans were enthusiastic supporters of religious reform and shared Cromwell's passion for building a godly society. They were powerful, but they were a minority – and an unpopular one. Most people disliked Puritan religious ideas, and the army was unpopular because it cost a huge amount of money to maintain, which meant heavy taxes.

Healing and settling

Cromwell believed that the wounds of Civil War needed to be healed. The best way to do that was through a return to order. This included re-establishing a clear social hierarchy. Cromwell believed that the people best placed to run the country and bring back the stability everyone wanted were those who owned land and property – the gentry.

The gentry shared Cromwell's desire for settlement and stability. However, they saw religious freedom and Puritan ideas as a threat to an ordered society. They believed that a strong Church, with power and influence, would help keep order. They also resented the power of the army and the Puritans, because these groups had usurped their rightful place in running the country.

ACTIVITY

Study the information on page 194. Here are three possible approaches Cromwell might have taken:
- He could have sided with the army and Puritans, demanding godly reform and ignoring the need for healing and settling.
- He could have focused on healing and settling and given up on establishing a godly society.
- He could have attempted to balance the two for the rest of his life.

1　Work in pairs or small groups. Based on what you have read about the situation in England at this time, what were the potential advantages and disadvantages of each approach?
2　If you were advising Cromwell, which option would you advise? Or would you advise a different option?
3　Based on what you have read so far, which of the approaches do you think Cromwell eventually chose?

Keep a note of your work. You will revisit this activity several times.

The Nominated Assembly (Barebones Parliament) 1653

When Cromwell dissolved the Rump Parliament, he thought that he would be able to achieve his aims with a new assembly. Its members were nominated by Cromwell and the army on the basis of their 'godly' outlook, although they also balanced these men with moderates who represented the gentry. The assembly was nicknamed the Barebones Parliament (after one of its more radical members, named Praise-God Barebones).

In some ways, the Barebones Parliament summed up Cromwell's problem. In the five months that it sat, the assembly passed over 30 laws. However, after just a few months, in December 1653, the moderates – alarmed by the ideas of the radicals – voted to dissolve parliament and hand power back to Cromwell.

Source 1 Richard Baxter, a Presbyterian minister, writing in 1696.

With the young Commonwealth being headless you might think there was nothing to stand between Cromwell and the Crown. But there was yet another pageant to be played out. Cromwell wanted to make the need for his rule undeniable and he also wanted to make his soldiers turn against the constitution. So he called a parliament, but a parliament deliberately made full of division and strife. After that parliament failed, who was there to rule but Cromwell and the army?

Source 2 Samuel Highland, a radical member of the Barebones Parliament.

It is generally told and widely believed that we radicals would have destroyed the church and clergy. In fact we were merely trying to fight the old and corrupt ways of paying for the clergy. Many a godly preacher lives on £20 per year while many undeserving preachers have £300 or more. We were godly and sober men trying to do our duty and we were rewarded by false reports and judged by hearsay without proof.

1　Read Source 1. What accusation is Baxter making against Cromwell?
2　Do you think this source is more useful about Cromwell or about Baxter?
3　How would a historian make use of Source 2?

Instrument of government: Cromwell's Protectorate

Cromwell must have seen the end of the Nominated Assembly coming, because for weeks his ally General Lambert had been drafting a written constitution called the Instrument of Government (see Factfile). In theory, the Instrument of Government seemed to solve all of England's political problems:

- It provided the country with a head of state, but limited his power.
- It aimed to keep the army happy by providing regular taxes to maintain a force of 30,000 men (the first standing army in English history).
- It set out a plan for a Church settlement. Protestant Christianity was to be the public faith of the nation, yet there was to be religious freedom (liberty of worship) for any Protestant sects that did not disturb the peace. The Church of England would exist but the role of the clergy would be to guide and encourage religious devotion, not to enforce rigid rules.

FACTFILE

The Instrument of Government December 1653

The Instrument of Government aimed to make government practical and possible. Cromwell was made Lord Protector and head of state. He could call and dissolve parliament, and control the armed forces, and he had the power to make war and peace. However, there were certain limits on his powers:

- The Lord Protector had to call parliament at least once every three years.
- Parliament had to sit for at least five months before it could be dissolved.
- The Lord Protector had to sign bills passed by parliament within 20 days or explain his reasons for not doing so. If he did not, they automatically became law.
- The Lord Protector was chosen (for life) by the Council of State (made up of between 13 and 21 members).
- The Council of State was selected by MPs and advised the Lord Protector in all matters.
- Parliament had the power to make laws, but not to change the Instrument of Government.

Source 3 An extract from the memoirs of Edmund Ludlow. Ludlow was an army officer and supporter of Cromwell, but turned against him over the Instrument of Government.

This important business [writing the Instrument of Government] that so concerned the nation was done in a secret manner by two or three persons, for no more were let into the secret of it. So it may justly be called a work of darkness.

ACTIVITY

Look back at the Activity on page 195. Which of the three options did Cromwell try with:

- the Nominated Assembly
- the Instrument of Government?

Note down at least one example to support your view for each.

---

1 How far does Source 3 support the views of Source 1 on page 195?
2 How far do Sources 1 and 3 agree or disagree with the information in the main text about the Nominated Assembly and the Instrument of Government? Which do you trust more?
3 Would you agree that Sources 1 and 3 are unreliable evidence about Cromwell but reliable evidence of the divisions in England at this time?

First Protectorate Parliament 1654–55

The elections for the first parliament were set for September 1654. In the months leading up to its first session, Cromwell and his Council of State worked hard producing new measures. He hoped that MPs would quickly approve these measures and make them law.

> **Source 4** Cromwell at the opening of the First Protectorate Parliament, 4 September 1654.
>
> *You are met here on the greatest occasion that, I believe, England ever saw; having upon your shoulders the interests of three great nations ... and truly, I believe I may say it ... you have upon your shoulders the interest of all the Christian people in the world. ... It's one of the great ends of calling this parliament that this ship of the Commonwealth may be brought into a safe harbour.*

Within days, Cromwell's hopes and expectations were dashed. Instead of passing all the laws he wanted, the new MPs attacked the Instrument of Government, claiming that it was an illegal document. The attack was led by Sir Arthur Hesilrige (one of the five MPs Charles I had tried to arrest in 1642) and the republican John Bradshaw (the presiding judge at the king's trial). These opponents were highly respected and influential. They said that the Instrument was illegal and criticised the fact that it was written by Cromwell's close ally General Lambert. They were also worried that Cromwell and the army were becoming too powerful.

Hesilrige and Bradshaw called for an immediate recall of the Rump Parliament and for the army to be placed under the Rump's control. They also refused to consider any of Cromwell's proposals for a Church of England that would allow Puritans and others some freedom in how they worshipped.

> **Source 5** A written order from Cromwell to one of his army commanders in London, November 1654.
>
> *Several pamphlets of scandal and rebellion are published from time to time. They dishonour this nation and disturb the peace. I am told that certain pamphlets of that nature have been, and are now about to be, printed by several persons within the city of London. I order you to immediately go to the homes or work houses of all such printers within the city that you suspect. Arrest all of them immediately and bring them before my Council at Whitehall. And you are to seize and bring away the [printing] presses and all the pamphlets and any other papers that are in any way harmful to me or the state. In order to do this, you are authorised to break open any locks or bolts whatsoever.*

Source 6 The Great Seal of the Protectorate. As well as being a statement of power, the seal was used for practical purposes – to show that documents had official approval. ▼

4 What can you infer from Source 5 about the popularity of Cromwell's rule and Cromwell's reaction to opponents?

5 Compare the seal in Source 6 with the Seal of the Commonwealth on page 191 and the seal of William the Conqueror on page 21. Which two are most similar?

6 What impression to you get of Cromwell from Sources 5 and 6?

7 Based on your knowledge, is this impression fair?

1 What can you infer from Source 7 about England at this time?

> **Source 7** An extract from Cromwell's speech dissolving the First Protectorate Parliament in January 1655.
>
> *If you had made a religious settlement which had created a godly clergy, and a Presbyterian church, and yet allowed men of the same Protestant faith such as Independents or Baptists some liberty in smaller matters of worship or faith then you might have settled peace and quietness among all godly folk. Have you done this? Or anything close to this? No. You are not satisfied unless you control the beliefs, the consciences, the very words of all your brethren. What hypocrisy that you who fought against being oppressed by bishops have now become greater oppressors.*

The four fundamentals

Cromwell tried to compromise with MPs, but he insisted on 'four fundamentals' that he would not change:

- Government must be by a single person and a parliament.
- Parliaments could not sit endlessly without dissolution or re-election.
- There must be LIBERTY OF CONSCIENCE in religion.
- Control of the army must be shared by the Lord Protector and parliament.

Cromwell insisted that the MPs take an Oath of Recognition, agreeing to the four fundamentals. Eighty MPs refused and were excluded from parliament. Even those who took the oath remained hostile, and continued to rewrite the Instrument of Government to give parliament greater powers. After five months, Cromwell's patience gave way, and on 22 January 1655 – at the earliest moment allowed by the Instrument of Government – he dissolved his First Protectorate Parliament.

Rule of the Major-Generals 1655–57

Cromwell was deeply troubled by the failure of the First Protectorate Parliament. In March 1655, a Royalist rebellion – Penruddock's Rising – broke out in Wiltshire. The army easily crushed the rebellion but it made Cromwell realise that the Royalist threat was still alive.

In April 1655, England's military force in the Caribbean (which was fighting the Spanish) suffered serious defeats. Once again, Cromwell saw the hand of Providence. He feared that God was punishing England; the nation needed a godly 'reformation of manners' in order to regain God's favour. To achieve this aim he turned to the army. England and Wales were divided into 11 military districts, each one commanded by a Major-General, including his old ally Lambert running northern England. These commanders would impose military discipline, crush any Royalist threat and impose a more godly lifestyle on the people. This meant shutting alehouses, stopping popular sports like cock-fighting and horse racing, and enforcing the ban on wild celebration and feasting during religious festivals like Christmas. The cost of using the army in this way, and of raising local militias to help them, was paid for by a new tax called the Decimation Tax. Paid by ex-Royalists, this cost them one-tenth of their income. For many, after years of war, this was an impossible price to pay. Some had to sell their homes and estates.

> **Source 8** An extract from a set of proposals sent to Cromwell by a Puritan lawyer, William Sheppard, in 1657.
>
> *It is disgraceful that there is no law against rude gestures, sluttish clothing, bare shoulders, powdering and painting of the face and curling of the hair. It is just as disgraceful that there is no clear law to punish rude jests, fiddling, piping, rhyming, juggling, fortune telling, dancing upon the rope, ballad-singing, sword playing, or playing of prizes, ape-carrying, puppet-playing, bear-baiting, bull-baiting, horse-racing, cock-fighting, carding, dicing and other gaming, especially the spending of much time and the betting of great sums on these things.*

Source 9 A pamphlet from 1652, criticising Cromwell's rule. He is accused of supporting Puritans who wanted to ban the celebration of Christmas. The Puritan is on the left, Father Christmas is in the middle and the man on the right represents ordinary people. Other complaints are aimed at the army (General Plunder and Major General Tax) and the ringworm (disease) called Excise (customs duties). This surviving copy of the pamphlet is from 1652 but it was reprinted several times, particularly during the rule of the Major-Generals. ▼

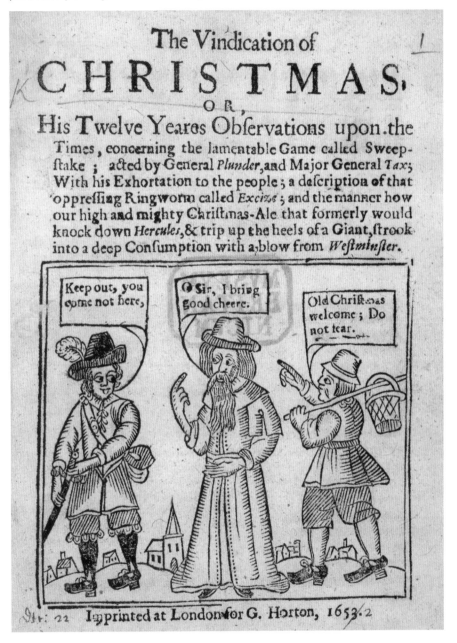

Look back at the Activity on page 195.

ACTIVITY

Look back at the Activity on page 195. Which of the three options did Cromwell try with:
- the First Protectorate Parliament
- the Major-Generals?

Note down at least one example to support your view for each.

The experiment failed. Most people did not embrace godly reform – in fact they were alienated by the loss of many of their leisure activities. Making Royalists pay the Decimation Tax opened up old rivalries and divisions, and did little to heal the wounds of the Civil Wars. Local magistrates, officials, and gentry were annoyed at having army officers telling them how to run local affairs. Many officers had risen through the ranks through merit, and were thus of lower social standing. The local elites resented the intrusion of these social upstarts. As an attempt at 'settling', it was a failure.

The recall of parliament and the end of the Major-Generals

By 1656 the Protectorate was facing a financial crisis. The Decimation Tax failed to cover the cost of the rule of the Major-Generals and an on-going war against Spain was proving expensive: outgoings were exceeding income by £230,000 every year. The Major-Generals confidently advised Cromwell to call another parliament in the hope that it would grant him new taxes. The Major-Generals assured the Lord Protector that they would be able to 'supervise' the elections so that only sympathetic MPs returned. Cromwell agreed.

When the MPs took their seats in the Second Protectorate Parliament, Cromwell soon realised the Major-Generals had failed in their mission to influence the elections. Cromwell excluded over 100 MPs from parliament, but even after this the remaining MPs refused to pass a Militia Bill that would have allowed the rule of the Major-Generals to continue. By January 1657, Cromwell recalled the Major-Generals from their localities, and the experiment in military rule fizzled out.

The Humble Petition and Advice 1657

By 1657, Cromwell was ageing but still he was being pulled in different directions. On one side were his army officers (the 'Old' or 'Radical' Cromwellians). They urged him to stick with the Instrument of Government. On the other side were civilian MPs (the 'New' or 'Conservative' Cromwellians), who were willing to support Cromwell's Protectorate so long as the power of the army was limited. They wanted the Instrument of Government (regarded as an army document) completely rewritten into a new constitution. These MPs – including Lord Broghill and Bulstrode Whitelocke – could be described as moderates who wished to return the nation to normality as soon as possible. They did not reject Cromwell's position as Lord Protector, but they wanted him to turn the Protectorate into a civilian system. They believed that the old system of monarchy had served England well for centuries and could now be used again to help bring stability – only this time Cromwell would be made king! These moderate MPs presented their new constitution, including the offer of the crown, in a document called the Humble Petition and Advice (see Factfile).

FACTFILE

The Humble Petition and Advice
The main terms of the Humble Petition and Advice included:
- Cromwell would be king, and would nominate his successor.
- A new House of Lords would be created, called the 'Upper House'. Cromwell would nominate its members in order to balance the power of MPs in the Commons.
- Parliament would control taxation.
- The army would be reduced in size to save money.
- Parliament would appoint key ministers of government.

Cromwell decides

Between February and May, Cromwell considered whether or not to accept the Humble Petition and Advice. There were arguments both for and against this:

- **For:** The offer of monarchy and the stability that it offered was certainly attractive. Englishmen understood monarchy well. Similarly, the Humble Petition and Advice had the advantage of being a settlement of parliament's own making – a truly civilian constitution, which also made his position legitimate and would gain him their support.
- **Against:** By accepting the petition, Cromwell could alienate the army and the loyal soldiers that had helped him get so far. Officers such as General Lambert were angry that the Humble Petition and Advice would make Cromwell king. They urged him to reject the offer. To accept would betray all they had fought for, and would appear as the sin of selfish ambition.

Despite his desire to accept the new constitution, it was the offer of the crown that led Cromwell to finally reject the Humble Petition and Advice, on 8 May 1657. God, he argued, had struck down the institution of monarchy, and Cromwell was not about to rebuild it.

'King, in all but name'

Instead, Cromwell decided to compromise. On 25 May 1657 he accepted a modified version of the Humble Petition and Advice, which allowed him to remain Lord Protector rather than king. He hoped this was a solution that everyone could accept.

In June 1657, Cromwell was reinstalled as Lord Protector in a ceremony that was essentially a coronation. He wore purple robes trimmed with ermine, and carried a golden sceptre. His household moved from Hampton Court Palace to the Palace at Whitehall and he was addressed thereafter as 'Your Highness'. Cromwell was king in all but name.

> **Source 10** Edmund Ludlow's account (see Source 3 on page 196) of conversations between Cromwell and army officers over the Humble Petition.
>
> *Cromwell was almost on his way to tell the MPs that he was prepared to accept the offer of the crown. He met with Colonel Desborough and told him his decision. Desborough said that he would not oppose Cromwell if he made this choice, but he would never serve him again. Desborough then met with Colonel Pride and told him what happened. Pride immediately declared that he would raise his fellow officers and petition Cromwell not to take this action.*

> **Source 11** Cromwell, writing about his role as Lord Protector, April 1657.
>
> *I am ready to serve, not as a king, but as an officer [of the law]. For truly, as before God, I have often thought that I could not say what my business or job was, except by comparing it with a good officer keeping the peace of the community. And truly, during the troubles that I have been through, it has made me content and happy that you have peace.*

Source 12 A contemporary engraving showing Cromwell accepting the role of Lord Protector after the Humble Petition and Advice, 1657. He is being presented with an ermine-lined robe, a gilt and embossed Bible, a sword of state and a gold sceptre. ▼

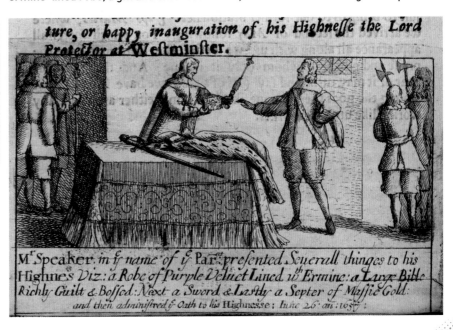

1. According to Source 10, why did Cromwell refuse the crown?
2. Study Sources 11 and 12. How would most MPs have reacted to them?
3. How would General Lambert or other army officers have reacted?

ACTIVITY

Look back at the Activity on page 195. Which of the three options did Cromwell follow with the Humble Petition and Advice? Note down at least one example to support your view.

Second Protectorate Parliament 1658

When the Second Protectorate Parliament reassembled in January 1658, it did so under the new rules laid down in the Humble Petition and Advice. Many of Cromwell's closest supporters had been promoted from the House of Commons and appointed to the new 'Upper House'. Cromwell hoped that, finally, all would proceed smoothly.

Once again he was to be disappointed. As soon as the new session of parliament opened, Cromwell faced vicious verbal assaults, this time from republican MPs, over the new constitution. These were the men like Hesilrige who had been excluded from previous parliaments but who, under the new rules, could once again take their seats. They were outraged at the fact that Cromwell had assumed the role of king in all but name. With many of his most loyal supporters now in the Upper House, the attacks in the Commons could not be silenced. When rumours circulated that members of the army were also unhappy, Cromwell realised he had to act, and he dissolved parliament. It had lasted only three weeks.

In Cromwell's final months, his relationship with the army deteriorated. General Lambert was dismissed for refusing to swear the new oath of allegiance demanded by the Humble Petition, and other officers lost their positions for publicly criticising Cromwell. Quite what Cromwell's next move would have been remains a mystery, as death intervened.

During the summer of 1658, Cromwell faced the deaths of both his son-in-law and his daughter, Elizabeth, from cancer. A month later, on 3 September (the anniversary of his great victories at Dunbar and Worcester), suffering from a recurring malarial-fever from his time in Ireland, Cromwell died.

Source 13 An extract from the memoirs of Colonel John Huthinson (see Source 3 on page 190). Originally a supporter of Cromwell, Hutchinson turned against him in the 1650s.

To speak the truth, Cromwell's personal courage and kindness supported him against all enemies and rebels. When they heard of the oath, 140 officers combined to oppose him with Lambert as leader. The Protector heard of it and frightened them all. They left Lambert to take the fall alone, none daring to support him publicly, though many in their hearts wished he were the leader.

Source 14 *The Royal Oak of Britain.* **This was published in 1649 by Clement Walker, one of the MPs excluded in Pride's Purge, and was reprinted several times in the 1650s. The tree is a symbol of the monarchy. It shows the royal crown, sceptre and coat of arms. Hanging off the branches are** *Eikon Basilike* **(see Source 1 on page 189), the Bible and Magna Carta, statutes and reports. Cromwell is standing just above the entrance to hell.** ▼

ACTIVITY

Look back at the Activity on page 195. Which of the three options did Cromwell follow with the Second Protectorate Parliament? Note down at least one example to support your view.

Source 15 An image of Oliver Cromwell published in 1658. Its title was 'The Emblem of England's distractions and her attained, and further expected freedom and happiness'. It shows the benefits of Cromwell's rule. In the top left you can see the holy mountain of Zion and Noah's Ark. The left pillar represents his religious goodness. The right pillar shows England, Ireland and Scotland offering loyalty to him. ▼

FOCUS TASK

Summing up Cromwell

1 Sources 13 and 14 present very different views of Cromwell. Work in pairs. Each of you take one source and analyse it. You should explain:
   ● whether it supports or attacks Cromwell
   ● how you know
   ● what this reveals about England at the time
   ● what it reveals about the difficulties of ruling England at this time
   ● whether you think the source is a convincing impression of Cromwell's rule in the 1650s; to do this you should compare the content of the source with what you have learnt in this section, and consider the provenance and purpose of the source.
   You could present your work as a written report or as an annotated presentation.

2 Work in pairs or small groups. Discuss the following statements and decide on a scale of 1–5 how far you agree with them:
   ● Cromwell wanted to be king.
   ● Cromwell wanted to rule like a king but not be a king.
   ● Cromwell ruled like a king for the good of the country, not because he wanted to.
   ● Cromwell failed to achieve his aims.
   ● It was impossible to unite England in the 1650s.

PRACTICE QUESTIONS

1 Explain why England was so divided in the 1650s. (10)
2 'Cromwell wanted the crown.' How far do the sources in this section convince you that this statement is correct? (20)

TOPIC SUMMARY

Parliament and the Protector 1653–58

1 Cromwell had two conflicting aims: to build a 'godly society' and to heal the wounds caused by the Civil War. The army supported him in the first; the gentry supported him in the second. Cromwell spent the next five years searching for an approach to government that might deliver both outcomes, but it proved impossible.

2 In the Nominated Parliament of 1653, Cromwell and the army nominated MPs who they thought were 'godly', balanced by moderates who represented the gentry. But the moderates were so alarmed by radicals they soon dissolved parliament and gave power back to Cromwell.

3 Cromwell's next solution was a written constitution (the Instrument of Government) that created new rules for parliament, with a head of state (called Lord Protector) with limited power – Cromwell took that role, of course. But instead of passing the laws Cromwell wanted, the new parliament challenged the Instrument itself. Cromwell dissolved the First Protectorate Parliament as soon as he could.

4 In March 1655, a Royalist rebellion and a defeat in the Caribbean made Cromwell fear that God was punishing England. He turned to the army to solve this problem. He divided England and Wales into districts commanded by Major-Generals, who imposed military discipline, crushed Royalist threats and imposed a godly lifestyle by, for example, shutting alehouses and banning popular sports. To pay for the Major-Generals, ex-Royalists were charged the Decimation Tax.

5 This experiment failed on all counts. People did not become more godly. They resented the control and the tax. The experiment ended by 1657.

6 Running out of ideas, moderate MPs planned to return to the system of government that had served England well for centuries. They presented the Humble Petition and Advice, inviting Cromwell to become king.

7 Cromwell thought about it, but eventually refused because of opposition from his army supporters. Instead he returned as Lord Protector. The Second Protectorate Parliament met under new rules laid down in the Humble Petition. But Cromwell now faced fierce criticism from his former supporters and even the army. Cromwell dissolved this parliament after only three weeks.

8 In Cromwell's final months his relationship with the army deteriorated further. On 3 September 1658 Cromwell died from malarial fever. The future course of English government remained unclear.

6.3 Restoration of the monarchy

FOCUS

Cromwell died in 1658. It was hard enough to run the country with Cromwell in charge in the 1650s, but without him it proved impossible. Cromwell had occupied a 'king-sized' role. For most of the people only another kingly figure would do. In this topic you will see why the only solution to this challenge proved to be the restoration of the monarchy.

Protectorate to Restoration 1658–60

Cromwell died in September 1658. He had nominated his son, Richard, as Lord Protector. Perhaps he was intending to found a dynasty of Lord Protectors, but no one can be sure. What we do know is that in less than two years the Protectorate had collapsed and the monarchy had been restored. How and why did this happen?

Richard Cromwell did not have his father's personality, ability or drive to run the country.

Richard's father had not involved him in politics, so he had little experience and no support in the army or parliament. The army generals Lambert and Fleetwood hoped to use him as a puppet and effectively rule themselves. However, like all rulers they needed parliament to agree taxes to pay for the army, government, etc. and parliament would not co-operate. Richard Cromwell gave up his leadership and retired to his lands in May 1659.

Parliament and the army could not work together.

The Rump Parliament was restored in May 1659, but in October that year the commander of the army in England, John Lambert, dismissed the MPs. He replaced the Rump with an army-dominated Committee of Public Safety.

The army was divided.

The commander of the army in Scotland, George Monck, refused to accept Lambert's actions and supported parliament. He also had the support of many troops and most of the navy. In December 1659, Lambert backed down and the Rump Parliament was restored a month later.

It was clear that government could not work without a king or a king-like figure.

Oliver Cromwell had been acceptable to both the army and parliament, but no one matched him in drive or stature. The Political Nation feared more conflict. The most obvious solution was to restore the monarchy.

Parliament began to negotiate with Charles I's son.

Charles accepted the terms parliament offered in the Declaration of Breda. In April 1660, Charles II returned as king, greeted by cheering crowds.

RESTORATION

Source 1 John Evelyn, an observer and writer who recorded events secretly in his diary, London, February 1660.

3rd February: General Monck came now to London out of Scotland; no man knew what he would do or whether he would declare for king or parliament; yet he was met on his way by the gentlemen of all the counties which he passed with petitions that he would recall the old ... parliament and settle the nation in some order. ...

11th February: Monck dispersed the nest of robbers [the army generals] and convened the old Parliament ... with ringing of bells, and universal jubilee [celebration].

Source 2 From the Petition of the Gentlemen of Devon, presented to General Monck as he marched south to London to help parliament gain control, 1659.

Since the death of the king, we have been governed by tumult; bandied from one faction to the other; this party up today, that tomorrow – but still the nation under, and a prey to, the strongest. So long as this violence continues over us, no other government can settle the nation. ... You speak of the necessity of a republic. We say it is not necessary, not even effectual, but if it were both, a free parliament ought to introduce it. The consent of the people must settle the nation, ... and interests of opinion and property must be secured by a free parliament.

Source 3 General Monck's declaration as he marched his troops south to protect parliament and make way for the Restoration of Charles II.

I have received a call from God and his people to march into England, to assist and maintain the liberty and being of our parliaments, our ancient constitution, and therein the freedom and rights of the people of these three nations from arbitrary and tyrannical usurpation.

1 What can you learn about John Evelyn from Source 1?
2 From your knowledge of the 1650s, the information on this page and Sources 2 and 3, do you think Evelyn was typical?

A remarkable turnaround?

When King Charles II rode into London on 29 May 1660, the Restoration was complete. Britain was a monarchy once again – and the people cheered! The political rollercoaster of the republic was now over and everyone hoped that stability and peace would return once more. As historians, however, we need to explore how such a dramatic transformation was able to take place. The diagram below summarises the factors that played a part.

The unpopularity of the regicide

As far back as 1649, many had seen the trial and execution of Charles I as an illegal act. Some believed that the pain and confusion of the 1650s was punishment from God for having allowed such a thing to happen. Charles I was seen as a martyr, so it was natural that people would support the return of his son.

The popular desire for stability

Many people were tired of the disorder that had followed Cromwell's death. Neither the army nor the republicans had been able to make things work.

The unpopularity of the republic

Many of Cromwell's actions had proved unpopular, especially the rule of the Major-Generals (see pages 198–200). People hoped for a less restrictive attitude. Charles was nicknamed 'the Merry Monarch'!

Why was the Restoration of the monarchy popular?

The role of General Monck and the army

Without Monck's troops the Rump could never have been reinstated. Similarly, Monck insisted that the old MPs who had supported the king be readmitted. He knew this would sway parliament towards to the Restoration. Lastly, he was in communication with Charles II, and advised him when to make his move.

The actions of Charles II

Charles II decided to sit back and wait for the republic to collapse. By doing this he was able to present himself as the popular and only logical choice. The Declaration of Breda reassured people that there would not be massive reprisals. The fact that parliament voted to accept this and declare him king meant that he was not imposing himself on the people – the people were pleading for his return.

Fear of radicals

The Civil War had seen a growth in radical groups, which threatened to disturb the order and stability of the English Church, and the order and hierarchy of society. In fact one group, the Fifth Monarchists, actually staged a rebellion against the restored Charles II soon after he took the throne (see Source 5 on page 207). Even though Charles promised 'liberty to tender consciences', many hoped that a strict Church would be returned to keep radicals under control.

ACTIVITY

Read the information in the diagram above.
1 Are any of these factors linked? If so, how?
2 Place the factors in order of importance according to your understanding. Compare your order with that of a partner and try to agree which factor was most important.
3 Do you think that the Restoration could have taken place without any one of these factors? If so, what does that reveal about the importance of that factor?

The Restoration Settlement

In the Declaration of Breda (see Source 4), Charles II promised to share power with parliament and maintain the religious freedoms offered during the Protectorate. Making such promises had helped overcome any fears that Charles II was going to install an absolute monarchy similar to that during Charles I's Personal Rule in the 1630s.

> **Source 4** From the Declaration of Breda to the people of England, by Charles II, 1660.
>
> *To all our loving subjects ... after this long silence, we have thought it our duty to contribute [to the peace of the nation] ... that all our subjects may enjoy what by law is theirs, by a full and entire administration of justice across the land, and by extending our mercy. ... We do declare a free and general pardon. ... Let all our subjects, how so ever faulty, rely upon the word of a king, solemnly given by this present declaration, that no crime whatsoever, committed against us or our royal father before the publication of this, shall ever rise in judgement, or be brought in question, against any of them. ... And we do further declare, that we will be ready to consent to any Act or Acts of Parliament to the purposes aforesaid.*

In reality, however, the Restoration Settlement imposed in the years after 1660 was much more hard-line than promised in the Declaration of Breda. This was not due to Charles II but, perhaps surprisingly, to his parliament.

In 1661, a new parliament was elected, nicknamed the Cavalier Parliament. MPs were so eager to prevent future disorder in society, politics and religion that they decided to create a Restoration Settlement that reinforced both the power of the king and of the Church of England. Rather than maintaining a broad Church that allowed freedom of worship for any Protestant sect, it imposed strict rules of uniformity. Everyone had to attend Church of England services; there was no freedom of worship. Anyone who was not Anglican (a practising member of the Church of England) was banned from holding office or dismissed from their posts.

FACTFILE

The Restoration Settlement

The king's power	The king was to appoint his own ministers/advisers.
	Prerogative Courts were still banned and nearly all the concessions made by Charles I in 1641 were kept in force.
	The king commanded the army and navy (but was once again reliant on parliament for funds).
Parliaments	The king had to convene a parliament every three years, but the new Triennial Act (1664) did not force him to hold new elections.
Finance	The king was expected to raise Ordinary Revenue from Crown lands.
	Parliament had to give permission to raise a tax.
	No agreement was made regarding a set/regular income for the Crown, so it remained in debt.
Religion	Parliament imposed the Clarendon Codes (see Factfile).
	There was a strict Church of England with compulsory attendance.
	Puritanism was discouraged.
	The Book of Common Prayer was reimposed.
	Radical sects were banned and punished. Radical leaders were imprisoned.
	Bishops were restored.
	Anti-Catholic laws were enforced.
Society	Popular sports and entertainments and pastimes were encouraged.
	The theatre was revived.
	The Royal Society was established to encourage scientific and artistic endeavour and discovery.

> **FACTFILE**
>
> **The Clarendon Codes**
>
> The Clarendon Codes were a set of laws designed to limit the influence and spread of radical groups like the Quakers and Baptists, and to create uniformity (everyone worshipping in the same way). Anyone who did not conform was termed a dissenter. Many of the Clarendon Codes expressly restricted the activity of radicals. For example:
>
> - **Corporation Act 1661:** Excluded religious radicals from holding public office. Officials had to be members of the Church of England and swear loyalty to the king.
> - **Licensing Act 1662:** Restricted the printing of religious pamphlets.
> - **Five Mile Act 1665:** Prevented dissenter clergymen/priests from coming within five miles of a town where they had formerly served.
> - **Conventicle Act 1664:** Imposed fines for not attending Church of England services.
> - **Quaker Act 1662:** Imprisoned leading Quakers.

Revenge

In the Declaration of Breda, Charles promised that he would not try to avenge himself on all of his enemies. Parliament passed the Indemnity and Oblivion Act, which pardoned the vast majority of those who had supported parliament or Cromwell during the Civil Wars and in the years that followed. However, Charles did take his revenge on some of those who had been responsible for the death of his father. Many of the regicides were dead, but the bodies of Cromwell, Ireton and other commanders were dug up and hanged. Cromwell's head was placed on a spike. Of the living regicides, 13 were executed, 19 were imprisoned and the remainder were pardoned.

Source 5 The title page of a book published soon after the Restoration. The bottom panel shows the rebellion of the radical group the Fifth Monarchists against Charles II in 1660. It was led by Thomas Venner. The rebellion was a failure and Venner and ten others were executed. ▶

How popular was the Restoration?

The Restoration seemed to solve several problems, but many others remained. Parliament began using taxes as a bargaining tool again. The king's finances remained insufficient to run the kingdom and tensions over religion, especially Catholicism, re-emerged repeatedly in the decades that followed. It would take another revolution to solve these.

Source 6 A painting from 1660, showing Charles II being welcomed on his return. ▶

Source 7 An extract from the diary of Thomas Rugg.

The end of April and beginning of May 1661 were spent in days of joy at his Majesty's coronation. The town of Bruton in Somerset rang the church bells day and night. And in Cambridge the town was strewn with ribbons, pictures and garlands.

PRACTICE QUESTIONS

1   Explain why the Restoration Settlement was comparatively harsh compared with the Declaration of Breda. (10)
2   'The Restoration of the monarchy was largely the result of the actions of General Monck.' How far do the sources in this section convince you that this statement is correct? (20)

Source 8 Extracts from court cases in London, in which people were prosecuted for criticising the government.

1660 A London lady was convicted for saying 'A pox on all kings. I do not give a turd for never a king in England.'

1661 A man from Wapping convicted for saying 'I would gladly spend five shillings to celebrate the execution of the king and would not mind being the executioner myself'.

1662 A London man convicted for saying 'I hope before long to trample in the king's and bishops' blood'.

TOPIC SUMMARY

Restoration of the monarchy

1   Cromwell nominated his son, Richard, to succeed him as Lord Protector, but he was unsuited to the role. He had no political experience and lacked support from parliament or the army. He soon retired.
2   The army generals were in charge, but they needed parliament to raise taxes and parliament would not co-operate. Lambert tried to replace parliament with an army-dominated Committee of Public Safety. But the commander of the army in Scotland, George Monck, refused to accept this and backed parliament.
3   War between army factions looked possible. It was clear that government could not work without a king or a king-like figure. The most obvious solution was to restore the monarchy. Parliament invited Charles's son to return as Charles II.
4   Charles accepted the terms parliament offered in the Declaration of Breda (notably to share power with parliament, maintain religious freedom and not punish his opponents).
5   In reality the Restoration Settlement was more hard-line because the new parliament was dominated by ex-Royalists. To prevent future disorder they strengthened the power of the king. Instead of freedom of worship they imposed strict uniformity.
6   The Indemnity and Oblivion Act pardoned most people who had supported parliament or Cromwell. However, Charles did take revenge on the regicides. The dead leaders were dug up and hanged. Cromwell's head was placed on a spike. Thirteen living regicides were executed.
7   The Restoration solved some problems but the others remained – particularly tension over religion.

ASSESSMENT FOCUS

How the depth study will be assessed

The British depth study on Personal Rule to Restoration will be examined in Paper 3, along with the study of the historic environment on castles. The British depth study is worth 35 marks – 20 per cent of your total GCSE. You should spend about 45 minutes on this part of the paper. The questions could be on any part of the content so you need to revise it all.

Question 1 will test the first two assessment objectives:
● AO1: Knowledge and understanding
● AO2: Explanation and analysis

Question 2 will test these objectives but it will also test AO3: Analyse, evaluate and make use of sources from the time.

Above all, the questions are designed to assess your ability to think and work like a historian. In the introduction, you looked at how historians work (page 4). There we set out some steps that historians take:
1 focus
2 ask questions
3 select
4 organise
5 fine tune.

The exam questions have already chosen the focus (Stage 1) and asked the questions (Stage 2). What the examiner wants from you is stages 3, 4 and 5.

Question 1

Question 1 will ask you to explain some important aspect of the period you have studied. This may involve explaining the range of reasons for an event or development, or possibly explaining the scale of the impact of an event or development. For example:

> ● **Explain why there was opposition to the rule of the Major-Generals. (10 marks)**

Aim of the question
The key word here is 'why'. Examiners are looking for an explanation of why there was opposition to the Major-Generals. It would be easy to miss this point and simply describe what the Major-Generals did.

The Question 1 medal ceremony

 Bronze (up to 25% of marks): You describe one or more examples of the actions of the Major-Generals (e.g. closing alehouses).

 Silver (up to 60% of marks): You explain one example of why the actions of the Major-Generals were unpopular.

Gold (up to 100% of marks): You explain two or more examples and make it really clear why the actions of the Major-Generals were so unpopular and generated opposition.

Even a Gold answer can be improved by ensuring you have:
● a clear conclusion that rounds off your argument
● provided a range of examples as supporting evidence and included relevant and detailed knowledge in your supporting examples
● given a balanced answer which shows you understand that there might be more than one view about the question or explains how the different factors are connected.

Advice

Select: Focus on the reasons why the actions of the Major-Generals caused opposition. Select at least two causes.

Organise: The important thing is to organise your knowledge in a relevant way to answer the question. Have a clear sense of what you are trying to say. In this question, a good way to organise your answer might be:

> There were several reasons why the rule of the Major-Generals caused so much opposition. The most important was that they represented the army, which was unpopular. Another reason was that they interfered with leisure activities.

Fine tune: Do all the usual checks, but make sure you say which of your reasons you think is more important.

Example answer

Comments

There is no need to improve this answer. It is a Gold medal response. It has a clear opening and it then sticks to the line that the opening suggests it will follow. There is a good analysis of two separate causes. In each case, the answer explains how the factor caused opposition. It would be an easy mistake to simply list the actions of the Major-Generals without explaining why these actions caused opposition.

> There were many reasons for opposition to the rule of the Major-Generals in the 1650s. Probably the two most important reasons were concerns about the religious restrictions they imposed and also the fact that many important people resented the power of the army. The army also cost a lot in taxes, which made it very unpopular.
>
> One of the main aims Cromwell had in appointing the Major-Generals was to make England a more godly place. The Major-Generals were enthusiastic about this role and they enforced laws against drunkenness (which included closing alehouses), swearing and entertainments like bear-baiting and horse racing. Not surprisingly, clamping down on many traditional entertainments made the rule of the Major-Generals very unpopular.
>
> Another form of opposition to the Major-Generals came from local officials, particularly magistrates or justices of the peace. They resented the army interfering in local issues such as the Poor Law or collection of taxes. This was made worse by the fact that the Major-Generals often came from humbler backgrounds and were not important nobles as many of the justices were.

Practice

We gave this answer a Gold medal. You can use the same idea to assess your own answers. There are plenty of practice questions at the end of every topic. Go back and try a couple of the 10-mark 'Explain...' questions. Then read over your answer and see which medal you might award yourself.

Question 2

Question 2 is a challenging question that requires effective use of knowledge and evaluation of sources. There will always be three sources and the question will ask you to explain how far the sources support a particular view. For example:

> *Study Sources A–C.*
>
> *'The poor relationship between Charles I and parliament in the period 1629–42 was caused by religion.' How far do Sources A–C convince you that this statement is correct? Use the sources and your knowledge to explain your answer. (20 marks)*
>
> *Spelling, punctuation and grammar and the use of specialist terminology. (5 marks)*

> **Source A** From a book by Sir George Croke about the 'Ship Money Trial' in 1637. Croke was one of five judges who ruled in favour of John Hampden in the trial. The book was based on notes taken at the time of the trial.
>
> *We are not to here to give judgements which support what the king wants as his policy. We are judging according to the law of England. We find it in our books, records and statutes. The law respects the property, goods and estates of the king's subjects. Without their consent (either their private actual consent or implicitly by agreeing to taxes in parliament) their property cannot be taken from them by the king or anyone else.*

Source B A Puritan woodcut circulated after the trial of William Prynne, which depicts Archbishop Laud, 1637. There is a plate of ears on the table. ▼

Source C An extract from the Grand Remonstrance, 1641.

We find that there is an evil conspiracy corrupting the laws and principles of government and attacking religion and justice in this kingdom. The men responsible are:

1. The Catholics who hate England's laws which prevent them imposing their own religion on England.

2. The bishops and corrupt members of our clergy who promote ritual and superstition and support only their own power and position.

3. Councillors and servants of the king who, for their own benefit, have been serving the interests of foreign powers to the great harm of His Majesty and the country.

Question 2 specialist advice

If you are not careful things could go badly wrong with this question. The question asks: 'How far do Sources A–C convince you…'. It does *not* ask how far *you personally agree* with the statement. Your answer should focus on the sources and relate them to the viewpoint. This means:

- Showing that you understand what each source is saying – that means comprehension *and* inference. Do both these things. An example of comprehension would be: 'Source A is saying that the law respects property.' An example of inference would be: 'Source A is showing that some people oppose Charles's policies such as his taxes.' This is inference because the source does not say this anywhere. The candidate has *inferred* what the source's author is really trying to say – similar to working out the message of a propaganda poster or a cartoon.

- Relating what the sources say to the view in the question (i.e. whether the source convinces you that the statement is right or not). Examiners often use the 'so what?' test when reading what candidates have written. If you only write 'Source A is showing that some people oppose Charles's policies such as his taxes' then the examiner will ask 'So what? What's your point?' You may have thought it was so obvious that some people disagree with Charles over taxes and that therefore religion was not the only reason for tension that you did not need to spell it out to the examiner. But you *do* need to spell it out! For example: 'Source A suggests that the statement is wrong. It is a court case against someone who is opposing the king's policies on taxes. Clearly it is money and taxes causing tension in this source, not religion.' Examiners cannot give marks for what you were probably thinking. They can only reward what you actually say.

- Evaluating the sources in terms of whether they provide convincing support for the statement. This is partly about judging the reliability of the sources. (But remember sources can never be reliable or unreliable in themselves. They can only be reliable or unreliable *about something*.) However, it is also much more, so in answering this question it is much better to use the words 'convincing' and 'unconvincing' and to use a range of tools to help you.

Evaluation tools	Convincing because...	Not convincing because...
Knowledge	It is supported by your own knowledge	It is contradicted by your own knowledge
Author	You know something about the author which makes it convincing	You know something about the author which makes it unconvincing
Purpose	It has a purpose which you think makes it convincing	It has a purpose which you think makes it unconvincing

Keys to success

1   Read the question carefully. Sometimes students answer the question they wish had been asked rather than the one that has actually been asked. So identify the skill focus (what it is asking you to do). Does it want you to write a description, an explanation or a comparison? Identify the content focus (what it is about) and select from your knowledge accordingly.

2   Note the marks available. This helps you work out how much time to spend on answering each question. Time is precious. If you spend too long on low-mark questions you will run out of time for the high-mark ones.

3   Plan your answer before you start writing. For essays this is particularly important. The golden rule is know what you are going to say, then to say it clearly and logically.

4   Aim for quality not quantity: in the time limits of an exam you will not be able to write down everything you know and can think of – even if it is relevant. The marker would much rather read a short answer that really tackles the question than page after page of material that is not relevant.

5   Check your work. You will never have time in an exam to rewrite an answer but try to leave some time at the end to check for obvious spelling mistakes, missing words or other writing errors that might cost you marks.

Comments

This answer is very good. It would probably get 17–18 marks. It shows good comprehension and inference working together and related to the statement in the question. Then the answer offers a range of ways in which the sources are evaluated, in relation to the question. Probably the only thing missing from this answer is a conclusion. It would be interesting to see which side of the argument the candidate found more convincing and why.

Advice

Before you start, be sure to read the statement carefully. In the stress of an exam it can be easy to misinterpret it. In this case, the statement is that the poor relationship between Charles and parliament was caused by religion. Make sure you are also clear about what the sources say (comprehension and inference).

Select: You need to select facts, events and developments that support or challenge the views in the sources. This question is about whether religion caused the poor relations, so select items from this part of your knowledge wardrobe.

Organise: A good way to start this question is to show you understand what the sources are saying at face value, then go on to evaluate them. This is probably the easiest approach. However, you could also organise your answer by setting out the arguments and evidence that the sources are convincing, then the counter-argument.

Fine tune: Do all the usual checks, but here it is worth making sure you have used at least two of the three evaluation methods (knowledge, author and purpose). You will get more credit for using Tools A and B than Tool C.

Example answer

Source A convinces me that the statement is completely wrong. It suggests that taxes caused the bad relationship between Charles I and parliament, not religion. In 1634, Charles brought in a new tax called Ship Money which he said he could collect without permission from parliament. Many of his opponents thought this was illegal, which was why John Hampden went to court over Ship Money and the judges ruled in his favour, shown by Source A. This source is very convincing to me that taxes were the causes of tension rather than religion. It is obviously critical of Charles, saying that the judges were supposed to follow the law not the king's policy and also emphasising that the king could not take property without permission. Hampden and other campaigners like John Pym constantly criticised Charles for acting this way.

On the other hand, Sources B and C do suggest that religion was a major cause of tension between Charles and parliament. Source B shows a Puritan propaganda picture. It is accusing the Archbishop of Canterbury, William Laud, of being vicious and cruel by showing him eating the ears of the Puritan speaker William Prynne. Prynne had been branded and had his ears cut off as a punishment. At this time there was strict censorship, so the fact that Prynne dared to speak out and the fact that other Puritans dared to publish this picture suggests that the religious divisions were very serious. Source B is obviously a very biased source but this helps us to see how strongly the Puritans felt against Laud.

Source C also convinces me that religion was a major source of tension. The language is extremely aggressive with terms like 'evil conspiracy' and accusing some of the king's ministers of trying to bring back the Catholic Church and even working for foreign powers. This shows how serious the religious divisions were, especially as blaming the king's ministers was simply a polite way of criticising the king himself.

On balance, I am not completely convinced by the statement. Religion was certainly one of the causes of tension and it was a very important cause. However, it is almost impossible to separate religion from the other causes of tension, particularly taxes and Charles's use of the law. For example, John Hampden, who appears in Source A, was also a Puritan so he opposed Charles over tax and religion. He was also one of the most important supporters of the Grand Remonstrance.

Practice

Once again we gave this answer a 'Gold medal'. You can use the same idea to assess your own answers. There are plenty of practice questions at the end of every topic. Go back and try a couple of the 20-mark source-based questions. Then read over your answer and see which medal you might award yourself.

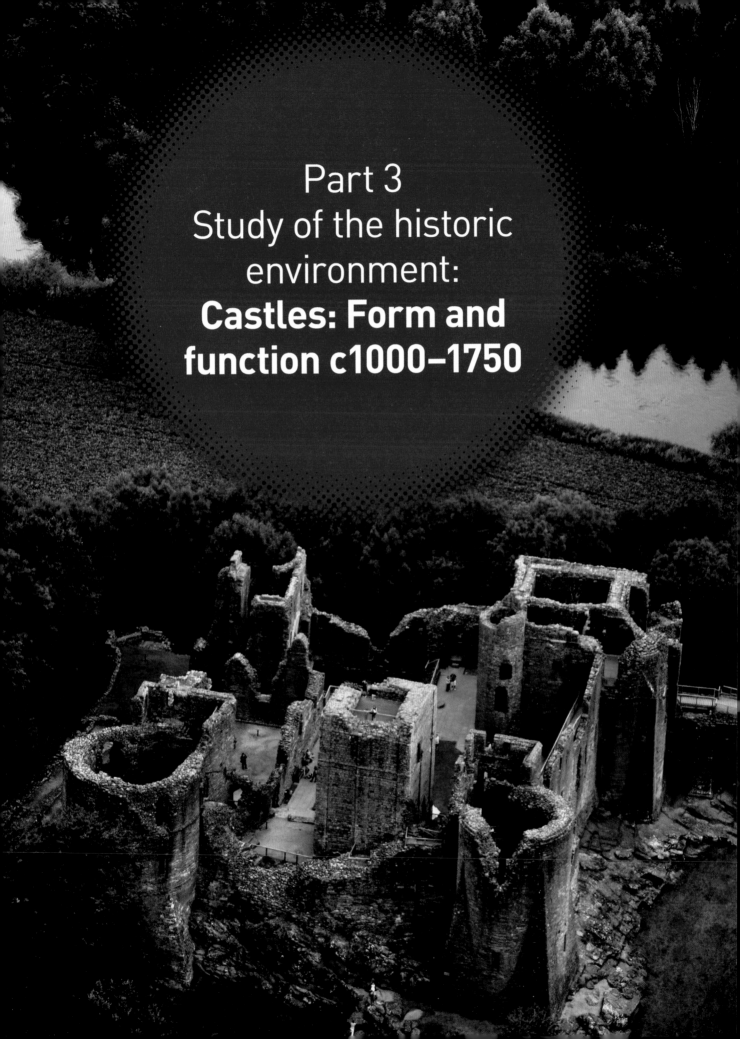

Part 3
Study of the historic environment:
Castles: Form and function c1000–1750

Introduction to the study of the historic environment

You will be familiar with using historical sources from your history lessons. You have used many written sources – chronicles, church records, official documents like Domesday Book or Magna Carta. You have used visual sources from the period you have been studying, and a few photographs and maps. In this study, the aim is to get you using another type of source – the historic environment.

Our focus is on castles, and how historians try to work out their story and that of the people who lived and worked in them. Experts can read castles and other buildings like you can read books or websites. When we put the evidence of buildings together with other evidence such as maps, photographs of the site, documents such as invoices and accounts, or letters to and from the people in the castle, it is possible to build up a detailed and interesting story.

You will be assessed on your knowledge of a key period of the castle – how and why it changed at particular times, for example. However, you will also be assessed on how historians use sources as evidence about the past. Remember – a source is *always* useful as evidence about something!

Countess Joan visits Goodrich Castle, 18 November 1296

Joan de Valence, the recently widowed Countess of Pembroke, spent the winter of 1296–97 at Goodrich Castle in Herefordshire, one of her main residences (see the photo on the previous page). She arrived on 18 November 1296, probably in a coach like the one pictured below. She had about 30 'upper servants' with her, who probably travelled with their families alongside them. Then there were about 15 'lower servants', plus carts (and carters) and pack animals for their luggage. This was a large group – perhaps 120 people.

Lords had their castles built in a particular spot for many reasons. They had to be convenient; they might need to defend an important place; and they needed to demonstrate the wealth and power of their owner (they were, in a way, propaganda in stone). Goodrich dominated an important crossing of the River Wye. The river itself, and the road that crossed it, were very important transport routes. As travellers entered the valley to cross the river, they would have been awed by the sight of the castle on top of the steep west side of the valley.

When Countess Joan's party settled into the castle, this sense of wealth and power probably increased. Four years of rebuilding had made Goodrich a state-of-the-art fortress palace. It had many comfortable rooms for the countess and her guests, as well as a new GREAT HALL and kitchens. Bright paint and tapestries decorated these rooms, which were heated by grand fireplaces. There was a series of large windows, most of which had seats so the countess and her guests could sit in comfort and look at the spectacular views. The first night's meal for this large party required 25 gallons of wine and three pigs.

How do we know all this detail from so long ago? This historic environment study shows you the range of skills and evidence you need to make statements like the ones you have just read.

7.1 How do we know about castles?

FOCUS

Source 1 shows two parts of Goodrich Castle. The keep is the tall, grey, rectangular building. In front of the keep there is another wall, built from a redder stone. Source 2 says the keep was built around 1150 and the outer wall was built around 1300. But how do we know?

In this topic, you will learn the skills needed to make plans like Source 2. You will see it is a combination of:

● looking very carefully at what survives – **the stones**
● fitting this into what you know about different fashions in castle-building at different times – **the styles**
● using the surviving documents – **the story**.

There are castles all over England – indeed all over Britain, Europe and the Middle East. People built them, lived in them, changed them and sometimes fought over them for hundreds of years. You can probably look at Source 1 and say it is a castle without ever having seen it before or knowing anything about it. Castles were not simply defensive structures. They were homes, sometimes palaces, centres of administration and a way of displaying power and wealth. In this topic, you will concentrate on Goodrich Castle and the nominated castle (the one in your exam).

A landowner named Godric built the first castle at Goodrich before 1100. There were major changes in about 1150, 1300 and 1450. This is typical of a castle's history. Over a period of 400 years, the needs and ideas of the people who owned and lived in the castle changed. These changes are a big part of the puzzle in trying to work out how people used the castle and why it was built the way it was. For any particular part of the castle, the answer might be different at different times in its history.

The difference between the 1150 and the 1300 buildings at Goodrich is easy to spot. The stone used in 1150 is light grey and is cut in large, rectangular blocks. The 1300 stone is darker and the blocks are smaller. So, it is easy to tell them apart – but how do we know which came first? Styles help here: the KEEP is of the type built in the first hundred years after the Norman Conquest. The wall in front is a CURTAIN WALL, of the type built in the twelfth to fourteenth centuries. So style suggests a date of around 1300, and documents we have available offer a more specific date of 1293–96, when royal workers seem to have helped. The work may have been finished by late 1296, because when Countess Joan visited more than 200 people were living in the castle.

Source 1 Part of the keep and curtain wall at Goodrich Castle. ▼

keep (c1150)

curtain wall (c1300)

Source 2 A phased plan of the same part of Goodrich Castle, showing the approximate dates when parts were built. ▼

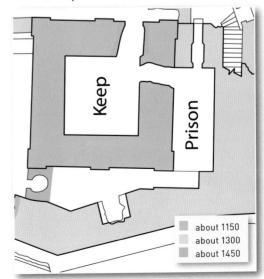

Keep

Prison

☐ about 1150
☐ about 1300
☐ about 1450

Reading a wall

Once you know what to look for, you can read a wall just like you can read a page in this book. We will start by looking at the clues in the stone in Source 3, which show that at different times this area looked like Source 4 and Source 5.

Source 3 The East Range (looking north) of Goodrich Castle. ▼

Corbels, beams and joists

JOISTS are long timbers that support walls or ceilings. Joists can be fixed to the walls or supported by beams, which are stronger timbers. Working out where the joists or beams joined the wall is the key to working out where the earlier floor levels were.

Corbels (stones that stick out from the wall), or neat holes or grooves to fit the joists into, or ledges to rest them on, are the things to look for.

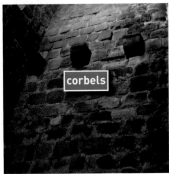

corbels

holes for joists

groove and ledge

Source 4 A single-storey hall from the late thirteenth century. ▼

Source 5 A later, three-storey building. ▼

The single-storey building

1 The scar of a roof-line runs diagonally between the two points marked 1 in Source 3. This is where the sloping roof joined the end wall of the (taller) gatehouse.
2 The stones in the outside wall have a gap where the door was.
3 The remains of the fireplace make sense with the floor level.

The three-storey building

4 This is a fireplace, with the chimney going up into the shadow. This means there must have been a floor at this level, and there cannot have been one in the single-storey building. The roof scar would cut through the fireplace.
5 This looks like a door that was cut in the tower after it was built – compare it with the original door (7). This could be an entrance to the same floor as the fireplace.
6 This looks like another door. This is the main evidence for this building having three floors.
8 This is a CORBEL (see Factfile), used to hold up a floor or a roof. It is a bit low to directly support the roof of this building, so the artist in Source 5 has suggested that a BEAM went up from the corbel to support the roof beams.
9 Two square holes have been cut in the wall, probably to fit two roof beams for the top of the ridged roof.
10 Another square hole, larger than the two at point 9. Again, these are probably for a roof beam, but one holding more weight.

An earlier version?

The windows marked 11 and 12, which originally provided light for the gatehouse behind this wall, do not really make sense with either of the buildings above. Window 12 was inside the roof of the single-storey building, which would be dark. The second floor of the three-storey building would cut across window 11 – a sure sign the window was from an earlier stage in the building. So originally, perhaps, there was no building here at all, or one with a lower roof.

FACTFILE

Fireplaces

Fireplaces give you different clues:

- A large fireplace probably means a large room.
- A fireplace with detailed carving probably means a grand room, or a private room for an important person.
- A fireplace is a good guide to where the floor was.

The best way to spot a fireplace is to look for a chimney. In early castles, the fire was often in the centre of the room, with no chimney. But for most of the period you are studying, fires were in fireplaces against the walls, and they had chimneys. In the top photo here, there was a stone hood over the fire and the smoke would have continued up through the top of the hood. In the smaller fireplace, you can see the remains of the start of the chimney going straight up.

Source 6 Inside the south-west tower, Goodrich Castle. ▼

FACTFILE

Doors and windows

Doors and windows are holes in the wall, and will always reveal a lot about the balance between defence and normal life in the part of a castle you are looking at.

For doors, look for evidence of hinges and slots for the locking bar (they confirm it was a door and tell you which side it might be locked from).

For windows, look for the balance between light and safety (see the contrast between pictures a and b). Also look to see how the window is finished internally (b has large windows with window seats – evidence that this was probably a grand room).

locking bar

Study Source 6.

1. Why is the bottom window so low? (Hint: either because medieval people were very strange or because the floor level has changed over time.)
2. What evidence can you find that there were changes to the tower at various times?

a

hinge

b

FACTFILE

Toilets

With over 200 people living in Goodrich, the castle needed a system for disposing of human waste. Toilets could just be a bucket with a seat, carried out and emptied when needed. But a better solution was to build permanent toilets (often called garderobes) and find a way of transporting the waste outside the castle. Building a toilet out from the top of an outside wall using corbelling was the simplest way (a). The seat was outside the base of the wall and waste simply dropped through. An alternative (b) was to build a toilet in the thickness of the wall, with a shaft running down inside the wall to a cesspit at the bottom. Look for:

- corbelled structures on an outside wall
- very small rooms, with evidence of a seat and a hole underneath it
- shafts through the thickness on the wall (c)
- holes on the outside wall (d) where waste could fall out, or where a child could be sent to climb in and empty the cesspit.

The big questions

When looking at any feature of a castle, there are several important questions you should always ask:

- Was it inside or outside the castle?
- Was it indoors or outdoors?
- What was its purpose – military, administrative, domestic or 'services'?
- Is there evidence that the answer to any of these questions changed during the life of the castle?

We will look at the military and administrative features later in this chapter.

Domestic features to look out for include the following:

- The Great Hall – a big room for feasts and day-to-day living and eating. Look for evidence of a high ceiling, large windows, a passage to the kitchen at one end, perhaps with two or three doors into the hall, a door and a passage or stairs to the private apartments of the lord and lady of the castle.
- Evidence that these private apartments may have included smaller rooms with high-quality features such as large windows (perhaps with a window seat), the remains of a well-carved fireplace and perhaps a private toilet. You may sometimes find the main private room, called a SOLAR, in plans.
- Castles usually had more than one set of private apartments. Most had a captain or governor who lived there all the time. They would need their own private apartments, as would important guests.

The service features might include a chapel, kitchens, storerooms, a BUTTERY (originally for keeping wine and beer, but later food as well), stables, toilets and a prison.

- Storerooms, the buttery and rooms used as a prison tend to be on the ground floor (or in cellars below). Look for evidence that a door was shut from the outside, and no or small windows.
- Stables would normally be away from the main living accommodation – they could be quite smelly!

Source 7 A part of the plan of Goodrich Castle. ▼

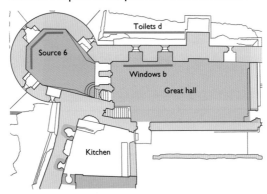

> **3** The areas shown in three photos showing parts of Goodrich are marked in red on Source 7 (the photos are Windows b, Toilets d and Source 6). What reasons can you find to support Source 7 that the blue not the green area was the great hall?

This photograph was taken looking down at what remains of the top of the north-west wall. Originally the wall was much higher. ▼

FACTFILE

Chapel

The castle community needed somewhere to worship, so castles usually had a church or large chapel. The lord's family might want a smaller private chapel – if so it was normally attached to their private apartments. Look for evidence of:

- a room that had an altar at the east end (sometimes the whole east end of a chapel might be raised a little)
- surviving features such as a sink for washing the vessels used in the mass, and a seat for the priest. The chapel in Goodrich has both, next to each other.

FACTFILE

Kitchens

A castle kitchen was big. It fed a large community. The kitchen was often in a detached building as they sometimes caught fire. Look for evidence of:

- at least one large fire (a) – meat would be roasted on a spit and pans could be held on hooks inside the fireplace.
- ovens for baking bread and pies (b). Medieval ovens were dome-shaped and heated by a fire of dry wood inside the oven.
- possibly a slightly sloping floor and a drain (c).

1 Source 8 shows the left-hand wall of the kitchen on the plan in Source 9. In what ways do the plan and the photo support the conclusion that it was a kitchen?

Source 9 A plan showing the kitchen at Goodrich. ▼

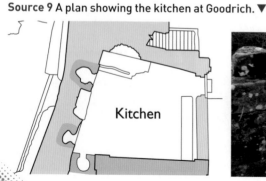

Kitchen

Source 8 The remains of the kitchen at Goodrich. ▼

Different styles of castle building

One of the functions of a castle was to resist attack and to provide ways to kill attackers from a position of relative safety. Castle builders – and attackers – were in a 600-year arms race to get the advantage. New methods of attack led to new styles and new features in castle-building. Occasionally, new castles were built in the latest style, but normally it was a case of looking to adapt what was there already to make it stronger through elements in the latest style. Knowing the broad pattern of styles and when they were fashionable is therefore very useful in understanding the development of any castle.

Motte and bailey (c1000–c1150): Common in Normandy before the conquest, the Normans built hundreds of MOTTE and BAILEY castles in the 50 years after 1066. The motte was a large mound of earth with a wooden fence and tower on the top. The bailey was a large enclosure, made by digging a ditch and making a bank with the earth, with a wooden fence on top of the bank. These were cheaper than stone castles and fairly quick to build. They kept a small group of people safe. The problems were that wooden buildings could be attacked with fire, and that wood in earth rots, so eventually they would need rebuilding. In addition, the space on top of the motte was quite small, so living conditions could be cramped. Carisbrooke is a good example of a motte and bailey castle.

Stone keep castles (1066–c1225): From the Norman Conquest, some castles were built from stone, for example the Tower of London. These were much stronger and bigger (and so more convenient to live in), and they stood as symbols of Norman power. There were two main weaknesses. Firstly, they were still rather small for the size of the household and garrison that made use of them. Secondly, it was difficult to kill attackers from a keep. Defence was a passive strategy and these castles were often captured when the people were starved out after a long siege. There were three main types of stone keep castles:

- **Square keeps'** main defensive feature was their massive stone walls, often 5 m thick. The holes in these walls were a weakness. The door was usually on the first floor, reached by an external staircase, and the windows were very small on the lower floors. Square keeps were too heavy to be built on a motte. Good examples include Rochester and Dover.
- **Shell keeps** were built on the top of mottes. The outer wooden fence of a SHELL KEEP was replaced by a stone wall, with rooms built against the inside of this wall. Because it was on top of the motte, the walls were not as thick as in a square keep, but living on top of the motte was still cramped and inconvenient. Carisbrooke and Windsor are good examples.
- **Round keeps** were a later development of square keeps. Some castles were taken when attackers broke through the corners of square keeps, and a round keep avoided this weakness. However, building technology could not make a round keep anywhere near as big as a square one, so they were often too cramped. Pembroke and Conisbrough are good examples.

Curtain wall castles (c1125–c1350): Wooden bailey walls were replaced by stone walls, called curtain walls. A curtain wall castle did not just have a stone wall. It had several of them – with a number of defensive features – usually enclosing a considerable area, which might be divided into more than one bailey. Most castles that existed in this time became curtain wall castles. They could be very large (see the plans on pages 222–23). This solved the problem of not having enough space, and grand buildings could be built in the baileys. However, the size brought its own problem. Defenders needed a very large garrison to hold a wall running all round these large castles. If an attack came at just a couple of points, many of the defending soldiers would not be in a position to join the fighting.

ACTIVITY

1 Make and fill in a data sheet for each style of castle, giving each one a whole page:
   - Motte and bailey
   - Square keep
   - Shell keep
   - Round keep
   - Curtain wall
   - Concentric
   - Courtyard
   - Post-gunpowder
   Use the following sub-headings on each data sheet:
   - Date
   - Description
   - Problems
   - Evidence of style at Goodrich
   - Evidence of style at … [your nominated castle]

2 Create a table for the defensive features on pages 222–23, using the following headings:
   - Description
   - Problems
   - Example at Goodrich
   - Example at … [your nominated castle]
   Note that not every feature may have an entry in the last two columns.

3 Using the internet or resources from your teacher, find pictures or plans for each style and feature. Where possible, choose examples from your nominated castle.

Source 10 A plan of Carisbrooke Castle. ▼

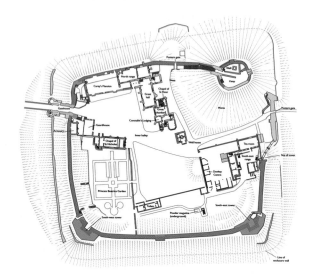

Source 11 A plan of Portchester Castle. ▼

FACTFILE

Defensive features

Merlons and embrasures

MERLONS (a) and EMBRASURES (b) were cheap, but not much good. The defender was safe behind the merlon, but to look out or shoot, he would need to be in the embrasure, which would make him a good target. Embrasures could be fitted with shutters (c). Look for evidence of slots or holes for the axle.

Bratticing

Attackers were most dangerous at the foot of the wall – and to see that far down defenders had to lean a long way out – making them a good target. BRATTICING (d) was a wooden extension built out from the top of the wall. It offered much more protection. Look for evidence of a line of holes or corbels near the top of the wall for the beams to go through. Bratticing needed a lot of maintenance, and could be set on fire or smashed by large catapults.

Machicolations

MACHICOLATIONS replaced bratticing with stone, corbelled out from the wall (e and f). They were expensive but stronger.

Source 12 A plan of Carlisle Castle. ▼

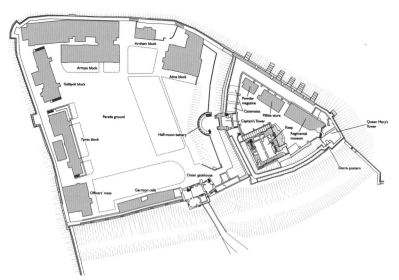

Source 13 A plan of Framlingham Castle. ▼

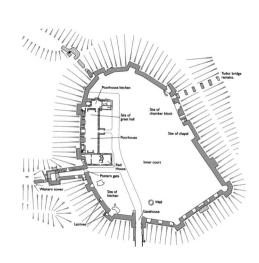

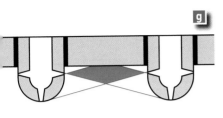

Towers and flanking fire
Fire from the side (FLANKING FIRE) was the best way to defend the base of the wall. Towers, sticking out from the wall, were the answer (g).

Barbicans
Castle designers created KILLING GROUNDS, crowding attackers together to make them an easy target. The entrance would always be a weak point because people needed to use it easily most of the time (when the castle was not being besieged), but they also needed to make it as safe as possible in case the castle was attacked. We call the defences of an entrance a BARBICAN. You can see them at all the castles on this page except Stokesay (Carlisle is hard to spot). At Goodrich, attackers were concentrated on two causeways then filed through a narrow tunnel (with 'murder holes' in the ceiling). Drawbridges, gates and portcullises slowed them down. It was a complex killing ground with well-protected firing places.

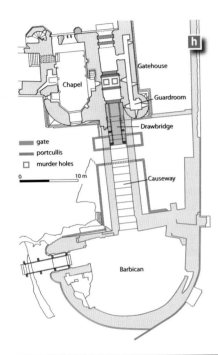

Gatehouse
Chapel
Guardroom
Drawbridge
Causeway
Barbican

gate
portcullis
murder holes

0   10 m

Source 14 A plan of Goodrich Castle. ▼

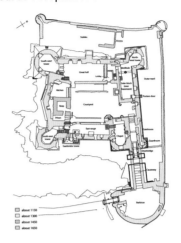

☐ about 1150
☐ about 1300
☐ about 1450
☐ about 1650

Source 15 A plan of Stokesay Castle. ▼

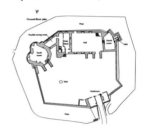

1 All these castle plans are to the same scale. What questions about these seven castles do their different sizes make you want to ask?
2 Compare the plan of your nominated castle on this page with the phased plans on pages 244–53. When was each of the styles used in your specified castle?

Source 16 A plan of Kenilworth Castle. ▼

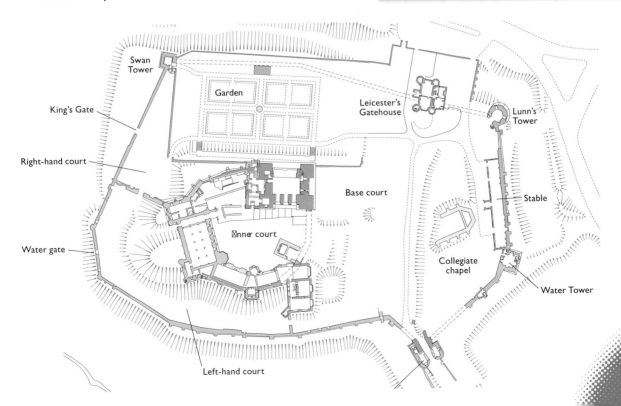

Swan Tower
King's Gate
Right-hand court
Water gate
Garden
Inner court
Leicester's Gatehouse
Base court
Lunn's Tower
Stable
Collegiate chapel
Water Tower
Left-hand court

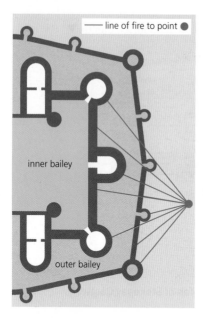

How a concentric castle concentrates fire on any point.

Castles c1200–c1500

Concentric castles (c1200–c1350) had at least two curtain walls, one inside the other, with the inner wall much taller than the outer wall. The idea was to concentrate firepower – wherever the castle was attacked from, many defenders could shoot. Should attackers break though the outer wall, they would be concentrated together in the small space between the outer and inner baileys, which became a good killing ground. Beaumaris is a good example of a concentric castle built from scratch, but many castles developed a concentric element by building a shorter outer wall or a taller inner one. Dover and Goodrich show this development.

Gunpowder was first used in the fourteenth century, but to begin with it did not have much impact on castle design. It gave the defenders a new weapon and gun loops began to be added, especially to barbicans. Queenborough Castle (built 1361–77) was the first castle with cannon planned into its defences. In 1405, Henry IV captured three powerful castles – Berwick, Alnwick and Warkworth – using siege cannon. The balance of power was shifting, and by the middle of the century it had shifted decisively – using cannon, the French captured 60 English castles in France in one year.

Courtyard castles (c1370–1500): There were not many new castles in this period, but those there were tended to be smaller and to move the balance more towards comfort and convenience and away from defence. They were usually built around courtyards (smaller than the earlier baileys). The outside wall of the living space was also the outside wall of the castle. Such castles provided status and relative safety for less money, both in terms of building and running costs. Bolton and Raglan are good examples. In existing castles, this style can been seen in more lean-to buildings against the inside of the curtain walls.

Post-gunpowder castles c1500–c1650

Medieval castles had been tall and thin. Defences against gunpowder needed to be short and fat. Stone walls were shattered by the force of cannon balls. The answer was low walls (which were harder to hit) and then walls filled with earth (which absorbed the impact of the ball). To use cannon as part of the defence also required thick walls – cannon recoil and need space. In the 1530s, Henry VIII built a series of castles to use cannon to protect the south coast from possible invasion. Later, some castles were given new earth-wall defences, some as late as the Civil Wars (1642–51). Many castles were besieged during this time and, because they had shown some military value, some were 'slighted' (made indefensible) or completely destroyed afterwards.

No medieval castle could withstand developments in artillery after 1650, and castles that continued to have a military function relied on new defences. Most were developed into grand homes or were abandoned. When the Duke of Marlborough won the Battle of Blenheim in 1704, his grateful nation built him not a castle, but a palace (Blenheim Palace, built 1705–33).

> **Source 17** A description of the wooden tower on top of the motte at Ardres, from a chronicle written about 1194. The motte was destroyed in 1855, so we do not know how big it was, but it was much larger than Abinger (Source 18).
>
> *On the ground floor were cellars and granaries, and great boxes, barrels, casks, and other domestic utensils. On the first floor were the living rooms, the rooms of the bakers and butlers, and the Great Chamber in which the Lord and his wife slept. Next to this was the dormitory of the waiting maids and children. In the inner part of the Great Chamber was a certain private room, where at early dawn, or in the evening, or during sickness, or for warming the maids and weaned children, they used to have a fire. On the upper floor were garret rooms in which, on the one side the sons (when they wished) and on the other side the daughters (because they were obliged) of the Lord of the House used to sleep. On this floor also the watchmen appointed to guard the house took their sleep. High up on the east side of the house was the chapel. There were stairs and passages from floor to floor, from the house into the kitchen, and from room to room.*

Using sources to tell the story of the castle

Historians use a range of sources to discover the story of a castle. Below are some of the different types of sources and the questions they can help us answer.

What was on the top of a motte?

Archaeology: Source 18 allows us to see what size and shape the buildings on the top of this motte were.

Chronicles: The history people wrote for themselves in medieval times sometimes includes descriptions (Source 17, which tells us things archaeology cannot).

Art: The art of the past can add to our picture. Source 19 shows a motte, with what is probably a wooden fence around the top (they are trying to set it on fire), and it shows a tower inside that fence.

Using the range of sources, we can see that sometimes they agree with each other – for example, Sources 17 and 19 on the fence around the top of the motte and the tower inside it. Each also brings something unique to help build our answer to the question.

Source 18 An archaeologist's plan of the top of the motte at Abinger. The marks show where wooden posts had been. ▼

1. Use Source 17 to make a possible plan for each of the three floors of the tower at Ardres. There is no right answer, because we do not know, but the best answers fit in everything the source tells you, use other knowledge about castles and interpret the source with common sense.
2. Using all three sources, explain what you would expect to find on top of the motte in a motte and bailey castle.
3. What are the strengths and weaknesses of each type of source?
4. Which source is most useful for answering the question of what was on top of a motte?

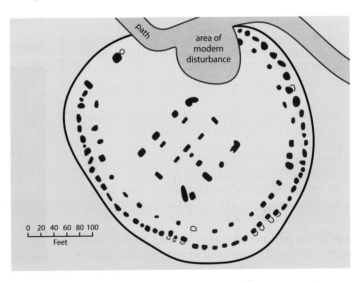

Source 19 A picture of an attack on a motte and bailey castle at Dinan, from the Bayeux Tapestry, made in the 1070s.

FACTFILE

Joan de Valence: 172 days at Goodrich Castle

Joan de Valence, who owned Goodrich, travelled between her different properties with a household of 50 or 60 people. During the visit to Goodrich:

- they drank about 25 gallons of wine and 60 gallons of beer a day; wine was bought in Bristol and beer in Monmouth as the castle's own brewery couldn't make enough
- they brought corn to bake bread from the surrounding area
- woodcutters on Joan's estates did 212 days' work cutting wood to heat the castle and cook the food, and 130 horses and a boat were used to bring the wood to the castle
- eleven important nobles visited Joan while she was at Goodrich – each would have brought their own household
- they ate 13,300 herrings during Lent (the six weeks before Easter)
- the Christmas Day feast involved 1½ beef cattle, 2 pigs, 12 ducks, 18 chickens, 2 peacocks, cheese, eggs and fish for those who would not eat meat for religious reasons
- she gave food for 20 poor people a day (and 61 on St Catherine's day)
- she sent a number of business letters, and employed a messenger to take them; London and her lands in Kent were a 12-day round trip for him
- a servant went to Bristol to buy new white robes for the entire household for Whitsun (six weeks after Easter).

---

1 What effect would a visit from Joan have on the castle?
2 What effect would a visit from Joan have on the surrounding area?
3 Make a sketch of the plan of the kitchen at Goodrich (see page 220). Mark on the fire and ovens.
4 How do these sources help you have a better answer than when you just had the plan and photo?

Source 22 The lord and his guests feasting, from a book made between 1320 and 1345 with many paintings of daily life. ▼

How did a lord live in a castle?

Private papers: These sometimes survive, like one small part of the papers of Joan de Valence. These enable us to find out about her time at Goodrich in 1296–97.

Art: This shows us, for example, a feast in the great hall, the fire cooks used, as well as what a baker's oven looked like in use.

Put this together with the plan and remains at Goodrich and it becomes clear that the archaeological evidence is actually the ghosts of a fireplace and an oven, which strongly suggests this is a kitchen.

Source 20 Cooks roasting fowl in front of the fire, from the same book as Source 22. ▼

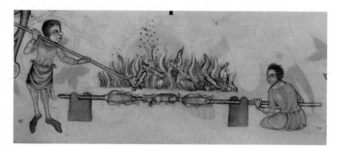

Source 21 A medieval baker putting bread in the oven. ▼

5 What does Source 23 suggest were the problems the constable of Dover Castle worried about?

6 List the things you can learn about Carlisle Castle from Source 24.

7 Does Source 25 prove more work was done on the Welsh castles in 1282 than in 1283?

8 Which of these sources is more useful for:
   a studying life in a castle?
   b understanding how royal castles were used?

Why do we know more about royal castles?

Just like the government today, the government in medieval times had lots of administrators – and they created a lot of records. The king's ministers sent orders to local government and to the constables of royal castles. Detailed accounts were kept showing how money was spent, and these accounts were sent back to London to be checked. Many of them survive today.

Legal documents: These were important at the time so they were kept carefully. They usually record the transfer of land, but Source 23 is unusual. It is a CHARTER listing the statutes of Dover Castle – the rules for the garrison.

Orders: Orders issued from the government – copies of which were kept in London – tell us a lot about the day-to-day running of castles, for example when money was spent for repairs or how they were garrisoned. Source 24 just picks out the orders for Carlisle Castle for one year, but hundreds of years of these documents survive.

Accounts: These are the lifeblood of government. Edward I built a series of mighty castles in Wales during his wars of conquest. Source 25 summarises what we can discover from the accounts of the building of these castles. The king took skilled and unskilled workers from all over England to work on this massive castle-building programme.

Castles owned by Joan de Valence probably generated almost as many orders and accounts as a royal castle, but they have been lost. Government records are more likely to survive.

Source 25 A map summarising the data in the royal accounts about the workers used on the Welsh castles, 1282–83. ▼

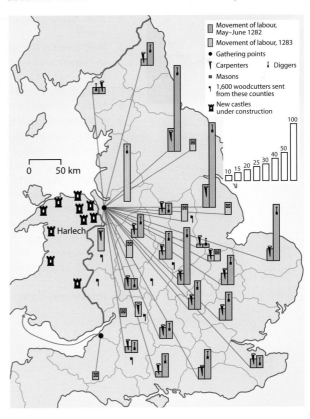

Source 26 The phased plan and remains of part of the kitchen at Goodrich Castle. ▼

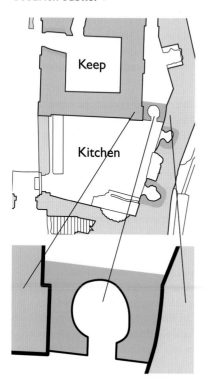

REVIEW TASKS

This topic has concentrated on what you can learn from the stones, the styles and the story. Your study of castles requires you to concentrate on your nominated castle as well as having a good general understanding of the subject.

You will need more information about your nominated castle. The castle Factfiles on pages 244–53 give you the key information to start you off – a copy of the phased plan, a view of the site today, information about its major events and a photo with evidence from the site.

1 Using materials from your teacher or an internet search for images of your castle, find photographs of parts of the castle that the phased plan says were built in different times. Source 26 on this page is another example. The starting point is the phased plan of the kitchen next to the keep. One small section of this plan has been enlarged and placed next to a photograph that shows the remains at this point. The keep (peach on the plan) has large rectangular stones. The oven (green on the plan) has stones that are smaller, a different colour and irregular.
   Find and explain at least three examples like this for your nominated castle.
2 Using the factfile, make a timeline of the main events in the story of your castle

TOPIC SUMMARY

How do we know about castles?

1 Historians have to work out a lot about the use and development of a castle from the remains as they are today.
2 Corbels, grooves, ledges and holes for beams are all evidence of where a floor or a roof might have been.
3 Fireplaces, doors and windows are all good clues about where floors were, and also about the social status of the people who used the room.
4 Toilets could just be a bucket with a seat, but later they were usually built-in and can be spotted by the remains of a seat over a shaft or a hole.
5 Most castles had chapels – they often had a small sink and/or a seat cut into a wall.
6 Kitchens were usually in a separate building because of the fire risk. Evidence includes very large fireplaces (a lot of cooking was over an open fire) and bread ovens.
7 Most castles started as motte and bailey castles, built from earth and wood.
8 Many castles had stone keeps added between c1070 and c1225.
9 Curtain wall castles (c1125–c1350) could be very large, with strong walls and additional defensive features.
10 Concentric castles (c1200–c1350) had higher walls and towers inside shorter outer walls to maximise firepower.
11 Siege cannon were first effective in about 1400 and by 1450 they could destroy any existing castle wall in time.
12 Courtyard castles (c1370–1500) were smaller and more comfortable. After siege cannon, it was hard for any castle to survive a determined siege.
13 Post–gunpowder castles (c1500–c1650) had low, thick walls, usually filled with earth.
14 Chronicles were history books written in medieval times, usually describing the recent past. They have stories of sieges and some descriptions of castles.
15 Private and state records, such as accounts, give us evidence of life in castles.

7.2 The functions of a castle

FOCUS

Castles had many different functions. Over time, the relative importance of these different functions changed. One of the main clues for understanding this is the changes made to the buildings at different times. In this topic, you will read about the various and changing functions of castles. All the time, you should try to relate what you are learning to your nominated castle.

FACTFILE

The development of Goodrich

c1070–c1125 Motte and bailey castle built by Godric.

c1125–50 Goodrich was close to the Welsh border, and raids into England were common. The stone keep was built.

1138–1247 Goodrich owned by powerful nobles who did not live there. A constable controlled the castle, which was home to a small community and garrison.

1216 Goodrich was besieged by the Welsh, but quickly relieved by English troops.

1247–1327 Goodrich owned by the de Valence family – major landowners who moved between various castles. Major works included a new curtain wall and much grander domestic buildings.

1277–95 Wales was conquered by Edward I in a series of wars and the border was strategically important.

1327–1421 Goodrich was owned by another powerful family, which spent less time there but strengthened the barbican, rebuilt the chapel and added a prison.

FOCUS TASK

What were the functions of a castle?

The table below lists the functions of a castle that are covered in this topic. Fill in the information below the heading 'Type' for Goodrich Castle and your nominated castle. Return to this table and fill in the information as you read about each function.

The functions of a castle	
Goodrich Castle	**Nominated castle**
Type (royal or baronial)	
Goodrich was first built as a baronial castle, but in 1176 ...	*e.g. First built by King William II in 1092, Carlisle was a royal castle ...*
Site	
Protection	
Power base	
Living and working	
Defensive	
Later uses	

Royal and baronial castles

An easy distinction to make is between a royal castle, controlled by the monarch, and a baronial castle, controlled by one of their subjects. It is an important distinction, and more documentary evidence survives about royal castles. So, why were some castles royal? The main reason is that they guarded (or dominated) strategically important places. The Tower of London was always a royal castle, and it dominated London. Dover (guarding the most important Channel crossing) and Carlisle (guarding the western end of the border with Scotland) were always royal castles. Others became royal castles for short periods. There were two main reasons for this:

- **Lack of an heir:** Goodrich was a royal castle between 1176 and 1204, because the owner died without an heir and it was only 28 years later that the king granted it to a new lord. Kenilworth also became a royal castle when the owner died in 1174. This was a time of civil war and the king, Henry II, decided it was strategically important so he garrisoned and strengthened it. Kenilworth remained a royal castle for 70 years and there was significant rebuilding in this time.
- **Confiscation:** Sometimes the monarch simply seized control of a castle, if its owner had been charged with treason, perhaps, or because it seemed strategically too important to leave in private hands. Henry II took Portchester in 1154 for strategic reasons. He ruled lands on both sides of the Channel and Portchester dominated a major cross-Channel harbour. It remained a royal castle.

FACTFILE

London's three castles

The castles built in London just after the Norman Conquest provide evidence that there was no great master plan for castle-building in England. As well as the Tower of London – the royal castle on the eastern edge of the city – there were two baronial castles, Baynard's Castle and Montfichet's Tower. These were both in the west of the city and stood right next to each other!

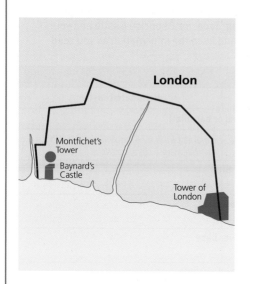

Montfichet's Tower was demolished in 1213. The original Castle Baynard was torn town before 1276 and a replacement built to the east of the site shown on the map. This castle was destroyed by fire in 1428 and rebuilt by the Duke of Gloucester as his London palace. The Great Fire of London (1666) destroyed this third Baynard's Castle.

Baynard's Castle in 1647.

Not all barons were equally rich and powerful, and not all baronial castles were the same. The plans on pages 222–23 show the difference in size of some of them. Stokesay, for example, was as much a fortified house as it was a castle. We would call Lawrence of Ludlow – who bought the manor in 1270 – a businessman. He was one of the richest men in the country and he wanted to keep both his family and his wealth safe. The years from 1250 to 1325 were a time of growing lawlessness and unrest. Taxes were high, harvests often poor and crime increasing. Stokesay was one of many new, smaller castles built in this period. They were not strong enough to hold out against a major siege, but they would keep the inhabitants safe from thieves or a peasant uprising.

At the other end of the scale, Framlingham and Kenilworth (from 1266 to 1399) were owned by powerful nobles who wanted large castles – part palace and part military stronghold. Just as the greatest nobles attended the king at his court, so the lesser nobles and knights would attend their lord in his castle. The castle therefore must be grand – reflecting the power and prestige of its owner. The great hall, where meals were taken and formal business often conducted, needed to be large and richly decorated. There must be accommodation for important guests and their followers. These castles also needed to be strong enough to withstand a major siege.

The site of the castle

There are nearly 2,000 castle sites in England and Wales. They were not built to any national master plan to make the country stronger. Some royal castles were built for strategic reasons immediately after the Norman Conquest, but individual lords built most castles wherever they wanted to on their lands.

Castle-building took place from the 1050s through to the 1540s, but there were some periods when many were built in a short time:

- In the first 40 years after the Norman Conquest (including Goodrich, Carlisle, Framlingham and Portchester).
- During the civil wars in the reigns of Stephen and Matilda (1135–54); the next king, Henry II, destroyed many of these when he restored order.
- From the late thirteenth century and through the fourteenth century, when trade and the profits of war with France made wider groups of people wealthy (Stokesay is in this group).

In the first 40 years after the Conquest, many castles were built in towns and, symbolically, existing houses were often torn down to make room. For example, in Lincoln 166 of the 970 houses in the town were torn down. Most of these town castles were royal castles. Later medieval towns often grew up around castles that had been built on rural sites. The castles provided security and a ready market of wealthy people.

The first builder of any castle had to answer two key questions:

- Where on my estate, roughly, do I want my castle?
- Once the area has been decided, which is the best exact spot to build on?

There were different criteria for each decision. After the Conquest, Norman lords were given large tracts of land, often a day's ride across. This land included villages and perhaps even small towns. The most important factors in deciding where on this land the castle might go were:

- **Strategic:** Was there an important river crossing or harbour to protect?
- **Communications:** From the castle, it would ideally be possible to get to all the important parts of the lord's estate and back within a day? Also, it should be reasonably convenient for a lord to get from his lands to other parts of the country that he may need to travel to.
- **Administration:** The castle would be the base for governing the area, collecting taxes and administering justice.
- **Economic:** Whether the wealth came from towns and trade or from farming, it was useful to be able to protect the economically significant parts of the territory.

Once the castle builder had decided on the general site, he had to home in on the specific spot for his castle. It is a mistake to think that most castles were built on hills. People lived in the castle all year round so being positioned high on a hill was not the most convenient location. Castles were rarely (if ever) attacked, so defence was not always the most important consideration. Obviously, the castle had to have a good water supply, both in case of attack and for convenience. The castle was usually much the tallest building in the area. This was significant for two reasons. It gave the garrison a good field of view, so they could see any threats a long way off. It also meant the castle could be seen from a large area – underlining the importance of the lord. Castle builders took care over the views of the castle people had as they approached it, going as far as moving roads or creating artificial lakes to make the castle look more impressive at first sight.

Protection

The Normans believed that castles did not just protect the people inside them; they protected the whole country. The lack of castles in Saxon England was one of the reasons they believed their conquest succeeded. The diagram shows what they thought. When you invaded a country, it would be dangerous to ignore enemy castles. The reason for this is the garrisons could come out once your army had passed and disrupt your communications back home. They could capture messages and supplies. The alternative, then, was to either besiege and capture every castle on the way, or leave enough troops behind to besiege each castle to keep the garrison inside. If you did the first, you advanced very slowly, and your enemy had time to gather a larger army. If you did the second, your army got smaller each time you left troops besieging a castle. This is what is shown in the diagram – how an attacking army nearly twice the size of the defending army could be brought down to the same size by the time they gave battle because of the number of troops left to besiege castles.

ACTIVITY

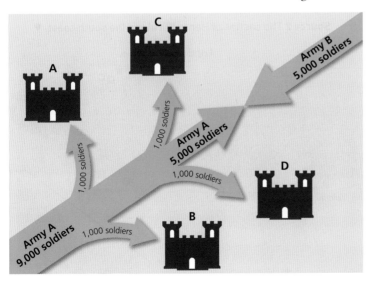

- 🏰 Possible castle site
- ⬛ Town
- ⬜ Hills — Main roads
- ⬜ Best farming land ⬌ Major trade routes

Draw a grid like the one below and give each factor a mark out of 10 for each of the three suggested sites.

	A	B	C
strategic			
communications			
administration			
economic			
Total			

How castles made a country safer from invasion.

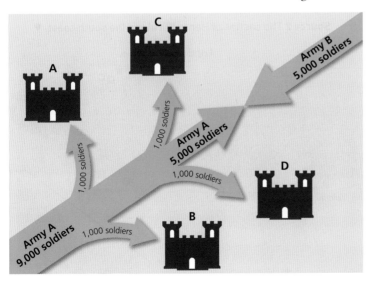

Henry VIII's coastal castles

Between 1539 and 1545, Henry VIII built a specialist group of castles. They were designed with one function in mind: to protect the country from invasion by installing cannon in castles positioned where a potential invasion fleet might land. These castles were built to be garrisoned by soldiers; there was no grand accommodation for a lord.

Source 1 A plan of Raglan Castle. All this was built after 1435. ▼

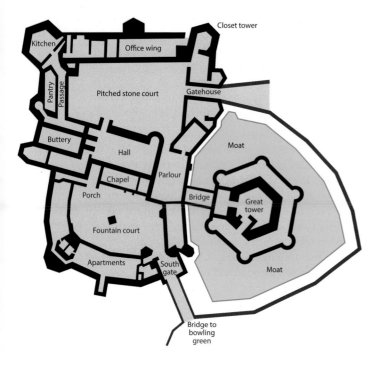

Protecting those inside the castle

Protecting those inside from those outside has been the most obvious function of a castle since the first motte and bailey castles. All the complicated defensive systems of curtain walls, flanking fire, machicolations and barbicans are just ways of keeping the people inside safe by making it easier to kill those outside.

Raglan Castle offers an interesting refinement in keeping people safe. The oldest part of the castle was built around 1435, yet it has a building that looks like a keep – and the mid-fifteenth century is too late for castle designers to build a keep. The Great Tower is a FINAL REFUGE, separated from the rest of the castle (and from the outside world) by a moat. It could be defended against the rest of the castle. There could be two reasons for this:

- It provided a final refuge for what remained of the garrison if the rest of the castle fell to the enemy.
- It provided a place for the lord's family and most trusted followers in the event that the garrison turned on the lord.

The idea of creating a final refuge was not new. Castle designers had been using it since motte and baileys. If attackers captured the bailey, the defenders could retreat to the motte. The fifteenth century was a dangerous time. It began with the overthrow and later murder of Richard II and in 1455–87 there was a series of civil wars. Perhaps these events influenced the designers of Raglan to make the final refuge just a little bit safer from the rest of the castle?

1 'Source 2 proves that Henry VIII thought invasion was a real threat in the years 1539–45.' Do you agree?
2 Look back at the plans of Goodrich and your nominated castle. Can you find a final refuge in each one?

Source 2 The castles of Henry VIII along the south coast. ▼

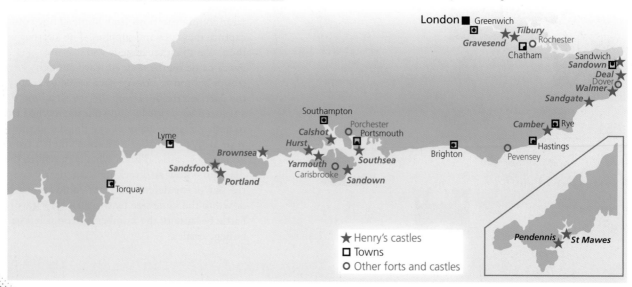

Power and symbolism

Castles provided a power base. In a castle, a lord (or constable) would have soldiers and the castle kept them relatively safe. Their power stretched at least half a day's ride or march. There was no police force and, for most of the time, no army. The lord's soldiers enforced the law and kept the area safe. All but the most serious crimes were tried in the lord's court, inside the castle. The castle, therefore, was the centre of both actual and legal power.

The castle was symbolic too. After the Norman Conquest, many castles were built where the previous Anglo-Saxon lord had lived. This emphasised that new people and customs had replaced the old. However, it also gave a sense of continuity: people would pay their taxes and come for justice to the same place.

At a time when most people lived in simple houses made from wood with a thatched roof, the multi-storey castles – usually made from stone – underlined the wealth, the power and the separateness of the upper classes. One way of emphasising this was to paint the outside of the castle. For example, the keep of the Tower of London is known as the White Tower because the outside was painted white to make it look more magnificent. Instructions from Henry III survive to whitewash the outside of the keeps of Corfe and Rochester Castles, and to mend the gutters of the White Tower to stop rainwater spoiling the whitewash.

Castle owners also wanted to show off to each other. Changing a castle by adding the latest features was a good way to show wealth and good taste. Men rising up the social scale, like Lawrence of Ludlow (who built Stokesay), built a castle as a way of demonstrating their new position and prestige.

Kings could use castles for symbolic and military reasons at the same time. When Edward I conquered northern Wales, he built a series of strong castles that both helped him control the land and demonstrated his new power (see the map on page 227). One of them, Conway, was built on the site of the grave of the Welsh national hero Llewellyn the Great.

Source 3 Historian Malcolm Hislop, writing in 2013.

Caernarfon Castle was intended to evoke Constantinople, capital of the Eastern Roman Empire. The princes of Gwynedd traced their ancestry to Magnus Maximus, who established himself as Roman Emperor in 383 BCE. Tradition associated Maximus with the Roman town of Segontium, close to Caernarfon. With this castle Edward was portraying himself as the successor of the Emperor and his supposed descendants the Welsh princes.

3 Look at Sources 4 and 5. What similarities are there between the walls of Constantinople and Caernarfon?

4 Do you agree with the judgement of the historian in Source 3? Explain your answer.

Source 4 Part of the surviving Roman walls of Constantinople (modern Istanbul). They were famous for the bands of colour, made by using courses of tile. ▼

Source 5 Part of the walls of Caernarfon Castle, built by Edward I in the 1280s. ▼

Living and working

Castles were both the home and the workplace of a large community that was divided into strict social levels. At the top was the lord or lady and his or her family, then any noble guests they may have, then their most important followers such as the constable of the castle. There was also a hierarchy among the servants, from the head cook and the butler (who was in charge of the wine) down to the unskilled labourers and kitchen skivvies. Life and work were very different depending where people were in this hierarchy.

Some parts of castle life were very formal. The great hall was often the site for ceremonial events. In the great hall the lord or the constable would:

- meet and greet noble guests
- eat – the lord's family ate on a stage (the DAIS) at one end of the hall, raised up so they could be seen
- conduct business, such as receiving payments of rent from the tenants
- hold court sessions to conduct trials and legal business.

Many others ate in the great hall, but lower down. In the first castles many people slept in the hall too, but that changed as more sleeping accommodation was added later. Another change was an increasing desire for privacy for the most important people in the castle. The lord's family started to spend time in private rooms. These were often reached from a door off the dais in the great hall.

Source 6 The remains of the east side of the great hall at Kenilworth Castle. ▼

> **Source 7** Extracts from *Sir Gawain and the Green Knight*, a poem written 1375–1400. The poem is more than 2,500 lines long and is set in the time of King Arthur. In this section, Gawain visits a perfect castle.
>
> *Knights and squires came to bring him to the Great Hall, where a fine fire fiercely burned. Then the lord came down from his chamber with good manners to greet Gawain there. He said, 'You are welcome, treat my home as your home'.*
>
> *The lord led him to a chamber, and chose a man to serve him, with several others to help. They took him to a bright bedroom with a beautiful bed, with a canopy of silk bordered with gold, and fur bedcovers, heavily embroidered. The curtains hung from golden curtain rings and ran on cords. The walls were hung with tapestries from Toulouse and Turkey, and, on the floor, were carpets too.*
>
> *In the Great Hall, he sat in a fine chair, and warmed himself. Soon servants set a table on trestles, with a clean white tablecloth, a saltcellar, and silver spoons. He washed well and went to the table. Servants served him with sumptuous food well-seasoned with costly spices, double helpings, as was right, and all kinds of fish – some baked in pies, some grilled over hot coals, some slowly boiled, some in spicy stews, and all the sauces were made just to his taste.*

1 Look at Source 7. List all the things you can learn about life in castles from this extract.

2 The castle described in Source 7 is fictional. Does this mean it is not a useful source for historians? Explain your answer.

Source 9 Instructions from Henry III to the constable of Dover Castle, about showing an important French nobleman round the castle, 1247.

When Gaucher de Châtillon shall come to Dover he shall take him into that castle and show the castle off to him in eloquent style, so that the magnificence of the castle shall be fully apparent to him, and that he shall see no defects in it.

3   Study Source 8 carefully. List all the things the artist has shown that are supported by evidence from this section.

4   Which of the sources in this section is most useful in helping you understand how a great hall was used? Explain your answer.

Source 8 An artist's reconstruction of the great hall at Kenilworth Castle in the fourteenth century. The cutaway in the lower right shows the cellars underneath. ▼

Source 10 An illustration from a fifteenth-century manuscript showing a king, bishops and great nobles eating in state on the dais of a great hall, while musicians play in a gallery. ▼

FACTFILE

Decoration

The walls of the main rooms would not have been left as bare stone in the way we see them today. Before c1250, the walls would normally be whitewashed, perhaps with the lines between the stones picked out in red. After c1250, walls were usually plastered and then painted, and some parts of the wall might be covered by wood panelling or tapestries. Colours could be very bright (see Source 10). Henry III's favourite colour scheme was gold stars on a green background. Floors were covered by rushes at first, and in the more public parts of the castle this continued. Increasingly, the private rooms of the lord, and certainly the dais in the great hall, would be floored with colourful glazed tiles.

> **Source 11 A description of dinner on a normal day at Raglan Castle in the 1640s.**
>
> *At eleven o'clock the Castle Gates were shut, and the tables laid; two in the Dining-Room; three in the Hall; one in Mrs Watson's Apartment, where the Chaplains eat, two in the Housekeeper's Room, for women.*
>
> *The Earl came into the Dining-Room, attended by his Gentlemen. At the first Table sat the noble Family, and such of the Nobility as come there. At the second Table sat Knights and honourable Gentlemen.*
>
> *In the Hall, at the first table sat the Steward, the Comptroller, the Master of the Horse, the Master of the Fish-ponds with such Gentlemen as came there under the degree of a knight. At the second table sat the Sewer [responsible for serving food], with the Gentlemen Waiters, and pages, to the number of twenty-four. At the third table sat the Clerk of the Kitchen, with the Yeoman Officers of the House, two Grooms of the Chambers.*

1 Sketch a plan of Raglan (see page 232), including the kitchen, buttery, great hall, dining room and the private apartments. Study Source 11. Mark on the tables, who ate where and the route the food would have taken.
2 'The dining room (above the parlour) at Raglan was for high-status people. It had large elaborate windows on to the courtyard and moat.' How far do Sources 12 and 13 support this statement?
3 Compare the impressions of castle life from the early twelfth century (Source 17 on page 225), the late fourteenth century (Source 7, page 234) and the mid-seventeenth century (Source 11, above). What changes, and what stays the same?

Castles were in use for hundreds of years and, during this time, the domestic accommodation of most castles changed more than the military features did. Two major trends in society show up in changes we can see in many castles:

- A move towards more **privacy**. You see it most in the accommodation for the high-status people in the castle, but also in things like adding towers with lots of toilets (which were for the soldiers and servants). At Raglan (Source 12) the grand private apartments were reached from a door off the dais in the great hall, and by the 1640s the owner (the Earl of Worcester) and his family normally ate in the private dining room. At Goodrich the GARDEROBE (toilet) tower was added about 1450.
- An **increase in the size of the household**. You see this in the increase in the accommodation, usually built against the inside of the curtain walls, from the late thirteenth century onwards. Households continued to get bigger in the fifteenth and sixteenth centuries, and you can often find more than one round of adding extra accommodation.

Look closely at the PHASED PLANS of your nominated castle. Can you see evidence of these two trends in society in its remains? If you can't, is there a reason? For example, later changes may have obliterated evidence of earlier changes.

Source 12 A phased plan of the private apartments at Raglan Castle (shaded beige). See the whole plan on page 232 to understand how this fits in to the rest of the castle. ▼

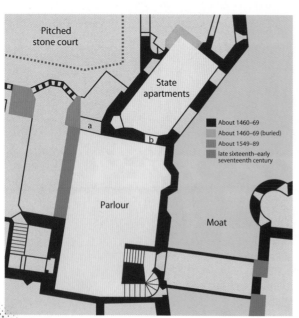

Source 13 The remains of the wall of the dining room over the parlour at Raglan Castle, showing the area between a and b on Source 12. ▼

FACTFILE

Smashing the castle walls

There were different ways to break a hole in the walls (called a breach), and different ways to defend against them.

- **Picks:** Men with pickaxes could take the wall down stone by stone. The best place to start was a right-angled corner. Defenders needed to be able to fire at the base of the wall – bratticing, machicolations or flanking towers.
- **Battering rams:** These were used to smash a hole in the wall. Defenders used flanking fire again, dropping things or setting the ram on fire.
- **Stone-throwing engines:** Set up at distance from the castle, these could fire heavy stones that would eventually smash a hole in the wall. Defenders had their own stone-throwing engines to smash the enemy's or they made a new wall behind where they expected the breach to be made.
- **Undermining:** Miners dug a tunnel under the wall itself. The roof of the tunnel was held up with wooden props. These were then set on fire, and without the props the tunnel (and the wall above it) would collapse. Defenders used the tactic of countermining – digging their own mine below the attacker's and capturing or destroying their mine.

Sieges – the castle at war

There is some disagreement among historians as to whether castle builders were much interested in war and the possibility of sieges. Castle revisionists point out that many castles were built over a 600-year period, but not many sieges took place. They suggest that castles were built in a military style, as bases for an upper class that wanted to reflect traditional military functions and traditions in the style of their castles. These historians suggest that the symbolism of castles and their peacetime functions were more important. As we look at the military functions of castles, keep the arguments of the revisionists in mind.

Historians have identified at least 1,897 castles that existed between 1066 and 1660. Some of them only stood for 20–50 years, but others survived for most of the 600 years we are studying. In all, we know of 1,022 sieges. Both these numbers are probably too small, because not all castles have left a written record or traces in the ground, and not all sieges were recorded either. Even so, the revisionists have a point – there were almost two castles to every one siege, and most sieges lasted a few weeks or months, not 600 years.

Besieging a castle – choices and tactics

The first choice for an attacking commander was whether to starve the garrison out or to STORM THE CASTLE (fight your way in). Starving could take a long time, and you probably did not know how much food and drink they had. But storming could cost you a lot of troops, and you might not even win. Luckily, there was a third option – CONDITIONAL RESPITE. Here you met with the commander of the castle and agreed that eventually you would win. The only thing that would save the castle would be a relief force – their side sending an army to rescue them. So, to avoid unnecessary bloodshed, you agreed a time (perhaps three months) and agreed that if a relief army did not arrive by then, the castle would surrender. During the period of conditional respite, the defenders were not supposed to do anything to strengthen the castle. In one famous siege, at Newbury in 1152, the castle commander, fitz Gilbert, agreed a period of respite and handed over his son as hostage. He then cheated and got in more stores. King Stephen had the son put in a catapult and threatened to fire him back into the castle unless fitz Gilbert handed over the stores. Fitz Gilbert shouted back from the battlements that he had the equipment to make another son, so Stephen could do what he liked. Stephen let the boy live.

Until about 1400, the range of tactics for smashing a hole in the wall and storming the castle were simple (see Factfile). After 1400, however, the availability of large siege cannon changed the balance of power. Cannon had much more force than stone-throwing engines, and they could BREACH the strongest walls with time, the right cannon and experienced gunners.

Figure 14 A graph showing the total number of sieges known to historians, 1060–1660. ▼

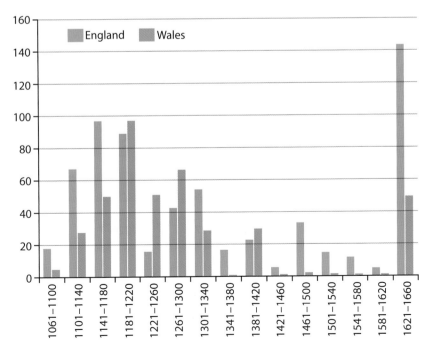

Rochester 1215: A medieval siege

In 1215, after his barons had forced him to sign Magna Carta, King John raised an army to fight them and win back the power he had lost. Rochester Castle was held by the barons and John's army was in Kent. He wanted to attack the barons in London, but felt he could not leave Rochester Castle behind him: it protected a fortified bridge over the River Medway, which was the main route to London. With a strong stone curtain wall and a square keep inside it, the castle had a garrison of about 100 knights plus their soldiers. The siege began on 11 October. John himself arrived on 13 October and had stone-throwing engines set up on a hill overlooking the castle.

> **Source 15 An extract from the account of Roger of Wendover, a monk and historian, writing between 1220 and 1231.**
>
> *The king did not allow the besieged any rest day or night. For, amidst the stones hurled from the engines, and the missiles of the crossbows and archers, frequent assaults were made by the knights and their followers, so that when some were tired, other fresh ones succeeded them in the assault; and with these changes the besieged had no rest.*
>
> *The besieged, too, tried to delay their own destruction. They were in great dread of the cruelty of the king. Therefore, that they might not die unavenged, they made no small slaughter amongst the attackers. The siege was prolonged many days owing to the great bravery and boldness of the besieged, who hurled stone for stone, weapon for weapon, from the walls on the enemy.*
>
> *At last, after great numbers of royal troops had been slain, the king, seeing his engines had little effect, employed miners, who soon threw down a great part of the walls. The provisions of the besieged failed them, and they were obliged to eat their horses. The soldiers of the king now rushed to the breaches in the walls, and by constant fierce assaults they forced the besieged to abandon the castle, though not without great loss on their own side. The besieged then entered the keep.*

If you read Source 15 carefully, you may think Roger's language shows some sympathy for the barons and a dislike of John ('dread of the cruelty of the king'; 'great bravery and boldness of the besieged'). Where we can check the facts of his account, this idea is supported although his time scheme might be slightly wrong. John sent orders on 14 October to the mayor of nearby Canterbury to make ('by day and night') and send to the king's army as many picks as they could. So mining was on his mind from the start of the siege. Once a breach was made, his troops stormed it and drove the defenders back into the keep, which became a last refuge.

> **Source 16 An extract describing the siege from the *Barnwell Chronicle*, another medieval history, written close to the time.**
>
> *King John put expert miners to work. They cut their way underground until at last they were under one of the great corner towers. As they moved soil and rock out, they put wooden beams in, with pits props underneath them, to hold up the roof above their heads. They worried every time the beams creaked from the great weight above them. The defenders worried too. Every night they heard tapping sounds under the ground but could do nothing about it. After two months, when the miners came out, brushwood and branches were carried into the tunnels and fat from 40 pigs. Then a fire was started. The fire crackled and sizzled as all the timbers caught fire and blazed until they collapsed. With a great roar the tower fell down.*
>
> *The defenders fell back behind a strong wall, for such was the structure of the keep that a very strong wall separated the half that had fallen from the other. The defenders did not give in until they had nothing but horseflesh and water to sustain them, which they found hard, having been brought up in luxury.*

At least one part of this story checks out. John sent an order from the siege to his chief supporter saying: 'Send us with all speed by day and night forty of the fattest pigs of the least good sort for eating, to bring fire beneath the tower.' The defenders surrendered on 30 November 1215.

Source 17 Phased plans of the first three floors of the keep of Rochester Castle. ▼

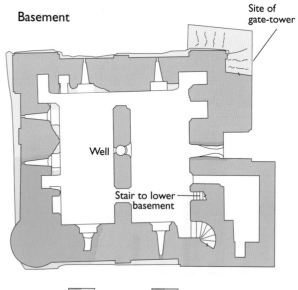

Basement

Site of gate-tower

Well

Stair to lower basement

 1127   1226–7

Source 18 The remains of the keep and curtain wall for Rochester Castle, taken from the south-east. ▼

First floor

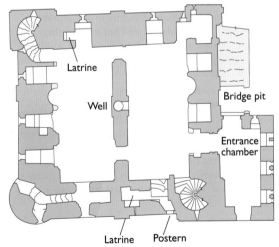

Second (principal) floor

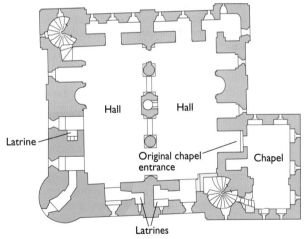

1 Does the language of Source 16 give you any reason to think the writer supported King John?

2 Study Source 17. Do the remains of the castle support the *Barnwell Chronicle*'s account of the capture of the keep? Explain your answer.

3 Rochester is one of the best surviving examples of a square keep. Study Source 17 carefully and explain how people entered the keep in 1127.

Source 19 The remains of Wardour Castle from the air. ▼

Wardour: A siege in the Civil War

When the English Civil War broke out in 1642, the country did not have many professional soldiers. Most of those involved in the fighting had to learn as they went. In the first years of the war, castles proved difficult to capture. By the 1640s, stone walls should not have been able to withstand siege with modern artillery, but there were not many siege cannon or officers trained to use them. The siege of Wardour Castle is typical. The only cannon available were far too small to do serious damage to the walls. Instead, the attackers used the traditional tactics of starving out the garrison, UNDERMINING and storming.

Strategically, castles helped each side control land – and controlling land meant being able to collect taxes. The garrison of a castle like Wardour could also raid enemy supply convoys and disrupt communications. Wardour was a very small castle, but it tied up Royalist forces for over three months until the siege was over.

By 1645, parliament had a well-equipped and professional army that was better able to attack castles. Increasingly, castles were unable to hold out against a proper siege unless they had low, earth-filled walls. Make sure you know what happened to your nominated castle during the Civil Wars of the 1640s.

Source 20 From an account of the siege of Wardour Castle, written by Edmund Ludlow, who commanded the parliamentary garrison defending the castle against the Royalist siege. The siege began in December 1643, and ended on 18 March 1644. These are extracts from a much longer account, and a gap of days (or weeks) is marked '…'.

The besiegers were commanded by Captain Bowyer, who offered us terms to leave the castle, which we declined. He threatened that great numbers of horse and foot, and several cannon, were on their way. He boasted of the right of his cause and spoke of our danger and inevitable ruin. Captain Bean, our cannoneer, told him we were sure of the right of our cause too, and would stay. He fired at Bowyer, and caught him in the heel. He fell to the ground. No one dared fetch him all day. By nightfall his wound had gangrene and he died. …

We now had no beer, only water in the well. Our corn was low and so we rationed it. There were now a hundred men. When our meat ran out we killed and ate one of the horses. The enemy then had a lucky shot, which broke the chain of our portcullis, so we could no longer use the gate. We barricaded it up on the inside; now we had no way out but through a window, for we had walled up our other doors earlier. …

The enemy now decided to dig a hole in the castle wall to blow the wall up, or to tunnel under it, supporting the tunnel with timber, then light a fire in the tunnel to bring the wall down. They brought up thick oak planks to the walls one dark night, on either side of the castle. Our men found them on one side and beat them off, forcing them to leave the planks behind. They had more luck on the other side, and got the planks set up to form a shelter. In the morning we heard them digging. We could not trace where the noise of digging was coming from. Then we found them and tried to shift them by pouring down hot water and melted lead, to little effect. We then threw hand grenadoes, and they were forced to go, leaving their tools and provisions. …

[About the middle of January, 1644] Now the King sent Sir Francis Doddington with more men to the castle, and among them an engineer to undermine the castle. As soon as we heard them beginning to dig, we began to try to undermine them, but the floor was too hard to break through. …

On the Thursday morning I lay down to sleep in my room. At some time between ten and eleven of the clock, the mine exploded. I was flung up as it exploded, amid clouds of dust.

As soon as the dust cleared I found my window towards the enemy blown open, with so big a hole as you could have driven a cart through it. They now made haste to storm the castle – the rubble from my window had made them a path to it. I could not get my pistols to fire. I had to trust to my sword to keep back the enemy. I was, at first, alone in holding them off. There was no way into my room but through the courtyard window. I called through this window to the men that were there requiring them to help at once. [Men] came to my assistance who I ordered to fill up the breach and the doors with the bed, chairs, tables and all else to hand. My room being made safe, I went to see what other breaches had been made. I found one breach, in the room under me, which was well defended, but there was one in the gun room that was not defended at all. I put a guard there, and ran to the upper rooms, which had many doors and windows blown open, at every one of which I placed a guard in some way proportional to the danger. …

We lost three of our men in the blast from the mine, but the rest were safe. But our corn supplies were blown up, as was much of our ammunition. We had some meat left, about enough for four days, so I thought it was best to hold out for as long as we could, hoping to get the best possible terms of surrender from the enemy. No one had been shot during the storm, though some had been slightly wounded, and I had an enemy bullet pierce my hat close to my head. The besiegers had lost ten of their men, killed by shot. …

The castle was now in such a poor state, as were we, that I said I would surrender on conditions. Firstly, no one was to be put to the sword. Secondly, none of my party was to be ill treated. Lastly, we would soon be exchanged for prisoners on their side. Sir Francis Doddington said they would agree to my terms, so I returned to the castle and ordered my soldiers to lay down their arms.

Source 21 A plan of the ground floor of Wardour Castle today. ▼

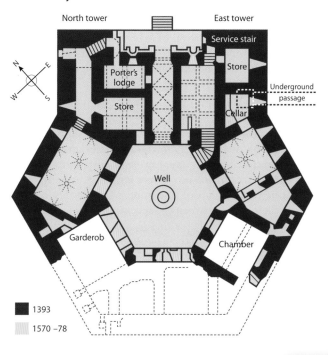

North tower

East tower

Service stair

Store

Porter's lodge

Underground passage

Store

Cellar

Well

Garderob

Chamber

■ 1393

▨ 1570–78

1 Study Source 19.
  a Was Wardour Castle built on high ground or lower ground?
  b Why might the original builder have made this decision?

2 Source 20 gives you seven incidents from the siege of Wardour, Make a table with three columns:
  a What the attackers did.
  b What the defenders did.
  c Were these tactics traditional or modern in 1643–44?
  Fill in the table for each incident.

3 How useful is Ludlow's account as a source for this siege?

4 Which of the other sources on this page is the most useful in addition to Ludlow's account?

5 Why were old-fashioned castles so significant in the Civil War?

6 Is the evidence of the sieges of Rochester and Wardour enough to prove wrong the revisionists' argument that castles were not mainly military?

Source 22 The remains of Wardour Castle from the south-west. ▼

The later history of the nominated castles

- **Carlisle** surrendered to the Jacobites without a fight in 1745 and was recaptured the same year by a royal army after a short siege. It became an army base, arsenal and – from 1819 until 1959 – a barracks.
- **Framlingham** was sold to a rich lawyer in 1635. He died childless, leaving the castle to his old Oxford college on condition that they pulled down parts of it and built a poorhouse. After a period of bad management, a new poorhouse was built in 1729, which lasted until a change in the national system caused its closure in 1839. The former poorhouse was used as a parish hall and the castle became popular with tourists. Ownership transferred to the state in 1913.
- **Kenilworth** was slighted in 1649–50, and the castle lands were converted into farmland, with the gatehouse as the farmhouse. From the 1780s it became popular with tourists, especially after Sir Walter Scott's novel *Kenilworth*, about Queen Elizabeth I, was published in 1821. It remains a tourist destination.
- **Portchester** was sold by Charles I in 1632 to a local landowner, who rented it back to the government to use as a prisoner-of-war camp in 1665. It was used for this purpose on and off until 1814. The army left in 1819 and it stood empty until the state took it over in 1926, caring for the site and opening it to the public.
- **Stokesay** was slighted but remained inhabited until the early eighteenth century. Until the early nineteenth century it was rented out as workshops, including a barrel-maker (in the hall) and a blacksmith (in the south tower, which caused a fire in 1830). It became popular with early tourists from the 1840s, and survived until it was bought and restored by a rich businessman in 1869.

Later uses

The end of the Civil War saw many castles slighted. This theoretically meant they were no longer defensible, but the living accommodation of many castles was badly damaged too. From the 1650s onwards, castles were much less likely to be inhabited. They were used in many different ways:

- **Prisons:** Buildings with strong walls to keep people out could easily be used to keep people in. Some bigger castles were prisons until very recently – Oxford Castle until 1996 and Lancaster until 2011.
- **Quarries:** Stone is expensive and difficult to quarry and all over the country were buildings nobody was using that had lots of fine stone. Many castles lost a lot of their walls between the seventeenth and nineteenth centuries as people – either legally or illegally – took the stones to use in their houses and farms.
- **Industrial uses:** Castle sites included large and strong buildings. Some of these were leased or bought for use in different industries. The keep of Canterbury Castle was used as a coke store for the gasworks (which were built in its bailey) until the 1920s.
- **Tourism:** Medieval ruins became fashionable in the late eighteenth century. People liked to visit them and enjoy these picturesque sites. Having ivy growing all over the walls added to the effect.

Goodrich Castle was abandoned after it was slighted in 1648. The ditch was used as a cattle enclosure, but the buildings seem to have been ignored until the 1780s, when it became a tourist site.

Source 23 The entrance to Goodrich Castle, from the barbican, in the nineteenth century. ▼

1 Compare the photo of Goodrich in Source 23 with the modern photos of the site in this chapter. How has the castle changed since 1872?

2 Why do you think these changes have happened?

3 How has tourism affected the later history of Goodrich and the five nominated castles?

4 Is tourism a better use for castles than using them as prisons, as quarries and for industry?

5 How typical is the later history of your nominated castle (see Factfile)?

PRACTICE QUESTIONS

Explain why Goodrich Castle was largely rebuilt just before 1300. (10)

TOPIC SUMMARY

What were the functions of a castle?

1. Royal castles were controlled by the monarch, baronial castles were owned by lords. Royal castles normally guarded somewhere strategically important, or the monarch controlled them for a short time before passing them on to a noble as a reward.
2. Castles were not always built on the highest ground – they had to be convenient to live and work in.
3. Castles could make a whole country harder to attack, because it was dangerous to ignore them and besieging them cost time or soldiers – or both.
4. Henry VIII built a series of castles on the south coast to use cannon to stop enemy ships landing an invasion force.
5. Many castles had a place of final refuge, which could be defended if the rest of the castle was captured.
6. Castles were important symbols of the power and prestige of a king or lord.
7. A castle was a hierarchical community, and there was a lot of ceremony in castle life – the great hall was important as a ceremonial space.
8. In most castles the domestic accommodation was changed more than the military features: larger households (so more accommodation) and more privacy (so private apartments for important people).
9. Sieges were very unusual.

Bringing it all together: remains, context and function

You have built up a lot of knowledge about castles – and about two castles in particular. A question like the one on the left requires you to pull all this knowledge together. Consider what you know:

- A phased plan gives you the best understanding of when different parts of the castle were built (the Goodrich plan is on page 223).
- The different styles of castle building, and roughly the times when they were fashionable (for Goodrich, stone keeps and curtain walls).
- The range of sources historians use to find out about individual castles (for Goodrich, the importance of the surviving manuscripts of Joan de Valence, page 226).
- The importance of the main events in the story of a particular castle (for Goodrich, page 229).
- The main functions of a castle and how some of them changed through time.

Which of these things really helps answer the question? Looking at the plan reveals that the big rebuilding around 1300 was in the curtain wall style. You should be able to explain some of the military and other factors that lay behind the decision to make these changes:

- The need for more living space in the castle, especially more space for the high-status people than the keep could provide.
- The need to replace earlier wooden structures.
- The desire to strengthen the defences of the bailey by building a strong wall with defensive features such as towers for flanking fire and a barbican.

The visit of Joan de Valence illustrates this and adds to the factors:

- Joan visited with a large household – which needed accommodation – and she was visited by other nobles who brought members of their households with them. So the need for accommodation was great.

From the story of Goodrich you could add:

- It had been owned by families that did not spend time there, then it came to the de Valence family, which did spend time there.
- This work was done around the end of Edward I's conquest of Wales, so perhaps it would be safe to improve the domestic features.

Then, from your understanding of the function of a castle, you might add:

- Goodrich was a baronial castle, owned at the time by a powerful noble family, which would have wanted to show off its power with a building appropriate to its importance and to administer its estates in the area.
- Goodrich had been besieged, so its owners might not want to ignore the need to make the castle safe – hence the strong towers and the barbican.

There is more here than you would be expected to remember in an exam, but it is a useful example of how you can bring together knowledge from each of the different ways of looking at castles covered in this chapter. Now you need to use the knowledge to support a good answer to the question. Remember: a list of facts and ideas is not an answer to a question. Plan out an argument, then use the facts and ideas to support your argument.

7.3 Castle factfiles

Portchester Castle

Source 1 Extracts from the phased plans of Portchester Castle. ▼

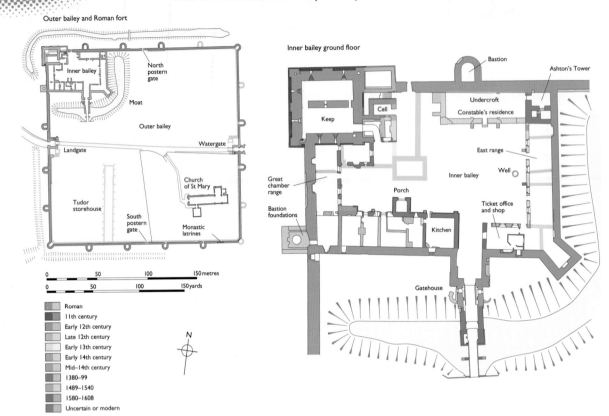

Roman
11th century
Early 12th century
Late 12th century
Early 13th century
Early 14th century
Mid–14th century
1380–99
1489–1540
1580–1608
Uncertain or modern

1 Explain where the area shown in Source 3 is in the plan (Source 1).
2 The plan shows different periods of building in this area. What evidence of this can you see in Source 3?

Portchester Castle is very unusual, in that it was built inside the walls of a Roman fort, which was already almost 800 years old and probably quite ruined. Inside the walls, the Roman buildings had been destroyed and a Saxon community lived and worked. Portchester became a royal castle because it guarded a great natural harbour, and remained important until Henry VIII's new castles defending the south coast superseded it. It continued to be valuable as a safe place for stores and then for prisoners of war.

Source 2 A painting showing the remains of Portchester Castle as they are today. ▼

1 Inner bailey
2 Keep
3 Richard II's palace
4 Exit ranges
5 Ashton's Tower
6 Moat
7 Gatehouse
8 North postern gate
9 Outer bailey
10 Landgate
11 Watergate
12 Parish church of St Mary
13 Outline of Tudor stonehouse

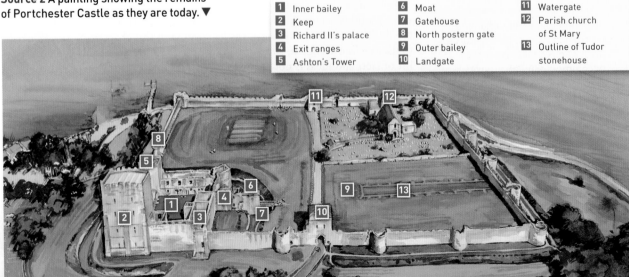

Source 3 A section of the remains today. The tall building is the keep. ▼

FACTFILE

Portchester Castle

285–290 Roman fort built at Portchester.

c1066–86 First Norman castle on the site, built by William Maudit. He probably had the moat to protect the inner bailey dug and built a wooden wall inside it.

c1120–48 William Pont de l'Arche rebuilt the keep and the inner bailey walls in stone.

1143 Priory founded inside the walls; its church later became St Mary's, the parish church.

c1154 Henry II took Portchester as a royal castle. He often visited, as it was a convenient port for France.

1173–74 Pipe rolls (royal accounts) show the gates, keep, walls and bridge were repaired. This included bratticing and catapults for defence. Garrisoned 10 (later 20) knights.

1183 Repairs to a royal residence in the inner bailey that was not the keep. This building was later replaced. *[Pipe rolls]*

1216 The castle was besieged and captured by Louis of France, who was fighting with the English barons against King John.

1217 Castle recaptured by Henry III, John's son and successor. The new king ordered that the castle be destroyed, but this did not happen. Instead repairs were made.

1256 Major repairs. *[Pipe rolls]*

1274 A survey reported the castle was in need of repair.

1289–96 Major repairs, including a new inner gate, a new drawbridge, bratticing and a tower on the sea wall.

1320–26 Over £1,100 spent on works – a massive sum. Work included repairs to the keep, the king's house, land gate and water gate, strengthening the gate of the inner bailey and building a new hall with floor tiles and painted walls.

1335–44 Significant repairs, including making some of the Roman walls useable and building a new wall to stop galleys entering from the sea.

1369 Repairs to some towers and to the wall walks and gates due to a threat of invasion from France.

1385 Ashton's Tower finished, barbican extended.

1390 Part of the west wall fell down.

1396–99 Richard II built new and better domestic accommodation, including the great hall and great chamber, kitchens and changes to the keep, plus decorated glass for the windows. Costs included candles to allow the builders to work at night.

1415 Portchester was Henry V's base for the invasion of France that led to the Battle of Agincourt.

1441 A royal surveyor described the castle as 'right ruinous and feeble'. Some repairs were started.

1450 The constable of the castle, Robert Fiennes, wrote to the king complaining: 'The gates have been broken, both within and without, the drawbridge fallen down, the towers, turrets and barbicans fallen down, and other houses of office [buildings] fail both in their roofs and floors.'

1489–1501 Repairs made.

1512 A gunpowder mill was established inside the walls.

1527 A large military storehouse was built, 73 m long by 9 m wide. Portchester was now mainly a military depot.

1535 Henry VIII visited the castle and agreed some repairs.

1583 With danger of invasion growing, £250 was allocated to the repair of Portchester. Some stone was taken from the castle for use in the new defences of Portsmouth.

c1605 The eastern range was rebuilt.

1609 A surveyor reported that most of the buildings, apart from the eastern range, were ruinous because the lead covering the roof had been stolen and rain had rotted the roof timbers. No repairs were made.

1628 Used as a stores depot for the navy.

1632 Sold by Charles I to Sir William Uvedale.

1644 Garrisoned for a while in the Civil War, but not attacked.

1665–1763 Used as a prisoner-of-war camp.

1763–94 Abandoned.

1794–1814 Used as a prisoner-of-war camp.

1819 Returned to the private owners.

1926 Passed back to the care of the government.

Carlisle Castle

Source 1 Extracts from the phased plans of Carlisle Castle.

12th century
13th–15th century
16th–early 19th century
Mid-19th–20th century

1. Explain where the area shown in Source 3 is in the plan (Source 1).
2. The plan shows different periods of building in this area. What evidence of this can you see in Source 3?

Carlisle Castle is unusual in that it was built as, and has always been, a royal castle. Built on the border between England and Scotland, it was besieged much more often than is usual. It was last besieged and captured as recently as 1745. Over hundreds of years it was ignored by the government when relations with Scotland were good, and strengthened when they were bad. It is a medieval castle that was modernised to use cannon in its defence. It became a barracks and army depot in the early nineteenth century, when the government was worried about social unrest during the Industrial Revolution.

Source 2 A painting showing the remains of Carlisle Castle as they are today. ▼

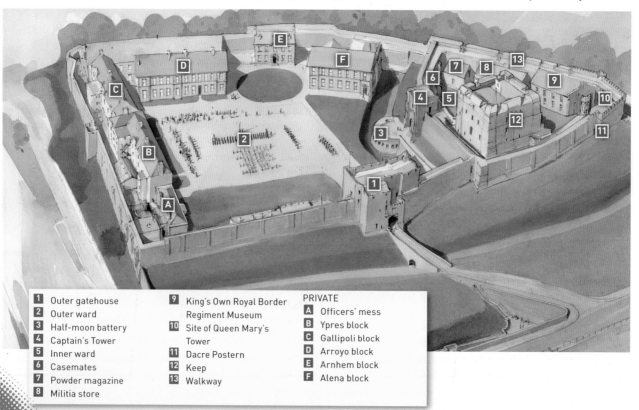

1	Outer gatehouse	9	King's Own Royal Border	PRIVATE	
2	Outer ward		Regiment Museum	A	Officers' mess
3	Half-moon battery	10	Site of Queen Mary's	B	Ypres block
4	Captain's Tower		Tower	C	Gallipoli block
5	Inner ward	11	Dacre Postern	D	Arroyo block
6	Casemates	12	Keep	E	Arnhem block
7	Powder magazine	13	Walkway	F	Alena block
8	Militia store				

FACTFILE

Carlisle Castle

1092 William II captured Carlisle from the Scots and built a castle there. This castle may just have been an earth bailey topped with a wooden wall. No remains survive.

1122 Henry I ordered new stone castle and city walls be built.

1136 Carlisle was taken by the Scots. Civil war in England meant no attempt to recapture it.

1136–57 Scottish king David I controlled the castle. The keep was probably begun in Henry I's time and finished during David's rule. David died in the castle in 1153.

1157 The Scots withdrew and Henry II of England took control. He strengthened the defences. Henry probably had the gatehouse of the inner ward built.

1174 William I of Scotland besieged the castle for three months. After some hard fighting, the constable of the castle and William agreed a period of conditional respite, during which Henry II defeated and captured William.

1186 Henry II visited the castle and ordered a new royal palace to be built against the north wall.

1186–88 Parts of the palace built – a chamber for the king, a small tower and a chapel.

1201 Worried by the possibility of war with Scotland, King John spent £214 strengthening the defences of the castle. War did not break out.

1216 King Alexander of Scotland besieged the castle. The south curtain wall was undermined, and the outer and inner gatehouses badly damaged by catapults. The castle was captured.

1217 The Scots returned the castle. The siege did so much damage it took years to make the castle strong again.

1226–27 Repairs to the keep after the damage of the siege.

1232–33 Repairs to the curtain wall.

1237 Scotland abandoned all claim to Carlisle.

1256 A survey: guttering, doors and windows of the keep missing; many of the floors rotten; outer and inner gates still unrepaired after the siege; the wood (doors, windows and bratticing) had been stolen or burned.

1264–69/1285–90 Some repairs were made, but not enough to return the castle to its pre-siege state.

1296 Edward I began his wars to conquer Scotland. This meant Carlisle was a key base for his operations.

1297–1303 The moats were cleared, new bratticing made and improvements to the great hall.

1307–12 New east gatehouse built, defences strengthened and a bath was installed in the palace for the queen.

1315 The Scots besieged the castle: well-organised, with a large catapult, attempted to undermine and fill in the moat for a siege tower to storm the walls. The castle had a strong garrison of almost 500 soldiers. The mines flooded, there was so much rain the Scots could not fill in the moat and the siege tower sank in the mud.

1321 & 1335 Surveys reported severe problems including (1321) two sections of the outer bailey wall had collapsed and (1335) the outer gatehouse 'ruinous'.

1363/1367–71 Some repairs to the keep and walls.

1378–83 New outer gatehouse built.

1380/1384 Five cannon added, two on the roof of the keep.

1430 The castle had six (more powerful) iron cannon.

1483 The tile tower built.

1488 Henry VII's master gunner modernised the defences.

1522/1523/1526 Surveys: partly ruinous, not enough cannon.

1532–33 Some money spent strengthening the defences.

1538 Survey: £1,000 needed for repairs; £53 was spent.

1541–42 Major work: cannon platform on keep roof, curtain walls strengthened for cannon, half-moon battery built.

1577–78 Significant repairs, including to the keep.

1603 James VI of Scotland became James I of England: no possibility of war between England and Scotland.

1617 James I visited the castle, saw it was badly decayed and did nothing to repair it.

1633 Most of the cannon removed.

1642 Castle refortified as a Royalist stronghold in the Civil War.

1644–45 City and castle besieged by Scots and parliamentary troops, a long siege until the garrison was starved out.

c1700 Garrison withdrawn.

1716 Used as a prison after the Jacobite rebellion failed.

1745 Surrendered to the Jacobites without fighting, the Jacobite garrison of 400 surrendered after the castle was attacked by powerful artillery in December.

1746 The castle used as a prison and storehouse.

1819 Worried by the possibility of revolution, the government built a barracks at the castle.

1945 Anti-aircraft gun installed on top of the keep.

1959 Carlisle barracks closed.

Source 3 A section of the remains of Carlisle Castle today. ▼

Framlingham Castle

Source 1 Extracts from the phased plans of Framlingham Castle.

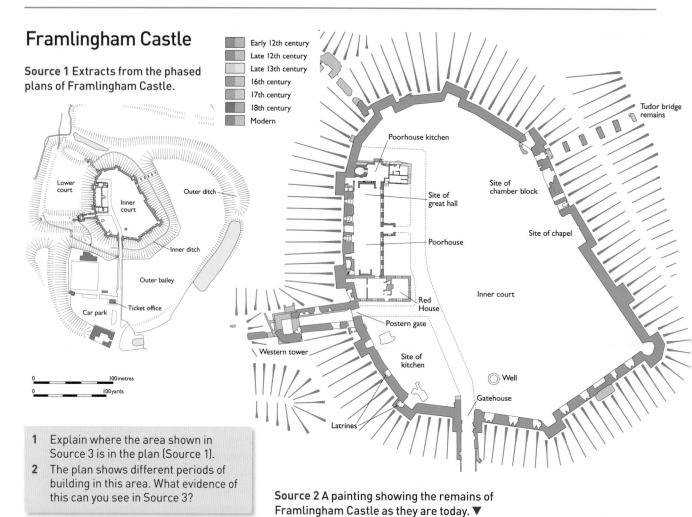

Key:
- Early 12th century
- Late 12th century
- Late 13th century
- 16th century
- 17th century
- 18th century
- Modern

Labels (left plan): Lower court, Inner court, Outer ditch, Inner ditch, Outer bailey, Ticket office, Car park, 0 100 metres, 0 100 yards

Labels (right plan): Poorhouse kitchen, Site of great hall, Poorhouse, Red House, Postern gate, Western tower, Site of kitchen, Latrines, Well, Gatehouse, Inner court, Site of chamber block, Site of chapel, Tudor bridge remains

1 Explain where the area shown in Source 3 is in the plan (Source 1).
2 The plan shows different periods of building in this area. What evidence of this can you see in Source 3?

Source 2 A painting showing the remains of Framlingham Castle as they are today. ▼

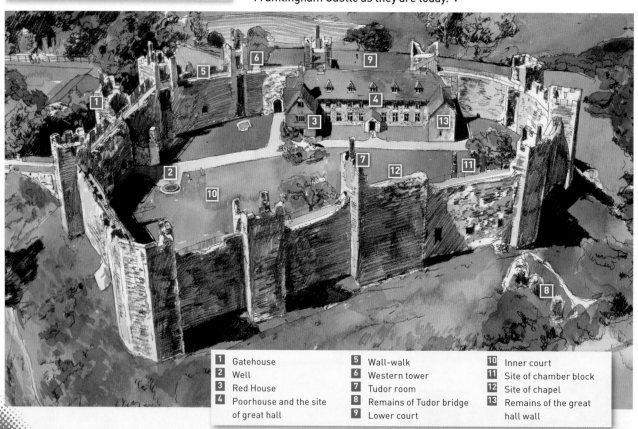

1	Gatehouse	5	Wall-walk	10	Inner court
2	Well	6	Western tower	11	Site of chamber block
3	Red House	7	Tudor room	12	Site of chapel
4	Poorhouse and the site of great hall	8	Remains of Tudor bridge	13	Remains of the great hall wall
		9	Lower court		

FACTFILE

Framlingham Castle

1066–1107 Roger Bigod built the first castle, made from wood.

1140 Hugh Bigod was made Earl of Norfolk.

1145–48 During the civil wars of Stephen's reign, Framlingham was big enough for the Archbishop of Canterbury and his court to live there.

c1150–57 First stone buildings, a chamber block and a chapel (later part of the eastern curtain wall) built.

1157–65 Henry II confiscated Framlingham from Hugh Bigod. Garrisoned by royal troops until given back to Hugh in 1165.

1173 Hugh Bigod rebelled against Henry II but was defeated and exiled. Walls of Framlingham destroyed.

1189 Hugh's son, Roger Bigod II, was given his title and castle back by Richard I. He started to build the stone curtain wall.

1216 Roger Bigod II was a leader of the barons who forced King John to sign Magna Carta. In the civil war that followed, John besieged Framlingham. Bigod was not there – the garrison was 26 knights, 20 sergeants-at-arms, seven crossbowmen, one chaplain and three others. The castle surrendered after two days. In the peace that followed Bigod got the castle back.

1248 Roger Bigod III became one of the richest barons in the country when he inherited lands and titles from his mother's father.

1270–1306 Roger Bigod IV made many improvements, including building new lodgings, re-roofing the knights' lodgings, adding some towers and the 'great dairy and cowshed'.

1306–12 Roger IV owed a huge debt of taxes and was virtually bankrupt. He made the king his heir and when he died in 1306 the castle passed to the Crown. In 1312, the king gave it to his half-brother, Thomas Brotherton.

1383 Framlingham was inherited by Margaret Brotherton, who became Duchess of Norfolk.

1483–89 Framlingham was inherited by John Howard, Duke of Norfolk, who started major repairs and rebuilding, but was killed (on the losing side) at the Battle of Bosworth in 1485. Framlingham was confiscated and then passed to Thomas Howard in 1489.

1489–1524 Framlingham was John Howard's main residence and he had much work done in the castle. When he died in 1524 his body lay in state in the castle chapel for four weeks, and the chapel and gatehouse were wrapped in 400 metres of black cloth.

1524 The new Duke of Norfolk did not live at Framlingham but at a grand house at Kenninghall, Norfolk.

1547 Thomas Howard was imprisoned for treason and Framlingham was confiscated by the king and passed to his sister Mary. The castle was in a poor state, a survey noted: 'Many houses of the same castle is in great decay, and [many] of them is like to fall down unless they be shortly repaired.'

1553 Edward VI died; a plan to replace him with Lady Jane Grey failed when Mary raised an army at Framlingham and Lady Jane's supporters deserted. Thomas Howard was released and given back his lands.

1572 Thomas Howard was executed for treason. The castle was confiscated by Elizabeth I and used as a prison.

1589 A survey of the castle reported: 'The castle of Framlingham is in great ruin and decay in divers places.'

1603 James I returned Framlingham to the Howard family, but they did not live there.

1635 Framlingham sold to Sir Robert Hitcham.

1636 Hitcham died, leaving Framlingham to Pembroke College, Cambridge, on condition it was used to benefit the poor of Framlingham and two other towns. This included setting up almshouses and a school for '30 or 40 of the poorest and neediest' children.

1654–66 The Red House was built, perhaps for the schoolmaster, then turned into a poorhouse. The castle was used for plague victims.

1669–99 The Red House was used as a pub, perhaps with some poor from the three towns living there.

1699–1729 The Red House used as a poorhouse for children.

1729–1839 A new poorhouse was built on the site of the great hall.

1839–1913 Local uses including as a parish hall and a local prison, increasing the number of tourists after the railway reached Framlingham in 1859.

1913 Given to the forerunner of English Heritage to run.

Source 3 A section of the remains of Framlingham Castle today. ▼

No evidence survives that there was a motte and bailey castle at Framlingham, but there probably was one. The first Norman lord may have used this site for his first castle and some of the existing earthworks could have been part of that castle.

What remains today is a very unusual castle. It was one of the great castle-palaces of the Middle Ages, with (presumably) grand accommodation within the existing curtain wall. However, all that has been demolished and some of it would have been under the Red House. It was certainly a castle designed to impress people when they saw it in the distance, with the castle reflected in the mere.

Kenilworth Castle

Source 1 Extracts from the phased plans of Kenilworth Castle.

▩	12th century
▩	13th century
▢	14th century
▩	15th century
▩	16th century
▩	modern

KENILWORTH CASTLE PLAN

Labels on the large plan: Kitchens · Great tower · Strong Tower · Site of Leicester's lodgings · Chapel · Inner court · Hall cellars · State apartments · Saintlowe Tower · Wardrobe · Privy kitchen · Gaunt's Tower · Leicester's Building

Labels on the small plan: Swan Tower · King's Gate · Garden · Leicester's Gatehouse · Lunn's Tower · Right-hand court · Water gate · Base court · Inner court · Stable · Collegiate chapel · Left-hand court · Water Tower · Mortimer's Tower · Site of Lower Pool · Site of the mere · Finham brook · Dam/shipyard · Gallery Tower

1 Explain where the area shown in Source 3 is in the plan (Source 1).

2 The plan shows different periods of building in this area. What evidence of this can you see in Source 3?

Kenilworth was one of the great castle palaces of medieval England. It was so powerful, and in such an important strategic position in the Midlands, that Henry II took it as a royal castle (although it was given back to great lords three times). Twice it was the headquarters of rebels, first Simon de Montfort and then the House of Lancaster in the Wars of the Roses. The Lancastrian John of Gaunt deliberately made it like a royal palace. The Earl of Leicester upgraded it again, trying to show himself a fit husband for Elizabeth I.

Source 2 A painting showing the remains of Kenilworth Castle as they are today. ▼

1	Outlying features	**7**	Great hall	**14**	Collegiate chapel
2	Mortimer's Tower	**8**	Saintlowe Tower	**15**	Lunn's Tower
3	Base court	**9**	State apartments	**16**	Water Tower
4	Inner court	**10**	Leicester's Building	**17**	Outer curtain wall
5	Great tower and forebuilding	**11**	Outer court	**18**	Elizabethan garden
6	Kitchens	**12**	Leicester's Gatehouse	**19**	Path to the Peasance
		13	Stable		

FACTFILE

Kenilworth Castle

1120s Geoffrey de Clinton built the first castle at Kenilworth. It is likely that the keep was built at this time because of the similarities between it and the keep of another castle owned by the de Clintons nearby at Brandon.

1173/4 The castle was so powerful and strategically important that Henry II took it as a royal castle.

1210–15 King John built domestic accommodation and parts of the outer curtain wall and gatehouse.

1241 Henry III ordered repairs and improvements to the king's chapel, the king's chamber, the queen's chamber, the keep, the gates and the southern curtain wall.

1244–65 Henry gave the castle to Simon de Montfort, who was killed leading a rebellion against Henry. His followers fled to Kenilworth.

1266 De Montfort's followers were besieged in Kenilworth. Archaeologists have found 140-kg stone balls fired by the besiegers' TREBUCHETS over 320 m from where they could have been set up. It was not possible to undermine the walls because of the water defences. An attempt to storm the castle failed. Starving, the garrison finally surrendered.

1267 Henry granted the castle to his son, Edmund of Lancaster.

1296–1322 Thomas of Lancaster, with about 500 retainers at the castle, entertained on a scale to rival the king. He probably had the water tower built to make more accommodation.

1314–22 A new chapel was built in the outer bailey.

1347 The great hall was improved and repaired.

1361 Kenilworth passed to John of Gaunt, a son of Edward III, who became Duke of Lancaster.

1371–83 Gaunt spent regularly on repairs and improvements.

1389–93 Gaunt built new accommodation, the state apartments, on the south and west sides of the inner court.

1399 Gaunt's son became king and Kenilworth a royal castle.

1414 Henry V ordered the building of the pleasance – pleasure gardens and royal apartments half a mile from the castle at the other end of the mere. It was probably a copy of the garden palaces of Islamic Spain.

1424/1461 New kitchens built in the castle.

1492–93 Henry VII, who often stayed at the castle, had a tennis court built and some other improvements made.

1524 Henry VIII picked Kenilworth as one of the four royal castles he wanted kept in good repair for his visits.

1524–26 The pleasance was abandoned and its timber-framed banqueting house re-erected in the base court.

1530–32 New royal accommodation was built (timber-framed) on the east side of the inner court.

1553 New stables built.

1563 Queen Elizabeth gave the castle to her favourite, Robert Dudley, Earl of Leicester.

1568–75 Leicester made extensive alterations to the keep, built a new gatehouse and a grand new domestic accommodation (Leicester's Building).

1575 Queen Elizabeth visited Kenilworth, staying for 17 days, with great pageants and entertainments.

1588–1642 Leicester died without an heir and the castle eventually returned to royal ownership. Both James I and Charles I visited it, and it remained an impressive palace.

1642–47 Kenilworth was abandoned by the royalists early in 1642 and garrisoned by parliament for the rest of the war.

1649–50 Parliament ordered the slighting of the castle – part of the keep and sections of the curtain wall were destroyed.

1650s Parliament granted the castle to officers in lieu of their arrears of pay – the gatehouse became a farmhouse and the domestic buildings were plundered for building material for other farms. Most was left as a roofless ruin.

1660–1860s The castle was a farm. Visiting the ruins became fashionable, especially after the publication of Sir Walter Scott's historical novel *Kenilworth* in 1821.

1860s–1958 The castle was cared for as a tourist attraction. In 1958, it was given to the Kenilworth town council.

Source 3 A section of the remains of Kenilworth Castle today. ▼

Stokesay Castle

Source 1 Extracts from the phased plans of Stokesay Castle.

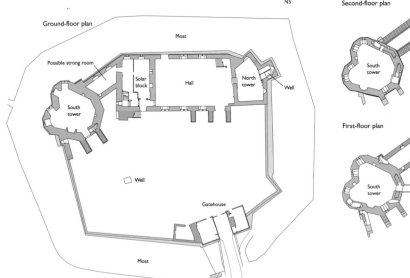

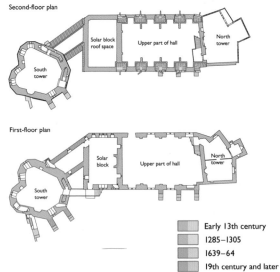

Early 13th century

1285–1305

1639–64

19th century and later

1 Explain where the area shown in Source 3 is in the plan (Source 1).

2 The plan shows different periods of building in this area. What evidence of this can you see in Source 3?

There was probably a fortified manor house at Stokesay before the castle was built in around 1285–91, but we have no evidence about it. Lawrence of Ludlow, a wool merchant and one of the richest men in England, built the current castle. He died soon after, commanding a trading fleet for the king that ran into a storm. For most of its history Stokesay was lived in by tenants of the owners and the tenants quietly got on with their lives. The castle was captured in the Civil War, but without any fighting. So much of it has survived relatively unchanged because the tenants were not rich enough to make major alterations.

Source 2 A painting showing the remains of Stokesay Castle as they are today. ▼

1 Gatehouse	6 North tower
2 Courtyard	7 Solar block
3 Curtain wall	8 Stairway
4 Well	9 South tower
5 Hall	10 Moat

FACTFILE

Stokesay Castle

1086 Stokesay, called 'Stoches', held by the Norman Lacy family.

1100–35 Stoches had been split into North and South Stoke. South Stoke was held by the Say family, known as Stokesay.

1241 Walter de Lacy died and Stokesay passed to John de Verdon, his daughter's husband. There was probably a castle at Stokesay at this point, but no trace of it remains.

1261–63 Wood cut in these years is used in the current solar block. It is likely this wood was used in the earlier castle, and reused when the new castle was built in 1285–91.

1264–81 Verdon was captured in the civil war between Henry III and Simon de Montfort. When freed he went on crusade, leaving a tenant in Stokesay.

1281 Lawrence of Ludlow bought Stokesay.

c1285 Work started on building the new castle. Lawrence probably lived in Shrewsbury until the castle was finished.

1291 Lawrence was granted a 'licence to crenellate' – this was official royal permission to build a castle and a sign of Lawrence's new social standing as a lord. He probably moved to the castle about this time.

1294 Lawrence drowned when a royal fleet he commanded taking wool to sell in the Netherlands was caught in a storm.

1294–1498 The Ludlow family – members of the local ruling class – continued to live in the castle.

1498 Sir Richard Ludlow died and his granddaughter Anne, who married Thomas Vernon, inherited Stokesay Castle.

c1577 Henry Vernon repaired the top floor of the tower.

1598 Henry Vernon, badly in debt, sold Stokesay Castle to Sir Richard Mainwaring for £6,000.

1620 Mainwaring sold Stokesay and other property in Shropshire to Dame Elizabeth Craven, widow of a former Lord Mayor of London.

1624 Dame Elizabeth died; the castle passed to her son William Craven (later the Earl of Craven), one of the richest men in the kingdom. He owned estates all over England and spent very little time at Stokesay.

1633 Craven is known to have visited Stokesay.

1640–41 Craven's accounts show he spent just over £500 on work on the castle. Tree-ring dating of the timbers used in the gatehouse shows that the wood used was cut in 1639–41, so we can be sure this was the new gatehouse.

1642 Royalists garrisoned the castle during the Civil War.

1645 In June, parliament's forces captured the castle. They outnumbered the garrison and summoned it to surrender. The garrison refused and the Parliamentarians prepared to storm the castle (which meant they could kill all the garrison according to the 'Laws of War'). Offered another chance to surrender, the garrison did – probably without a shot being fired. Parliamentarians garrisoned the castle.

1646–47 The castle was slighted – the curtain walls considerably reduced in height.

1647 The Baldwyn family had the tenancy of the castle.

1709–1830 The Baldwyns moved away and sub-let the castle.

1813 A visitor, John Britton, described the castle as 'abandoned to neglect, and rapidly advancing to ruin: the glass is destroyed, the ceilings and floors are falling, and the rain streams through the opening roof on the damp and mouldering walls.' The hall was being used as a barrel-making workshop and the solar as a grain store.

1830 The basement of the South Tower was a blacksmith's workshop. A fire destroyed all the floors of the tower.

1853 Lord Craven, whose family still owned the freehold of the castle, made repairs to stop it decaying any further.

1869 The castle was bought by John Allcroft, who built a grand house to live in nearby and also restored the castle.

Source 3 A section of the remains of Stokesay Castle today. ▼

7.4

The development of a castle

What is the story of *your* castle?

English Heritage plans to commission a series of websites about major castles. Each castle's site will follow the same structure (see Figure 1). You have been invited to pitch for the job of creating the content for the site for your nominated castle. To pitch well, you need to plan the following:

- **The main castle landing page:** This must hook people's interest and make them want to know more. It should include: a single image to sum up the castle, with an explanation of why this was chosen; introductory text (maximum 100 words); navigation text.
- **History pages:** Three sample pages:
  - The site, where it is, why it was built there.
  - Main changes landing page: an overview of the main changes to the castle, with block text and image for each change discussed on a linked page. Maximum 70 words per block. Linked pages are not needed at this stage.
  - Main functions landing page: an overview of the main functions of the castle, with block text and image for each function to be shown discussed on a linked page. Maximum 70 words per block. Linked pages are not needed at this stage.
- **The tour:** Four sample pages:
  - Landing page: this should be a plan with the areas highlighted that will hyperlink to a page on a particular feature.
  - Three sample feature pages.
- **The argument:** English Heritage wants visitors to know there is a disagreement between historians about why castles were built. You must use the standard introductory text (Source 1) and then explain how far the evidence of your castle supports either argument.

To keep costs under control, English Heritage has developed three wireframes of different page designs that the website will use (see Figure 2). For each page apart from the tour landing page, you must work with one of these three page designs.

You should use the material on your nominated castle in this book and any other material about the castle you have been given. Wherever you can, explain on web pages *how* you know what you are describing. Historians do two different types of work: researching and communicating. When they have finished their research and know what they think, the job is not over. It is just as hard to work out the best way of explaining something – and that is what this task requires you to do.

Source 1 The revisionist's view.

Originally historians thought that castles were mainly military buildings, and that changes in the way castles were designed and built were as a result of an 'arms race' between new methods of attacking castles, and defences to nullify those new measures.

More recently, some historians, called revisionists, have seen castles as symbols of the power of the castle owner, with this symbolism, domestic comfort, and administrative convenience the main reasons for changes in castle design.

Figure 1

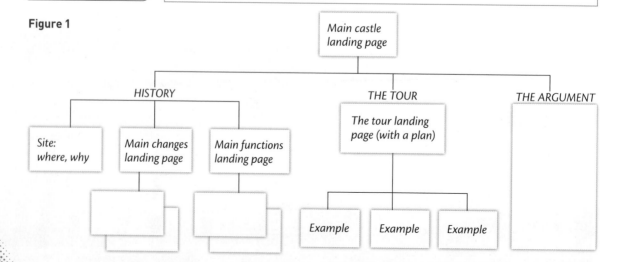

Figure 2

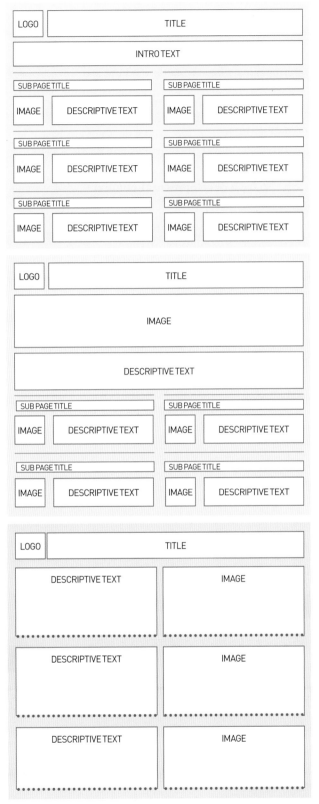

The functions of the castle

The best way to do this task, and to prepare for your examination, is to relate the nominated castle to what you have learned about castles in this chapter. The place to start is with the functions of the castle – be clear about them and this will give you a good base from which to work. You looked at the different functions of a castle in Topic 7.2.

Royal or baronial: This is the first thing to be sure about. When was the castle first built, and who by? If it started life as a baronial castle, was it taken over by the Crown at any point? If it was, be clear whether this was because of its strategic importance, as a punishment or because the owner's family died out with no heirs. If it ever was a royal castle, how long did it stay one? Topic 7.3 is a good place to check if you are unsure of any of the answers to these questions.

Site: Does the castle guard something of clear strategic value, like a harbour or a bridge? Was it built on a major transport route? Did it protect a town or did a town grow up because there was a castle? Was it built on the highest ground available or was the site a compromise between convenience and safety?

Symbolism: What effect would the castle have had on the people who lived near it? Is there any evidence to suggest it was built with any thought as to how it looked from nearby roads and rivers? Did it replace something? Can you explain any of the changes made to the castle because they make its owner look richer and more powerful?

Administration: Is there any evidence of how the castle was used as a centre from which to run the lord's estates? Is it possible to work out what parts of the castle would be used for a court or formal meetings?

Accommodation: To what extent was it a barracks for soldiers, and to what extent was it a palace for the rich and the powerful? Were there special parts of the castle for the rich and powerful, and if so when were they built or changed? How did the castle change as a living space over hundreds of years?

Castle life: What do you know about life in the castle? Was there a great hall? If so, did it change? Did the provision of toilets change? Where were the kitchens? How big were they?

Defensive features: How would the castle have been defended? Did these defensive features change over time?

The phased plan you can find in Topic 7.3 is a key source for starting to answer most of these questions. Also, if you can, you should explain how evidence for what you say can still be found in the remains of the castle.

Source 2 A list of the servants of Joan de Valence at Goodrich Castle who were given money for new shoes at Easter 1297.

The chapel clerk,

Humphrey [of the mistress's chamber],

John of the Wardrobe,

Richard the usher,

the mistress's laundress,

Waiter the farrier [who shoed horses],

John Bendogeda,

John Cely,

Richard the Sauserer [a specialist chef],

John the Baker,

the mistress's herald,

Isaac [of the kitchen],

Richard of Stanes,

John the mistress's palfreyman [groom],

Hec the coachman,

Burgeys,

Adam the carter,

the groom of Edward Burnel,

Davy the coachman

John the carter,

a half-rate to Henry Pendyn.

Fitting the castle into its contexts

Notice the plural in the title. A castle does not have just one context – it has several.

It has **historical contexts** – the things that were happening when the castle was built and when major changes were made to it. The top half of the timeline below gives you some starting points, but some specific research about the castle at different times will probably help, too. And it does not just have one historical context, there will be one for each major change.

It also has a **developmental context** – what were the up-to-date styles and fashions in castle-building when the changes were made? Do the changes fit neatly into this pattern or not? What about some of the trends in society? Do the changes give more privacy to the most powerful? Is there evidence that the castle needed to house more people as the typical size of noble households grew?

Again, you will find that the castle factfile and the phased plan are good places to start. It is worth looking at the main events and building periods in the castle's history against the timeline. Do not expect everything to fit neatly. The timeline needs to have a lot of generalisations. Sometimes when something does not fit, the reasons may be very interesting!

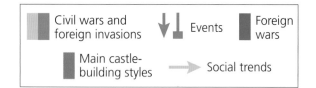

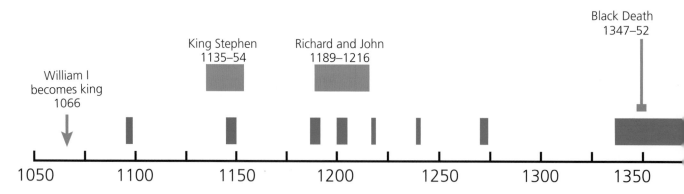

REVIEW TASKS

1 Study Source 2 (opposite) and Source 3 (on page 258). Which of these sources is more useful to a historian studying the domestic accommodation at Goodrich Castle?

The best way to answer this type of question is to:
● focus on the subject, in this case *domestic accommodation*
● consider what you can learn from each source; write a paragraph with examples about each source
● consider possible limitations or problems with the source; again, write a paragraph about the limitations of each source
● make sure you have a conclusion; you have been asked a question, so answer it. Sometimes it can help to start with the conclusion: 'A historian would find Source 2 more useful because ...'

There are two historical skills you should remember and use:
● **Inference:** This requires making a deduction. If you simply said 'There was a coachman called Hec and another called Davy', that would be comprehension. A deduction would be: 'There was a farrier, a groom, two carters and two coachmen, *so horses were an important part of the life of Joan's household, and the accommodation would have needed to include stables.*'
● **Distinguish between information and evidence:** This is very important (and making an inference usually means you are using the source as evidence not for information). You use a source as *evidence* when you make a statement about the past, and back it up by using the source. *'So horses were important'* is a *statement*, and the farrier, groom, two carters and two coachmen are *evidence* from the source to support it.

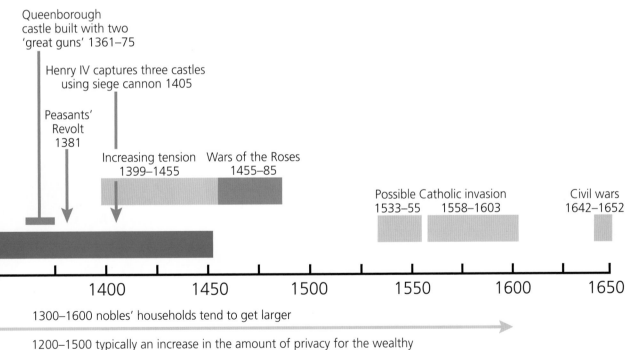

Queenborough castle built with two 'great guns' 1361–75

Henry IV captures three castles using siege cannon 1405

Peasants' Revolt 1381

Increasing tension 1399–1455

Wars of the Roses 1455–85

Possible Catholic invasion 1533–55   1558–1603

Civil wars 1642–1652

1400   1450   1500   1550   1600   1650

1300–1600 nobles' households tend to get larger

1200–1500 typically an increase in the amount of privacy for the wealthy

PRACTICE QUESTIONS

1   Explain why Goodrich Castle has a stone keep (built in about 1150). (10)

2   Study Sources 3 and 4. Which of these is more useful for a historian studying the rebuilding of Goodrich Castle in the late thirteenth century? (10)

The final exam

You know what to expect: two sources and two questions. But do not make the mistake of thinking this means you know what to do and you should just get started. You need to study the two sources closely. The examiner has picked these exact two sources for a reason – for the particular things you can learn from them. So look, read, and think!

Source 3 An aerial photograph of the remains of Goodrich Castle, near the English border with Wales. ▼

KEY TERMS

Make sure you know what these terms mean and are able to use them confidently in your writing.

- bailey
- baronial castle
- beam
- bratticing
- breach (in a wall)
- buttery
- chronicle
- conditional respite
- corbel
- curtain wall
- dais
- embrasure
- final refuge
- flanking fire
- garderobe
- garderobe tower
- great hall
- joist
- machicolations
- merlon
- motte
- oilet
- phased plan
- royal castle
- shell keep
- solar
- storm a castle
- undermining

Source 4 Extracts from the accounts of Joan de Valence on 18 November 1296, the day she arrived at Goodrich Castle for a long stay.

Item 10 shillings 6 pence in procuring 3 carts to transport the mistress's property by road.

Item 6 pence for a horse to carry the mistress's money by road.

Item 2 shillings, 5 pence for 8 horses and 4 carters, loaned by the abbot of Gloucester and the abbot of Nutley for transporting the mistress's property by road, staying a night across the river Wye, unable to get across.

Item 16 pence to John the baker for 8 days travelling from Exning to Goodrich Castle to bake bread there before the mistress's arrival, and 16 pence to Isaac [of the kitchen] travelling to Goodrich Castle to prepare the larder there.

Source 3 will not have been the only photograph the examiner had to choose from – so what is there in this one you should notice? What exactly can you see?

- the barbican
- how large the gatehouse is
- the curtain walls with flanking towers
- the GARDEROBE TOWER
- the keep – which shows up as a different colour stone
- the inner courtyard.

Question 1 asks you about the *keep*, so that will be part of it. Question 2 focuses you on *rebuilding*, so what does the photograph tell you about that?

It is the same with Source 4. Do not just think about what you learn with reading – that they used candles, ate fish, the coachman's name was Hamo. What can you *infer* – Joan took a lot of possessions with her (three carts and a horse for the money); her arrival was carefully planned (sending ahead the baker and Isaac of the kitchen). The examiner thinks you should be able to use some of this in your answer to Question 2 – so do not disappoint them!

ASSESSMENT FOCUS

How the study of the historic environment will be assessed

The historic environment study on castles will be examined in Paper 3, along with the British depth study on the Reformation. The historic environment part is worth 20 marks – 10 per cent of your total GCSE. You should spend about 30 minutes on this part of the paper. Each year the exam is on a different site – and you will have studied it in depth.

Question 1 will test the first two assessment objectives:
- AO1: Knowledge and understanding
- AO2: Explanation and analysis.

Question 2 will test AO1 and AO2, but it will also test:
- AO3: Analyse, evaluate and make use of sources from the time.

Above all, the paper is assessing your ability to think and work like a historian. In the introduction, you looked at how historians work (page 4). There we set out some steps that historians take:
1. focus
2. ask questions
3. select
4. organise
5. fine tune.

The exam questions have already chosen a focus (stage 1) and they have asked questions (stage 2). What the examiner wants from you is stages 3, 4 and 5.

Question 1

Question 1 will ask you to explain an important aspect of the history of the castle you have studied. This will cover a period in the history of the castle but not its whole history. For example:

> **Explain why Conwy Castle fell into disrepair in the period 1400–1600. (10 marks)**

Aim of the question
The key word here is 'why'. Examiners are looking for an explanation of why the castle fell into disrepair. It would be easy to miss this point and simply describe what happened to the castle.

 Bronze (up to 25% of the marks): You describe a few events relating to the castle (e.g. no money was spent on the castle after 1400 and in 1406 there were only 12 archers).

 Silver (up to 60% of the marks): You explain how the castle fell into disrepair (e.g. after 1400 no money was spent on the castle; by the early 1500s it was used for storage but mostly unmanned; local people started to steal the stone).

 Gold (up to 100% of the marks): You build on the Silver level to make it really clear why the castle fell into disrepair (e.g. Wales was no longer a war zone). This will probably involve several reasons.

Even a Gold answer can be improved by ensuring you have:
- a clear conclusion that rounds off your argument
- used a range of examples as supporting evidence and included relevant and detailed knowledge in your supporting examples
- a balanced answer which shows you understand that there might be more than one view about the question or explains how the different factors are connected.

Advice

Select: Focus on the reasons why the castle fell into disrepair. Select at least two causes.

Organise: The important thing is to organise your knowledge in a relevant way to answer the question. Have a clear sense of what you are trying to say. In this question a good way to organise your answer might be:

> There were several reasons why Conwy Castle fell into disrepair in this period.
>
> First of all ...
>
> Another reason why Conwy declined was ...

Fine tune: Do all the usual checking but make sure you say which of your reasons you think is more important.

Example answer

Comments

There is no need to improve this answer – it is a Gold medal response. It has a clear opening and then sticks to the line that the opening suggests it will follow. The final sentence is not necessary but it is a nice ending to the answer. There is a good analysis of two separate reasons. In each case the answer explains how the factor sent Conwy into decline.

> By 1400, English rulers believed that their control of Wales was relatively secure. For most of that time England was torn by the Wars of the Roses and the battles in this war were not fought in Wales.
>
> Another reason why Conwy declined was that English rulers no longer needed a military outpost there. By the 1520s, Conwy was being used again but not really as a military building. Henry VIII did carry out repair work on the castle but not on a big scale. The castle was used as a prison and as a place for storing goods and as a place where official visitors could stay. Henry was fighting wars in Ireland, and Conwy was a useful staging post for armies and officials on their way to Ireland but it did not have an important military role.
>
> So the combination of location and changing political situation meant that English rulers did not need or want to spend money on Conwy Castle in the period 1400–1600. This view is supported by the fact that when the English Civil War began in the 1640s and troops from Ireland were brought into England through North Wales Conwy was repaired and played an important military role again.

Practice

We gave this answer a Gold medal. You can use the same idea to assess your own answers on your nominated castle. Afterwards, read over your answer and see which medal you might award yourself.

Question 2

Question 2 is a challenging question that requires effective use of knowledge and an understanding of how historians use sources. There will always be two sources. One will usually be a document and the other a visual source such as a map, a photograph or a plan. For example:

> *Study Sources A and B. Which of these sources is more useful to a historian studying the first hundred years of Conwy Castle (from the 1280s to the 1380s)? (10 marks)*

Bronze (up to 25% of the marks): You summarise the sources or pick out a few details from the sources.

Silver (up to 60% of the marks): You make an inference to explain how the content of each source is useful about the history of the castle (e.g. A is useful as it shows the size and scale of Conwy Castle).

Gold (up to 100% of the marks): You make an inference to explain how the content of each source is useful about the history of the castle and the role of the castle at particular times (e.g. A is useful as it shows the size and scale of Conwy Castle. The fact that it was so big tells us ...).

Source A An aerial photograph of the remains of Conwy Castle in North Wales.

Source B Extracts from accounts showing spending on Conwy Castle in the period 1283–1330.

March 1283 to November 1284 £5819

December 1284 to December 1292 £7870

February 1296 to February 1301 £500

December 1304 to December 1330 £88

Question 2 specialist advice

This question asks you to compare two sources and explain whether you think one source is more useful than the other. There are a few essential points to bear in mind.

All sources are useful for investigating some aspect of the past. Do not try to argue that one source is useful and the other one is *not*.

Examiners want you to show how each source is useful. They are not interested in how it is not useful. You will get no credit for this. Candidates often argue that a source is biased so it is not useful. But actually if a source is biased then that makes it useful – it tells us about the author of the source. It is a good idea to think 'How is it useful ...?' rather than 'How useful is it ...?'

Comparing the sources is quite difficult so examiners will give you a bit of leeway. It is acceptable to explain how each source is useful about different things. You will not be penalised if you do not argue that one is more useful.

Even a Gold medal answer can be improved by ensuring you have:
- a valid conclusion that rounds off your argument
- evaluated several sources in your answer
- clearly explained why historians hold particular views.

Advice

Before you start, make sure you are clear about what the sources say (comprehension and inference).

Select: You need to select facts, events and developments that support or challenge the views in the sources. So select items from this part of your knowledge wardrobe.

Organise: A good way to start this question is to show you understand what the sources are saying at face value and then go on to explain why historians find this information useful.

Fine tune: Do all the usual checks, but above all make sure that you have made inferences, and that your inferences are supported.

Example answer

Both sources can be useful to historians studying Conwy Castle in this period. Source A is extremely useful because it can tell us many things about why Conwy Castle was built and why it was built in that particular place. We can see from the photograph that Conwy was built at the mouth of the River Conwy. This was so that the castle could be supplied effectively, even if it was under attack from the land. It was also so that the castle could control trade going up and down the river.

Comments

This answer is very good – a Gold medal again! It would probably get 10 marks. For each source comprehension and inference work together well and relate to the question. As well as pointing out how the source is useful about the castle, the candidate has used knowledge effectively to show how the castle was important in the events of the time.

Probably the only thing you could criticise about this answer is that it is too long. It is probably worth about 17 out of 10! This is not as good as it sounds. When you over-answer, you usually run short of time for other questions.

When Edward I chose this site he went against the usual policy of putting castles on high ground so that the Castle could control the river. Source A is also useful in showing how determined Edward I was to conquer Wales and hold on to it. The massive fortifications and towers we can see were designed to intimidate and oppress the Welsh as well as to provide English forces with a secure base. Source A has its limitations of course. As it is a modern photograph it shows the road layout and the railway bridge next to the castle. This modern development obscures features and details which might have been visible in earlier maps or plans. And obviously the castle is now a ruin and so the photograph cannot show us what it was like in the period 1280–1380 when it was a thriving and important site with many troops and officials. On the other hand Source A does show us the basic layout of the castle and so we know that this is what it looked like then and now.

Source B is also useful to historians. Obviously it shows how much was spent on the castle at different times. From this we can tell that the castle must have been important to Edward I. The first two figures show the main cost of the castle when it was being built. This would be hundreds of millions of pounds today. This shows how serious Edward I was about conquering Wales and how important Conwy was in his plans to do that. The other figures are also useful. The £500 shows us what the running costs were for the castle once it had been built. This was actually relatively cheap because castles this size could cost a lot more. The figures from 1304 to 1330 suggest that the castle was not really being used much and that there were few soldiers or servants running it. We know that in the 1300s the conquest of Wales was fairly successful and this source is useful evidence to support that view. As with Source A, the source does have its limitations. The most obvious one is that it covers a limited time period. Also we need to use other sources such as chronicles to check some of the points we make, such as Wales being more peaceful in the early 1300s.

On balance I think that Source A is the more useful source because it provides evidence that does not need to be checked and it covers a longer time span than Source B. Source B is very useful but for different purposes and overall Source A is better.

Practice

Once again we gave this answer a Gold medal. You can use the same idea to assess your own answers on your nominated castle. Afterwards, read over your answer and see which medal you might award yourself.

Keys to success

As long as you know the content and have learned how to think, this exam should not be too scary. The keys to success are:

1   Read the question carefully. This may sound obvious, but there is a skill to it. Sometimes students answer the question they *wish* had been asked rather than the one that has *actually* been asked. So identify the skill focus (what they are asking you to do). Do they want you to write a description, an explanation or a comparison? Identify the content focus (what it is about) and select from your knowledge accordingly.

2   Note the marks available. This helps you work out how much time to spend on answering each question. Time is precious – if you spend too long on low-mark questions you will run out of time for the high-mark ones.

3   Plan your answer before you start writing. For essays this is particularly important. The golden rule is: know what you are going to say, then say it clearly and logically.

4   Aim for quality not quantity: in the time limits of an exam you will not be able to write down everything you know and can think of – even if it is relevant. The marker would much rather read a short answer that really tackles the question than page after page of material that is not relevant.

5   Check your work. You will never have time in an exam to rewrite an answer but try to leave some time at the end to check for obvious spelling mistakes, missing words or other writing errors that might cost you marks.

Glossary

absolutist monarchy a king or queen whose authority is not limited by any laws or customs, so they have complete power

allegory a story designed to make a point through representations (e.g. representing ordinary people as a flock of sheep or an enemy as a demon)

altar the table in a church where the priest says most of the service

Anarchy the name given to the period of civil war between Matilda and Stephen from the 1130s to the 1150s

Anglo-Saxon Chronicle a history of Anglo-Saxon England written by a series of authors (probably monks) from the mid-ninth century to 1154

annul to end a marriage by saying that it had never been legal in the first place; people talk about Henry VIII seeking a divorce, but actually he sought an annulment – the concept of divorce did not exist in Tudor times

archbishop a senior churchman, who answered only to a cardinal or the pope

artillery heavy missile weapons; usually refers to cannon but could include catapults

atheling a prince of the royal family in Anglo-Saxon England

authority the right to command or rule

autocrat someone who rules completely by themselves, with absolute power

Axis Powers the name given to Germany and its allies Italy and Japan in the Second World War

bailey an area of open ground in a Norman castle, usually surrounded by a defensive wall

barbican a fortified gatehouse

baron a nobleman from the medieval period; barons usually owned land from the monarch and in return served in government or provided troops in times of war

baronial castle a castle belonging to a baron rather than the monarch (barons usually had to get permission to build or develop their own castles)

Bayeux Tapestry a visual representation of the events of 1066, probably commissioned by Odo, the bishop of Bayeux

beam a strong strip of wood designed to hold up floors or other parts of buildings

bishop a senior churchman, usually in charge of a cathedral

Blitz spirit a way of describing the attitude of the British people during the Second World War, characterised by cheerfulness and a determination to carry on with life in the face of hardship

Book of Common Prayer the prayer book introduced by Charles I and William Laud, designed to ensure that church services and worship would be the same across the whole country

bratticing a protective wooden extension built out from the top of a castle wall

breach a hole made in a defensive wall, usually by artillery

burh a fortified town, manned by soldiers; Alfred the Great established a series of burhs across southern England

buttery a food store

caliphate the area ruled by a caliph (a Muslim leader)

charter a document issued by a monarch, usually giving authority to an individual (such as a royal official) or group to act in a certain way or collect a tax

chivalry a set of rules and code of behaviour that knights were supposed to follow, including showing mercy to defeated enemies and respect for women

Christendom countries where the main faith was Christianity, mostly in western Europe

chronicle a history, usually of royal families or the history of countries; chronicles could be completed by more than one author

churchmen officials of the Church, including the pope, cardinals, archbishops, bishops, priests, curates, monks and many others

civil defence civilians who volunteered or were conscripted to help in matters of defence on the home front during the Second World War

clergy any officials of the Church (priests, monks, etc.)

colonial troops Soldiers and sailors from the colonies of the British Empire, who fought on Britain's side in war

colony a region or country that comes under the control of another country and is ruled by it

common law law that is based on tradition and custom rather than written down in statute or Acts of Parliament; the common law was particularly important to the gentry

communist a supporter of communism – a political, economic and social system involving state control of the economy and less emphasis on individual rights than under capitalism

conditional respite an agreement between forces attacking and defending a castle that the castle would be surrendered after a certain period of time if the defenders were not helped by other forces

conscientious objector someone who refuses to fight in a war for moral reasons

conscription compulsory service in armed forces or related work

Continental System a system introduced by French leader Napoleon Bonaparte in 1806, in which French territories were forbidden to trade with Britain

corbel a bracket on a building, usually supporting a floor above

Council of the North a group of senior nobles who represented the king's authority in the north of England

Court of Exchequer one of the king's courts, in which people accused of not paying taxes were tried

crusade a religious war

curtain wall the outer defensive wall in a castle

dais a raised platform

Danegeld money paid by Anglo-Saxon rulers to stop attacks by Viking forces

Danelaw an area in eastern England with a substantial population of Danes and other Vikings

deposed removed from power

Direct Rule the rule of Northern Ireland by the government in London, rather than having its own government

Domesday Book a collection of information about landholding in England, created in 1086

Domesday survey the survey that gathered the information in the Domesday Book

earl a senior member of the nobility

Elizabethan Settlement the agreement reached in the reign of Elizabeth I about religion in England – England was a Protestant country; Catholics were not persecuted but they faced mistrust and discrimination

embrasure the space between battlements on a castle (for firing at attackers)

fascism a set of beliefs based on the importance of loyalty to a leader and using force to solve disputes

feudalism a system of land ownership and duties in medieval times (not a term used at the time)

final refuge the most secure part of a castle

flanking fire attacking an opponent from the side

fyrd the militia force of Anglo-Saxon England – part-time fighters who were called up when needed

garderobe the toilet in a castle

garderobe tower the tower containing the garderobe

gentry the lesser nobles, lower in rank than barons, earls or dukes – mostly knights

great hall the main hall of a castle, usually the main space for eating and entertaining

guerrilla a type of warfare that avoids large-scale battles and relies instead on hit-and-run raids

Hanoverian someone who belonged to the ruling House of Hanover in Germany; a Hanoverian prince became King George I of Britain

Harrying of the North a series of attacks on northern England by William the Conqueror in 1069–70

House of Commons initially described the lesser nobles and other members of parliament, but by the twentieth century the term was also used for the building where they met

House of Lords initially described the greater nobles and senior churchmen, but by the twentieth century the term was also used for the building where they met

housecarl professional soldiers of Anglo-Saxon rulers

hundred a division of land in Anglo-Saxon England, usually with enough people and resources to provide the king with 100 troops

ideology a set of beliefs, usually political beliefs or religious beliefs that have a political element

imam a Muslim leader

impeach to be accused of wrongdoing and investigated

impress to force someone to join the armed services against their will

indenture a contract between a knight and the king, setting out the terms by which a man-at-arms would serve the king in war and what he would get in return

insurgency an uprising, usually against a government

Islamist someone who supports Islamic fundamentalism or militancy

Jacobite someone who continued to support James II after he was deposed and who believed he should be restored to the throne

joist a wooden beam, usually supporting a floor

keep the major fortification inside most castles

killing grounds areas around or in castles designed to trap attackers

knight an important landowner, usually given lands by a more senior noble (e.g. an earl) and who then owed the earl a certain number of days of military service per year

legitimate legal (although sometimes the term was used to mean reasonable)

lesser nobles noblemen who were below barons in rank and importance, usually knights

liberty of conscience a declaration that people should be free to worship as their conscience dictated (i.e. granting freedom of religion)

lord-lieutenant a senior nobleman who was commissioned to organise the military forces of particular counties

Low Countries a region along the coast of western Europe, made up of parts of the Netherlands and Belgium

machicolation an opening in the floor of a castle which allowed defenders to drop stones or liquids or other missiles on attackers

magistrate also known as justices, these were important local people who judged court cases for less serious crimes

Magna Carta a charter issued in 1215 by King John under pressure from rebel barons, which granted some important rights and agreed to other changes to the power structure in England

March one of several regions on either side of the border between England and Scotland; each March had a warden who was supposed to help keep peace in the border region

marksman a soldier who is especially trained and skilled at shooting

mass media all forms of publication and communication that reach large numbers of the general public – for example, newspapers, television and radio

member of parliament someone chosen to represent an area (constituency) and help make laws

merlon the solid section of a battlement in a castle

motte a large man-made mound used as the foundation of a castle, with a tower usually placed on top

National Debt the amount of money owed by the government; the National Debt is usually larger in times of war

NATO the North Atlantic Treaty Organization – a political and military alliance of countries established in 1949 with the aim of preventing another World War by providing mutual defence and support to member nations

nobles important members of society, usually landowners

oilet a specially shaped opening in a castle wall to allow defenders to fire crossbows

ordinary revenue money raised from customs duties, fines and land belonging to the king

pacifist someone who believes that conflict should be avoided at all costs

paramilitary a group that uses armed force but is not a normal army

parliament a group of people commanded by the monarch to advise them; parliament developed from the medieval period to become the main power in Britain in the nineteenth century

Parliamentarian someone who supported parliament and the army during the English Civil Wars of the seventeenth century

phased plan a map or diagram that shows the different stages of building and rebuilding of a castle or other structure

plunder money or goods that are stolen, often using violence, during times of war or civil unrest

Policy of Thorough the term used to describe the strict and harsh control of the country under the Personal Rule

Political Nation the people who have some say in how the country is run; the Political Nation changes over time

pope the head of the Roman Catholic Church, based in Rome, Italy

prerogative court a court, such as the Star Chamber, through which the king exercised his personal powers and privileges

privateering the use of privately owned ships as warships, commissioned by the Crown to attack an enemy; in theory this was meant to be in retaliation for offences against England, but often these ships would attack others just to take their valuable cargo

Privy Council a group of high-ranking officials or nobles who advise the monarch

propaganda a particular set of ideas or information that is spread for a political purpose; propaganda can come in many different forms

Protestant the term given to Christians in Europe who protested against some aspects of the Catholic Church in the fifteenth century

Puritans radical Christians who believed in simple church services and studying the Bible rather than following the Catholic Church, priests or bishops

radicalised to have religious or political views that have become more extreme than those of others who share a particular ideology

recusancy refusing to attend Church of England services

regicide the killing of a king or queen

reivers bands of men from Scottish border clans that conducted raids on other clans and areas outside their own region

remonstrance a strong objection to something in parliament

requisition to demand the use of something for a specific purpose (usually an order from a government, monarch or similar authority)

royal assent the king's or queen's approval for a bill that has been put forward and passed by parliament; a bill cannot become an Act of Parliament or be passed into law without royal assent

royal castle a castle owned by the monarch

Royalist someone who supported the king during the English Civil Wars of the seventeenth century

sacrilegious something that destroys or harms something that is considered sacred

scorched-earth policy a tactic used during times of conflict in which a retreating army destroys everything in its path, such as goods or crops, so that the enemy cannot use it

scutage money that someone paid to their lord instead of performing military service

sectarian violence conflict and violence between people belonging to different sects of the same religion or ideology

serf a low-ranking member of society

shell keep a type of castle, essentially a stone tower on top of a motte

sheriff a key royal official, responsible for justice, taxes and many other roles within a local area

Ship Money a tax established in medieval times, usually paid by coastal counties to cover the cost of the navy in times of war, but extended in the reign of Charles I to all counties and not just for emergencies

shire an area under the control of an earl in Anglo-Saxon England

solar a lord's private room in a castle

sovereignty supreme power over something or someone; often used to refer to one country or its ruler claiming control of or leadership over another

Speaker of the House the chief officer in the House of Commons; the Speaker maintains order in the House and, although an MP, is supposed to be impartial during debates

standard a flag or banner that is raised in front of troops to mark a gathering place for troops before a battle begins

storm (a castle) to attack a castle

tax money or goods paid by the population to a monarch or government

thegn a noble in Anglo-Saxon society

treason to speak or take action against the ruler of a country

trebuchet a type of artillery used against castles

undermining tunnelling underneath the walls of a castle to make them collapse

unilateral disarmament the complete elimination of all nuclear weapons by every country that has them

vassal someone who lived on land owned by the king

veldt large areas of open, uncultivated grassland in southern Africa

Vikings people from northern Europe who raided and settled in England from the eighth to the eleventh centuries

villein a low-ranking member of medieval society

war of attrition a form of warfare in which each side tries to win by wearing down the other side through loss of soldiers or supplies

Wessex a southern Anglo-Saxon kingdom

Witan the council of senior nobles in Anglo-Saxon England

writ an instruction sent by the monarch to one of his officials, usually a sheriff

Index

Acknowledgements

The Publishers would like to thank the following for permission to reproduce copyright material.

Photo credits
p.4 Illustration by David Parkins for The Economist; **p.7** © Everett Historical/Shutterstock; **p.12** © Armands Pharyos/Alamy Stock Photo; **p.12** t © Granger Historical Picture Archive/Alamy Stock Photo, b © Photo Researchers, Inc/Alamy Stock Photo; **p.16** t Queens Aethelswitha and Aethelflaed. / British Library, London, UK / © British Library Board. All Rights Reserved / Bridgeman Images, b © The Trustees of the British Museum; **p.18** Wikimedia/Berig; **p.23** Interfoto/Alamy Stock Photo; **p.26** © Historic England Archive; **p.28** © Skyscan.co.uk; **p.31** t © North Wind Picture Archives/Alamy Stock Photo, b © Everett Historical/Shutterstock; **p.32** © North Wind Picture Archives/Alamy Stock Photo; **p.33** © English Heritage. NMR; **p.34** Drawing Of The Battle Of Lincoln. Captions identify the man to the left as Baldwin FitzGilbert and the central crowned figure as King Stephen; the king is directing Baldwin to address the army of his behalf. / British Library, London, UK / © British Library Board. All Rights Reserved / Bridgeman Images; **p.35** © Mathew Lodge/lodgephoto.com/Alamy Stock Photo; **p.36** © mirrormere/Shutterstock; **p.38** l © Lebrecht Music and Arts Photo Library/Alamy Stock Photo, r © Historic England Archive; **p.40** © 2003 Topham Picturepoint; **p.43** © Peter Lane/Alamy Stock Photo; **p.44** Royal 20 C.V11 John Baliol before Edward I, illustration from the 'Chroniques de France ou de St. Denis', French School, (14th century) / British Library, London, UK / © British Library Board. All Rights Reserved / Bridgeman Images; **p.46** Roy 20 C VII f.41v Rioters pillage a house in Paris (vellum), French School, (14th century) / British Library, London, UK / © British Library Board. All Rights Reserved / Bridgeman Images; **p.47** © National Archives, E 32/12 rot3d, Exchequer, and its related bodies, with those of the Office of First Fruits and Tenths, and the Court of Augmentations; **p.56** t © Interfoto/Alamy Stock Photo, b © Interfoto/Alamy Stock Photo; **p.59** l © Granger Historical Picture Archive/Alamy Stock Photo, r © Granger Historical Picture Archive/Alamy Stock Photo; **p.60** t Queen Elizabeth I, c.1578 (oil on panel), Geeraerts, Marcus, the younger (1561-1635) / The Portland Collection, Harley Gallery, Welbeck Estate, Nottinghamshire / Bridgeman Images, b © Artokoloro Quint Lox Limited/Alamy Stock Photo; **p.62** © The Newberry Library; **p.63** College of Arms MS:~Sidney Funeral Roll. Reproduced by permission of the Kings, Heralds and Pursuivants of Arms; **p.66** © Library of Congress, Rare Book and Special Collections Division, The Hans P. Kraus Collection of Sir Francis Drake; **p.67** © Universal History Archive/UIG via Getty Images; **p.71** The Kingdom's Monster Uncloaked from Heaven, c.1640-43 (woodcut) (b/w photo), English School, (17th century) / Private Collection / Bridgeman Images; **p.74** The Battle Plan of Naseby / British Library, London, UK / © British Library Board. All Rights Reserved / Bridgeman Images; **p.75** © Hampshire County Council; provided by Hampshire Cultural Trust; **p.76** The English Irish Soldier, 1642 (print), English School, (17th century) / British Library, London, UK / © British Library Board. All Rights Reserved / Bridgeman Images; **p.77** Incident During Tyrone's Rebellion at Portadown, in 1641-42 (engraving), English School, (17th century) / Private Collection / Bridgeman Images; **p.78** © World History Archive/Topfoto; **p.82** © English Heritage Photo Library; **p.84** © Take 27 Ltd; **p.85** © John Morrison/Alamy Stock Photo; **p.88** © Chronicle/Alamy Stock Photo; **p.89** © Niday Picture Library/Alamy Stock Photo; **p.90** Scaling the Heights of Abraham, illustration from 'Glorious Battles of English History' by Major C.H. Wylly, 1920s (colour litho), Payne, Henry A. (Harry) (1868-1940) / Private Collection / Bridgeman Images; **p.97** A View of the Taking of Quebec, September 13th 1759 (colour engraving), English School, (18th century) / Private Collection / Bridgeman Images; **p.98** © World History Archive/Alamy Stock Photo; **p.99** © DeAgostini/Getty Images; **p.100** © Crown DfC; **p.103** British Library/745.a.6 (Public Domain); **p.105** © Pictorial Press Ltd/Alamy Stock Photo; **p.106** © Roger Fenton/Getty Images; p.107 © Wellcome Library, London; **p.109** t © Pictorial Press Ltd/Alamy Stock Photo, b © Photo12/UIG via Getty Images; **p.110** t © Photo12/Alamy Stock Photo, b © Mary Evans/Roger Worsley Archive; **p.113** Peter Scholey/Alamy Stock Photo; **p114** © The Print Collector/Print Collector/Getty Images; **p.115** © IWM (Q 70214); **p.116** Library of Congress; **p.119** t © The National Archives, b © Everett Historical/Shutterstock; **p.122** l © The National Army Museum/Mary Evans Picture Library, r Wikimedia/National Archives; **p.123** l © Chronicle/Alamy Stock Photo, r © The National Archives; **p.124** © George W. Hales/Stringer/Getty Images; **p.125** Reproduced by permission of The Labour Party; **p.129** t © Rick Strange/Alamy Stock Phot, bl © National Archives/Central Office of Information, br © Rick Strange/Alamy Stock Photo; **p.131** t © Victor Weisz, 'Intolerable having your rockets on my doorstep!', 24 Oct 1962, *Evening Standard*, Associated Newspapers Ltd. / Solo Syndication, British Cartoon Archive, University of Kent, b © A. Jones/Evening Standard/Getty Images; **p.132** © Popperfoto/Getty Images; **p.133** © John Downing/Getty Images; **p.134** © John Cole/Alamy Stock Photo; **p.135** © Raymond Jackson, The Irish, 29 Oct 1982, *Evening Standard*, Associated Newspapers Ltd. /